A nation in arms

A nation in arms

A social study of the British army
in the First World War

edited by
*Ian F. W. Beckett
and Keith Simpson*

Manchester University Press

Published by
Manchester University Press
Oxford Road, Manchester M13 9PL, U.K.
51 Washington Street, Dover, N.H. 03820, U.S.A.

British Library cataloguing in publication data
A Nation in arms : a social study of the
  British Army in the First World War.
  1. Great Britain, *Army* – History   2. World
  War, 1914–1918 – Great Britain
  I. Beckett, I. F. W.   II. Simpson, Keith, *1949–*
355′.00941   UA649

Library of Congress cataloging in publication data
A Nation in arms.
  Bibliography: p. 238
  Includes index.
    1. Sociology, Military – Great Britain – History – 20th
century. 2. Great Britain. Army . History – European War,
1914–1918. I. Beckett, I. F. W. (Ian Frederick William)
II. Simpson, Keith.
  UA649.3.N38   1985   306′.27′0941   84–25048

ISBN 0–7190–1737–8 (*cased*)

Photoset in Century Schoolbook
by Northern Phototypesetting Co., Bolton
Printed in Great Britain by
Butler & Tanner Ltd, Frome and London

Contents

Illustrations

Editorial acknowledgement

The editors wish to express their thanks to all their fellow contributors, who have been so willing to share their particular knowledge of the British army in the Great War. Especial thanks go to Peter Simkins and Clive Hughes as well as Rod Suddaby and the staff of the Department of Documents at the Imperial War Museum for their assistance with the archive sources of that institution. Thanks also to Mr John Hunt and the staff of the Royal Military Academy, Sandhurst, Library for all their support for this project. Lieutenant Commander (Retd) Tony Thomas of the Department of War Studies and International Affairs at Sandhurst and Mrs. J. Isaac were kind enough to draw the maps, while John Keegan also agreed to grace the volume with a foreword.

Sandhurst   I.F.W.B.
May 1984   K.R.S.

Foreword

John Keegan

It is a great pleasure to be invited to contribute the foreword to a book that tackles a neglected aspect of the First World War, the nature and composition of the British army and its relationship with the nation from which it was drawn. Much has been written about the French, German, Russian or Austro-Hungarian armies of 1914–18, on their leaders and their operations. Much also has been written about British operations in the war – one thinks, particularly, of those endlessly controversial episodes, Gallipoli and Passchendaele – and about British generals. But the British army has been the subject of scarcely any study since Ian Hay produced *The First Hundred Thousand* in the thick of the fight seventy years ago.

Ian Hay's propagandistic but still readable novel was devoted to the raising of the first of the Kitchener armies – K One, as the jargon of the day had it. That reminds us that Britain, between 1914 and 1918, put four armies into the field in succession, each representing a different strand of the nation's military tradition.

The Kitchener armies came third, at least chronologically. First to take the field was the regular army, which, since 1908, had been organised in large part to provide an expeditionary force in time of war. Its concentration area in 1914 was Aldershot, whence six infantry divisions and a large cavalry division were by plan to be sent abroad. Political considerations limited this number initially to four, but eventually eight altogether were to go to France, while in 1915 a Guards division was also formed in imitation of those in the German and Russian armies. Moreover, by substituting Territorial for regular battalions in India and the colonies, three more divisions, the 27th, 28th and 29th, were eventually raised from the imperial garrisons. Thus the regular army, though only 200,000 strong in 1914, was ultimately able to field twelve divisions of infantry, all of which were deployed either on the western front or at Gallipoli.

It did so, however, only by absorbing its reserves, which were inadequate to make good losses suffered when the fighting became intense. That was soon. By December 1914 the regular army in France had lost 80,000 killed and wounded. Its units and formations were skeletons and could hardly hold the sector of the line allotted to them, east and south of Ypres, during the harsh winter of 1914–15. Fortunately the Germans, too, had exhausted their reserves, both of men and of *matériel*, and so left the survivors of the original BEF largely in peace during those months.

And there was relief at hand. The Territorial Force, with its fourteen divisions of infantry and fourteen brigades of yeomanry cavalry, was by November 1914 just reaching a state of training and equipment where it could be sent abroad. The TF was an oddity by international military standards: a voluntary militia only tenuously attached to the regular army. Originating in the Volunteer movement of 1859 – itself a spontaneous phenonemon historians still find difficult to explain – it had gradually been regularised, and equipped to regular standards, though too often it made do with what the regulars had just discarded. In the crisis of 1914–15, however, such defects had to be overlooked. During the winter months the TF divisions came gradually into line. By the autumn of 1915 they were numerous and experienced enough to supply much of the strength of the Loos offensive.

At Loos the Territorials suffered heavily. But it was not such losses that put a check on their further expansion. Kitchener, the Secretary of State for War, had taken steps on his appointment in 1914 to divert reserves of manpower in a direction away from the Territorials. In part he anticipated, perhaps wrongly, an incapacity among the Territorial County Associations, the organising bodies, to raise reserves quickly. In part he wanted the creation of a great new national army under his own hand. The result was the First Hundred Thousand of September 1914 – 100,000 volunteers, engaged to serve 'three years or the duration' – followed, such was youthful British enthusiasm, by four more 'hundred thousands'. Each produced six divisions of infantry, many of them recruited on the 'Pals' or 'Chums' principle, which would see whole streets, factories, football clubs and Boy Scout troops devastated by grief when such units eventually entered combat and left their quota of dead in No Man's Land.

These quotas became huge during and after the Kitchener divisions' great contribution to the British, and Allied, effort on the western front, the Somme offensive of July–November 1916. The 20,000 dead of the first day, the 300,000 casualty total of the whole campaign eventually succeeded in drying up the hitherto apparently inexhaustible flow of volunteer manpower. Throughout 1915 as the government watched its reservoir of men emptying, it flirted with the prospect of introducing compulsion. Its first implementation of a principle never before admitted in British civic life, was tentative – the Derby Scheme. But by December 1915 it could avoid conscription in all its rigour no longer – if the war was to be prosecuted.

Britain's fourth army – though it materialised as a host of

replacements, not as a body of formed units – was thus new in several senses. But 'pressed men' – the term harked back to the strictly local but limited naval draft system of sailing ship days – turned out in practice to be as loyal and brave as those who had gone before. And as prone to casualties. The British army lost as heavily in 1918 as in both the previous years of fighting.

Its four incarnations are the subject of this book. (Purists who remember that the ancient *posse comitatus* and county militias were hidden in the 3rd Special Reserve battalions of infantry regiments in 1914 may rightly claim that a fifth manifestation has been ignored.) But the incarnations were not, of course, purely military. They were also social in the widest sense – regional, economic and cultural. To study them is to learn a great deal about the Britain of 1914–15, what it was before the war began, how it became what it did after 'the war to end wars'. This book is an original and fascinating introduction to that study.

Ian Beckett **1**

The nation in arms, 1914–18

It is now seventy years since the outbreak of the Great War, a conflict that has generated millions of words in print: in Britain, a critical bibliography of 'war books' appeared as early as 1930.[1] Yet historical understanding has been constantly extended and revised by new interpretation, and the historical evaluation of the war is clearly far from complete. The historiography of the British army in the First World War affords a good example of how great the gaps in knowledge still are.

There have been many studies of the army's battles and campaigns over the years, and for 'popular' historians the increasingly stale debate on British generalship has apparently lost none of its intrinsic interest. Scholarship has, however, moved inexorably forward, at least as far as other armies are concerned, and, influenced by the burgeoning status of the study of the impact of war upon society and its institutions, historians have produced fine modern accounts of the armies of the other main protagonists between 1914 and 1918. Neglect of the British army has perhaps been all the more surprising in view of the excellent research in recent years on the forces of the dominions and colonies[2] but most modern scholarly accounts of the British army have tended either to terminate in 1914 or to commence in 1919.

Fortunately, there has been increasing interest in the army as an institution during the First World War itself, ranging from the 'life in the trenches' approach to more sophisticated treatment of such problems as the motivation for and pattern of enlistment, morale and discipline, and demobilisation and veterans' organisations. As yet no single volume has drawn this work together to assess the overall impact of the war upon the army, upon those who served in its ranks and upon those civilians who came into contact with it. This book is therefore intended to make that attempt and to explain precisely what happened to the army and to its relationship with society as a result of its massive expansion between 1914 and 1918. Starting as a small force of less than 250,000 regulars, the army had absorbed over five million men by 1918 and, in the process, Britain at least temporarily became a 'nation in arms' for the first time in a century.

Such expansion was always likely to have greater impact upon the British army than others because, alone among the major European powers, Britain had maintained a voluntary system of enlistment prior to the war. In Europe the modern concept of 'a nation in arms' can be said to date from the proclamation of the law of *réquisition*, popularly known as the *levée en masse*, by the French Committee of Public Safety in August 1793, although forms of conscription for a standing army had existed previously and the idea of a mass citizen army had attracted earlier support from French philosophers and military theorists. The creation of the French citizen armies transformed the very nature of war itself and the example was emulated by those powers defeated by France, most notably Prussia. To the Prussian military reformers led by Scharnhorst the adoption of universal service was more than a military innovation, it was a catalyst of social and political change. It would 'bring the army and nation into a more intimate union', the army becoming a school of the nation in statehood and service in it a route to the franchise.

After the Napoleonic Wars the concept of a nation in arms came under widespread attack as monarchs and restored monarchs preferred the political reliability of professional long-service armies, although in Prussia the actual system of short-service conscription survived. The military effectiveness of short service in providing a large reserve upon mobilisation was convincingly demonstrated by Prussian victories in the wars of 1864, 1866 and 1870. In tribute to Prussia's ascendancy, the armies of Europe once more hastened to adopt short-service conscription, which was again seen as having wider social and political implications, but now in the service of absolutism and the control and moulding of the individual by the State. The rhetoric of the new concept of the nation in arms was thus not to be taken too literally in social and political terms. Nor did it imply that all available manpower would be conscripted, since all such forms of universal military service were, of necessity, selective in practice. In so far as a genuine mass citizen army existed it was to be found only in Switzerland and in the imagination of socialists such as Jaurès.[3]

In Britain the idea of universal military service also had its exponents, the pressure for the introduction of some form of conscription increasing as Britain's political isolation became more apparent and as her position in relation to the other major powers came under threat. By 1900 she had been outstripped by both imperial Germany and the United States in terms of industrial production, her continued superiority resting more on financial capital, shipping and primary products than upon manufactured goods or new technology. To some extent unrivalled financial primacy in world trade and the existence of the empire masked the long-term political and strategic implications, but Britain was less and less able to outbuild naval opponents with her former ease and could not hope to compete realistically where numbers secured by conscription were now the yardstick of military power.

The South African War was undoubtedly a shock to complacency, not least in the claims that the 'imperial race' itself was declining in physical terms. Little comfort was derived from the suggestion by the subsequent Interdepartmental Committee on Physical Deterioration, reporting in July 1904, that the physique of army recruits during the war was not necessarily an accurate representation of the nation as a whole. The concern with the physical and moral condition of the nation as well as a declining birth rate not only fuelled such movements as Baden Powell's Boy Scouts and the National Social Purity Crusade but contributed to the appeal of eugenics and the demand for 'efficiency'. The latter in particular enjoyed a broad constituency until the issue of tariff reform drove a wedge between the Liberals and the radical right.[4] Conscription formed part of the efficiency programme, appearing as such in Lloyd George's stillborn plans for a coalition government in 1910, but its advocacy was principally in the hands of the National Service League.

It is possible but misplaced to assume from the campaigns of the League and other apparent manifestations that Britain was a militarised society prior to 1914. The National Service League, founded in 1902, claimed over 91,000 members by 1911 but it was always more Anglican than Nonconformist, always more Unionist than Liberal. As its most recent historian has written, 'for an organisation which aimed at realising its objective through the force of public opinion, the implications were disquieting'. Even when disguised as universal military service or national service, conscription was never likely to prove popular with the public at large. There was military support for some form of conscription, its introduction being endorsed by the Wantage Commission in 1892, by the Norfolk Commission in 1904 and by the Army Council in April 1913. Similarly, the League could draw inspiration from the respect accorded Lord Roberts, who had become its president in 1905; from the controversy over the efficiency of the Territorial Force after 1908; and from the introduction of forms of universal service in Australia and New Zealand in 1909.

Short-service conscription was in fact unsuitable for the defence of a far-flung empire, as the League readily conceded in embracing older ideas for long and short-service armies to exist side by side. However, the programme it adopted as politically acceptable – four months' initial training for a conscript, followed by only fifteen days in each of the next three years – was equally unlikely to provide an adequate army for home defence. There was some indication of public support for compulsion in the 1910 elections and at some subsequent by-elections, but all five of the parliamentary Bills introduced to implement conscription between 1908 and 1914, only one of which was actually supported by the League, failed.[5]

If conscription was always going to arouse 'violent prejudices', as Lloyd George recognised in 1910, what then of other forms of militarism? Certainly there was more support for the compulsory training of youth, and by 1914 British youth had become highly organised. Quasi-military bodies of a denominational nature such as the Boys' Brigade or non-denominational groups such as the Lads' Drill Association had enjoyed considerable growth in the late nineteenth century and, with the addition of the Boy Scouts from 1907, it is possible that as many as 41 per cent of all male adolescents may have belonged to some form of youth organisation by 1914. However, there is evidence to suggest that those most susceptible to the appeal of such organisations tended to be the upwardly mobile youth of the outer suburbs rather than the disadvantaged for whom they were conceived as an antidote to restlessness and parental vice.[6]

To a large extent the moral purpose underlying the Boys' Brigade and the working-class cadet battalions that had originated in the 1880s mirrored the cults of athleticism and muscular Christianity which had developed in the public schools. There were well over a hundred public school cadet corps by 1914, Haldane remarking of the public schools that 'the spirit of militarism already runs fairly high both there and at the universities', but it seems remarkably unlikely that the creation of the Officers' Training Corps from such groups could ever have brought the army into a 'close and organic relation with the life of the nation' as Haldane hoped. It is true, of course, that military drill was widely accepted as the most appropriate form of physical training in the majority of Board schools, and that the regimented discipline and the content of the syllabus in such schools was likely to instil military virtues. Pressure groups such as the Navy League and the National Service League were undoubtedly active within both schools and youth organisations.

Beyond the schoolroom and adolescence, popular writers such as Henty and Haggard, the popular press, popular entertainment such as the music hall and even the infant cinema did similar service in transmitting nationalistic themes. There were few on the left of the political spectrum beyond Will Thorne, MP, and the maverick Robert Blatchford, who supported compulsion, but the industrial strife of the Edwardian age made militancy as much a part of the 'emotional baggage' of the left as of the right. There was also a well developed theme of 'Nonconformist militarism' stemming from such sources as idolatry of Garibaldi for his exploits during the unification of Italy, the evangelical acceptance of imperialism as a prelude to missionary conquest and the Victorian discovery of 'Christian heroes' such as Henry Havelock and Charles Gordon.[7]

Similarly, the constant recurrence of invasion scares in Victorian and Edwardian Britain continued to generate much popular literature. There were, indeed, more contributions to this genre between 1900 and 1914 than in the preceding thirty years, while the possibility of foreign espionage provoked near paranoia. Invasion also promoted serious discussion of military matters in periodicals and books which extended to debate on the nature of war itself. Almost inevitably this was overlaid with the assumptions of Social Darwinism, so prevalent throughout

Europe, these assumptions being disseminated to a wider audience by authors such as Benjamin Kidd. By contrast the 'peace movement' in Britain was fragmented and impotent, and for many the prospect of war appeared far from intimidating. Yet, although society was clearly conditioned at many levels 'to accept military activity as necessary or desirable or both', militarism as such existed, in the words of Michael Howard, only in 'mild solution'.[8] This may be further illustrated in the general attitude displayed towards the regular army; in the peculiarly 'British' nature of Haldane's version of the 'nation in arms'; and in the actual response of society to the outbreak of war in August 1914.

As the National Service League argued, the regular army prior to 1914 was hardly representative of society as a whole and was forced to depend for the recruitment of its rank and file upon a 'compulsion of destitution'. The ranks were overwhelmingly English, working-class and at least nominally Anglican. Although the auxiliary military forces were far from being the middle-class bastions of popular imagination, the Militia, Yeomanry and Volunteers had always been more genuinely representative of society at large than regulars. Indeed, if a nation in arms existed in Britain prior to the First World War it must be sought in the auxiliaries, since, as historians in the employ of the National Service League continually stressed, there was a tradition of compulsion for home defence. Despite being recruited by voluntary enlistment since 1852, compulsion for the Militia was still technically feasible and it is significant that, when converted to the need for compulsion after the battle of Loos, Kitchener contemplated a quota system remarkably close to the old militia ballot. Increasingly from 1866 the Militia had attracted the same kind of recruit as the regular army, a situation recognised in its translation into the Special Reserve in 1908, but the Volunteers and Yeomanry had continued to recruit their ranks and file from those elements of society who would not otherwise have become involved in military affairs. Thus the Volunteers were drawn mostly from the skilled working class who enjoyed higher wages and greater security of employment than the average regular or Militia recruit, while the Yeomanry was highly though not exclusively dependent upon the farming community.[9]

Not surprisingly, when Haldane's second memorandum on army reform in February 1906 envisaged the creation of a 'real national army, formed by the people', the essential point of contact in welding a unity of army and society was depicted as being the new Territorial Force, which would replace, absorb and improve upon the older auxiliaries. The idea of educating the nation in its responsibilities for defence was carried further in Haldane's fourth memorandum of April 1906, which suggested that the new Territorial county associations might promote military virtues in schools through encouraging drill, physical exercise, cadet units and rifle clubs. The composition of associations would also forge links between army and society through a distinctive elective element provided by borough and county councils. Fear of political opposition led Haldane to compromise his original intentions but it can be noted that he believed that his version of a nation in arms would negate rather than encourage militarism and that the long-term nature of his proposals also indicates that he was unaware of any deep attachment to military virtues in the country as a whole. It is undeniable that the auxiliary forces did contribute to the promotion of military values, and that large numbers of men – perhaps 8 per cent of the male population as a whole – had experienced some form of military training in them by 1914, but the failure of the Territorials to match Haldane's unrealistic manpower targets or to sustain popularity after a waning of the invasion scare of 1909 must contribute to the impression that Britain was not consciously militarised and was primarily concerned with its apparent weaknesses.[10]

Just as the British army as it existed in 1914 represented the 'exigency of peacetime acceptability' so the response to the outbreak of war can be interpreted as less than wholeheartedly enthusiastic. Public opinion had hardly become aware of the impending crisis in Europe until 29 July, at which time there was both panic in financial markets and at least some initial willingness on the workers' part to heed the admonitions of their leaders. Of all the peoples involved in August 1914 the British had the least time to react, and it seems more than likely that public opinion reflected that 'general metamorphosis' observed of other Europeans 'from passivity, through pacifism, to patriotism'.[11]

As indicated in Table 1.1, some 15 per cent of all enlistment took place in the first two months of the war, but the 'first rush' was not immediate and can be almost precisely dated to the period between 25 August and 15 September 1914. There was much initial confusion, not least among would-be recruiters, and there was equally little news of events until the publication of the sensational despatches of Arthur Moore and Hamilton Fyfe on 30 August 1914 reporting the retreat from Mons. German atrocity stories had also begun to surface, and on 24 August the Earl of Derby approached the War Office with his suggestion for the 'Pals' battalions, although in fact the idea had originated in the War Office as early as 12 August and the "Stockbrokers" battalion of the Royal Fusiliers had already begun to recruit on 21 August. These factors together appear to have accounted for the great increase in recruits in early September: the 30,000 recorded on one day in that month exceeded the pre-war total for the regular army in one year. By 9 September 1914 the most fruitful recruiting period of the war was over, and the same enthusiasm was never to recur, fewer men enlisting in October than in the first four days of September. The news from France

Table 1.1. *Enlistments in the regular army and Territorial Force, 1914–18*

Month	Total
August 1914	298,923
September	462,901
October	136,811
November	169,862
December	117,860
January 1915	156,290
February	87,896
March	113,907
April	119,087
May	135,263
June	114,679
July	95,413
August	95,980
September	71,617
October	113,285
November	121,793
December	55,152
Total	2,466,719
January 1916 to November 1918	2,504,183
August 1914 to November 1918	4,970,902
Strength of British army, Territorials and Reserves, August 1914	733,514
Total serving in British army, 1914–18	5,704,416

Source. Statistics of the Military Effort of the British Empire during the Great War, HMSO, London, March 1922, p. 364.

had improved, with the first reports of the German retreat, while there were increasing rumours that recruits were suffering discomfort in improvised accommodation, the pre-war recruiting machinery having been totally swamped and an *ad hoc* 'voluntary recruiting movement' having sprung up in its stead. It also appeared that men were no longer actually required, deferred enlistment having been introduced, under which they were enlisted in the Reserve and sent home until they could be accommodated on 6*d* a day. Many had, however, already given up their job to enlist, and on 10 September Asquith was compelled to announce an increase to 3*s* a day to deferred entrants. More significantly, the following day the War Office attempted to assert control over the flow of recruits by raising the height requirement from the 5 ft 3 in. of 8 August 1914 to 5 ft 6 in., although the age limit for enlistment was increased from the original nineteen to thirty years to an upper limit of thirty-five. Some 10,000 men already enlisted were rejected on arrival at their units under the new regulation, and there is little doubt that it had an immediate impact upon recruiting.

When the War Office lowered the height requirement to 5 ft 4 in. on 23 October 1914 and extended the age limit to thirty-eight years, or forty-five for former soldiers, it was soon apparent that recruiting could not be run on a 'stop-go' basis. On 14 November 1914 the height requirement was dropped again, to 5 ft 3 in. and the first 'Bantam' regiments were raised of men below even this standard. It was lowered again in July 1915, to 5 ft 2 in., and the age limit extended to forty years, but by then the voluntary system had been reduced to 'recruitment by insult'.[12]

The response to war was also extremely uneven, as indicated in Table 1.2. The implication, as Jay Winter has noted, was that 'men engaged in commercial or distributive trades were in uniform and at risk for longer periods and in relatively larger numbers than were industrial workers, transport workers or agricultural workers'. The lowest response was among textile and clothing workers, industries which were shortly to enjoy a considerable boom. A number of groups came under attack for their alleged unwillingness to enlist, such as professional sportsmen, particularly footballers, while the Harmsworth Committee of April 1915 fixed its sights on the retail trade as ripe for combing out. High wages may have discouraged enlistment among dockers, railway workers and miners, while low rates of employment may have stimulated recruiting among building workers, but it must also be borne in mind that the actual age structure of the labour force varied considerably from industry to industry, and this may well have been 'the single most important determinant in the first year of the war'. There was also from

Table 1.2. *Sectoral distribution of enlistment in the British forces, August 1914 to February 1916*

Occupation	Men employed July 1914 ('000)	Men who joined ('000)	% of pre-war labour force volunteering
Industry	6,165	1,743	28·3
(Mines and quarries)	(1,266)	(313)	(24·7)
Agriculture	920	259	28·2
Transport	1,041	233	22·4
Finance and commerce	1,249	501	40·1
Professions	144	60	41·7
Entertainment	177	74	41·8
Central government	311	85	27·3
Local government	477	126	26·4
All occupations	10,484	3,081	29·4

Source. PRO, Reconstruction Papers, 1/832, tabulated in J. M. Winter, 'Britain's lost generation of the First World War', *Population Studies*, 31, 3, 1977, p. 454.

the very beginning a degree of 'protectionism' for workers in key occupations such as the railways or the many individuals 'badged' by the Admiralty before December 1914. With the introduction of conscription, of course, protectionism increased, particularly in areas such as agriculture and transport, thus ensuring that some sectors of society would throughout the war bear a disproportionately low share of the military effort while others, such as those involved in commerce, would bear a disproportionately high share through their lack of protection from compulsion or the attention of the recruiters.

The reasons for such variations must also be sought at local rather than national level. There were wide regional variations, with Wales and Scotland, for example, finding proportionally more recruits than England, while, within England, the East Midlands and Yorkshire registered lower enlistment than elsewhere. Comparison of rates of enlistment in Norwich, Nottingham and Hull or in Bristol, Liverpool and Glasgow shows wide discrepancies. In Bristol some 10 per cent of the work force had been laid off in July 1914 and a further 26 per cent placed on short time in a prevailing mood of industrial and commercial uncertainty; the approaching autumn was a traditional time of lay-offs in agriculture and the building trade through the winter months. In August, too, the Local Government Board instructed charities not to grant relief to those eligible for enlistment. As a result, nine out of every ten men laid off enlisted, and the city's unemployment rate fell by a full $1\frac{1}{2}$ per cent, but by November its industries were buoyant with wartime orders and recruiting dropped. In Birmingham some 78 per cent of all recruits in August 1914 came from the same classes who had supplied the regular army in peacetime, the majority from less secure employment that experienced seasonal labour changes: August was a particularly bad time for Birmingham trades every year. Over the country as a whole at least 480,000 men had lost their jobs by the end of August, and it is logical to assume that many enlisted, although equally there was a high rate of enlistment by men in industries such as engineering, chemicals and iron and steel that were not threatened by unemployment.[13]

In December 1914 the *Manchester Guardian* expressed the hope that Britain would fight the entire war without recourse to conscription, an achievement which would be 'well worth trying for'. In reality the limits of voluntary enlistment were soon realised, while the reluctance of many Territorials to undertake overseas service in 1914 and the undeniable attraction of enlistment for home service, which continued to be sanctioned in the Territorials until March 1915, equally suggest that the idea of a 'rush to the colours' needs serious revision. The numbers who could be found by voluntary means inevitably failed to match the manpower requirements of mass modern war. Precisely what numbers

Table 1.3. Enlistments in the United Kingdom, by country, 1914–18

	Voluntary Enlistments to Dec. 1915	Proportion of males aged 15–49 enlisted to Dec. 1915	Enlistments after Jan. 1916	Proportion of males aged 15–49 enlisted after Jan. 1916	Total enlistments 1914–18	Proportion of males 15–49 enlisted 1914–18	Proportion of all males enlisted 1914–18	% of regular army 1913
England	2,092,242	24·2	1,913,916	22·1	4,006,158	46·2	24·0	78·6
Wales	145,255		127,669		272,924		21·5	1·4
Scotland	320,589	26·9	237,029	14·6	557,618	41·4	23·7	7·6
Ireland	117,063	10·7	17,139	1·6	134,202	12·3	6·1	9·1

Source. Statistics of the Military Effort of the British Empire during the Great War, HMSO, London, 1922; J. M. Winter, 'Britain's lost generation of the First World War', *Population Studies*, 31, 3, 1977, p. 451; *General Annual Report of the British Army for the year ending 30 September 1913*, Cmd 725 (1914).

might be required was unknown, and manpower policy remained less than exact. Pre-war assumptions had dictated that a future war would be short and that Britain would adopt the 'business as usual' approach of a limited maritime commitment resting principally on a naval blockade.

All such assumptions were swept aside by Kitchener's appointment as Secretary of State for War on 5 August 1914. Kitchener believed not only that the war would be prolonged but that Britain must have a large enough army to be able to dictate terms at any post-war settlement. Accordingly, on 6 August Parliament was asked to sanction an immediate increase of 500,000 men, with Kitchener making his appeal for the 'first 100,000' of his 'New Armies' on 7 August.

Yet Kitchener himself had no clear idea of how many men might be needed, the confusion being apparent in the conflicting figures emanating from accounts of the Cabinet meeting on 24 August at which the New Armies were first discussed. A figure of seventy divisions is usually cited as the ultimate intention, presumably chosen as it was approximately the size of the German and French armies prior to mobilisation. The figure of seventy divisions was not, however, arrived at immediately. On 25 August Kitchener spoke of thirty divisions, a figure that had risen to fifty by mid-September and to sixty by June 1915. The figure of seventy was accepted by a Cabinet sub-committee in August 1915 but adjusted to sixty-two divisions abroad and five at home in February 1916 and subsequently altered to fifty-seven divisions abroad and ten at home in April 1916. In terms of overall numbers, Parliament sanctioned a further increase of 500,000 on 9 September 1914, another million on 12 November 1914 and an upper limit of 4 million men in December 1915. The figure was adjusted for the last time, and in effect retrospectively, to 5 million in December 1916.[14]

The effective limit of 2.5 million volunteers was reached by December 1915. Conscription thus followed from what Arthur Henderson was to call a 'process of exhaustion'. It was simply not a practical proposition in August 1914, and the fact that it took another two years to be implemented is testimony enough to the depth of opposition within society. The long and agonised wartime debate is sufficiently well known to require little amplification here,[15] the organisational milestones being the Householders' Return of November and December 1914, the National Register in July 1915 and the Derby Scheme of October to December 1915. It was, of course, the results of the latter, in which only 1,150,000 out of 2,179,000 single men attested a willingness to enlist if called upon, with only 343,000 of those willing actually available, that forced Asquith's hand after his promise of 10 November 1915 that no married man would be called up before all single men had been taken. Receiving the royal assent on 27 January 1916, the first

Military Service Act deemed that all single men and childless widowers between the ages of eighteen and forty-one had enlisted. However, the wide discrepancies in medical examination which were to lead to the establishment of the Ministry of National Service in November 1917, and the numerous exemptions granted by tribunals, resulted in fewer men becoming available than expected. Between 1 March 1916 and 31 March 1917, for example, only 371,500 were compulsorily enlisted while some 779,936 were exempted for various reasons.

The resulting attempt to call up married men who had attested under the Derby Scheme in contradiction to Asquith's pledge led to increasing pressure. In the wake of the Easter Rising, which required yet more manpower to suppress, the Military Service Act (No. 2) passed all its parliamentary stages in nine days and received the royal assent on 25 May 1916. Subsequent legislation, as indicated in Table 1.4, further extended the reach of conscription, although it should be noted that its application was remarkably tolerant by comparison with other countries, Britain alone recognising a legal right to exemption on the grounds of conscience.[16]

Nor did conscription equalise the burden of military service within society, owing to the continued exemption of large numbers of the working class through physical unfitness. The Ministry of National Service medical boards exempted on medical grounds over a million men out of the 2.5 million examined in the last year of the war, although there was a tendency among practitioners to equate fitness with stature and to display prejudice against certain sections of society, such as Jews, particularly Russian-born Jews.[17] Ironically, conscription also failed to solve the long-term manpower shortage, although enlistment exceeded wastage until the last third of 1917, since as the war economy evolved the army was but one of several agencies competing for manpower and frequently came at the bottom of the list of priorities. The allocation of manpower resources was not within the army's control and was subject to political manoeuvring between politicians and soldiers. The question of manpower shortages in France and Flanders has been exhaustively examined elsewhere[18] but it can be said that the army did not always distribute its manpower as economically as it might have done.

In all over 5·7 million passed through the British army during the First World War, the wartime enlistments of 4.·9 million representing some 22.11 per cent of the male population of the United Kingdom and 10·73 per cent of the population as a whole.[19] This figure does not represent the full extent of military participation. Excluding the contribution of the white dominions, India and other colonies, which together provided another 2,881,786 enlistments in the forces of the empire, the strength of the army in France and Flanders also included

Table 1.4. *The Military Service Acts, 1916–18*

Act	Date	Provisions
Military Service Act, 1916	January 1916	Conscripts all single men and childless widowers aged 18–41
Military Service Act (No. 2), 1916	May 1916	Conscripts all men aged 18–41
Military Service (Review) of Exceptions) Act, 1917	April 1917	Combs out more men from industry, agriculture and the mines, including many previously judged unfit, notably those born between 1895 and 1898
Military Service (Conventions with Allied States) Act, 1917	July 1917	Allows for conscription of British subjects living abroad and of Allied citizens in Britain. Convention signed with Russia (July) and with France (October)
Military Service Act, 1918	February 1918	Removes a variety of exemptions
Military Service (No. 2) Act, 1918	April 1918	Conscripts men aged 41 to 50 and allows for extension of the age limit to 56 and cancellation of most exemptions if the need arises. Also allows for the extension of conscription to Ireland
Naval, Military and Air Force Service Act, 1919	April 1919	Retains compulsory military service until 30 April 1920

from 1916 onwards some 193,500 native labourers drawn from China, India, South Africa, Egypt, the West Indies, Malta, Mauritius, the Seychelles and Fiji. There were similar labour corps in Mesopotamia, East Africa, Egypt, Italy and at Salonika.[20] In Britain itself two other groups participated in the armed forces, namely women and a revived Volunteer Force.

Traditionally the army had employed women only as nurses prior to 1914, and this pattern continued with the Queen Alexandra's Imperial Military Nursing Service, the Territorial Force Nursing Service and the Voluntary Aid Detachments, which contained both men and women and were administered by the Territorial county associations. Excluding the VADs, some 74,000 by 1914, the number of military nurses expanded from some 2,600 in 1914 to over 18,000 by 1918. There was undoubted reluctance to use women in any other capacity, but their work in the munitions industry forced the army to reconsider, and in April 1915 an Army Council instruction authorised the employment of cooks and waitresses in Britain, the Women's Legion receiving official recognition in February 1916 and numbering some 6,000 by the end of the year. If women could replace men at home, then, as an official report concluded in January 1917, there was no logical reason why they could not do so abroad, and in March 1917 the first cooks from the new Women's Army Auxiliary Corps arrived in France. Unlike the civilian volunteers such as the VADs, the First Aid Nursing Yeomanry or military nurses generally, the 41,000 women who served in the WAAC were mostly working or lower middle-class girls who enjoyed a totally unjustified reputation for immorality. This may have derived from the resentment that the WAAC, who were replacing men in the ratio of four to three as clerks, typists, cooks, drivers, telegraphists, storemen and so on, were releasing men for the front, but the military as a whole never quite came to terms with the concept of women in uniform and their status within the army remained ambiguous.[21]

Almost as soon as the war began, unofficial and illegal bodies of 'Town Guards' appeared in many areas. Rather more formally, Percy Harris suggested in a letter to *The Times* on 6 August 1914 that a 'London Defence Force' be established, Lord Desborough agreeing to become president of a preliminary committee three days later. Subsequent correspondence with the War Office led to authorisation on 4 September 1914 for the committee to instruct men not of military age in drill and musketry. In view of the considerable number of requests for information emanating from other parts of the country, the committee transformed itself into the Central Association of Volunteer Training Corps and on 19 November 1914 was given official status. Certain conditions were attached, including the stipulation that men of military age should not be enlisted unless they had 'genuine' reasons for not joining the army; that eligible volunteers would undertake to enlist in the army if required; that no military ranks or uniforms be utilised other than an armlet; that no expense should fall on the State, and that a recognised military adviser be appointed. Rather like the WAAC, the VTC attracted its share of controversy, since, on occasion, it was accused of shielding men who might otherwise have enlisted, while the traditional ridicule of the amateur soldier was resurrected in the epithets ascribed to the VTC of 'George's Wrecks', 'Georgeous Wrecks' and 'Genuine Relics' from the GR on the armlet.

The Marquess of Lincolnshire made an attempt to improve the status of the VTC with a short Bill in October 1915 to enable the War Office to regulate the force more closely, but it ran out of parliamentary time and

in March 1916 the provisions of the Volunteer Act of 1863 were applied.
The Central Association now became one of Volunteer Regiments and
an advisory council to the Director-General of the Territorial Force,
whose staff Harris and Desborough joined, while local administration
was devolved to Territorial county associations. With the introduction
of conscription and the decision by the Local Government Board in July
1916 that tribunals could grant exemption from military service on
condition that men joined the Volunteers, the 1863 legislation became
unsatisfactory, since it stipulated that men could resign on fourteen
days' notice. A new Volunteer Act in December 1916 closed the loophole
and compelled men both to serve for the duration and to undertake a
statutory minimum number of drills per month.

The advent of the 'tribunal men' changed the character of the
Volunteers, since they formed an increasingly large proportion of the
force. In February 1918, for example, some 101,000 out of 285,000
Volunteers, or approximately 35 per cent had been directed by
tribunals, while by November 1918, after the new military service
legislation had swept up older Volunteers, the proportion increased to 44
per cent. From the point of view of the Volunteers this was highly
unsatisfactory, as many tribunal men employed in industry or
agriculture were unable or unwilling to complete the drills required, and
tribunals proved unhelpful in compelling them to do so. From the point
of view of the War Office, the Volunteers had become an escape route,
the Adjutant-General claiming in the summer of 1917 that 100,000 men
had been lost to the army.

Nevertheless, although incapable of totally replacing regular
formations in home defence, the Volunteers did give useful service in a
variety of tasks ranging from guarding vulnerable points to munitions
work, digging the London defences, assisting with the harvest, running a
pay office on Victoria Station, supplementing London's firemen and
providing transport for soldiers on leave or invalided home. In the
summer of 1918 over 13,000 Volunteers served in special service
companies on the east coast in three-month tours to release more
regulars for France and Ireland. For all this the Volunteer Force, which
may have embraced up to a million men during the war, received little
reward, being allowed almost to wither away in December 1918 when a
state of suspended animation was effected. Formal disbandment began
in January 1920, the units of Motor Volunteer Corps, which were seen as
potentially useful for strike-breaking, being retained until March 1921.[22]

Thus, if the extent of participation among males in the United
Kingdom of military age is added to that among those under, of or above
military age who served in the Volunteers or Special Constabulary, as
well as the participation of women and the growth that took place in
youth organisation membership among both boys and girls, then Britain

was truly a nation in arms between 1914 and 1918. What, then, was the impact of that participation on society, the individual and the army itself?

The extent of military participation could not fail to have an impact upon civilian perceptions of the army. What might loosely be termed an 'official' image was assiduously cultivated in a number of ways. There were, of course, the efforts of the voluntary and official recruiters to stir patriotism and present a traditionally heroic image of the soldier serving a noble cause. A week-long recruiting campaign at Preston in Lancashire in August 1915, for example, included marching bands and pipers, a 'moving picture van', garden parties and fetes and the prominent exhibition of a local VC winner.

The recruiting movement embraced much of the establishment in each locality, including, wherever possible, representatives of local labour. Thus in Lancashire the Earl of Derby made much of a miners' agent, Joe Tinker, who, though strongly anti-militarist before the war, had accepted Derby's sponsorship to obtain a place in the Inns of Court OTC. The clergy were specially prominent in encouraging recruitment, and the great majority of the 20,000 local agents who acted for the Inns of Court in providing information on obtaining commissions were clergymen. The Archbishop of Canterbury had refused to sanction the use of the pulpit for recruiting, but many diocesan bishops were highly effective recruiters outside it, notably the Bishop of London, A. F. Winnington-Ingram, who 'did much to popularise the belief that the nation was engaged in a Holy War'. In Wales even Nonconformist ministers spoke so strongly in favour of the war that many ultimately lost their congregations. Once conscription had replaced the voluntary system the local establishment tended to preside over the tribunals, which have been characterised as 'civilian, middle-class and public-minded'.[23]

The nobler military virtues were also presented to the public at large through the pictorial representation of the soldier by artists such as R. Caton Woodville, W. B. Wollen and Fortunio Matania, whose work, appearing in popular illustrated periodicals and children's literature, invariably depicted gallantry, self-sacrifice and determination, while death somehow contrived to be tasteful. The majority of rank-and-file soldiers did not have the literary skill to describe their experiences accurately in letters home, even had they wished to do so, the unconscious humour and simplicity of such letters striking many of the officers who censored them.

Even less reality was derived from the popular press. After the Moore and Fyfe despatches the army quickly rounded up freelance journalists and sent them back to England, Ernest Swinton becoming 'Eyewitness' (or, 'Eyewash', as he was more popularly known) in September 1914, to be succeeded in July 1915 by five official war correspondents. The correspondents were chiefly characterised by their extreme discretion, almost an entirely new language developing to disguise setback and defeat. On those rare occasions when mavericks like Ashmead-Bartlett or Repington did not observe discretion, the newspaper proprietors and editors themselves operated a self-censorship far more effective than that of the official Press Bureau. Editors like Gwynne of the *Morning Post*, Garvin of the *Observer*, Blumenfeld of the *Daily Express* and Strachey of the *Spectator* needed little encouragement to pronounce the infallibility of GHQ. *The Times* under Northcliffe's proprietorship continued to support the generals after Northcliffe himself had ceased to believe in them, although, in the end, the *Daily Mail* and *The Times* swung against them too – at which point Repington departed the latter for the *Morning Post*. The national and provincial press was overwhelmingly patriotic, its customary outrage at censorship being immediately muted when the victims were socialist or pacifist journals.[24]

Contact with the soldier was not, however, confined to the sight of recruiting bands, reading letters and newspapers or to hearing the sound of the guns across the Channel. For the first time in a century very large numbers of troops were permanently visible to society and, with the delay in providing hutted accommodation in the autumn of 1914, in close proximity to civilians. Reactions naturally varied on both sides but in many cases the influx of men from different regions and classes was undoubtedly a cultural shock for householders, although the troops appear to have been welcomed at first. In autumn 1914, for example, 'the army was all over Watford' but, on leaving, an officer noted that 'The people have been awfully good and took to our fellows wonderfully.' The War Office was deluged by complaints from 'well-meaning' civilians at the plight in which many troops allegedly found themselves, one letter received by Southern Command in August 1915 claiming that troops at Bulford were begging for food.

On the other hand, one billeting officer touring country parks in February 1915 'was not received with any excessive cordiality by the owners', while by February 1916 the inhabitants of Chelmsford were so disillusioned with the presence of troops that they 'either went to bed and locked the doors, or went to the seaside and left their houses "not available for billets" '. The wartime diary of the town clerk of Southwold in Suffolk is a catalogue of civil–military friction ranging from the 'horrible mess' made by the Lincolnshire Yeomanry on the common in October 1914 to the cutting off of water to the 101st Provisional Battalion during their fourteen-month sojourn between September 1915 and November 1916 because the men were 'stealing' it.[25] Another problem was the encouragement of prostitution, both professional and amateur. The GOCs at Portsmouth and Plymouth, for example, were much exercised by the rate of venereal disease in their commands in November 1914, the latter reporting that an ill lit stretch of road near the barracks and huts at Crownhill enabled prostitutes to solicit while rendering respectable women liable to molestation.

The official medical history of the war was later to claim that, of the considerable number of hospital admissions for venereal disease in France and Flanders, the numbers thus incapacitated being the equivalent of a division a day by 1918, some 50 per cent had contracted the disease in England rather than in France. However, the controversy that had surrounded the Contagious Diseases Acts, repealed in 1886, left the military authorities wary of new legislation and it was only the pressure of the dominions, whose troops recorded far higher venereal disease rates than the British, that finally forced the insertion of clauses in DORA in March 1918. They were promptly withdrawn in November.[26]

But if the intrusion of troops could be harmful, it could also prove beneficial. The recruitment of the New Armies disrupted industry and ultimately brought trade unions face to face with the realities of dilution but, by contrast, large numbers of troops could be made available, as they were in the summer of 1915, to assist with harvesting. The presence of troops also generated trade, Welsh seaside resorts actually competing to attract the camps of the Welsh Army Corps during the slack autumn period of 1914. The conflicting efforts of War Office, Territorial associations, corporations and individuals to equip units in 1914 also benefited businesses, as did the erection of the many new army camps that sprang up in the first autumn and winter of the war and the provision of supplies to them. Official army contractors such as Cox and Co., Dickenson and Co. and Messrs Powling made handsome profits through grossly inflated prices, although local contractors often did equally well by undercutting them.

There were innumerable local scandals. In the case of Southern Command, for example, complaints were investigated in March 1915 that ASC men from Winchester were selling off oats to farmers, while a farmer at Hungerford in August 1915 was buying swill for his pigs from the army and reselling 'the least damaged loaves at 1*d* per piece'. At Sutton Veny camp in November 1915 a soldier was selling freshly roasted meat to the Dickenson canteen manager, who then sold it back to the troops as faggots. Another major investigation at the same time discovered that private veterinary surgeons were making profits by subcontracting out sick horses.[27]

The impact of the army upon those who enlisted would vary as much as the impact upon civilian communities in districts where troops were located. For all recruits there was some adjustment to make between civilian life and life in the services. For the many recruits of middle-class origin or from sheltered homes, enlistment could spell an end to innocence in its widest sense. For the working-class recruits the army might not be far different from the regimentation of the factory, and in some respects they might be better-off in the ranks than in the slum conditions in civilian life. Former soldiers, such as the 60 per cent of the BEF infantry in 1914 who were recalled reservists, had to come to terms with a march discipline introduced only in 1912 which induced considerable exhaustion in the opening campaign of the war.[28] For some of the 'class corps' of the Territorial Force, with their choral societies, penny readings and other social activities in camp, the introduction to military service could be almost pleasurable, but camp life in England in the autumn and winter of 1914 also brought frequent complaints of poor food and the outbreak of disease.

At Bedford measles killed eighty-five men of the 51st (Highland) Division in December, 10 per cent of those who contracted it, with men from the remoter islands and far north being the most badly affected. There were cases of cerebral meningitis at Halton in Buckinghamshire, an outbreak of the 'itch' at St Anthony in Cornwall, pneumonia and pleurisy at Lulworth and Bovington in Dorset; in all, over 29,000 men were returned as sick each month in the camps on Salisbury Plain between October and December 1914, leading to wildly exaggerated rumours that 2,000 Canadians alone had died of pneumonia or meningitis.[29] Ironically, one of the few rights of the servicemen was to refuse inoculation, and many did so, despite an official campaign, until the concession was withdrawn by means of refusing leave to those who had not been inoculated. There was also an official campaign to persuade younger recruits on health grounds not to start smoking cigarettes.[30]

The contrast with civilian life was, of course, greatest on active service, and there has been some debate whether a 'war generation' subsequently existed, based on universality of experience among officers and men in the front line. Before the war one of the main features of British society was the extent to which divisions existed at almost every level. Such divisions, whether primarily economic or social, were certainly perpetuated at least initially among the rank and file of the greatly expanded army. Thus individuals had to come to terms not only with service life itself but with the social traits of fellow recruits from widely different backgrounds. The journalist W. L. Andrews and his fellow 'bun-wallahs', having purchased their own cutlery, were astonished to be told that 'it was bad taste for us to differentiate ourselves in that way from the rougher men'. Similarly, a trooper of the 1/2nd County of London Yeomanry (Westminster Dragoons) sharing accommodation on a troopship in September 1914 with fellow

Territorials of the 1/9th Manchesters recorded that 'their lack of manners and their filthy habits are more than we can stand'. His amazement at the conduct of the officers of the Manchesters speaks volumes:

I don't wonder our officers, who are nearly all regular Army Cavalry officers and gentlemen, don't get on with theirs as their officers all say 'thee' and 'thou', even the Captains. They are the commonest lot of men I ever saw. They live most of the day with their sergeants and I heard one officer ask a man what he was doing and, on being told, he said, 'You'd better shoot up and 'op it!' Another officer said, 'B.g. . r off,' to one of his men.[31]

Inevitably divisions were eroded, for, as the historian of the 1/6th West Yorkshires put it, 'A few months in an infantry battalion on active service was a liberal education. The artificial distinctions of civilian life were broken down, and a man lived in intimacy with different types and classes.' There were clearly, too, commonly shared views, such as a distaste for 'slackers' or for civilians whose concept of trench warfare was restricted to the ruined village erected in Trafalgar Square or the model trench dug in Kensington Gardens which proved such a source of amusement to soldiers on leave.[32]

There are many accounts which indicate the unease soldiers often experienced in civilian company whilst on leave and the sense of escape on returning to France. At the front the development of 'ritualisation' and 'live and let live', whereby there was a tacit acceptance of an unofficial truce between the opposing front lines, has been depicted as a kind of conspiracy involving both the rank and file and junior officer, united in the desire to survive.[33] The enemy of ritualisation, it has been argued, was not the opponent across No Man's Land but the 'staff'. Certainly there is plenty of evidence of resentment against staff officers, the future Major-General Essame testifying to the contempt engendered by the nightly contrast at Victoria Station between the crowded leave trains of regimental officers and men and the dining cars of the staff train. Of course, there is an element of myth in the characterisation of the staff in the Great War. Many difficulties arose because some 49 per cent of all pre-war-trained staff officers were killed or died of wounds, well over a third of them before the end of 1915. Their replacements were often inexperienced, while the over-centralisation of authority at higher levels stifled initiative among regimental officers and lowered the latter's prestige.[34]

In some respects, then, there was a fellowship 'fused by the action of war . . . beyond the understanding of those who have not known it',[35] but this should not be pushed too far, since many gulfs existed at the front. There were the divisions between the infantry and the artillery and, within units, between specialists such as snipers or machine-gunners and the others. Specialists like the trench mortar crews could endanger the survival of others in a 'live and let live' situation, since the infantry could expect to receive a 'tit for tat' barrage from across 'No Man's Land. The greatest gulf of all existed between officer and man. It was not necessarily one of class, since officers were increasingly promoted from the ranks, but one of status and privilege. Officers might well share front-line dangers, play football with the men or offer themselves up as objects of ridicule at concert parties but, as a survey of trench newspaper literature suggests, this was far from being recognised as a universality of experience by the rank and file.

Officers were differentiated in innumerable ways, ranging from their separate brothels and cinemas to the very different treatment of those suffering shell shock. It was assumed that a 'healthy brain' would respond to treatment. In fact the rate of return to duty by officers suffering from some form of neurosis was 36 per cent higher than that of other ranks, and this only encouraged 'lightly veiled class analysis of mental disorder' such as that by Sir Frederick Mott and W. H. Rivers, who believed that enlisted men were more liable to hysteria than officers. Equally the Graves Registration Commission, later the Imperial War Graves Commission, had a constant battle during and after hostilities to ensure equality of treatment for officers and men.[36] The 'celebration of community' identified as deriving from the 'social knowledge' imparted by the war was largely confined to the better educated. There are thus distinct dangers in accepting the post-war disillusionment of a Robert Graves or a Siegfried Sassoon and their longing for the unity of the front line as in any way representative. In Britain as elsewhere the war generation existed, as a more recent review article concludes, 'only for so long as it remained under fire . . .'[37]

While those enlisting underwent a process of socialisation into military life, the regular army, equally, had to adjust to the influx of recruits of a very different stamp from those of peacetime service. The vast majority of wartime servicemen were just that: they did not seek a permanent military career and brought into the army civilian perceptions. The lack of understanding of the army's code of discipline resulted in many initial lapses. The New Armies suffered two distinct waves of unrest, the first upon arrival in camps where lack of equipment and tents led many to attempt to go home, as at Purfleet, Shoreham and Preston; and the second when more permanent hutted accommodation was still being constructed while winter weather struck exposed sites such as Codford and Shoreham. Men readily communicated their grievances to their families, the press and MPs, as in the case of the 'strike' by men of the 24th (Service) Battalion, Royal Fusiliers ('2nd Sportsman's') at Tidworth in September 1915 over poor food. Unfamiliarity with military custom led to incidents unknown to the peacetime army, such as the 'siege' of Hoxton barracks in August 1914 by hundreds of women when the men of the 1/7th London were unexpectedly compelled to remain in barracks overnight for the first time, or the absence of up to 250 men at a time in December 1914 and January 1915 among Welsh Territorials recruited from the Llanberis and Penygroes slate quarries who slipped away to tend their allotments.[38] Yet the fact that most servicemen were civilians first and foremost was a significant factor both in maintaining the army's morale during the war and in preventing any large scale post-war revolutionary unrest.

The British army did suffer morale problems much like any other army during the First World War but it survived them where other armies faltered. There was a crisis of morale in the BEF during the first winter of the war and again in the winter of 1917/18. Indices utilised by GHQ such as the incidence of trench feet, shell shock and crime were not reliable as a means of assessing morale. Crime invariably rose after heavy casualties, while medical advances progressively reduced the number of cases of trench feet and shell shock. Nevertheless, the available statistics and the more sophisticated surveillance developed later in the war, in so far as they can be interpreted meaningfully, do give an impression of a less than compliant soldiery.

Desertion remained relatively high throughout, as did drunkenness. Self-mutilation was not a significant problem but there were those who were intent on avoiding danger; the Army Suspension of Sentences Act, 1915, was devised to prevent crime being committed to avoid the front line. The ratio of military police rose steadily, while the Darling Committee discovered in 1919 that there had been an average of 160 courts-martial a day during the war, compared to ten a day in 1913. Major-General Childs directly attributed the increase in crimes relatively unknown in the pre-war army like sodomy and murder to the influx of wartime recruits and officers. There were also instances of collective indiscipline, the best known being at Etaples base camp in September 1917. The Adjutant-General's Department became particularly skilled at negotiating the termination of such disturbances, a lenient policy which was not applied where native labourers or troops were concerned.[39] There was also something of a moral collapse in March 1918, with flight, panic and premature surrender in the Fifth Army. It has been suggested that such a crisis of morale tended to occur in all armies, except the German, between two and a half and three years after real entry into the war, Britain's baptism being counted from the battle of Loos in September 1915. Again with the exception of Germany, there is a correlation between the occurrence of collapse and the total number of deaths equalling the number of fighting infantry.[40] March 1918 fits the pattern well but, unlike the armies of France, Italy, imperial Russia and ultimately even Germany, the British army did not collapse totally.

A comparison with the French army, which suffered its large-scale collapse in spring 1917, is instructive. Both armies shared the privations of the trenches and misgivings about their military leadership but it might be argued that on the face of it the French rather than the British were the better motivated. Whereas the British soldier was not consciously in direct defence of his homeland, the French *poilu* was fighting on his own soil to regain occupied territory, although admittedly this could adversely affect the morale of those whose home lay behind German lines. There is no evidence that the British soldier was better fed than the French, who were allowed more leave, while the dominion contingents all received better pay. British troops had grievances over most material factors of importance such as food, leave and pay allowances, as both Horatio Bottomley, whose *John Bull* proclaimed itself a soldier's champion like the *Daily Mail*, and the War Cabinet recognised in September 1917.

Disturbances at Shoreham that month were prompted by the scale of rations, the higher pay of nearby Canadians and the cancellation of leave trains to Brighton in order to save fuel. Similarly, the only two known Soldiers' Councils in Britain during the war – those at Birmingham and Tunbridge Wells in 1917 – were concerned with bread-and-butter issues far removed from revolutionary intent. It is, of course, a misnomer that British troops were constantly in the front line or even in active sectors of line, but French troops behind the lines were not harassed by their officers in the way that British troops 'at rest' were regarded almost as an affront. The French were also spared the 'bull' of which British trench newspapers so frequently complained. Nor did the French believe in the 'active front' policy pursued by the British high command, the extent to which British trench raiding in particular raised morale being highly problematical.

In fact the British trench press attacked all those features of military life that were distinctly British, but clearly there were differences which contributed to the greater stability of British morale. Drill and the element of compulsion undoubtedly assisted, for all that MPs at Westminster increasingly complained about draconian punishments fundamentally unsuited to a citizen army. One cannot entirely discount the rum issue but this alone can hardly explain the upkeep of morale. Religious belief appears to have been of little effect, but British troops do appear to have had a greater sense of duty and loyalty than some others, and here the impact of regimental tradition and its local identity cannot be overestimated. The rallying call of Lieutenant-Colonel Elstob on 21 March 1918 ('The Manchester Regiment will hold Manchester Hill to the last') or the notice in Mansel Copse cemetery on the Somme ('The Devons held this trench, the Devons hold it still') are essentially British in their expression. British medical care was certainly far superior to that of the French, while the French officer showed none of that concern for the welfare of his men that was so inculcated in the British tradition of junior leadership, whether regular or wartime commissioned officers. The French had their *marraines de guerre* or wartime 'godmothers' but did not enjoy that great welfare network of divisional and regimental canteens, YMCA, Church Army and comfort funds that saw some 800,000 parcels reaching the BEF each week by April 1917. The bath arrangements and concert parties so often mentioned in British memoirs do not figure in French accounts; nor do the divisional sports meetings, boxing tournaments, inter-battalion football and cricket matches that characterised the British army.

Current research suggests that entertainment was of particular significance, the mass export of British popular culture and the civilian pattern of recreation that resulted being far different from those of the other armies, including the dominion forces who unsuccessfully tried to emulate it. Subordination and tedium were commonplace in British industrial society, while popular culture made light of hardship and enabled men to normalise their emotions under stress. In effect it comes down to the characteristics of the British working-class civilian soldier – perhaps a phlegmatic acceptance of fate or sheer bloodymindedness but always with a sardonic humour. If some did become disillusioned, then there were always newcomers, from the New Armies of 1915 and 1916 to the optimistic youths of 1918. As Dominick Graham has written, 'fresh men in the ranks, ignorant and easily killed though they often were, blended with surviving natural leaders to keep the show going'.[41]

Just as the fact that British servicemen were only temporarily in uniform had a bearing on morale, it also affected the post war situation. There were large numbers of pre-war trade unionists in the army's ranks but despite official fears they rarely figured in wartime disturbances. By contrast, survivors of the regular army do appear prominently and suffered a disproportionate number of wartime executions for all crimes. Significantly, where trade unionists did emerge clearly was in the demobilisation disturbances which reached a climax between 3 and 16 January 1919. Some of these incidents had a political element linked to the possibility of service in Russia but the great majority were related solely to demobilisation demands and familiar grievances over food, compulsory church parades or, as at Calais, working hours. Those involved wanted not only to leave the army but to sever all contact with it. Thus most were indifferent to the attempt by some veterans' organisations to forge a radical political movement. Ex-servicemen certainly had grievances, but even members of the radical groups baulked at close co-operation with industrial militants who had stayed at home while they fought. The veterans' movement was also fragmented, with six different organisations, the bitter rivalry resulting in a riot at Luton in July 1919. Much of the basis for grievance was removed by government concessions on pensions in mid-1919, and by 1921 the three main organisations had combined in a British Legion which rejected political partisanship, while the radical organisations disbanded.[42]

The rapid process of demobilisation even at a time of increased commitment – the war did not officially end until the Order-in-Council of 31 August 1921 – was probably greeted with relief by those regular officers who expressed that apocryphal desire to return to 'real soldiering'. The army certainly returned to its pre-war style of life but, in a sense, remarkably little had changed during the war itself.

The officer corps is a case in point, for although over 200,000 commissions were granted during the war, of which only 16,000 were permanent, the ethos of the corps as a whole remained dominated by the surviving pre-war regulars. Thus the officer corps continued to display considerable difficulty in adjusting to new and changing conditions. There was little attempt to learn from the Great War either during or after it, no official effort being made to absorb the lessons until the Kirke Committee of 1932 and then primarily to provide a commentary on the *Official History*. Indeed, the CIGS, Sir George Milne, remarked in 1926 that the war was 'abnormal'.[43] There were some adjustments in the structure of the army but only gradually, the most significant

Table 1.5. *Demobilisation of the regular army and territorial force, 1918–20*

Year	Month	Total strength under arms
1918	October	3,817,837
	November	3,759,471
	December	3,717,445
1919	January	3,656,258
	February	3,451,566
	March	2,962,288
	April	2,250,275
	May	1,853,517
	June	1,598,167
	July	1,441,093
	August	1,320,834
	September	1,204,834
	October	1,058,566
	November	882,794
	December	689,446
1920	January	580,746
	February	517,881
	March	458,630
	April	381,056

Source. Statistics of the Military Effort of the British Empire, HMSO, London, 1922, pp. 89, 231–3.

change being that forced in disciplinary procedure by civilian pressures. The greatest impact of military participation was thus not on the army but upon those individuals who had temporarily served in it.

The best estimate of deaths of British servicemen is 722,785, of which over 673,000 occurred in the army. This represents a slightly higher rate of loss among the total mobilised than in the German or Austrian armies but lower than that of France, Romania or Serbia. Not surprisingly, since 70 per cent of those who served were under the age of thirty, the loss was greatest among the young, some 74 per cent of all British war deaths being those aged under thirty and some 38 per cent among those aged under twenty-four. As Jay Winter's detailed studies have shown, the war was 'dysgenic' in its effects through uneven participation among social groups. Thus, since the middle and upper classes did suffer proportionately heavy losses, the concept of the 'lost generation' is no myth.[44] Of course, the loss of life is but one manifestation of the war's effect, since there were also those maimed physically and mentally, many wounds of the latter type not becoming apparent for some years. Disability awards totalled 1·7 million in 1921 but had risen to 2·4 million by 1929, and in 1980 there were still some 27,000 men disabled between 1914 and 1918 receiving a pension. In 1927 the British Legion calculated that 160,000 women had lost their husbands and 300,000 children had lost fathers. The sense of loss could also hit hard later when men listed as missing, were found dead, some 25 per cent of the 28,000 bodies discovered for the first time between 1921 and 1928 being identifiable.[45]

The Great War was not a unique experience for British society. Similar manpower problems had been encountered during the Crimean War, while, although participation and loss were far greater in the First World War than in either the Crimean or the South African wars, British losses in the Napoleonic Wars were almost certainly higher proportionately in terms of men under arms than between 1914 and 1918. Military participation itself, in regular and auxiliary forces, was also probably greater in proportion to the male population between 1793 and 1815. Nevertheless, it is what contemporaries believed that is important and, as Paul Fussell has demonstrated, the popular memory of the Great War persists in innumerable ways. To apply to the British army between 1914 and 1918 that now classic model of Arthur Marwick on the effects of total war: clearly the war did have destructive, test, participation and pyschological aspects.[46] That more lasting change did not result from the army's experience is perhaps a reflection of its peculiar status in society; or, conceivably, wars change societies more than the armies that defend them.

Notes

Crown copyright material in the Public Record Office appears by permission of Her Majesty's Stationery Office. The author also gratefully acknowledges the generosity of the following in allowing him to consult and utilise archives in their possession: the Trustees of the Imperial War Museum; the Ministry of Defence Library (Old War Office); the National Army Museum; the University of Reading Library; the Lambeth Public Library; the Staffordshire Record Office; the Hereford and Worcs. Record Office; the Guildhall Library; the Board of Trustees of the Inns of Court and City Yeomanry; Jeremy Chance Esq; Colonel John Christie-Miller; and Mrs Eileen Luscombe.

1. Cyril Falls, *War Books: a Critical Guide*, Peter Davies, London, 1930.
2   For Australia and New Zealand, see L. L. Robson, *The First A.I.F.: a Study of its Recruitment, 1914–18*, Melbourne University Press, 1970; L. L. Robson, 'The origin and character of the first A.I.F., 1914–18: some statistical evidence', *Historical Studies*, 15,61, 1977, pp. 737–49; Patsy Adam-Smith, *The Anzacs*, Hamish Hamilton, London, 1978; M. McKernan, *The Australian People and the Great War*, Thomas Nelson, Melbourne, 1980. For Canada, see D. Morton, *Canada and War: a Military and Political History*, Butterworths, Toronto, 1981; D. Morton, 'Exerting control: the development of Canadian authority over the Canadian Expeditionary Force, 1914–19', in T. Travers and C. Archer, *Men at War: Politics, Technology and Innovation in the Twentieth Century*, Precedent, Chicago, 1982, pp. 7–19; R. C. Brown and D. Loveridge, 'Unrequited faith: recruiting the CEF, 1914–18', *Revue Internationale d'Histoire Militaire*, 51, 1982, pp. 53–79. For India, see D. C. Ellinwood, 'Ethnicity in a colonial Asian army: British policy, the war and the Indian Army, 1914–18', in De Witt, D. C. Ellinwood and C. Enloe (eds.), *Ethnicity and the Military*, New Brunswick, 1981, pp. 89–114; J. Greenhut, 'Race, sex and war', *Military Affairs*, 45, 2, 1981, pp. 71–4; J. Greenhut, 'Sahib and society', *Military Affairs*, 48, 1, 1984, pp. 15–18. For other colonies, see P. McLaughlin, *Ragtime Soldiers: the Rhodesian Experience of the First World War*, Books of Zimbabwe, Bulawayo, 1980; J. Barrett, 'The rank and file of the colonial army in Nigeria, 1914–18', *Journal of Modern African Studies*, 15, 1, 1977, pp. 105–15.
3   For the evolution of conscription in Europe, see V. G. Kiernan, 'Conscription and society in Europe before the war of 1914 to 1918', in M. R. D. Foot (ed.), *War and Society*, Paul Elek, London, 1973, pp. 143–58; Michael Howard, *War in European History*, Oxford University Press, 1976; John Gooch, *Armies in Europe*, Routledge and Kegan Paul, London, 1979; Hew Strachan, *European Armies and the Conduct of War*, Allen & Unwin, London, 1983; Brian Bond, *War and Society in Europe, 1870–1970*, Fontana, London, 1984.
4   S. Hynes, *The Edwardian Turn of Mind*, Princeton University Press, 1968; G. R. Searle, *The Quest for National Efficiency*, Basil Blackwell, Oxford, 1971; R. Hyam, *Britain's Imperial Century, 1815–1914*, Batsford, London, 1976, pp. 129–34; G. R. Searle, *Eugenics and Politics in Britain, 1900–1914*, Sijthoff, The Hague, 1976; G. R. Searle, 'Critics of Edwardian society: the case of the radical right' in A. O'Day (ed.), *The Edwardian Age: Conflict and Stability, 1900–1914*, Macmillan, London, 1979, pp. 79–96.
5   D. Hayes, *Conscription Conflict*, Sheppard Press, London, 1949, and T. Ropp, 'Conscription in Great Britain, 1900–1914: a failure in civil–military communication?', *Military Affairs*, 20, 1956, pp. 71–6, provide useful summaries of the pre-war debate but they have been superseded by Michael Allison, 'The National Service Issue, 1900–1914', unpub. Ph.D., London, 1975. Previous ideas on long and short service armies are outlined in Ian F. W. Beckett, 'H. O. Arnold-Forster and the Volunteers' in Ian F. W. Beckett and John Gooch (eds.), *Politicians and Defence: Studies in the Formulation of British Defence Policy, 1840–1970*, Manchester University Press, 1980, pp. 47–68.

6 Youth organisations are discussed in J. O. Springhall, 'The Boy Scouts, class and militarism in relation to British youth movements, 1908–1930', *International Review of Social History*, 16, 2, 1971, pp. 125–58; J. O. Springhall, 'Lord Meath, youth and empire', *Journal of Contemporary History*, 5, 4, 1970, pp. 97–111; P. Wilkinson, 'English youth movements, 1908–30', *Journal of Contemporary History*, 4, 2, 1969, pp. 3–24; M. D. Blanch, 'Imperialism, nationalism and organised youth', in J. Clarke, C. Critcher and R. Johnson (eds.), *Working Class Culture*, Hutchinson, London, 1979, pp. 103–20; J. O. Springhall, *Youth, Empire and Society*, Croom Helm, London, 1977.

7 Geoffrey Best, 'Militarism and the Victorian public school', in B. Simon and I. Bradley (eds.), *The Victorian Public School*, Gill and Macmillan, London, 1975, pp. 129–46; A. Vance, 'The ideal of manliness', *ibid.*, pp. 115–28; J. A. Mangan, 'Athleticism', *ibid.*, pp. 147–67; D. Newsome, *Godliness and Good Learning*, John Murray, London, 1961; M. D. Blanch, 'British society and the war', in P. Warwick (ed.), *The South African War*, Longman, London, 1980, pp. 210–38; H. Hanham, 'Religion and nationality in the mid-Victorian army', in Foot, *War and Society*, pp. 159–82; Olive Anderson, 'The growth of Christian militarism in mid-Victorian Britain', *English Historical Review*, 86, 338, 1971, pp. 46–72; Anne Summers, 'Militarism in Britain before the Great War', *History Workshop*, 2, 1976, pp. 104–23; C. Nicholson, 'Edwardian England and the coming of the First World War', in O'Day, *Edwardian Age*, pp. 144–68; Zara Steiner, *Britain and the Origins of the First World War*, Macmillan, London, 1977, pp. 154–63; M. Girouard, *The Return to Camelot: Chivalry and the English Gentleman*, Yale University Press, New Haven, 1981.

8 Invasion is discussed at length by Howard Moon, 'The Invasion of the United Kingdom: Public Controversy and Official Planning, 1888–1918', unpub. Ph.D., London, 1968, two volumes; and, more succinctly, by John Gooch, 'The bolt from the blue', in John Gooch (ed.), *The Prospect of War*, Frank Cass, London, 1981, pp. 1–34. Dr. Gooch also discusses its impact on periodical literature and intellectual thought in the same volume in his essay on 'Attitudes to war in late Victorian and Edwardian England', *Prospect of War*, pp. 35–51. Spy mania is discussed by David French, 'Spy fever in Britain, 1900–1915', *Historical Journal*, 21, 2, 1978, pp. 355–70, while Social Darwinism is covered in James Joll, '1914: the unspoken assumptions', and H. W. Koch, 'Social Darwinism as a factor in the New Imperialism', in H. W. Koch (ed.), *The Origins of the First World War*, Papermac, London, 1972, pp. 307–28 and 329–54 respectively. The 'peace movement' has been recently examined in K. Robbins, *The Abolition of War*, University of Wales Press, Cardiff, 1976, while an overall view of militarism is provided by Michael Howard, 'Empire, race and war', *History Today*, 31, 12, 1981, pp. 4–11.

9 The Victorian Militia is covered by Duncan Anderson, 'The English Militia in the mid Nineteenth Century: a Study of its Military, Social and Political Significance', unpub. D.Phil., Oxford, 1982, while the Volunteers are examined in Ian F. W. Beckett, *Riflemen Form: a Study of the Rifle Volunteer Movement, 1859–1908*, Ogilby Trusts, Aldershot, 1982. As yet the Yeomanry lacks a modern study or, indeed, any general survey.

10 Haldane's motivation with respect to the creation of the Territorial Force is examined in detail in Edward M. Spiers, *Haldane: an Army Reformer*, Edinburgh University Press, 1980, pp. 92–115, and summarised in his *Army and Society, 1815–1914*, Longman, London, 1980, pp. 265–87. John Gooch has also contributed to the debate in 'Mr. Haldane's army, in Gooch, *Prospect of War*, pp. 92–115, and 'Haldane and the National Army', in

Beckett and Gooch, *Politicians and Defence*, pp. 69–86.

11   L. L. Farrar, 'Reluctant warriors: public opinion during the July crisis, 1914', *Eastern European Quarterly*, 16, 4, 1982, pp. 417–46, provides a general survey of research on public attitudes to the outbreak of war. For a masterly revision of previous interpretations of the response of the French, see J. J. Becker, *1914: Comment les français sont entrés dans la guerre*, Presses de la Fondation Nationale des Sciences Politiques, Paris, 1977.

12   J. M. Osborne, *The Voluntary Recruiting Movement in Britain, 1914–16*, Garland, New York and London, 1982, pp. 73–105; Peter Simkins, 'Kitchener and the expansion of the army', in Beckett and Gooch, *Politicians and Defence*, pp. 87–105; David French, *British Economic and Strategic Planning, 1905–1915*, Allen and Unwin, London, 1982, pp. 124–37; F. W. Perry, 'Manpower and Organisational Problems in the Expansion of the British and other Commonwealth Armies during the two World Wars', unpub. Ph.D., London, 1982, pp. 14–80; S. Allison, *The Bantams*, Howard Baker, London, 1981.

13   J. M. Winter, 'Britain's lost generation of the First World War', *Population Studies*, 31, 3, 1977, pp. 449–66; P. E. Dewey, 'Military recruiting and the British labour force during the First World War', *Historical Journal*, 27, 1, 1984, pp. 199–224; Osborne, *Voluntary Recruiting*, pp. 106–29, 138–44; Clive Hughes, 'Army Recruitment in Gwynedd, 1914–16', unpub. M.A., Wales, 1983, pp. 336–39; M. D. Blanch, 'Nation, Empire and the Birmingham Working Class, 1899–1914', unpub. Ph.D., Birmingham, 1975, pp. 341–67. For an example of the pressure upon professional sportsmen to set an example, see Guildhall Library, Mss 17710, 1, letter of P. F. Warner, 14 September 1914. The complexity of local factors in recruitment can also be traced in the correspondence of Gershom Stewart, MP, who raised the 13th Battalion, the Cheshire Regiment – see PRO, Cab. 45/207(i). The thorny question of Irish recruiting has been studied by Dr Keith Jeffery, whose paper, 'War, revolution and recruitment; the Irish and the British army, 1910–1922', was delivered at the Social History Society of the United Kingdom's 'War and Society' conference at the University of Sheffield in January 1984.

14   David French, 'The rise and fall of Business as Usual' in K. Burk (ed.), *War and the State: the Transformation of British Government, 1914–19*, Allen and Unwin, London, 1982, pp. 7–31; G. Cassar, *Kitchener: Architect of Victory*, William Kimber, London, 1977, pp. 195–212; Perry, 'Manpower', pp. 14–80.

15   A useful summary of the wartime debate is Hayes, *Conscription Conflict*, *passim*, while more recent surveys have been included in Cassar, *Kitchener*, pp. 443–456, and Martin Gilbert, *Winston S. Churchill: the Challenge of War, 1914–16*, Heinemann, London, 1971. The Householders' Returns, National Register and Derby Scheme are fully covered in Roy Douglas, 'Voluntary enlistment in the First World War and the work of the Parliamentary Recruiting Committee', *Journal of Modern History*, 42, 1970, pp. 564–85.

16   For the application of conscription, see John Rae, *Conscience and Politics: the British Government and the Conscientious Objectors to Military Service, 1916–19*, Oxford University Press, 1970; T. C. Kennedy, *The Hound of Conscience: a History of the No Conscription Fellowship, 1914–19*, University of Arkansas Press, Fayetteville, 1981.

17   J. M. Winter, 'Some aspects of the demographic consequences of the First World War in Britain', *Population Studies*, 30, 3, 1976, pp. 539–52; J. M. Winter, 'Military fitness and civilian health in Britain during the First

World War', *Journal of Contemporary History*, 15, 1980, pp. 211–44.

18   David R. Woodward, *Lloyd George and the Generals*, University of Delaware Press, Newark, 1983, *passim*; Perry, 'Manpower', pp. 14–80. Woodward's book is, of course, the latest in a long line to examine civil–military relations during the war. See also John Gooch, *The Plans of War*, Routledge and Kegan Paul, London, 1974, and his 'Soldiers, strategy and war aims in Britain, 1914–1918', in B. Hunt and A. Preston (eds.), *War Aims and Strategic Policy in the Great War, 1914–18*, Croom Helm, London, 1976.

19   *Statistics of the Military Effort of the British Empire, during the Great War, 1914–1920*, HMSO, London, 1922, pp. 30, 156–9, 363–4. It should be noted that the figures in the latter differ in some respect from those in *The General Annual Reports of the British Army, 1913–19*, Cmd 1193 (1921).

20   PRO, WO 162/6, 'History of the Development and Work of the Directorate of Organisation, 1914–18', pp. 619–22; Michael Summerskill, *China on the Western Front: Britain's Chinese Work Force in the First World War*, privately published, London, 1982, p. 163; B. P. Willan, 'The South African native labour contingent in France, 1916–18', *Journal of African History*, XIX, 1, 1978, pp. 61–86; G. W. T. Hodges, 'African manpower statistics for British forces in East Africa, 1914–1918', *Journal of African History*, XIX, 1, 1978, pp. 101–16; R. T. Edgar, 'Lesotho and the First World War: recruiting, resistance and the South African Native Labour Corps', *Mohlomi*, 3–5, 1981, pp. 94–108. For the dominions, see note 2 above.

21   The military employment of women has attracted increasing attention, notably Lyn Macdonald, *The Roses of No Man's Land*, Michael Joseph, London, 1980, and more scholarly contributions from Elizabeth Crosthwait, 'The Girl behind the Man behind the Gun: the Position of the Women's Army Auxiliary Corps in World War One', unpub. M.A., Essex, 1980; N. L. Goldman and R. Stites, 'Great Britain and the world wars' in N. L. Goldman (ed.), *Female Soldiers: Combatants or Non-combatants*, Greenwood Press, Westport and London, 1982, pp. 21–46. See also Gail Braybon, *Women Workers in the First World War*, Croom Helm, London, 1981, which reveals precisely similar attitudes being adopted towards women in industry as in the army.

22   PRO, WO 161/105, 107, 108, 109, 111; *ibid*, WO 32/5048, 5049, 5050; MOD, W(ar) O(ffice) L(ibrary), *Volunteer Force Precedent Book, 1916–21*, three volumes; *ibid, Returns of Strength of the Volunteer Force, 1917–18*; *The Volunteer Force and the Volunteer Training Corps during the Great War*, Central Association of Volunteer Regiments, 1920; Ian F. W. Beckett, 'The local community and the Great War: aspects of military participation', *Records of Bucks*, XX, 4, 1978, pp. 503–15. There is an abundance of material relating to the Volunteer Training Corps in county record offices but the force has yet to find a modern historian. Ian F. W. Beckett will, however, examine the volunteers in more detail in 'Aspects of a nation in arms: Britain's Volunteer Training Corps in the Great War' in the forthcoming special volume of *Revue Internationale d'Histoire Militaire* accompanying the International Commission of Military History's symposium on the First World War at Stuttgart in 1985.

23   PRO, WO 161/112, Winder to Williams, 17 October 1917, for Lancashire recruiting methods during the war; Randolph S. Churchill, *Lord Derby; King of Lancashire*, Heinemann, London, 1959, p. 189; Guildhall Library, Mss 17710, 3, Derby to Errington, 3 September 1915; *ibid*., Mss 17686, Inns of Court OTC, 'Press Cuttings'; *ibid*., Mss 17710, 1, Errington to Haldane, 13 February 1916; A. Wilkinson, *The Church of England and the First World War*, SPCK, London, 1978, pp. 32–46, 109–35, 251–5, especially p. 252;

Hughes, 'Recruitment in Gwynned', pp. 269–71, 319; Rae, *Conscience and Politics*, p. 57.

24   C. J. Lovelace, 'Control and Censorship of the Press during the First World War, unpub. Ph.D., London, 1982, especially pp. 162–99. For a summary of Lovelace's work see his earlier 'British press censorship during the First World War', in C. Boyce *et al.* (eds.), *Newspaper History: from the 17th Century to the Present Day*, Constable, London, 1978, pp. 307–19.

25   Diary of H. J. Harris, 1/8th London, 2 January 1915 (by courtesy of Mrs E. Luscombe); I(mperial) W(ar) M(useum), Mss of Captain A. Roberts, letter of 24th March 1915; R(eading) U(niversity) L(ibrary), Astor Mss, 1066/1/618, Ancutt to Macnamara, 11 August 1915; N(ational) A(rmy) M(useum), 7908–62–2, Mss of E. W. S. K. Maconchy, p. 437; IWM, 80/32/2, Christie-Miller Mss, p. 48; *ibid.*, Mss of E. R. Cooper, pp. 2b, 3b, 5b, 7a, 10a, 13a.

26   RUL, Astor Mss, 1066/1/620, Astor to Landon, 5 November 1914; *ibid.*, 1066/1/621, Astor to Landon, 11 November 1914; *OFH: Medical Services, Hygiene of the War*, I, HMSO, London, 1923, p. 20; *ibid, Casualties and Medical Statistics*, HMSO, London, 1931, p. 74; Suzann Buckley, 'The failure to resolve the problem of venereal disease among the troops in Britain during World War One', in Brian Bond and Ian Roy (eds.), *War and Society: a Yearbook of Military History*, Croom Helm, London, 1977, pp. 65–85; McKernan, *Australian People at War*, pp. 116–49.

27   WOL, *Circular Instructions affecting the Territorial Force and County Associations Issued by the War Office*, HMSO, July 1915, Order of 10 July 1915; *ibid.*, TF2, *Miscellaneous Letters during the War Period*, No. 911, Order of 11 June 1915; Hughes, 'Recruitment in Gwynedd', pp. 75–6; RUL, Astor Mss, 1066/1/617, Chapman-Huston to Astor, 2 December 1915; *ibid.*, 1066/1/619, Astor report on 102nd Infantry Brigade, 25 November 1915; *ibid.*, 1066/1/621, Report on 19th Division, 13 December 1914; *ibid.*, 1066/1/623, Breadman to Kitchener, 20 January 1915, and Gilby to Kitchener, 3 February 1915; *ibid*, 1066/1/626, Astor to OC, 339 Coy, ASC, 21 August 1915; *ibid.*, 1066/1/629, Astor to Pitcairn Campbell, 5 August 1915; *ibid.*, 1066/1/634, Correspondence on the case of A. F. S. Jackson, MRCVS. The Astor Mss (1066/1/616–634) are an invaluable collection on the administration of the army in Southern Command, 1914 to 1916.

28   For examples of the shock to sensitive recruits, see F. A. J. Taylor, *The Bottom of the Barrel*, Regency Press, London and New York, 1978, p. 34; N. Gladden, *The Somme, 1916*, William Kimber, London, 1974, pp. 24, 29; IWM, 79/3/1, Diaries of I. L. Meo, especially entry for 18 May 1915; *ibid.*, Mss of F. H. Kibblewhite, pp. 6–7, 16; Worcs. RO, 899:116, BA 5225, Mss of Hugh Chance, pp. 1–2. On reservists, see A. A. Hanbury-Sparrow, 'Discipline or enthusiasm', *British Army Review*, 20, 1965, pp. 8–13, and Spiers, *Army and Society*, p. 289.

29   The range of social activities in Territorial units can be seen in A. A. Taylor (ed.), *From Ypres to Cambrai*, Elmfield Press, Morley, 1974; IWM, P246, Mss of P. H. Jones; *ibid.*, 76/51/1, Mss of W. T. Colyer; diary of H. J. Harris (see note 25 above). For complaints of bad food see RUL, Astor Mss, 1066/1/616–634, *passim*. Outbreaks of disease are recorded in W. N. Nicholson, *Behind the Lines*, Cape, London, 1939, p. 51; F. W. Bewsher, *The History of the 51st (Highland) Division, 1914–18*, Blackwood, Edinburgh and London, 1921, p. 4; S. Cloete, *A Victorian Son*, Collins, London, 1972, p. 200; RUL, Astor Mss, 1066/1/622, Report on Falmouth area, 4 February 1915; *ibid.*, 1066/1/620, Astor to Landon, 28 October 1914; *ibid.*, 1066/1/621, Astor to Landon, 3 January 1915, and sickness records for October to December

1914.

30 On inoculation see RUL, Astor Mss, 1066/1/624, Report on visit to Sutton Veny, 28 April 1915; *ibid*., 1066/1/630, leaflets prepared by the Board of Education for the Research Defence Society and by the British Union for the Abolition of Vivisection, for and against inoculation respectively, which were circulated to Commands in September and October 1914; WOL, *Miscellaneous Letters*, No. 517, Memorandum by the Surgeon-General, 23 August 1914; A. Behrend, *Make me a Soldier*, Eyre and Spottiswoode, London, 1961, p. 29; IWM, 80/32/2, Christie-Miller Mss, pp. 39–41. For evidence of an anti-smoking campaign see Lambeth Public Library, Acc. B08710, IV/36/1/16, Orders of 2/21st London, 29 October 1914 and 3 November 1914; Staffs. RO, D1300/1/8, Orders of 1/1st Staffs. Yeomanry, 17 November 1914.

31 B. A. Waites, 'The effect of the First World War on class and status in England, 1910–1920', *Journal of Contemporary History*, 11, 1, 1976, pp. 27–48; W. L. Andrews, *Haunting Years*, Hutchinson, London, n.d., pp. 14–25; IWM, P430, H. E. Politzer Mss, unidentified letter from RMS *Aragon*, 14 September 1914. For examples of comments derived from the experience of censoring letters see IWM, L. R. Grant Diary, entry for 25 June 1915; R. Palmer, *Letters from Mesopotamia*, Women's Printing Society, London, n.d. p. 53.

32 E. V. Tempest, *History of the 1/6th Battalion, the West Yorkshire Regiment*, Lund Humphries, London and Bradford, 1921, p. 282; E. G. Godfrey, *The Cast Iron Sixth: a History of the 6th Battalion, London Regiment*, F. S. Stapleton, London, 1938, pp. 207–8; J. Nettleton, *The Anger of the Guns*, William Kimber, London, 1979, p. 126; IWM, 79/54/1, C. J. Low Mss, letter of 18 December 1914; Guildhall Library Mss, 17710, 3, letter of Errington, 28 January 1916; Staffs. RO, D1549, J. H. Turner Mss, p. 265.

33 A. E. Ashworth, 'The sociology of trench warfare, 1914–18', *British Journal of Sociology*, XIX, 4, 1968, pp. 407–23; A. E. Ashworth, *Trench Warfare, 1914–18: the Live and Let Live System*, Macmillan, London, 1980.

34 H. Essame, *The Battle for Europe, 1918*, Batsford, London, 1972, pp. 19–20; Brian Bond, *The Victorian Army and the Staff College, 1854–1914*, Eyre Methuen, London, 1972, p. 324; J. Brent Wilson, 'The Morale and Discipline of the BEF, 1914–18', unpub. M.A., New Brunswick, 1978, pp. 121–33, 310–13; T. Travers, 'Learning and decision-making on the western front, 1915–16: the British example', *Canadian Journal of History*, April 1983, pp. 87–97.

35 R. H. Haigh and P. W. Turner (eds.), *The Long Carry*, Pergamon, Oxford, 1970, p. 231. See also R. H. Haigh and P. W. Turner, *World War One and the Serving British Soldier*, MA/AH Publishing, Kansas State University, 1979, a miscellaneous collection of occasional papers which is repetitive but contains some useful information.

36 John Fuller, 'Industrial Entertainments for Industrial War: the British Army Overseas, 1914–1918', paper presented to the University of Cambridge War Studies seminar at Corpus Christi, 14 March 1984 (Mr Fuller is preparing a doctoral dissertation entitled 'Popular Culture and the Problem of Troop Morale in the British and Dominion Forces, 1914–18'); P. J. Lynch, 'The Exploitation of Courage: Psychiatric Care in the British Army, 1914–18', unpub. M.Phil., London, 1977, pp. 108–9, 136–53, 182–3, 221; P. Longworth, *The Unending Vigil*, Constable, London, 1967, pp. 13–14, 32–3, 42, 45–6, 51–5.

37 E. J. Leed, 'Class and disillusionment in World War One', *Journal of Modern History*, 50, 4, 1978, pp. 680–99; E. J. Leed, *No Man's Land*,

Cambridge University Press, 1979; Paul Fussell, *The Great War and Modern Memory*, Oxford University Press, 1975; R. Wohl, *The Generation of 1914*, Weidenfeld and Nicolson, London, 1980; Richard Bessel and David Englander, 'up from the trenches: some recent writing on the soldiers of the Great War', *European Studies Review*, 11, 3, 1981, pp. 387–95.

38   Peter Simkins, 'Kitchener's armies', paper presented to the 'British Army in the Great War' conference at RMA, Sandhurst, November 1978; PRO, Cab. 45/207(i), Statement by J. H. Shields, 17 September 1914; RUL, Astor Mss, 1066/1/618, Astor report on the Tidworth strike, 2 September 1915; *ibid.*, 1066/1/632, Altham to Brade, 18 June 1915, Pitcairn Campbell to Brade, 4 November 1915, and Brade to Pitcairn Campbell, 10 December 1915, for an exchange on the continuing flood of complaints to be investigated from clergymen, MPs and others writing on behalf of troops; IWM, PP/MCR/175, E. C. Palmer Mss, pp. 16–18; Hughes, 'Recruitment in Gwynedd', p. 173.

39   Brent Wilson, 'Morale and discipline', pp. 67–117, 212–62; David Englander and James Osborne, 'Jack, Tommy and Henry Dubb: the armed forces and the working class', *Historical Journal*, 21, 3, 1978, pp. 593–621; D. Gill and G. Dallas, 'Mutiny at Etaples base, 1917', *Past and Present*, LXIX, 1975, pp. 88–112. The opinion of Childs is quoted by Brent Wilson, *op. cit.*, p. 49, but see also Sir W. Childs, *Episodes and Reflections*, Cassell, London, 1930, which contains a chapter of his memoirs of crime and punishment in the field. Examples of the rather different treatment of native mutineers can be found in W. F. Elkins, 'A source of black nationalism in the Caribbean: the revolt of the British West Indies Regiment at Taranto, Italy, in 1918', *Science and Society*, spring 1970, pp. 99–103 (the only mutiny mentioned in any British official history), and Ian F. W. Beckett, 'A serious *émeute*: the Singapore mutiny of February 1915', forthcoming in *Journal of the Society for Army Historical Research*.

40   John Keegan, *The Face of Battle*, Harmondsworth, 1978, p. 276. Keegan provides a masterful descriptive piece on the experience of the Somme, pp. 207–89. Rather less satisfactory treatments of morale and discipline can be found in W. Moore, *The Thin Yellow Line*, Leo Cooper, London, 1974; W. Allison and J. Fairley, *The Monocled Mutineer*, Quartet, London, 1978, which gives no source notes of any description; and D. Lamb, *Mutinies, 1917–20*, Solidarity, n.d., the general inaccuracy of which can be illustrated by comparing the account of the Canadian mutiny at Kinmel Park in 1918 with the scholarly reconstruction in Desmond Morton, 'Kicking and complaining: demobilisation riots in the Canadian forces, 1918–19', *Canadian History Review*, LXI, 3, 1980, pp. 334–60.

41   In addition to those sources already cited in note 39 above, comments on morale also derive from John Baynes, *Morale: a Study of Men and Courage*, Cassell, London, 1967; A. Babington, *For the Sake of Example*, Leo Cooper at Secker and Warburg, London, 1983; Wilkinson, *Church of England*, pp. 109–35, 153–68; John Fuller's research cited at note 36 above, which contains information culled from over a hundred different trench newspapers; F. W. Hirst, *The Consequences of the War to Great Britain*, Oxford University Press, 1934, pp. 80–2; and, especially, a paper by the late Antony Brett-James, 'Some Aspects of British and French Morale on the Western Front, 1914–18', presented to the 'British Army in the Great War' conference at RMA, Sandhurst, in November 1978. See also S. Bidwell and D. Graham, *Fire-power*, Allen and Unwin, London, 1982, p. 117. The Kirke Committee in 1932 concluded that raids had not increased morale – see PRO, WO 32/3116, Report of the Committee on the Lessons of the Great War, appendix I, p. 15.

42   Post-war demobilisation disturbances are well covered in Andrew Rothstein,

The Soldiers' Strikes of 1919, Macmillan, London, 1980, which is more reliable than Lamb or Tom Wintringham, *Mutiny*, London, 1937. Individual disturbances are examined in J. Williams, *Byng of Vimy*, Leo Cooper at Secker and Warburg, London, 1984, pp. 260–61; A. Boyle, *Trenchard*, Collins, London, 1962, p. 320; and D. Killick, *The Calais Mutiny, 1918*, Militant, 1976, which inspires little confidence by getting the date wrong (there was a separate mutiny at Calais in July 1918, while Killick's account refers to that of January 1919) and is, in any case, based on issues of *Worker's Life* dated 29 March and 5 April 1929. The veterans' organisations are covered in Englander and Osborne, 'Jack, Tommy and Henry Dubb', pp. 593–621, and especially by S. R. Ward, 'Intelligence surveillance of British ex-servicemen, 1918–20', *Historical Journal*, XVI, 1, 1973, pp. 179–88, and his 'Great Britain: land fit for heroes lost' in S. R. Ward (ed.), *The War Generation*, Kennikat Press, Port Washington and London, 1975. The Luton disturbances are studied in detail by J. G. Dony, 'The 1919 peace riots in Luton', *Bedfordshire Historical Record Society*, 57, 1978, pp. 205–33. David Englander and Tony Mason are preparing a comparative study of the impact of the world wars upon the political attitude of servicemen entitled *War and Politics: the Experience of Servicemen in two World Wars*, forthcoming from Macmillan, while Julian Putkowski, formerly of Essex University and now at South Cheshire College, is completing a doctoral dissertation on First World War disturbances in the British army.

43 Brian Bond, *British Military Policy between the two World Wars*, Oxford University Press, 1980, contains a chapter on the ethos of the post-war army (pp. 35–71), while the unchanging nature of the officer corps before and after the war can be seen in the sociological analyses of P. E. Razzell, 'The social origins of officers in the Indian and British home armies, 1758–1962', *British Journal of Sociology*, XIV, 3, 1963, pp. 248–61; C. B. Otley, 'The social origins of British army officers', *Sociological Review*, 18, 2, 1970, pp. 213–40; and C. B. Otley, 'The educational background of British army officers', *Sociology*, 7, 2, 1973, pp. 191–209. The attitude of the wartime officer corps to the learning process and to change has been examined by T. H. E. Travers, 'The offensive and the problem of innovation in British military thought, 1870–1915', *Journal of Contemporary History*, 13, 3, 1978, pp. 531–53; Tim Travers, 'The hidden structural problem in the British officer corps, 1900–1918', *Journal of Contemporary History*, 17, 1982, pp. 523–44; Tim Travers, 'Learning and decision-making', pp. 88–97; Bidwell and Graham, *Fire-power*, *passim*; D. Graham, 'Sans doctrine: British army tactics in the First World War', in Travers and Archer, *Men at War*, pp. 69–92.

44 J. M. Winter, 'Some aspects of the demographic consequences', pp. 539–52; J. M. Winter, 'Britain's lost generation', pp. 449–66; J. M. Winter, 'The impact of the First World War on civilian health in Britain', *Economic History Review*, 30, 3, 1977, pp. 487–507.

45 Pension and disability statistics are given in Hirst, *Consequences of the War*, pp. 297–9; Macdonald, *Roses of No Man's Land*, pp. 217–19, 293–304; and Denis Winter, *Death's Men*, Allen Lane, London, 1978, pp. 242–54. Details of burials come from *War Graves of the Empire*, Times Publishing Co., London, 1928, p. 5.

46 Olive Anderson, 'Early experiences of manpower problems in an industrial society at war: Great Britain, 1854–56', *Political Science Quarterly*, LXXXII, 4, 1967, pp. 526–45; Clive Emsley, *British Society and the French Wars, 1793–1815*, Macmillan, London, 1979, pp. 133, 169; Fussell, *Great War and Modern Memory*, *passim*; Arthur Marwick, *War and Social Change in the Twentieth Century*, Macmillan, London, 1974, pp. 1–23.

Edward M. Spiers **2**

The regular army in 1914

'In every respect the Expeditionary Force in 1914 was incomparably the best trained, best organized, and best equipped British Army which ever went forth to war'.[1] This assessment, though proffered in 1925, is still palpably true. Several years of reform, commenced during the South African War and completed under the direction of Richard Burdon Haldane (Secretary of State for War, 1905–12), had produced a thoroughly professional military body. Yet Haldane had never simply intended that his military reorganization should bring about an *armée d'élite*: he had a broader purpose, namely the creation of a 'nation in arms' in which the army would be brought 'into a close and organic relation with the life of the nation'.[2] Since Haldane would claim in his post-war memoirs, 'what we set ourselves to accomplish, we did accomplish',[3] it is worth considering how far the regular army in 1914 reflected his aims.

Haldane likened his reforms to the creation of one national army in the shape of a metal cone. The regulars, he declared, would comprise 'a sharp point of finely tempered steel', backed by a second line of troops (later known as the Special Reserve) and reinforced ultimately by a broad base of expansion and support (the Territorial Force). Haldane argued that this reorganisation, if undertaken, would raise the status of military service, improve the efficiency of the auxiliary forces, and provide a long-term means of expansion through the development of rifle clubs and school and university cadet corps. Ultimately, he asserted, the army and the nation would be welded together, conscious of the demands of imperial defence.[4] In promoting this idea Haldane was trying to reform not merely the army but, more important, public attitudes towards the army. He had perceived, possibly from his reading of Clausewitz and almost certainly from his memories of the South African War, that the conduct of war and the wartime role of the army requires both social consent and political cohesion. As a Liberal imperialist he had supported Britain's military effort in South Africa, but he knew that nothing had more alarmed his fellow Liberals than the passions and fervour evoked by the war. He rejoiced that such feelings had failed to permeate the villages and towns of East Lothian, and that his constituents had 'left the flaunting of Jingo watchwords to the London music halls, and to the more extreme organs of the warlike press'.[5] Creating a nation in arms, he believed, would help to avoid a recrudescence of such feelings and bitter divisions. As he assured his constituents at Haddington:

There was nothing that had a more steady and sober influence on the mind of the population than to be brought closely into contact with the machinery of war. The phrase, 'a nation in arms', did not mean a nation permeated by the spirit of militarism, but it meant a nation that realized what arms signified, what a terrible resort that appeal was if come it must and caused them to pursue their business more soberly, more steadily, more wisely, because they knew it touched themselves in their hearths and homes.[6]

Fulfilling this lofty objective was never likely to be easy, but Haldane's limited remit virtually ensured that the quest would founder. He could not imitate Continental practice and introduce conscription. Despite the campaigning of the National Service League,[7] he regarded compulsory service as politically unacceptable and doubted that it met the unique requirements of British strategy. He repeatedly adumbrated Britain's military priorities: first, the protection of the Channel and the maintenance of a formidable navy, so obviating dependence upon a mass conscript army for home defence; secondly, the garrison requirements of a vast and diverse empire, which relied upon troops who were willing to serve for at least seven years in the colours; and thirdly the hazards which might befall any mingling of the voluntary and compulsory systems, particularly the suspicion, which the General Staff endorsed, that Britain could not sustain its voluntary army of 260,000 men if it also introduced conscription.[8]

Constricted by voluntary recruiting, the regular army could not expect any additional funding either. From the outset of his military planning, Haldane had insisted that the Army Estimates should remain within a ceiling of £28 million.[9] He had realised that his reforms would not be accepted on a lasting basis unless he kept military expenditure within a politically acceptable level. To meet this requirement, he reduced the army by about 16,000 men in 1906; restored the old terms of service (seven years in the colours followed by five years in the Reserve for infantry and cavalry, three years in the colours and nine years in the Reserve for the Guards, six and six for the horse and field artillery, eight and four for the garrison artillery); and produced a balance between the linked battalions at home and abroad, so ensuring the requisite flow of drafts to the overseas units. From the seventy-one home battalions, he earmarked sixty-six to serve in his Expeditionary Force of six large divisions of 154,000 men. In other words, the Expeditionary Force was not determined by any strategic requirements; it was merely a rationalisation of existing resources, the largest body which could be formed out of the units retained at home.[10]

Small in number, the regular army was also unrepresentative of society as a whole. The officer corps was still heavily dependent upon its traditional sources of supply (the peerage, gentry, military families, and to a lesser extent, the clergy and the professions), with only a small minority coming from business, commercial and industrial families. The social composition of the senior officers barely changed between 1899 and 1914 (Table 2.1). Such recruitment was not as rigid as it may superficially appear. The landed interest was a relatively open group; while some established families lost their fortunes and vacated their estates, the *nouveaux riches*, having made their money in industry, commerce and speculation, moved on to the land. During the first half

Table 2.1. *The social composition of the military leadership in 1899 and 1914 (%)*

	Colonels		Generals	
	1899	1914	1899	1914
Peerage and baronetage	12	7	12	10
Gentry	26	26	39	32
Armed services	23	23	19	25
Clergy	12	14	9	6
Professional	9	12	7	6
Others	13	15	18	18
'Don't know'	5	3	8	3
Total (%)	100	100	100	100
Total number	129	118	113	116

Note. The names of officers, excluding those who had retired or were placed on half-pay, were obtained from the relevant Army Lists. For 1899 and 1914 the 'military leadership' includes all field-marshals, generals, lieutenant-generals and major-generals and a random sample of one-third of each list of active colonels.

of the nineteenth century such movement had been particularly apparent when land had not lost its value as an economic and political asset. These new landowners were often in search of status, respectability, or an *entrée* into the activities and gatherings of county society. Serving Crown and country was one method by which aspirants or their descendants might court the approval of local society.[11]

Military service carried such status because it had already become a traditional and respected career for many families. Perpetuating a distinguished family tradition, often stretching back over several generations in the same regiment, was powerful career motivation. In many instances it was a wholly positive influence, motivating both parents and children. Sometimes it was preserved by filial determination despite a parental preference for another career. And in some families it was maintained by the meek acquiescence of the son concerned. Lord Wavell, for example, who entered the 2nd Battalion, Black Watch, in 1901 recalls that:

I never felt any special inclination to a military career, but it would have taken more independence of character than I possessed at the time, to avoid it. Nearly all my relations were military. I had been brought up amongst soldiers; and my father, while professing to give me complete liberty of choice, was determined that I should be a soldier. I had no particular bent towards any other profession, and I took the line of least resistance.[12]

The motivations also varied for those officers who came from non-service families, with or without their parental approval. Some were lured by the appeal of military life, others were faced with little alternative, having failed in their university or civil service examinations. For the sons, particularly the younger sons, of self-assigned gentlemen, the career opportunities could be extremely limited. As Wavell recollects, 'it was quite natural that some of those who failed for the Indian Civil Service should turn to the Army for a career; in fact, other openings were limited, for commercial business was not those days considered a suitable occupation for a gentleman'.[13]

Compounding this relative homogenity of social intake was the connection between the army and the land (Table 2.2). The county communities continued to provide the bulk of officers in the early twentieth century. Within their confines an uncomplicated patriotism and sense of duty flourished alongside an unbridled enthusiasm for field sports. These instincts and aptitudes seemed all too relevant for a pre-technological army. By offering abundant opportunities for sporting and social enjoyment, regiments sustained their appeal for the sons of county families. This exclusivity was preserved still further by the recruitment from the public schools. During the South African War some 62 per cent of regular officers had come from public schools, with 41 per cent from the ten great public schools and 11 per cent from Eton alone.[14] Several public schools had 'army classes' and specialised in training boys for admission into the professional military colleges (Sandhurst for entry into the cavalry and infantry, Woolwich for entry into the artillery and engineers). Their success rate was variable; many boys required three or six months at a crammer before they could pass the examinations for Sandhurst and Woolwich, while those with less intellectual ability sought regular commissions through the 'back door'

Table 2.2. *The rural/urban background of the military leadership in 1899 and 1914 (%)*

	Colonels		Generals	
	1899	1914	1899	1914
Estates, farms, villages under 1,000 population	38	46	40	43
Villages and towns 1,000–5,000 population	25	19	22	22
Total rural	63	65	62	65
Towns over 5,000 population	29	26	30	27
Abroad	8	9	8	8
Total (%)	100	100	100	100
Total number	107	87	91	91

of the Militia until 1908. Many schools fostered martial enthusiasm through their cadet corps, whose appeal had flourished in the wake of the Boer War and on account of the general anxiety about Britain's relative standing in the international arena. New corps were formed, more boys enlisted in them, and a surge of keenness was evident in the field days and annual camps. The corps were allocated more time for their activities and were frequently encouraged by visiting speakers from the Navy League and the National Service League.[15]

Haldane had sought to harness this enthusiasm directly. Requiring an additional 4,000 regular officers for his Expeditionary Force and another 6,000 auxiliary officers, he hoped to find them from the school and university cadet corps. In 1908 he launched the Officers' Training Corps to provide an organisation for the corps under the supervision of the War Office. Henceforth cadets could gain certificates for their service in school and/or in university corps which would entitle them to a reduction in their period of training with a regular unit before receiving a commission. The inducement was none too attractive. By 1912, 18,000 had already completed their service in the corps, of whom only 283 had joined the Special Reserve. Instead of a scientifically planned mobilisation, Haldane was forced to admit that it would be a rather 'ragged business', dependent upon the commissioning of NCOs, reserve officers and Sandhurst cadets. Many others, he forecast, would volunteer, especially former OTC cadets:

it is not too much to expect that, in the event of a supreme national emergency, feelings of patriotism would, as has always been the case in the past, induce a certain number of gentlemen to come forward and take commissions . . . many of whom would have had the advantage of the improved training now given in the Officers' Training Corps.[16]

Yet the army had never valued a public school education simply on account of the army classes and cadet corps. Of much more importance were the qualities of character which the schools were thought to develop. The cult of team games, so prevalent within the public school system, reflected these assumptions. Playing rugby and cricket, it was thought, developed not merely the physical attributes of health, strength, co-ordination and a quickness of eye – all essential military requirements – but also moral virtues like self-discipline, the submersion of the individual for the sake of the team, and the enhancement of team spirit – all qualities which could be transferred to regimental service. Above all, perhaps, the public schools inculcated loyalty – loyalty which, as Geoffrey Best describes, 'began with loyalty to your house . . . and rose through loyalty to your school (a paradigm of the nation) to loyalty to your country, faith and leaders'.[17] Boys possessing such attitudes were readily welcomed as potential officers.

Neither a suitable family background nor a public school education,

however, guaranteed entry into the regular army. For those who wished
to serve in a home-based regiment, private means were virtually
essential, as officers could not live on their pay. On joining his regiment
each subaltern had to provide his own uniform, cases, furniture, mufti,
servant's outfit and incoming mess contribution. Thereafter he had to
meet the annual mess expenses, the upkeep of his uniform, the cost of
field sports, social events and the constant moving that army life
entailed. The expenses varied from regiment to regiment; they were
fairly well known and they roughly reflected the regiments' order of
status. By 1914 the average officer in the Cameronians (2nd Scottish
Rifles) required a private income of about £250 per annum, while the
Coldstream Guards expected an income of £400 per annum. The cavalry
regiments were even more expensive because the officers had to provide
at least one charger as well as two hunters and three polo ponies.[18]
Although poorer young men generally sought service in India, where
they could enjoy the sport and social life of the home-based officer at
much less cost, some served in the most expensive regiments because of
exceptional promise, or skill at games, or ability as horsemen.
Meanwhile more affluent contemporaries sometimes failed to enter the
regiment of their choice if better qualified candidates blocked their way
or they had foundered at Sandhurst.

Once in their regiments or corps, officers led a fairly controlled life
centred around the officers' mess. Strictly run, the mess operated upon
the acceptance of numerous rules and customs, particularly rules which
curbed the conduct of junior officers. 'Shop' could never be mentioned
in the mess, and subalterns who displayed excessive diligence were
liable to comradely rebuke (to dampen such enthusiasm, Lord Gort was
thrown into the Basingstoke Canal).[19] Officers could use their ample
leisure to indulge their passion for field sports, polo, point-to-point
racing, team games, social entertainment and local travel, if stationed
abroad. As Viscount Montgomery recalls, 'it was not fashionable to
study war and we were not allowed to talk about our profession in the
Officers' Mess'.[20]

Regular officers were not a caste, set apart from the rest of society nor
did they comprise a separate 'corps' in the Continental sense, since
British military service was not centred upon the army as an institution
but upon the various regiments. The regimental tradition, in which
NCOs and private soldiers fully shared, provided a cohesive identity
based upon a history of collective service and sacrifice. Regimental
esprit de corps, declared Sir John Spencer Ewart (Adjutant-General
1910–14), was the 'priceless possession' of the British army. 'Nobody,' he
affirmed, 'who has not served in a British regiment can quite realise
what this espirit de corps really means . . . . It makes every man from the
Colonel to the last joined drummer feel that it is far better to lose his life

than do anything to discredit his regiment.'[21] Nevertheless, some officers moved beyond their regimental confines; by August 1914, 447 had graduated from the staff colleges at Camberley or Quetta. Staff college graduates had also obtained the majority of the high command and senior staff appointments in the BEF. Under the direction of two impressive commandants (Brigadier-General H. H. Wilson, 1907–10, and Major-General W. R. Robertson, 1910–13), the staff college had grown in size and stature. And staff training, though defective in some important respects, such as the maintenance of morale and logistics, would prove its worth in the mobilisation of the BEF and its subsequent movements against the German right wing.[22]

The other ranks, like their officers, had experienced relatively little change in social composition (Table 2.3). Unskilled labour, especially 'town casuals', continued to provide the largest single contribution to the annual intake. These trades were only those which were claimed by or ascribed to potential recruits: the vast majority of men lacked any employment before they offered themselves for enlistment. Although the army never recorded its dependence upon the unemployed, the Health Report of 1909 estimated that 'well over 90 per cent' of those who had been inspected were out of work.[23] Nor was there any improvement in the physical condition of the potential recruits. Coming largely from a poverty-stricken urban background, their health and physique reflected those ailments and the want of physical development which characterised the urban poor. The majority failed to meet the army's meagre medical standards – infantry recruits had to measure 5 ft 3 in. in height, 33 in. round the chest and 112 lb in weight. Even the decline of rejections by medical officers only indicated that a larger number of men were being rejected prior to medical inspection, and that medical standards were being altered (for example, the provision of dental treatment on inspection)[24] or ignored as the army tried to overcome its recruiting shortage.

By 1 May 1914 the regular army was 10,932 men, or approximately 6 per cent, short of its peacetime establishment.[25] Recruiting had failed to sustain the reduced Haldanian establishment: whereas the army required an annual intake of 34,000 to 35,000 recruits, only in 1907–08 had recruiting reached this target, with an average annual intake of 29,626 recruits from 1909 to 1913. By 1914–15 infantrymen, who had enlisted in 1904–05 to serve for nine years in the colours, would pass into the reserve alongside men who had served for seven years under the terms of service restored by Haldane. To offset this wastage, the War Office actuaries forecast, 50,000 recruits would be required in the next recruiting year. In view of recent trends in recruiting, the actuaries predicted that the army would incur a further deficit of at least 19,000 men[26] – a problem which was only averted by the outbreak of war.

Table 2.3. *Trades of men who offered themselves for enlistment* (%)

Year ending:	30.9.07	30.9.08	30.9.09	30.9.10	30.9.11	30.9.12	30.9.13
All unskilled	47	48	47	46	48	46	45
Town casuals	19	20	19	21	20	16	16
Agricultural unskilled	11	11	11	11	12	12	11
Other unskilled	17	17	17	14	16	18	12
Skilled	22	23	24	23	22	24	24
Other occupations	26	24	24	26	25	25	26
Professions and students	1	1	1	1	1	1	1
Boys under 17 years	4	4	4	4	4	4	4
Total	100	100	100	100	100	100	100
Number	(58,764)	(61,182)	(56,327)	(45,085)	(47,421)	(47,008)	(42,977)

Note. The categories included in:
Unskilled: agricultural and other outdoor labourers, railway workers, factory and indoor labourers, town and country casuals.
Skilled: coal miners, smiths, farriers, carpenters, butchers, etc.
Other occupations: carmen, town carters, clerks, tradesmen's assistants, servants, porters.
Professions: musicians and students.
The tables were collated and percentaged from the relevant numerical tables of the men who were medically examined in each of the Annual Reports for the years in question.

Military service had very limited appeal. Neither the pay nor the conditions nor the image of military life were particularly attractive, at least to workers in regular employment. Although a soldier's pay had been increased during the Boer War (giving him a clear shilling a day plus messing allowance, gratuities and service pay – later renamed proficiency pay – of 6d a day), the rates were not competitive. An infantry private, in receipt of proficiency pay, could earn 1s 11d daily, less 3½d stoppages – a net weekly pay of 11s 4½d – but this was over 2s less than the average weekly wage of an agricultural labourer in Caithness, the poorest paid in mainland Britain.[27] Soldiers were also indifferently housed. When serving in the United Kingdom they were quartered in barracks which varied enormously in size and in amenities. Some, like the new barracks at Colchester and Tidworth, were reasonably well appointed, but others, especially those located in manufacturing towns (for the purpose of riot control in the early nineteenth century), lacked either adequate accommodation or training facilities. Soldiers lived without privacy, rarely left their barracks, and often ate in the rooms in which they slept. Their life, too, could be dull and monotonous. After early morning drills and inspections they frequently spent more time on fatigues and employments than in military training. Rarely leaving the barracks, their relaxation all too often centred upon the wet canteen. Drunkenness, if much less prevalent than in the Victorian army, was still the most prominent of military crimes (9,230 men were fined for it in 1912–13).[28]

However disciplined and dreary the image of army life, there were compensations, particularly for the men who had escaped from the urban slums. They earned regular, though small, wages and some received extra duty payments as officers' servants. They lived in clean quarters, undertook physical exercise, and ate ample (if unappetising) meals. They had to attend army schools until they obtained a third-class certificate of education (equivalent to Standard III in elementary schools). Above all, they gained a sense of security and purpose from their comradeship and regimental service. Yet these considerations barely dented the prejudice against military service, so deeply rooted within respectable working-class families. Compounding the miserable rates of pay were limited opportunities to learn a skill or trade and scant provision for the ex-soldier, one in four of whom became an unemployed or unemployable vagrant.[29] Even more important were the emotions aroused by the distinctive features of army life – enforced discipline, communal living and a sacrifice of individual liberty. Many felt that a boy, once enlisted, was lost to family and friends. As Wavell recalled, 'There was in the minds of the ordinary God-fearing citizen no such thing as a good soldier; to have a member who had gone for a soldier was for many families a crowning disgrace.'[30]

Where army life had changed significantly was in matters of training and tactics. By 1914 training had become established as a cumulative process, beginning with individual instruction in winter, followed by squadron, company and battery training in the spring; regimental, battalion and brigade training in the summer; and, finally, divisional or inter-divisional exercises and army manoeuvres in late summer and early autumn. Such training was more comprehensive in scope and larger in scale than that undertaken before the Boer War. It was, nonetheless, devalued by the perennial shortage of men (occasioned by the annual provision of drafts, the instruction of raw recruits who were unavailable for field service, and the employment of men either casually or permanently upon non-military duties – as cooks, waiters, servants, labourers, etc.). Although training, as Sir William Robertson remembers, was 'largely a case of trying to make bricks without straw',[31] mobilisation was regularly practised and every winter selected units were brought up to war establishment. In 1910 one of the two Aldershot divisions was mobilised at the expense of the other, not only in front-line forces but also in ancillary services. Despite the persistent manpower problems, manoeuvres were conducted on as realistic a basis as possible.

Training had radically altered in content, too. The South African War had indicated the dangers posed by fire zones swept by long-range, small-calibre magazine rifles. In place of volley firing, frontal and flank attacks, there was greater emphasis upon operations in extended order, the use of cover, artillery support, and flank and converging attacks. Known as the doctrine of fire and movement, it was encapsulated in *Field Service Regulations: Part 1 (Operations)*. Fire action, though vitally important, remained subsidiary to the forward movement of troops. Sustaining the offensive was the vital objective, an aim seemingly buttressed by the outcome of the Russo-Japanese War, in which Japan's successes were attributed to moral superiority, the spirit of the offensive, and final assaults with the bayonet.[32] The British concept envisaged a firing line, advancing as far as possible without opening fire to conceal its position and conserve ammunition. Thereafter it had to attack in successive waves, regarding fire positions as transitory objectives, before closing with the enemy in the decisive attack, 'cost what it may'.[33]

Certain fundamentals still remained the bases of training. Whatever his talents in fieldcraft, the soldier was expected to be smart and steady on parade, to shoot accurately, and to be able to march. As Sir Ian Hamilton declared, the

South African and Manchurian experiences equally tend to show that men who are smart on parade are more alert, more readily controlled, more obedient, and move more rapidly and with less tendency to confusion or panic than troops which depend entirely on their individual qualities.[34]

The cavalry had also resisted the sweeping reforms which some critics, including Lord Roberts and Erskine Childers, the author of *War and the Arme Blanche* (1910), had advocated. Through the influence of its senior commanders, particularly Sir John French and Sir Douglas Haig, the cavalry had preserved the supremacy of shock tactics based upon the lance and sword. Although squadrons practised their reconnaissance and dismounted duties more regularly, they devoted the bulk of their training, possibly as much as 80 per cent, to perfecting their traditional tactics.[35] Finally the artillery, which had rearmed with quick-firing guns, was not prepared to imitate the rapid-fire tactics of the French gunners as some critics urged. Artillery commanders, like their French counterparts, had accepted that the classical artillery duel and independent artillery action must give way to a more subordinate role in battle, with the aim of supporting the infantry and ensuring its success. But they could not emulate French standards, because their guns possessed neither an automatic fuse setter nor a carriage as stable as the French 75 mm gun. They feared, moreover, that reduction of their battery formations from six guns to four (to facilitate faster methods of ranging) would simply enable the government to economise by reducing one-third of the guns.[36]

By judiciously blending new tactical requirements with traditional priorities, a radical improvement had occurred in training. By frequent practice on the rifle range, rates of fire were developed (fifteen rounds per minute at 300 yards) which markedly exceeded the equivalent rates in conscript armies. By combining rapid shooting with reasonable standards of accuracy the army compensated, at least partially, for the cuts in the ammunition allowance and for the refusal to concede more than two machine-guns per battalion.[37] Using squads or sections to attack each other in company training, the ability to fire and move in attack and to regulate fire from defensive positions was regularly practised. Often the exercises were conducted without orders from officers or non-commissioned officers to ensure that the ranks would act increasingly on their own initiative. By the last army exercise before the outbreak of war, the progress had become abundantly apparent. The infantry, noted Commandant de Thomasson, 'makes wonderful use of the ground, advances as a rule by short rushes and always at the double, and almost invariably fires from a lying down position'.[38]

Underpinning this improvement was a flourishing of more professional attitudes within the army. The service had responded to its experience in South Africa, and to the criticisms aired in Parliament and the press, by preparing more thoroughly for its next engagement. To improve professionally, the army had neither changed its social composition nor developed closer links with the rest of society. It had developed a new sense of professionalism by the prescription and practice of training and tactical skills which seemed more relevant to the altered conditions of warfare. Most battalions had a core of officers and NCOs who had served in South Africa and knew the rigours of protracted conflict. Like the artillery and cavalry, they had new equipment with which to practise – the short Lee Enfield rifle, loaded on a clip system. They had new tactical precepts to apply in unit training, and knew that their effectiveness could be tested in divisional and inter-divisional exercises. Officers and men could take pride not simply from the historic achievements of their battery, battalion or regiment but from their ability to meet and sustain professional standards.

The 1st Battalion, Black Watch,[39] exemplified many of these points. Since the South African War the battalion had moved round various stations in the United Kingdom (Edinburgh, Fort George, the Curragh, Limerick and Edinburgh) before joining the 1st Brigade, 1st Division, at Aldershot in February 1913. For the next eighteen months the battalion remained at the army's principal training station. The battalion was still part of another larger formation, the Black Watch Regiment, whose depot was in Perth and whose recruiting area included the counties of Perth, Angus and Fife. The 2nd Battalion was quartered in Bareilly, India, and received drafts from the 1st Battalion. The 3rd Battalion, based in Perth, was a Special Reserve battalion which held civilians who had agreed to serve in war. This was largely a paper formation, as the reservists only undertook six months' training as recruits, followed by a commitment to attend an annual camp. The other four battalions were viable formations, they were Territorial battalions composed of part-time soldiers who not only attended annual camp but trained each week and at some weekends. The 4th Battalion was based on the city of Dundee, the 5th on Angus and Dundee, the 6th on Perthshire and the 7th on Fife.

The 1st Battalion had two commanding officers in 1914. During May Lieutenant-Colonel Hugh Rose completed his four years in command, to be succeeded by Lieutenant-Colonel Adrian Grant-Duff. Rose had served on the ill fated Nile expedition of 1884–85, winning a medal with four clasps and a bronze star, and in South Africa (1901–02), winning the Queen's Medal with four clasps. A tough and extremely fit man, he appreciated the importance of physical resilience in any campaign. He instituted a regime of physical training and early morning runs in Ireland and set a personal example on the athletic field (in July 1913 he won the veteran officers' race at the annual army athletic meeting at Aldershot – an immensely popular win).[40] His successor was a man of a rather different stamp. Like Rose he had an excellent war record. Mentioned in despatches for his duties in the Chitral (1895), he served in the North West Frontier campaign (1897–98) and in the South African War, where at least one of his contemporaries regarded him as the 'best soldier' in either the 1st or the 2nd Battalions.[41] A staff college graduate, he had displayed his staff skills in South Africa and had received various non-regimental postings in the post-war years, culminating with his appointment as the military assistant secretary to the Committee of Imperial Defence (October 1910 – August 1913).

At the CID Grant-Duff was largely responsible for preparing *The War Book*, a catalogue of procedures which government departments would have to follow at the outbreak of war. While engaged on this 'slow and tedious pastime'[42] he kept a frank and reflective diary. It confirmed not merely his intellectual gifts and prodigious energy but also his acceptance of a strict code of personal ethics. A believer in absolute standards of morality, sobriety and religious fundamentalism, he wrote that 'the service of God is perfect freedom, and I suppose it is the service of God which most of us are striving for in various blundering and unconscious ways'.[43] From this perspective, coupled with fairly rigid views on how society should function, he brooded over the nation's decline. Strikes, suffragettes and 'crude social legislation' caused him much despair. By 11 March 1912 he could see 'no sign of improvement in the steady degradation of national life'.[44] He 'devoutedly' hoped that the employers would 'flatly refuse to be coerced' even by the government in the dock strike, and viewed 'the entry of women into politics' as 'very serious, and not the least serious effect is the lowering of the chivalrous instinct in men'.[45] By 26 July 1912 he feared that 'respect for Law and Order, for soberness, for intellect, for truth, for honesty is waning not increasing'.[46]

Grant-Duff was profoundly contemptuous of most politicians. Although the son of a former Liberal MP, he deprecated the policies of Asquith's administration and the attitudes of leading Liberals. He was by no means the only officer from a Liberal family who evinced such feelings. Sir John Spencer Ewart, though 'a Liberal by instinct', neither forgot nor forgave the calumnies which Campbell-Bannerman, Lloyd George and the pro-Boers had hurled at the army during the Boer War.[47] But in Grant-Duff's case the estrangement from contemporary Liberalism was particularly deep. He deplored 'the tyrannical spirit of modern "liberalism" ', as reflected in the National Insurance legislation and the views of 'sentimental radicals' who prated about 'International Peace' while 'preaching the Social War'.[48] He regularly castigated the Liberal Secretaries of State for War. After an army debate in the House of Lords he described the speech of Haldane as 'much as usual – woolly!' A month later he described a meeting of the Imperial Conference in which Haldane had 'poured out his usual torrent of muddled and somewhat disingenuous haziness'.[49] He regarded Haldane's successor as even worse, 'Seely,' he asserted, 'seems to me a very inferior intellect and a dangerous creature in every way'.[50] Finally, he was none too impressed with the Unionists, especially in view of their commitment to tariff reform.[51]

This jaundiced outlook coloured Grant-Duff's assessment of Haldane's reforms. Like Sir Henry Wilson, he doubted that the Expeditionary Force was large enough to fulfil its likely military mission. He took issue with Wilson's querulous enquiry, 'Why six divisions?' only in as much as it was 'badly worded'. 'There is no logical reason', added Grant-Duff, 'why we send that number or any other. Despite all our clear thinking our Army is *organized* for peace purposes – while those of our possible enemies are *organized* for war.'[52] But he was not in favour of conscription, which he likened to a tyranny acceptable only in a socialist society.[53] Instead of raising a vast army of untrained men, to be armed with rifles and earmarked for home defence, he believed that 'more valuable results' would accrue from spending 'the same amount of money . . . on organized and trained troops'.[54] Whether such views commanded widespread support is by no means clear, but there was certainly a gulf between the priorities of some army officers and those of the Asquith government, possibly substantiating the view of the army 'as part of the conservative wing of public opinion in Edwardian Britain'.[55]

But neither army reform nor national politics were of prime concern at regimental level, where officers had more immediate interests. Those who served in the 1st Battalion, Black Watch, were a fairly homogeneous body (see Table 2.4). Save for the absence of any sons of the manse and a fairly small proportion of officer's sons in the battalion, the composition compares with the military leadership in 1914 (Table 2.1). Some three-quarters of the recruitment was still coming from the traditional sources of officer supply. The peerage and baronetage was formidably represented, including Major Lord George Stewart-Murray, third son of the Duke of Atholl (the honorary colonel of the 3rd Battalion, Black Watch); Captain the Hon. Maurice Charles Andrew Drummond, brother of the Earl of Perth and third son of the Viscount Strathallan; Second Lieutenant John Eric Henry Rollo, grandson of the tenth Baron Rollo and later the twelfth baron himself; and Lieutenant Robert E. Anstruther, son of Sir Robert Anstruther, Bart., a wealthy landowner in Fife who also represented the county in Parliament. Officers from the gentry came from families with a wide range of interests and investments: Second Lieutenants Reginald Don and John Rennie came from families which had originally made their capital in trade – the former as a linen manufacturer, the latter as a ship owner. Army sons, though fairly small as a proportion, included the offspring of some distinguished officers – Captain William Green, son of General Sir W. Green and Second Lieutenant Julian N. O. Rycroft, only son of Major-General Sir W. H. Rycroft. Many other officers came from

Table 2.4. The social composition of the officer corps of the 1st Battalion, Black Watch, in August 1914

Rank (and number)	Peerage and baronet- age	Gentry	Army	Profes- sional	Church	Others	Don't know
Lieutenant-colonel (1)	–	–	–	1	–	–	–
Majors (2)	1	1	–	–	–	–	–
Captains (6)	1	–	1	2	–	1	1
Lieutenants (11)	1	3	3	2	–	2	–
Second lieutenants (8)	1	3	–	2	–	2	–
Total (28)	4	7	4	7	–	5	1
Percentage (100)	14	25	14	25	–	18	4

Note. The officers include only those who embarked with the 1st Battalion in August 1914 (Major-General A. G. Wauchope, ed., A History of the Black Watch, 1914–18, London, 1925, I, pp. 2–3). Background information was acquired from the service records of some officers, the birth records of others and the registers of Woolwich and Sandhurst. It was supplemented by details from the standard reference works, Who's Who, Who Was Who, Burke's Peerage, J. Bateman, Great Landowners of England, E. Walford, County Families of the United Kingdom, The Dictionary of National Biography, J. Irving, The Book of Scotsmen, some printed obituaries, and the registers of twenty-five public schools.

families with strong service connections, even if their fathers had not regarded the army as a career.[56] Those who came from professional families had fathers who were in branches of the law, accountancy and the civil service. Of the remainder, apart from Quartermaster William Fowler, who had risen from the ranks, all were the sons of businessmen, some of whom were extremely successful.[57]

The battalion was overwhelmingly Scots. Some 92 per cent of officers and men were Scottish,[58] with at least half the officers coming from rural estates or small county towns. Only six, however, came directly from the Black Watch area (of the remainder, eight came from addresses in England, three from Edinburgh, four from other parts of the Highlands and five from the Lowlands). Uniformity was much more evident in their schooling (Table 2.5), where the vast majority had attended an English public school. Eight were old Etonians. The four sons of businessmen had attended Eton, Rugby, Charterhouse and Berkhamstead. Nearly half the officers had gone to Sandhurst (and Woolwich in the case of Captain Axel Krook). However valuable as a means of ensuring that officers shared certain values, assumptions and codes of behaviour, schooling was probably of less relevance than war experience for the development of professional attitudes. Twelve of the officers had served in the Boer War, both Lord George Stewart-Murray and Captain Drummond being mentioned in despatches.[59]

A social analysis of non commissioned officers and other ranks is more difficult to proffer because so many service records have failed to survive. A small random sample can be examined from the company book of A Company, which catalogued the intake of men from 1895 to 1912. Of the 133 men, 92 per cent were Scots, and some 90 per cent were of a Protestant persuasion (77 per cent were listed as Presbyterians). Just over half the men (53 per cent) were recruited from the Black Watch area, reflecting the difficulty of Highland regiments in finding sufficient men from their prescribed area of recruitment. Only 8 per cent came from rural communities and 21 per cent from small towns (that is, towns whose population ranged from 1,000 to 5,000 people). Of the 69 per cent who had left an urban environment, the largest numbers were the twenty-one from Dundee and fifteen from Edinburgh. Like the army nationally, the Battalion did not catalogue its dependence upon the unemployed, preferring to list the 'previous occupations' of its recruits. In this respect A Company differed sharply from the national statistics, finding its largest proportion of men from the ranks of skilled labour, 8 per cent from shopmen and clerks, and 10 per cent as 'boys'. Whereas mining provided twenty recruits – the largest single category – the agricultural trades produced fourteen, labouring eleven, and the mills nine.[60]

To wield these men into a fighting unit, the battalion rightly stressed

Table 2.5. *The educational background of the officers of the 1st Battalion, Black Watch, in August 1914*

Rank (and number)	Eton	Other English public schools	Scottish public schools	Non-public schools	Not formally educated	Don't know
Lieutenant-colonel (1)	–	1	–	–	–	–
Majors (2)	1	–	–	–	–	1
Captains (6)	2	2	1	1	1	1
Lieutenants (11)	3	6	–	1	1	–
Second lieutenants (8)	2	5	1	–	–	–
Total (28)	8	15	2	1	1	2
Percentage (100)	28	50	7	4	4	7

Note. The other English public schools included Wellington (two), Harrow (two), Rugby (two), Winchester (two), Berkhamstead, Blundells, Cheltenham, Charterhouse, Radley and Haileybury.

the importance of group loyalty and *esprit de corps*. It nurtured loyalty not simply to the battalion and regiment but also to the eight separate companies. As these companies had historic nicknames like the Grenadiers, Lawson's Men, Springers, etc., and competed with each other in work and in sport, the battalion deeply resented the introduction of the four-company system in 1913, with each company divided into platoons (irreverently christened 'spittoons' by the other ranks). Nevertheless, the battalion reorganised its competitions into an All-round Championship which was intended to encourage all branches of musketry and sports, including the less popular competitions of boxing and bayonet fighting. The battalion was none too successful in inter-regimental sports (with the exception of golf) but participation was considered more important than proficiency. Officers joined the ranks in hockey and cricket matches, while Lieutenant Robert Anderson excelled in athletics. Officers generally preferred field sports – hunting where possible,[61] shooting and fishing in the Highlands (an attractive fringe benefit of guard duty at Balmoral) and riding from point to point.[62]

Since the end of the Boer War the battalion had sustained an excellent training record – an achievement rendered even more remarkable by virtue of two postings in Edinburgh Castle. The Scottish capital was a prestigious posting, but the accommodation was uncomfortable, the training ground terribly restricted, and the temptations which greeted the soldier on leaving the Esplanade were all too obvious. But the battalion's discipline was maintained; its musketry met with the approval of the General Officer Commanding the Scottish Command in 1904 and, out of twelve selected regiments in the following year, the battalion had the highest percentage of first-class shots, the lowest percentage of second-class shots, and smallest proportion (2·96 per cent) who were permanently sick. This standard was sustained in Ireland, despite the presence of 331 soldiers under twenty years in a strength of 776 men. In his inspection of 1908 Brigadier-General A. W. Thorneycroft observed that:

The Battalion is quick and handy and moves with great spirit and dash; taking cover and covering long distances at the double when necessary.
  Company and Battalion training are well carried out, and included a great deal of night work and co-operation with other arms. The men dig well, and are efficient at bridging expedients for crossing rivers.[63]

An account of the battalion's training was compiled by Private W. Wilson. He recalls that the men were taught the signals for advance, close, retire and extend; the good places behind which they could take cover; how to judge distance, especially over hollows and water; and how to pass messages down the line. For five days a week, over several weeks, they practised different ways of advancing, the techniques of fire

control, night picquets, scouting, and signalling to one another while
under cover. The training was then extended on to a company basis. The
mornings were devoted to fieldwork – more practice in extensions,
scouting, and the seizing and holding of positions by digging in.
Frequently there were lectures in the afternoon, and occasionally
practice at night in the use of the North Star and outpost duty.[64]

By the eve of war the hours of preparation and practice had paid off.
Musketry standards had continued to improve. Compared with the
results in 1911, when it had 140 marksmen, 263 first-class shots, 155
second-class and two third-class, the battalion had in the following year
(under more stringent rules) 184 marksmen, 248 first-class shots,
eighty-nine second-class and four third-class. In a competition with the
King's Own Scottish Borderers, firing over distances of 200, 300, 500 and
600 yards, the 1st Battalion won decisively, with each of its eight best
teams outscoring their opponents from the KOSB. In the Scottish army
rifle meeting (15 – 16 August 1912) the proficiency of the Black Watch
was even more apparent, winning a host of cups in the team events and
individual competitions.[65] Although standards declined slightly the
following year (partly on account of the loss of some training
opportunities occasioned by the move to Aldershot) the battalion
performed creditably in the army exercise of 1913. It gained a 'good
name for march discipline, for keenness, and for the speed with which it
covered the ground'.[66]

When the battalion mobilised in the autumn of 1914 it was not the
body of men who had been training at Aldershot for the previous
eighteen months. Some 200 soldiers had to be left behind, as they were
under twenty years of age and hence ineligible for active service.
Another 500 reservists were required to bring the battalion up to its war
establishment of twenty-eight officers and 1,031 other ranks. The
efficient organisation of Lieutenant William Fowler, the quartermaster,
and his staff, coupled with the regular practice of mobilisation
procedures, ensured a comparatively smooth transition from peace to
war. The battalion mobilised ahead of schedule. All reservists had
arrived by 8 August, enabling them to spend the next five days in
training and in improving their musketry. Bade farewell by King George
V, the regiment's colonel-in-chief, on 11 August, the battalion left
Southampton two days later.[67] It was indicative of its discipline that the
men, who were forbidden wine or cider *en route*, heeded the order. 'The
French people', recalled Major A. D. C. Krook, 'were so astonished at
the men refusing the drink.'[68]

Several points are worth stressing about the 1st Battalion, Black
Watch, and indeed about the regular army as a whole, in 1914. In the
first place, it was a small elite force of professional soldiers. The army
had responded to the experience in South Africa in a thoroughly

pragmatic fashion. It had adduced certain lessons (which often differed from those aired by war correspondents and civilian pundits) and endeavoured to apply those lessons in peacetime training. It still revered the traditional military requirements of parade-ground discipline, musketry skills and marching ability. But it added the techniques of fire and movement, combined arms operations, the use of cover and much greater emphasis upon fieldwork whether by sections, companies, battalions or larger formations. The relevance of the peacetime training and its absorption by the rank and file would be confirmed in Flanders, where the reservists would encounter the rigours of warfare, within days of their arrival, amid the sweltering heat of a French autumn.

Secondly the army had improved professionally without becoming more representative of the rest of society. This was still a pre-technological army inasmuch as the bulk of its transport was horse-drawn, and so it contained a smaller proportion of technically skilled personnel than it would require in future years. Officers and men were drawn from fairly narrow segments of the community but they were still capable of taking a pride in their profession. While the distinctive ethos and life style remained, the fierce loyalties, based upon regimental customs, traditions and histories, were coupled with a real interest in the performance of particular units. Undoubtedly the bitterness aroused by the Boer War had left its mark. The various arms deeply resented the aspersions which had been hurled at them by journalists[69] and certain politicians. They were determined to maximise their state of military readiness.

Finally it was apparent that Britain, in August 1914, was anything but a nation in arms. The BEF of some 160,000 men was superbly trained but under-equipped in many vital respects, especially when the belligerents commenced large-scale position warfare for which the British lacked sufficient entrenching tools, barbed wire and sandbags as well as heavy artillery, machine-guns and adequate reserves of shell and ammunition. Despite the zealous campaigning of Haldane, the Territorial Force had never reached its peacetime establishment of about 312,000 men. By 30 September 1913 it had dwindled to 9,390 officers and 236,389 other ranks, of whom only 1,090 officers and 17,788 NCOs and men had volunteered to serve overseas on mobilisation.[70] The appeal of a military career had not increased, nor had the suspicions eased between some of the military and political leaders.

Indeed, the latter had been exacerbated by the events at the Curragh in March 1914, when Brigadier-General Hubert Gough and fifty-seven officers of the 3rd Cavalry Brigade stated that they would prefer dismissal rather than obey any order to enforce Home Rule on Ulster. The written assurance which was sent to Gough precipitated a furious row in Parliament, whereupon the government repudiated any notion of a private bargain with a few rebellious officers and Seely, French (the CIGS) and Ewart (the Adjutant-General) proferred their resignations. The affair was more of an 'incident' than a mutiny. Unlike the cavalry officers, some 280 officers from other units at the Curragh had resolved to do their duty. Nor were the careers of the senior officers involved blighted; French assumed command of the BEF, Gough led his brigade to France, and Ewart received the Scottish command.[71] Nevertheless, the incident had aroused great controversy, reflecting the doubts which many officers felt about the trend of government policies and the integrity of some senior politicians. It was hardly an auspicious basis on which to lauch a war effort of unprecedented proportions.

Notes

1 Brigadier-General J. E. Edmonds, *Military Operations, France and Belgium, 1914*, 2 Volumes, HMSO, London, 1925, I, pp. 10–11.
2 *The Scotsman*, 22 May 1908, p. 5.
3 Lord Haldane, *Before the War*, Cassell, London, 1920, p. 34.
4 *Newcastle Daily Chronicle*, 15 September 1906, p. 7.
5 *Scotsman*, 8 January 1900, p. 5.
6 *Scotsman*, 29 September 1906, p. 10.
7 M. J. Allison, 'The National Service Issue, 1899–1914', unpub. Ph.D., London, 1975.
8 *Glasgow Herald*, 12 January 1909, p. 10; *Scotsman*, 9 January 1912, p. 5; and *Army Review*, 3 July 1912, pp. 1–18.
9 N(ational) L(ibrary of) S(cotland), Haldane papers, Ms 5,918, ff. 44–5, Haldane, 'A Preliminary Memorandum on the Present Situation. Being a rough note for consideration by the Members of the Army Council', 1 January 1906.
10 E. M. Spiers, *Haldane: an Army Reformer*, Edinburgh University Press, 1980, pp. 48–73.
11 G. Harries-Jenkins, *The Army in Victorian Society*, Routledge and Kegan Paul, London, 1977, pp. 24–5.
12 J. Connell, *Wavell, Scholar and Soldier*, Collins, London, 1964, p. 34.
13 Field-Marshal Lord Wavell, *Allenby: Soldier and Statesman*, Harrap, London, 1964, p. 25.
14 A. H. H. MacLean, *Public Schools and the War in South Africa*, Stanford, London, 1902, p. 12.
15 G. Best, 'Militarism and the Victorian public school', in *The Victorian Public School*, ed. B. Simon and I. Bradley, Gill and Macmillan, London, 1975, pp. 131–7.
16 *Parl. Deb.*, Fifth Ser., 11, 13 May 1912, col. 989. See also Spiers, *Haldane*, pp. 135–43.
17 Best, 'Militarism', p. 143. See also T. H. E. Travers, 'Technology, tactics and morale: Jean de Bloch, the Boer War and British military theory, 1900–1914', *Journal of Modern History*, 51, June 1979, p. 286.
18 J. Baynes, *Morale: a Study of Men and Courage*, Cassell, London, 1967, pp. 29–30.
19 J. R. Colville, *Man of Valour*, Collins, London, 1972, p. 18.
20 Viscount Montgomery, *The Memoirs of Field Marshal the Viscount Montgomery of Alamein*, Collins, London, 1958, p. 80.
21 S(cottish) R(ecord) O(ffice), Ewart papers, Sir J. S. Ewart, speech to officer

cadets, n.d.

22 B. J. Bond, *The Victorian Army and the Staff College*, Eyre Methuen, London, 1972, pp. 305–6, 310, 324, and J. Connell, *Wavell*, pp. 62–3. Wavell's comment about morale is instructive. Had the army been as concerned about 'the loyalty, patriotism and determination to win of the city-bred masses' as one scholar argues, the maintenance of morale might have figured more prominently on the Staff College curriculum. T. H. E. Travers, 'The offensive and the problem of innovation in British military thought, 1870–1915', *Journal of Contemporary History*, 13, 1978, p. 539.

23 *Report of the Health of the Army for the year 1909*, Cd5477, 1911, XLVII, p. 2.

24 'The loss or decay of many teeth' was the largest single cause of medical rejections in the years from 1903 to 1910. This proportion (19 per cent) was nearly halved to 10 per cent by the provision of dental treatment from 1910 to 1913. *Parl. Deb.*, Fifth Ser., 1, 4 August 1909, col. 1,599.

25 *Parl. Deb.*, Fifth Ser., 63, 25 May 1914, col. 37.

26 PRO, WO 163/20, 167th meeting of the Army Council, 22 May 1914, and Precis No. 815.

27 J. H. Clapham, *An Economic History of Modern Britain*, 3 volumes, Cambridge University Press, London, 1926, 3, pp. 98–9.

28 *General Annual Return of the British Army for the year ending 30 September 1913*, Cd 7252, 1914, LII, pp. 74–8.

29 E. M. Spiers, 'The Reform of the Front-line Forces of the Regular Army in the United Kingdom, 1895–1914', unpub. Ph.D., Edinburgh, 1974, appendix XI.

30 Field Marshal Sir A. Wavell, *Soldiers and Soldiering*, Cape, London, 1953, p. 125.

31 Field Marshal Sir W. Robertson, *From Private to Field Marshal*, Constable, London, 1921, p. 159.

32 Major-General Altham, *Principles of War*, I, Macmillan, London, 1914, p. 205. For a good review of the changes in British tactical thought, see T. H. E. Travers, 'The offensive and problem of innovation', pp. 531–53.

33 *Infantry Training* (1914), p. 134.

34 Liddell Hart Centre for Military Archives, King's College, University of London, Hamilton papers 7/1/10, 'The following remarks by the Lieutenant-General Commander-in-Chief Southern Command are circulated to Volunteer Brigades for their perusal and guidance, 1 August 1906.'

35 N(ational) A(rmy) M(useum), Roberts papers, R/223, Colonel de Lisle to Lord Roberts, 7 June 1910. See also E. M. Spiers, 'The British cavalry, 1902–1914', *Journal of the Society for Army Historical Research*, LVII, summer 1979, pp. 71–9, and B. Bond, 'Doctrine and training in the British cavalry, 1870–1914', *The Theory and Practice of War*, ed. M. Howard, Cassell, London, 1965, pp. 97–119.

36 Liddell Hart Centre for Military Archives, King's College, University of London, Hamilton papers, 7/3/14/3, Hamilton to Repington, 27 October 1910.

37 Lieutenant-Colonel J. Campbell, 'Fire action', *Aldershot Military Society*, CXII, 14 March 1911, p. 6, and General Sir G. Barrow, *The Life of General Sir Charles Carmichael Monro*, Hutchinson, London, 1931, p. 29.

38 Commandant de Thomasson, 'The British army exercise of 1913', *Army Review*, 6, January 1914, p. 149.

39 Having worked in the B(lack) W(atch) A(rchive) at Balhousie Castle, this author would like to pay tribute to the excellent facilities there and to the

co-operation of Mr James Macmillan and his assistants.

40 D. L. Wilson-Farquharson (ed.), *The Chronicle of the Royal Highland Regiment, the Black Watch*, Edinburgh, 1914, p. 134. See also E. and A. Linklater, *The Black Watch: the History of the Royal Highland Regiment*, Barrie and Jenkins, London, 1977, p. 135.

41 BWA, Cameron letter books, item 186, Captain A. R. Cameron to his father, 31 July 1900.

42 I(mperial) W(ar) M(useum), Grant-Duff diaries, DS/MISC/77, 2 April 1913.

43 IWM, Grant-Duff diaries, 15 March 1913.

44 IWM, Grant-Duff diaries, 11 March 1912.

45 IWM, Grant-Duff diaries, 1 and 23 July 1912.

46 IWM, Grant-Duff diaries, 26 July 1912.

47 SRO, Ewart papers, item 122, diary entries, 16 February, 3 and 10 March, 24 May, 10 July, 12 August 1901, 1 January 1902 and 16 January 1906.

48 IWM, Grant-Duff diaries, 26 July 1912 and 15 March 1913.

49 IWM, Grant-Duff diaries, 3 April and 29 May 1911.

50 IWM, Grant-Duff diaries, 19 December 1911.

51 IWM, Grant-Duff diaries, 26 November 1912.

52 IWM, Grant-Duff diaries, 6 October 1910.

53 IWM, Grant-Duff diaries, 17 January 1911 and 15 March 1913.

54 IWM, Grant-Duff diaries, 2 April 1913.

55 T. H. E. Travers, 'Technology, tactics, and morale', p. 286.

56 Anstruther's father was once a captain in the Royal Engineers, Rollo was related to the late General the Hon. Robert Rollo, a former colonel of the Black Watch, and Second Lieutenant Kenneth S. MacRae had two uncles who formerly served in the regiment.

57 For example, Second Lieutenant Geoffrey W. Polson was the son of Daniel Polson, the corn flour manufacturer, and Lieutenant Lewis R. Cumming's father was a wealthy distiller from Aberlour, Banffshire.

58 Major General A. G. Wauchope (ed.), *A History of the Black Watch 1914–18*, Medici Society, London, 1925, I, p. 3.

59 Marchioness of Tullibardine (ed.), *A Military History of Perthshire 1899–1902*, R. A. and J. Hay, Perth, 1908, II, appendix 1.

60 BWA, item 36, Company book, 'A' Company, The Black Watch, 1895–1912. The data was assembled and percentaged by the author.

61 BWA, item 464, Diary of the Curragh Camp, 1908–09.

62 For accounts of the battalion's sporting interests see D. L. Wilson-Farquharson (ed.), *The Chronicle of The Royal Highland Regiment the Black Watch 1913*, Edinburgh, 1913, p. 45–6, 56–71, and 1914, pp. 94–7, 126–175.

63 BWA, item 37, Historical Record: 1st Battalion, The Black Watch, 1892–1908.

64 BWA, item 34, Private W. Wilson, Diary describing training in Ireland, 16 March to 19 May 1910.

65 *The Chronicle . . . 1913*, pp. 72–81.

66 *The Chronicle . . . 1914*, pp. 122 and 176–81.

67 Wauchope, *Black Watch*, p. 1.

68 BWA, item 237, Diary of Major A. D. C. Krook in France (1914).

69 Not least in the 2nd Battalion, Black Watch, after Magersfontein. BWA, item 186, Letter book of Captain A. R. Cameron, 16 January 1900 and 4 February 1900.

70 *The Annual Return of the Territorial Force for the year 1913*, Cd 7 254, 1914, LII, pp. 5 and 125.

71 Sir J. Fergusson, *The Curragh Incident*, Faber, London, 1964, pp. 187–202.

Locations of garrisons, camps and billeting centres in England and Wales, December 1914.

Keith Simpson **3**

The officers

The 1914–18 war *did*, of course bring the army right into the forefront of national awareness. Millions were involved in military service for the first time, and tens of thousands were commissioned from the ranks. The apparent failure of 'traditional' military leadership helped to destroy neo-feudal myths about the unique compatibility of officering with gentlemanly status.[1]

During the First World War a total of 229,316 combatant commissions were awarded in the British army. The pre-war officer strength of the regular army had been approximately 12,738, with the addition of 2,557 on the Special Reserve and 3,202 in the Reserve of Officers.[2] A combination of heavy casualties among the regular officers and the influx of vast numbers of civilians awarded 'temporary' commissions in the regular army would suggest that the British officer class[3] might have changed fundamentally with regard to social origins, methods of recruitment, training and education and professional expertise and ethos. And yet, by 1924, the regular officer class, numbering some 12,974, appeared to have reverted, at least superficially, to its pre-war characteristics.

There were five main routes to a commission in the regular army before 1914. Candidates for the cavalry, infantry, Indian Army and the Army Service Corps were selected by competitive examination for an eighteen-month course at the Royal Military College, Sandhurst. In 1913 67 per cent of all regular officers commissioned into these units were from Sandhurst. Candidates for the Royal Engineers and the Royal Artillery were selected by competitive examination for a two-year course at the Royal Military Academy, Woolwich. In 1913 99 per cent of all regular officers commissioned into these units were from Woolwich. Some 15 per cent of all regular officers commissioned into the cavalry and infantry in 1913 came direct from the universities, where they had undertaken some military training in the Senior Division of the Officers' Training Corps. The Special Reserve and Territorial Force provided another 15 per cent of all regular officers commissioned in 1913, candidates having undertaken military training in an OTC, Special Reserve or Territorial unit. Finally, some 2 per cent of all regular officers commissioned in 1913 were directly from the ranks, over and above the quite separate category of quartermasters and riding masters.

However, the importance of Sandhurst as a route to a commission in the cavalry, infantry, Indian Army or Army Service Corps was less significant for the officer class as a whole than the percentage indicates. For the period 1876–1914 Sandhurst trained only 55 per cent of all new officers for these units, as many regular officers were commissioned through the back door of the Militia. In contrast, for the same period, Woolwich never trained less than 75 per cent of all officers commissioned into the Royal Engineers and Royal Artillery. The importance of Woolwich for potential sappers and gunners is explained by the need for a sound basic technical education and training for officers of those arms.[4]

Before the First World War the officer class was characterised by its social and financial exclusiveness. By 1914 the overwhelming majority of candidates for a commission in the regular army were products of the public schools.[5] Attendance at and passage through a recognised public school met the army's requirements in educational and social terms for a potential officer. Neither Sandhurst nor Woolwich 'taught' leadership. It was assumed that by the time a candidate reached either of these two institutions, or alternatively went direct to his regiment, he had already acquired the necessary social and moral qualities thought necessary for an officer and gentleman and thus a military leader.[6] Time spent at Sandhurst and Woolwich, and, more important, as a subaltern at regimental duty, would develop these qualities and supplement them with certain military skills and ethos.

As far as the officer class was concerned it was almost impossible for someone who had not been through this system to become an officer and a gentleman. An exclusive social and educational background, the gentlemanly ethos, a commitment to country pursuits, loyalty to institutions, self-confidence and physical courage were the qualities required, and they were almost totally associated with select areas of the middle class and definitely the upper class. Regular soldiers were almost entirely recruited from the working and lower middle classes and thus regarded by the officers as demonstrably lacking in the most important qualities of an officer and gentleman. Furthermore, it was the belief of most officers that soldiers preferred to be officered by gentlemen rather than by those of their own class whatever their narrow technical and educational abilities.

Thus it was not simply a question of social snobbery or financial exclusiveness which restricted the number of officers commissioned from the ranks to insignificance, but a widely held view on the part of the officer class about the qualities required in an officer. William Robertson was very much the exception to the rule, and his achievement in reaching the rank of field-marshal was based upon his own considerable personal qualities, careful tutoring by his wife, the support of powerful and influential contemporaries such as Douglas Haig and later King George V, and promotion through the staff rather than the regimental system.[7]

The social exclusiveness of the officer class was reinforced by financial obstacles that were formidable. Given that by 1914 the army recruited potential officers largely from the public schools, it required some considerable initial expenditure, usually from parental resources, for a candidate to acquire the necessary education. Apart from a few special exceptions, the majority of candidates then had to pay £100 p.a. for their training at Sandhurst or Woolwich. Then, depending upon his regiment or corps, an officer frequently needed an allowance or private income over and above his pay to meet the obligations of sporting and social life.[8]

A potential officer's social and financial background, combined with his personal qualities and abilities, helped determine his choice of regiment or corps. The link between an individual potential officer and a particular regiment might be explained in terms of social competitiveness. Even before the abolition of purchase and the establishment of a regimental system based upon county and borough affiliations, a form of regimental pecking order had been established, with infantry regiments making up more than half the total. Regimental position in the pecking order depended upon historical precedent, close association with the royal family, ancient lineage, tradition of social exclusiveness, regional affiliation, military reputation and the distinction between regiments and corps.[9]

Over several decades there could be variations in the pecking order, but it is possible to establish a reasonably accurate one before 1914.[10] The Foot Guards, the Household Cavalry, four to five regiments of cavalry of the line and the Rifle Brigade would be at the top. The rest of the cavalry next, with probably most of the Highland regiments slightly below them, then the light infantry and fusilier regiments, following those the southern English county and Lowland Scots regiments, and then the Irish, Welsh, Northern and Midland regiments. Somewhere in the middle would come the Royal Artillery, with the Royal Horse Artillery above and the Royal Garrison Artillery well below, and also the Royal Engineers. At the bottom would come the Army Service Corps, Army Ordnance Corps and the Army Pay Department, all of whom were regarded by many regimental officers as being 'trades.' In a somewhat separate category was the Indian Army, with its own pecking order of regiments. Generally speaking, the majority of these regiments would be placed high in the main pecking order.

What two scholars have referred to as the 'pair bonding' between potential officers and regiments sometimes began when a candidate was christened or later at school.[11] Family connections or cultivation by a regimental officer began a process which would be formalised when the candidate had successfully passed through Sandhurst or Woolwich. Uncommitted candidates could enhance their chances of being accepted by a desirable regiment through personal achievement at either institution. However, the 'pair bonding' between a gentleman cadet and a regiment was a matter of mutual choice, and although the War Office could ultimately sanction or deny the king's commission it could rarely force a regiment to accept a candidate it did not want. A potential candidate would be interviewed by the colonel and would visit the regiment to be assessed by its officers. In the decade before the First World War there was a shortage of candidates for regular commissions, and some regiments had to accept officers who might not fully reach their desired standard. Usually, however, a regiment could rely upon its own very thorough socialisation process to effect the necessary changes. Individual outsiders were only too willing to conform and soon became the fiercest advocates of this regimental selection system.

Poor but worthy candidates attempted to pass out high enough at Sandhurst for the Indian Army and at Woolwich for the Royal Engineers. Both were socially as well as militarily acceptable and had the additional advantage of enabling officers to live comfortably on their pay and allowances. Failing to do well enough at Sandhurst to gain a commission in the Indian Army, Bernard Montgomery went to the Royal Warwickshire Regiment, which was unfashionable but sound and inexpensive.

It would be wrong to assume that most junior officers were wealthy scions of the aristocracy. There was a considerable element of 'shabby gentility', with much personal discomfort for the sake of appearances. E. G. W. Harrison was a gunner subaltern in 1913 whose father gave him an allowance of £18 p.a. 'This gave me a yearly income of £92. Mess Bill without a drink or cigarette £6 monthly, soldier servant and washing £1 a month, so a penny bus fare was a matter of deep consideration.'[12] P. R. Mundy, a subaltern with the South Wales Borderers, found 'There was not much opportunity for any social amusements as the pay was 5s 3d. per day out of which 4s 6d. was the cost of messing. No rations being given to officers or up-keep of uniform leaving 9d. per day for any amusement apart from the allowance.'[13] Loss of an allowance after commissioning could mean transfer to another regiment or corps, or secondment overseas. H. D. Thwaytes was commissioned into the Dorset Regiment in 1909, and his father, a colonel in the Army Pay Department, gave him an allowance of £100 p.a. When in 1912 his father retired and told him he could no longer continue the allowance, Thwaytes had to seek a secondment in the Army Pay Department. He reverted to the Dorsets in August 1914.[14]

For at least the first six months of regimental duty the newly joined subaltern was of social and military insignificance. Experience varied from regiment to regiment and, from regiment to corps, but basically the new officer went back to initial training, being drilled on the square with recruits, taught musketry and basic tactics, and after about six months was passed off the square by the adjutant.[15] In the mess, he reverted to the lowest form of social life, something he had already experienced at preparatory school, public school and Sandhurst or Woolwich. After a period of initiation, which usually meant being ignored, his brother officers either accepted him as a member of the regiment or ruthlessly rejected him.

Although, unlike previous generations, officers were expected to know their soldiers and work closely with NCOs, there was still a considerable social divide between the ranks. In most regiments a soldier could only speak to an officer via an NCO. John Lucy, a pre-war regular in the Royal Irish Rifles, thought that 'the pre-war officer, despite his pleasant fancy to the contrary, was not very much in touch with his men, whose temper and habits were better known to the non-commissioned officers'.[16]

Despite the fact that the officer class were encouraged to follow the pursuits and life style of country gentlemen and refrain from any vulgar displays of militarism, few knew many beyond their own social and professional class, and regimental society dominated the thinking of the majority. R. C. Money, who was commissioned into the 2nd Cameronians before the war, reflected later in life that:

We were, I suppose, very innocent by modern standards. Psychologists, sociologists and the like had not been invented so there was no pernicious jargon to cloud simple issues. Right was right, and wrong was wrong and the Ten Commandments were an admirable guide. There was no obsession with sex, drink and drugs. The approach to sex was perfectly normal, whilst the horror of V.D. was very real. A 'homosexual' was a bugger and beyond the Pale. A drunk was a drunk and quite useless. A coward was not someone with a 'complex' (we would not have known what it was!) but just a despicable creature. Drugs were unheard of, and I personally never heard of a lesbian until I was over forty. Frugality, austerity and self-control were then perfectly acceptable. We believed honour, patriotism, self-sacrifice and duty, and we clearly understood what was meant by 'being a gentleman.'[17]

However, the more adventurous or impecunious could broaden their experience by seeking a secondment with the Egyptian army or the King's African Rifles, or perhaps through a posting as adjutant to a Territorial unit. But the majority of officers had little contact with civil society. Nothing like the American Civil War had occurred to disturb their traditions or attitudes. No citizen army had had to be absorbed by the regular army, and few serving officers before the war supported the campaign for the introduction of conscription. The Territorial Force was regarded as a military irrelevance whose officers were social climbers.[18] For the pre-war officer class life in the army was more about soldiering than about fighting.

Within a few weeks of mobilisation in August 1914, and following Kitchener's appeal for volunteers, the army faced immediate shortages in the supply of officer replacements for casualties in the BEF and considerable organisational difficulties relating to the recruitment and training of potential officers for the New Army. To bring the BEF up to war establishment in officers it had been necessary to utilise the

majority of the 2,557 officers of the Special Reserve and those officers
holding staff and administrative appointments in the War Office, staff
college, command headquarters and various army schools. Between 23
August and 30 November 1914 the BEF sustained some 3,627 officer
casualties, of whom the majority were regulars. Although 2,097 of these
were only wounded and would eventually return to duty it still meant
that a quarter of the pre-war officer class had become casualties within
four months of mobilisation. The greater proportion of these casualties
had been sustained by infantry battalions.[19]

To meet the immediate requirements for regular officer replacements
in the BEF it was decided to continue the system of granting
commissions through Sandhurst, Woolwich and the Special Reserve. To
increase the output of both Sandhurst and Woolwich the courses were
shortened considerably, initially to three months at Sandhurst and to
six months at Woolwich, and the age limit was raised from nineteen and
a half to twenty-five. By these measures the yearly output of officers to
replace casualties in the old regular army was quadrupled.[20] Candidates
for permanent regular commissions still sat the entrance examinations
and competed for their regimental choice. Although as the war
continued regiments were grateful to get whom they could, socially elite
regiments still carefully selected those who were to be offered permanent
commissions. By continuous stages through the war the courses at

Table 3.1. *Officer casualties in four infantry battalions of the BEF between 23
August and 30 November 1914*

1st Queen's (I Corps, 1st Division, 3rd Brigade)	26 officers on mobilisation 9 killed in action 13 wounded 1 evacuated sick 1 P.O.W.
1st Norfolk Regiment (II Corps, 5th Division, 15th Brigade)	26 officers on mobilisation 8 killed in action 7 wounded
3rd Worcestershire Regiment (II Corps, 3rd Division, 7th Brigade)	28 officers on mobilisation 8 killed in action 7 wounded
1st Northamptonshire Regiment (I Corps, 1st Division, 2nd Brigade)	26 officers on mobilisation 13 killed in action 12 wounded 1 invalided

Sources. Figures calculated from three regimental histories and one private
account. Colonel H. C. Wylly, *History of the Queens' Royal Regiment*, VII, Gale
and Polden, 1927; F. Loraine Petre, *The History of the Norfolk Regiment,
1685–1918*, II, Jarrold, n.d.; E. J. Needham, *The First Three Months: the
Impressions of an Amateur Infantry Subaltern, the Northamptonshire Regiment*,
Gale and Polden, 1933; Captain H. Stacke, *The Worcestershire Regiment in the
Great War*, G. T. Cheshire, n.d.

Table 3.2. *The number of permanent commissions in the regular army as second lieutenant granted during the period 5 August 1914 to 1 December 1918 (figures in brackets show the intake in 1913)*

Royal Military Academy	1,928	(112)
Royal Military College	5,013	(343)
Royal Military College, Canada	172	(6)
Special Reserve	1,008	(67)
Territorial Force	335	(9)
Temporary commissions	1,109	–
Universities	246	(78)
Colonial	20	(3)
Ranks	6,713	(7)
Total	16,544	(625)

Source. Statistics of the Military Effort of the British Empire during the Great War, 1914–1920, HMSO, 1922, p. 234.

Sandhurst and Woolwich were lengthened until by 1918 they lasted a year. The lengthening of the course reflected growing concern about the quality of new officers for permanent commissions.

But Sandhurst and Woolwich could provide only about a third of the replacement officers required for the regular army, so candidates for a permanent commission were taken from dominion and colonial military colleges, and a certain number of commissions were granted direct to university candidates. A considerable number of suitable young men who had passed through the OTC before the war were commissioned into the Special Reserve and were available almost immediately for service with the regular army. The extent of this supplement for the regular and later the Territorial and New Armies can be seen from the fact that 30,376 permanent commissions in the Special Reserve were granted between 4 August 1914 and 1 December 1918.[21] A number of warrant officers and NCOs were granted permanent commissions in the field and suitable candidates were promoted from the ranks of Territorial units in France such as the Inns of Court and London Scottish. Later in the war a number of officers with 'temporary' commissions were given the opportunity to convert.[22]

Casualties and the expansion of the army altered the pattern of recruitment and the social and educational background of regular officers holding permanent commissions during the First World War. By 1917 the parental background of entrants to Sandhurst and Woolwich showed a marked decrease in 'gentlemen' and military professionals and a marked increase in businessmen, managers and civilian professionals, and 'others' in comparison to those of 1910. Thus by 1917 there was a greater lower middle-class parental background to candidates at Sandhurst and Woolwich.[23] Although Woolwich was able to provide never less than 75 per cent of all new permanent regular army officers during the war, Sandhurst was able to provide only some 30 per cent. No less than 41 per cent of all permanent commissions in the regular army were awarded to NCOs during the war.[24] However, it would be wrong to assume that this was a dramatic change in recruitment away from the pre-war 2 per cent from the ranks, because many of the wartime NCOs were volunteers with middle-class backgrounds.

When Kitchener launched his appeal for 100,000 volunteers, serving for three years or the duration of the war, he decided to create New Armies separate from the regulars and Territorials.[25] As a result of some 500,000 volunteers enlisting by the end of September, he was able to form eventually over 500 battalions in thirty divisions. The new battalions were raised as additional battalions of the regiments of the infantry of the line, sharing their traditions and regimental spirit. They were numbered consecutively after the existing battalions of their regiments and were distinguished by the word 'service' in brackets after their number. For example, by the end of the war the East Yorkshire Regiment had raised two regular battalions, a third reserve battalion, four Territorial battalions, ten service battalions and two garrison service battalions, giving a total of nineteen.[26] In addition, a large number of new units were raised of artillery, engineers, transport and medical services. The formation of service battalions took some time to organise and regiment from the diverse city, county, works and 'Pals' battalions which were formed in the enthusiastic response to Kitchener's appeal.

Large numbers of officers were required for the New Army, and these had to be found from a variety of sources.[27] A small cadre of regular officers was available because the regimental depots usually still had three officers on strength, the senior of whom was a major. In almost every case he was promoted to the rank of temporary lieutenant-colonel and given the command of the senior service battalion of his regiment, whilst the other two took up positions as a company commander and adjutant. Three regular officers from each battalion making up the BEF had been detached for service with the New Armies before embarkation. After the early battles fought by the BEF, wounded officers from the front, not yet fit for active service but well enough for training duties, were also attached to service battalions.[28] Finally, there were some 500 officers of the Indian Army who were home on leave in England, and the majority of them were posted to the New Armies. A certain number of officers from the reserve were also available for service along with others who had retired but were no longer liable for recall. Many of them were men of forty-five or fifty years of age who had left the army after the South African War or even earlier, and were soon unkindly nicknamed, 'dug-outs'. The first Kitchener battalions absorbed most of the regular and retired officers available.

The great and immediate requirement was to obtain junior officers for the thousands of recruits arriving daily who were being formed into the service battalions. To obtain the supply at once and in sufficient numbers, it was necessary to waive the preliminary training, either at a military college or in the ranks, which was required for officers holding permanent commissions. Instead, it was decided to offer temporary rather than permanent commissions in the regular army to suitable young men.

One likely source of potential officers was the OTC. Although established by Haldane in 1907 with a senior division based on the universities and a junior division based on the public schools and certain grammar schools, by 1914 several thousand young men had passed through and acquired some elementary military knowledge. As important, in the view of one contemporary observer, was the fact that the OTC was composed of men and boys of 'the intellectual and moral attainments likely to fit them for the rank of officers'.[29] Not only did the OTC provide a reservoir of suitable candidates but their training organisation could be utilised to give crash courses of basic instruction to other potential officers who after a few weeks could then be commissioned. Between August 1914 and March 1915 some 20,577 junior officers were commissioned from the OTCs and, in addition, 12,290 men who had been trained in the OTCs, served in the ranks.[30]

After the outbreak of war thousands of men who had emigrated or were working abroad came back to enlist. Many of them were quite happy to serve in the ranks, but a considerable proportion were awarded temporary commissions. Regular officers believed that even given a wide range of social and educational backgrounds these men made good officers, 'for they had taken some risks, they had been on their own responsibility, and had generally had men under them and experienced dangers by flood and field'.[31]

In locally raised and later in 'Pals' battalions, considerable latitude was given to the raisers over the question of the appointment of officers. Thus for 'Pals' battalions recruited in urban areas or from specific occupational groups the managers or foremen were appointed officers, with the professional classes providing a useful supplement. In rural areas it was the local gentry and the professional classes combined who made up the overwhelming majority of officers, particularly if there had been social contacts with the officer class. Almost invariably those chosen had their commissions confirmed by the War Office.

For officers of the technical corps, such as the Royal Engineers, the Army Service Corps and the Army Ordnance Corps, technical qualifications were required rather than merely a general education. The heads of the corresponding civilian professions drew up lists of likely candidates, who were then interviewed, and if suitable, commissioned. As far as the Royal Engineers were concerned, a qualified engineer of good health and physique, with practical experience in supervising some form of engineering, scientific or constructive work, already possessed four-fifths of the qualifications required by an engineer officer in war.[32]

During the month following Kitchener's appeal for volunteers there was considerable confusion over the appointment of temporary officers, with very few guidelines established by the War Office and considerable freedom of appointment given to local commanding officers, adjutants and civic dignitaries. Gaining a commission was something of an uncertain business, with qualifications, luck and influence all playing a part. R. C. Sherriff found that when he first applied for a temporary commission with his county regiment he was not considered suitable, as he had been to a grammar rather than a public school. It made no difference that his grammar school had been established several hundred years before the majority of the public schools. The criterion used by the adjutant of that particular regiment was the traditional social and educational background of the officer class.[33]

At thirty-one Clement Attlee was told that he was too old to enlist. However, he joined the Inns of Court Regiment and drilled for a fortnight with other recruits. He was soon commissioned as a temporary officer in the 6th South Lancashire Regiment because the commanding officer was a relative of one of his pupils and had applied for him personally.[34] Harold Macmillan, an undergraduate at Oxford, volunteered and joined the Artists' Rifles. After some cursory training in London he was commissioned as a temporary officer in a service battalion of the King's Royal Rifle Corps. Becoming bored with interminable training and few weapons or equipment, and desperately wanting to get to France, he used his mother and some university friends to get an interview with the regimental lieutenant-colonel of the Grenadier Guards and obtained a transfer.[35]

The first service battalions were the most fortunate in that they had the pick of the few experienced officers available and a good proportion of potentially able young officers. The 10th (Irish) Division was one of the first six New Army divisions, was formed from service battalions of all the Irish line regiments and was quite fortunate in its complement of officers. The GOC was Major-General Sir Bryan Mahon, a serving officer who happened to be home on leave, having earlier in the year relinquished command of the Lucknow Division in India. The three infantry brigadiers were all experienced regular officers. Two of the brigade majors were Indian Army officers home on leave. Each of the senior service battalions of the regiments making up the division was commanded by the promoted major of the regimental depot. The other battalions were commanded by a lieutenant-colonel from the Reserve of Officers. Every battalion had a regular adjutant, and the four company commanders had as a rule some military experience. Most of the junior officers were selected by the commanding officers and were drawn from the professional and trading classes – barristers, solicitors, civil engineers, medical students, undergraduates and schoolboys. Some had been through the OTC, and at the end of the year many of them attended young officers' classes at Trinity College, Dublin.[36]

The 50th Brigade formed part of the 17th (Northern) Division, which in turn was part of the Second New Army. Some of the battalion commanders were regulars, but apart from a few retired officers the majority of field and junior officers were civilians from business, university or school.[37] Matters were even worse in the 21st Division, which was part of the Third New Army. Every one of the battalion commanders had been retired on the outbreak of war, and, of the other officers, only fourteen had had any experience of the army at all. The remainder, almost 400 officers, were almost totally without military experience.[38]

Circumstances varied between service battalions, but there were certain continuities of experience. When Guy Chapman joined the 13th Royal Fusiliers as a temporary second lieutenant in December 1914 he found that there were only three regular officers, very senior and very retired, two from the Indian Army and not one from the Royal Fusiliers. The rest of the officers came from every walk of life, 'colonial policemen, solicitors, ex-irregulars, planters, ex-rankers, and in three cases pure *chevaliers d'industrie'.*[39] H. W. Yoxall was a temporary officer in the 18th King's Royal Rifle Corps. As it was one of the later service battalions, by the time it was formed the regulars were nearly all 'dug-outs' from the Boer War, except for the adjutant and the quartermaster, who had been NCOs with the 1st Battalion with the BEF until wounded. These two the temporary officers respected because of their recent war experience. The 'dug-outs' were tolerated as amiable old buffers. Yoxall believed that the real differences were between the new officers who had joined straight from school and older new officers who had been in commercial and industrial life and who, for some reason, had not joined up earlier. That was where the professional and social differences were felt; differences of breeding and education, and to some extent of money, in favour of the older men.[40]

For the technical arms in the New Armies the situation with regard to the supply of suitable officers was similar. As far as the Royal Engineers were concerned, the amalgam of the regular and the temporary or Territorial engineer officers in the proportion of about one to eight appeared to be successful. A typical New Army sapper unit was 82nd Field Company, 19th (Western) Division. The commanding officer was a thirty-eight year-old regular, who at the outbreak of war was the Staff Officer, RE, Malta. Although he had no field company or war experience, he had served, however, four years as adjutant of a Territorial RE unit, which had given him valuable experience in dealing with civilians. On 16 October 1914 at Chatham he was given charge of 200 men who were to form his new company. At first he had the assistance of only two time-expired RE NCOs, but after a few days two temporary subalterns arrived. Both had experience with engineering firms, one as a structural engineer, the other building bridges. A month later two more temporary subalterns arrived, both having just finished engineering school. Although the commanding officer could rely upon the technical knowledge of his new officers, he had to train them at the same time as the men in military administration and discipline.[41]

The reaction of regular officers to temporary ones depended upon a mixture of military and social factors and whether a regular officer served in a regular or service battalion. A lot of initial prejudice shown by regular officers against temporary officers was the professional reaction of the regular against the amateur, and it also included the Territorials. Major-General Henry Wilson was not alone in regarding Kitchener's New Armies as a joke. Many regular officers could not believe that the hastily raised, barely trained and equipped volunteers would be able to match the pre-war regulars of the BEF against the 'magnificent German Army'.[42] The highly professional Captain Jack of the 2nd Cameronians noted that the courage of the semi-trained temporary officers was excellent. But their professional standards of junior leadership, of soldierliness and battle efficiency fell far short of the pre-war regulars. He believed they had lacked proper grounding as cadets and recruits and could seldom handle their men quickly and with instinctive good judgement in an emergency. Later, when they were sent on short courses of instruction, it was too little and too late and delayed them in getting to know their soldiers intimately. All this combined to make the task of the regular officer more difficult, as he had to nurse the temporary officers.[43]

But regular officers soon appreciated the enthusiasm, intelligence and courage of temporary officers. C. A. F. Drummond, a pre-war gunner subaltern, believed that most of them were very good and keen and efficient. Some who had returned from overseas he thought had much wider experience than himself, both of the world and of the handling of men.[44] I. M. Stewart, a pre-war regular subaltern in the Argyll and Sutherland Highlanders, made a similar appreciation. After being wounded serving with a regular battalion, and following convalescence in Britain, he was posted to the 10th Battalion in France in 1915. As someone with battle experience he felt very much superior to the majority of the new officers in the battalion. At the age of nineteen he was given command of a company and found that one of his platoon commanders was aged about thirty and an important man in civilian life. Stewart soon realised that he had a lot to learn from this type of man, and concluded that, as one of the early New Army service battalions, the 10th Argyll and Sutherland Highlanders were as good as any regular battalion for trench warfare.[45]

The initial reaction of some regular officers towards temporary officers also depended upon social factors combined with the conviction that to lead men in battle an officer also had to be a gentleman. A. A. Hanbury-Sparrow spent a short time attached to a North Country battalion of the New Army in 1915. As a pre-war regular officer of the 1st Royal Berkshire Regiment he was shocked to hear 'these queer Yorkshire lads' boasting about embracing girls in public whilst wearing uniform, and the fact that the other officers saw nothing wrong with such behaviour. It was impossible for Hanbury-Sparrow to believe that 'officers of this class could ever hold the men in battle'.[46] Later in the war he was to modify this opinion. Siegfried Sassoon noted that the regular adjutant of a training camp in Britain in 1915 criticised the manners and accents of a number of temporary officers which clashed with those of the more carefully selected Special Reserve officers like himself, and with the public schoolboys from Sandhurst. But then Sassoon realised that the adjutant was trying to make them conform to a pattern of pre-war officer, which the adjutant himself exemplified.[47] Sassoon found that it was to his advantage when joining the 1st Royal Welsh Fusiliers in France in 1915 that he was known as a hunting man.[48] Certainly those temporary officers who had a similar social and educational background to the regulars found it far easier to gain acceptance. Arthur Osburn, a pre-war regular officer in the RAMC, observed that some regular officers were rather contemptuous of temporary officers through a combination of professional and social prejudices against 'outsiders'. This attitude began to change as soon as they realised that the grocer's assistant, the young chemist or architect could make, with a minimum of training, quite a brave and efficient officer.[49]

At first a degree of social snobbery was directed towards temporary officers, who were dubbed 'temporary gentlemen' by some regulars and the press, who considered them not quite 'pukka'. *Punch* had a field day mocking the professional and social inadequacies of the new officers, but in fairness it should be pointed out that the press had always enjoyed making fun of the amateur military tradition. Apart from setting a personal example and attempting to instruct the temporary officers in how to be officers and gentlemen, the officer class, through the War Office, issued a number of pamphlets on the subject and encouraged serving and retired regular officers to put pen to paper. So there appeared such publications as *The Making of an Officer, Straight Tips for Subs, Customs of the Army* and *Notes for Young Officers*, which became 'bluffers' guides' for many temporary officers. Although the contents of these publications were regarded as insensitive and irrelevant by some regular officers, they do reflect the concern of the officer class about the social behaviour of temporary officers and their ability to lead men in battle.

Social behaviour was of particular concern, and young officers were advised not to smoke a pipe in public, be rowdy or drink too much, or 'be seen walking about with one of the opposite sex with whom you would not care for your colonel or men to see you with'.[50] Young officers were warned against wasting their time riding motor bicycles with a girl on the carrier, spending time as a 'kinema creeper', becoming a bookworm or a bar loafer.[51] It was also feared that many temporary officers did not know how to command men or look after their interests: 'An officer must not think that his duties end with the dismissal of his platoon after the parade. The life of an average private soldier is a dull one, the class from which he comes has not much time for amusement, and it is his officers who have to teach him to amuse himself in the right way.'[52] Perhaps as revealing as the concern about the competence of temporary officers to look after their men is the class prejudice displayed in this official publication of 1917.

The temporary officer was assisted in his task of acquiring the necessary authority and ethos through his pay and dress. He received the pay of a subaltern, which was soon increased by a government anxious to see that new officers could meet their financial obligations and maintain the correct life style. Many of the expenses of peacetime soldiering disappeared after mobilisation, and, with extra allowances and supplementary pay, young officers found they could live reasonably well. By 1916 a subaltern was being paid 7s 6d a day. When commissioned he received a £50 kit allowance. Lodging allowance of 2s per day was given when there were no military quarters. Field allowance for a subaltern was 2s 6d a day, and when living in a mess he received a free ration allowance. When travelling on duty an officer received either a free warrant or an allowance.[53] Once on active service a subaltern was quite comfortably off. Some temporary officers, like Harold Knee, received in addition half-pay from the civilian employers. In his case this amounted to 17s 6d per week.[54]

As soon as he was commissioned the temporary officer was desperate to acquire his uniform of service dress, Sam Browne belt and, the symbol of his rank, a sword. Local tailors began to offer off-the-peg service dress at £1.10s. Pope and Bradley sold officers' breeches at £2 12s 6d and the service dress tunic at £1 7s 6d. But these were only the basic items and, as one parody put it relating the experience of 'tired Arthur'.:

Many pounds spent Tiadatha,
On valises, baths and camp beds,

Spent on wash-hand stands and kit bags,
Macs and British warms and great-coats,
And a gent's complete revolver.[55]

Some temporary officers were also surprised to find that they were
assigned a batman, although in more socially exclusive regiments they
were referred to as orderlies. Those from middle-class homes were used
to servants, but others found it an uncomfortable experience, and
regular officers were horrified to see how familiar some temporary
officers were with their batmen or, alternatively, how they failed to look
after their welfare. Slowly the temporary officer acquired some of the
professional and social manners of the regular officer class.

In turn a temporary officer's assessment of the regulars would depend
on whether he was with a service or regular battalion. In a service
battalion regular officers were few and far between, and in their desire to
learn about soldiering and how to behave temporary officers frequently
overlooked instances of social snobbery or the fact that the regular
officer was dug-out or a dud. As a temporary officer in the 9th York and
Lancaster Regiment Charles Carrington found that he and the other
temporary officers dined in the mess and paid excruciating attention to
details of etiquette in the way they assumed regular officers did.[56]

But the majority of temporary officers were impressed by the regulars
and stood in awe of their knowledge, particularly those with recent
battle experience. Harold Macmillan, attached as a temporary officer in
March 1915 to the reserve battalion of the Grenadier Guards, was
greatly impressed by the way in which he and other young officers – 'and
this term applied to anyone between the age of eighteen and forty-five
who had no previous military experience' – were introduced to
regimental traditions, forms of behaviour and the mystique of drill.[57]
Although Macmillan was from a similar social and educational
background as the regular Grenadier officers, he had no family
connections with the army. At first he regarded the regular officers as
men of limited outlook, interested only in sport, horses and women.
Only after a considerable time did he find out that they had perhaps an
expertise and interests beyond those traditionally associated with the
military. Like so many temporary officers who in the normal course of
events never would have considered soldiering, Macmillan was to learn
gratefully what he believed were the military virtues of smartness and
the belief that if a thing was to be done at all it had to be done well.[58]

Robert Graves, like Siegfried Sassoon, was commissioned into the
Special Reserve of the Royal Welsh Fusiliers and posted to the 2nd
Battalion in France. Although initially Graves was treated coldly, if not
rudely, by the regular officers, a continuation of peacetime ritual for any
new officer, he had at least a considerable social and military advantage
over any temporary officer or outsider posted to the battalion. In the

spring of 1915 the 2nd Royal Welsh Fusiliers was a fairly unique battalion in the BEF, as it still had almost a full complement of regular officers. Graves recalls how he was briefed on arrival by a Special Reserve officer of the East Surrey Regiment attached to the battalion and contemptuously known as 'the Surrey man'. After being told how traditional and conservative life was in the mess and how Graves would probably be ignored, the East Surrey officer concluded, 'in the trenches I'd rather be with this battalion than with any other I have met. The senior officers do know their job, whatever else one may say about them.'[59]

The best regular officers were admired by temporary officers for their professionalism. Sidney Rogerson served as a junior officer with J. Jack when he commanded the 2nd West Yorkshire Regiment in 1916. Although he was ultimately to serve as Jack's adjutant, Rogerson admits he never really knew him, however much he grew to admire and love him. Jack's sense of duty was far too strict for most of the young officers to understand, and he had an exasperating punctiliousness for what appeared to be unimportant details of military etiquette and discipline. It was only later that Rogerson fully appreciated Jack's professional virtues.[60] Philip Gibbs, a war correspondent who wrote scathingly about British military leadership during the war, did, however, praise the virtues of the regular officer, which he saw as courage and leadership in battle, a gentlemanly code of conduct, *noblesse oblige* and 'the stern sense of justice of a Roman centurion'.[61]

Many of the professional and social differences between regular, temporary and Territorial officers disappeared or seemed less important on active service. This was particularly true for the technical arms. Sir John Cadman, an eminent engineer in civil life, was called upon as a consultant by the Royal Engineers, which required him to make frequent visits to the various theatres of war. He said he could never tell whether he was talking to a regular or temporary engineer officer.[62] For junior officers serving at the front it became more important to judge fellow officers by criteria other than purely social ones. Qualities admired were those of courage, steadfastness, loyalty, comradeship and stoicism.[63] The test of war revealed surprising strengths and weaknesses in all types of officers, and the attritional nature of some battles inflicted stress which many refused to recognise or understand either in themselves or others. As a result of increasing casualties and the continuing expansion of the army the War Office decided in February 1916 to establish a new system for selecting and training junior officers.

As early as January 1915 it had been recognised that there were a number of potential officers serving in the ranks, so it was decided that NCOs and other ranks who were recommended by their commanding officers would be given a short course of officer training for four weeks.

This training was to be in units such as the Inns of Court, Artists' Rifles and university OTCs, and, if suitable, the candidates were commissioned. By the end of the year it had become necessary to establish a more uniform system of selecting and training junior officers for temporary commissions, and such a system was established in February 1916 with the formation of the Officer Cadet Battalions. Under the new system temporary commissions were granted only to those who had passed through the ranks, unless they had previous experience as an officer or some specialist qualification. With the introduction of compulsory military service a few months later this system replaced the OTCs as the route to a temporary commission.

A candidate for a commission had to be recommended by his commanding officer, and whilst under training he retained his former rank, so that if at any stage he was found unsuitable he could be returned to his unit. The course lasted four months, and whilst a certain amount of specific military training was provided, the stress was on developing leadership and the cultivation of initiative and self-confidence. In the words of one contemporary writer the tone was 'intended to be that of Sandhurst or Woolwich or of the best public schools'.[64]

By July 1917 there were twenty-three Officer Cadet Battalions, of which the majority provided officers for the infantry.[65] The Officer Cadet Battalions were housed in university colleges, former barracks and country houses. Between February 1916 and December 1918 107,929 temporary commissions were granted from Officer Cadet Battalions.[66]

Despite the commitment of British forces in the Mediterranean and the Middle East, the most important theatre of operations was north-west Europe. Throughout the war the overwhelming proportion of officer casualties occurred on the western front. Between 30 September 1915 and 30 September 1917, the period covering the battles of the Somme and Arras, the total officer casualties in France amounted to 49,147. For the period from the 30 September 1917 until 30 September 1919, covering the third battle of Ypres, the German spring offensive of 1918 and then the allied advances in the summer and autumn, the total officer casualties in France amounted to 42,466. These figures do not include those reporting sick or being removed from France for other reasons. Although a proportion of the wounded officer casualties would return to duty, most contemporary observers agreed that a fundamental change occurred in the professional and social quality of new officers over the period June 1916 to November 1917, and that this continued dramatically into 1918.

The battles of the Somme and Third Ypres eroded any original differences there might have been between regular, Territorial and service battalions. With the introduction of compulsory military service

Table 3.3. *Officer Cadet Battalions, July 1917*

Household Brigade	Bushey, Herts.
No. 1	Newton Ferrers, Devon
No. 2	Pembroke College, Cambridge
No. 3	Bristol
No. 4	Oxford
No. 5	Trinity College, Cambridge
No. 6	Balliol College, Oxford
No. 7	Moore Park, Co. Cork
No. 8	Lichfield
No. 9	Gailes, Ayrshire
No. 10	Gailes, Ayrshire
No. 11	Pirbright
No. 12	Newmarket
No. 13	Newmarket
No. 14	Berkhamsted, Herts.
No. 15	Romford
No. 16	Kinmel, Rhyl
No. 17	Kinmel, Rhyl
No. 18	Bath
No. 19	Pirbright
No. 20	Crookham, Aldershot
No. 21	Crookham, Aldershot
Garrison	Jesus College, Cambridge

Note. Before the end of the war No. 3 Officer Cadet Battalion moved to Parkhurst, Isle of Wight, in 1918; No. 14 Officer Cadet Battalion moved to Catterick in January 1918; the Garrison Battalion became No. 22 (Garrison) Officer Cadet Battalion in August 1918; No. 23 Officer Cadet Battalion was at Catterick, having been converted from a Machine Gun Corps Officer Cadet Battalion.

Source. Brigadier E. A. James, *British Regiments, 1914–1918*, Samson Books, 1978, p. 119.

in 1916, battalions increasingly contained a mixture of all elements, although some units were able to retain a higher proportion of the original cadre than others. J. Jack noticed in July 1918 when in command of the 1st Cameronians that 'although my battalion is labelled "Regular" it contains no greater number of trained personnel than Territorial or New Army battalions. Perhaps we have one or two more experienced warrant and noncommissioned officers than they.'[67]

When Robert Graves rejoined the 2nd Royal Welsh Fusiliers on the Somme in January 1917 he found a very different battalion to the one he had left: 'No riding school, no battalion mess, no Quetta manners, no regular officers, except for a couple of newly arrived Sandhurst boys.'[68] In September 1917 Guy Chapman noted in his own battalion, the 13th Royal Fusiliers, that 'the officers in degree were as the men. Very few of the pre-Somme vintage remained, the rest were either very young or had served in the ranks.'[69] This change was reflected in the professional and social backgrounds of brigade and battalion commanders. F. P. Crozier,

Table 3.4. *Summary of officer casualties, 1914–19*

| Theatre | No. of casualties[a] | | | |
	A	B	C	Total
France	29,889	68,241	8,440	106,570
Dardanelles	1,084	1,817	263	3,164
Salonika	336	824	81	1,241
Italy	116	289	30	435
Mesopotamia	739	949	400	2,188
Egypt	917	1,726	106	2,749
East Africa	114	115	7	236
North Russia and				
Vladivostok	40	45	27	112
Other theatres	100	61	6	167
Total				116,781

a Note. A Killed in action, died from wounds and other causes, *B* Wounded, *C* Missing (including prisoners).

Source. General Annual Reports on The British Army for the period 1 October 1913 to 30 September 1919, HMSO, 1921, pp. 71–2.

who commanded the 119th Brigade in 1917, was a retired pre-war regular officer who in 1914 had been second-in-command of a battalion of the Ulster Volunteer Force. He noted that by the middle of 1917:

The four battalions were commanded by Plunkett, who had been Sergeant-Major of the Royal Irish Regiment in 1914, and had received his commission into the regiment early in the war; Benzie, a Scotsman who had been in civil engineering in Ceylon and who had been to Gallipoli with the Ceylon Planters' Corps, in which he was a Second Lieutenant; Andrews, a man who had taken part in many revolutions in South America, and who had run away from school in 1900, to fight in South Africa in the ranks of the Yeomanry; and Kennedy a lecturer at the London School of Economics.[70]

In 1918 Clement Attlee was serving with the 5th South Lancashire Regiment, and he contrasted the officers in that battalion with those of the 6th battalion in 1914. Whereas in 1914 the majority of officers were from public schools and many were from Oxford or Cambridge, in the 5th Battalion in 1918 there was a greater variety, including a Lancashire miner and an errand boy.[71] In A Battery, 190th Brigade, Royal Field Artillery, the background of the officers in 1918 were as follows: the major and battery commander, a pre-war regular; the captain, New Army and a lawyer; lieutenant, Special Reserve and Canadian rancher; three subalterns, all temporary officers, a banker, a footballer and a 'gentleman'.[72]

By spring 1918 in France the overall manpower shortages, particularly among the infantry, meant that many battalions were disbanded and cannibalised, and brigades were reduced from four to three battalions. Furthermore, there was frequently a marked discrepancy between establishment and actual strength. In October 1918 battalions with an establishment of twenty officers and 800 other ranks had barely half that strength. In 190th Brigade, Royal Field Artillery, the total officer establishment in 1918 was fifty-three, but the actual strength at any one time was twenty-eight.[73]

As the majority of new temporary officers from February 1916 were selected from the ranks and trained at Officer Cadet Battalions, some of the criticism about the deterioration in the quality was laid against the new system. Some 10,000 officers were required yearly by 1917, and a division was ordered to find fifty suitable candidates a month who had to be recommended by their commanding officers. However, it was by no means certain that the best possible candidates were put forward. Many commanding officers were reluctant to put forward their best NCOs, and not only would they lose their services but it was unlikely they would return to the unit as officers. Some NCOs refused the opportunity to become a candidate for a commission, as they preferred serving in a unit they knew, were confident as NCOs and less sure they would be so as junior officers, and may have calculated that they would have a lower life expectancy. Certain commanding officers put forward the names of unsuitable NCOs whom they wished to remove from their units. Some men put in for a commission simply to get away from the war for a few months, hoping that it might be over before they were commissioned.[74]

There are certain implied assumptions behind the opinion that the quality of new officers deteriorated after 1916. Some temporary officers who had been volunteers questioned the commitment of those who were commissioned after the introduction of compulsory military service. There is an assumption that the quality of new officers deteriorated uniformly and in every arm of service. But the shortage of officers and the criticism of their quality both refer mainly to front-line infantry, artillery and engineer units. The fact is there was not an overall shortage of officers after 1916, just one among the infantry overseas and particularly in France. Many regular officers and original temporary officers who had been wounded, or had some particular expertise or influence, remained on home service or obtained staff and administrative appointments.[75]

But the most interesting assumption relates to the connection between social and educational background and class and the ability to be an officer and a gentleman and thus a military leader. In the first few months of the war the regular officer class generally displayed traditional leadership qualities, although they frequently found it difficult to adapt to the requirements of modern warfare. For many regular and some temporary officers the requirements of leadership in battle were more than narrow professional expertise and bravery. To be an officer still required a certain style of dress, behaviour and speech which had to be quite different from that of the rank and file.

A. A. Hanbury-Sparrow had been critical of the social behaviour of some temporary officers in 1915 and questioned their ability to lead men in battle. By 1917 he was prepared to accept the 'somewhat uncouth but very willing officer reinforcements'. He thought it was no good blaming the Officer Cadet Battalions for the type of new officer who was being commissioned, as it was obvious that the supply of gentlemen was on the verge of exhaustion. Hanbury-Sparrow worked on the dictum that 'You can't make a silk purse out of a sow's ear, but you can make a good leather one.' Hence his attention to social behaviour and the need to instruct the new officers by having a 'properly run officers' mess out of the line and insisting that officers change into slacks for dinner'.[76] J. Jack, commanding the 1st Cameronians in September 1918, turned his eye for detail to the dress of his officers, insisting that they were properly turned out and an example to their men. He had them discard non-regulation articles of uniform and presented them all with proper canes.[77]

Officers' uniform and dress during the First World War symbolised the struggle between class identification, sartorial elegance and fashion on the one hand, and on the other the functional requirements of soldiering. In 1914 the British officer had gone to war in a uniform that was impractical for active service, with rank badges conspicuously displayed on the cuff, and wearing a sword. The effects of firepower, and the requirement to live literally in the field, meant that uniform was gradually adapted. Rank badges were made less conspicuous, swords were discarded, the Sam Browne belt was replaced by webbing, and the service dress hat by the steel helmet. However, many officers, disregarding the increased dangers and discomfort, either failed to adapt their uniforms or adopted new articles of dress and equipment, such as brassards, walking sticks and burnished steel helmets.[78]

Harold Macmillan found that Colonel C. R. C. de Crespigny, of the 2nd Grenadier Guards, disregarded any order of which he disapproved in the matter of uniform. 'Crawley' regarded any suggestion that he should discard his Sam Browne belt, wear the same webbing as other ranks, and even carry a rifle in an attack as degrading: 'He always wore a gold-peaked cap, belt, boots and gold spurs.' Amazingly, he survived the war.[79] Graham Greenwell, a young temporary officer, noted in 1917 the new brigadier's insistence that all officers were to wear Tommies' tunics, 'among other fads'.[80] Then as now, and throughout history, officers made themselves distinctive from their men by the quality of their uniform and by the symbolic but ineffectual nature of their personal weapons. In European armies this distinction has been gradually eroded by the nature of modern war and the decline in social differences between officers and rank and file.

To a certain extent an officer's behaviour was determined by his relationship with his soldiers. Some had few expectations of their men, and regarded them 'like children moving in a haze of their own dreams, unconnected with practical things'.[81] The robust Hanbury-Sparrow thought that the men were 'wonderful, marvellous in the docility, their cheerfulness, and the fewness of their wants'. But that didn't stop him from thinking that the duty of an officer was to lead:

Talk about the officer being worthy of his men you esteemed as clap-trap; for the men, you held, were definitely inferior beings and you'd no illusions about them ... But their very helplessness made it more than ever necessary for the leaders to equip themselves mentally and morally.[82]

Charles Carrington resented the barrier between officer and man. He found the most satisfying moments when he and his men were isolated as a unit in conditions where rank could claim no privilege: 'where the primacy I exhibited was due only to my superior knowledge. I did not want to belong to a distinct caste, though I accepted the social necessity of the military hierarchy; I wanted to identify myself "with the lads".'[83]

Soldiers looked for a number of things in their officers, including professional competence, a degree of understanding, confidence and a certain style. But above all they respected courage. Frank Richards put it simply when he wrote, 'We always judged a new officer by the way he conducted himself in a trench, and if he had guts we always respected him.'[84] John Lucy, a regular who thought his officers were not very much in touch with their men, did believe, however, that they were 'extraordinarily gallant, and their displays of valour, often uncalled for, though thought necessary by them, coupled with the respect engendered in the old army for its corps of officers, won the greatest devotion, and very often the affection of the men'.[85]

If at times there appeared to be social and professional differences between regular and temporary offices, and officers and other ranks, there seemed to be an even greater divide between regimental officers and soldiers and generals and their staffs. Field Marshal Wavell has pointed out that this division between the planners and the participants of battles was a historical one:

The feeling between the regimental officer and the staff officer is as old as the history of fighting. I have been a regimental officer in two minor wars and realised what a poor hand the staff made of things and what a safe luxurious life they led; I was a staff officer in the First World War and realised that the staff were worked to the bone to try and keep the regimental officer on the rails; I have been a Higher Commander in one minor and one major war and have sympathised with the views of both staff and regimental officer.[86]

Criticism of both generals and staffs alike during the First World War abounds in memoirs, letters and diaries. Regular, Territorial and temporary regimental officers and soldiers were equally strident in their views.[87] The generals and their staffs have been accused of being

incompetent and at the same time out of touch with the realities faced
by the regimental soldier. This condemnation has to include the whole
pre-war officer class because it overwhelmingly provided almost all
officers at and above the rank of brigadier-general and the majority of
staff officers above brigade level.

The competence and professional efficiency of British generals and
their staffs is a more complex question than that raised by traditional
generalisations and caricatures.[88] The transition from amateur to
professional proved a lengthy and difficult business. It was a struggle
between the technical, professional approach to war and the traditional,
amateur one; it produced tensions within individual officers, like
Douglas Haig, and the officer class as a whole, as one ideal replaced the
other or both tried to coexist. This process had begun in the nineteenth
century and was evident during and after the South African War. The
conduct and the management of the First World War intensified these
tensions within the officer class.[89]

The physical and spiritual separation of the generals and their staffs
from the front line was partly due to command and control problems.
Unfortunately the country-house life style of many generals and their
staffs and the incestuous nature of their self-promotion did not endear
them to the regimental soldier. It was not that British generals or their
staffs lacked courage – seventy brigadier-generals and above were killed
in action or died of their wounds during the war.[90] Rather, they became
isolated from the front line by new managerial problems which they had
not mastered, and at the same time they continued to live the life style
of traditional commanders and their staffs who in the past had been
able to live physically close to the battlefield. These lessons were not lost
on junior regimental officers such as Richard O'Connor, Bill Slim and
Bernard Montgomery, who as generals in the Second World War made
certain that, as far as possible, no such division appeared between the
high command and regimental soldiers.

When measured against the total numbers of men serving in the army
during the First World War, officers suffered higher casualties than the
rank and file. Proportionally, junior officers below the rank of
lieutenant-colonel suffered heavier casualties than did more senior
officers, hence the requirement for a constant supply of new ones.
Statistically speaking, a man increased his chances of becoming a
casualty, firstly by serving in the infantry, secondly by being an infantry
officer, and thirdly by serving on the western front.[91] However, the
legend of the 'three-week subaltern' is largely a myth. Although
experiences varied between one battalion and another, it is possible to
estimate in general terms that if a battalion served in France over a
period of some forty months the average subaltern spent six months of
front-line service before becoming a casualty or leaving for some other

Table 3.5. *Officer/other rank casualties, 1914–18 (%)*

Period	Killed		Wounded		Missing/P.O.W.s	
	Officers	ORs	Officers	ORs	Officers	ORs
1 October 1914– 30 September 1915	14·2	5·8	24·4	17·4	3·7	2·9
1 October 1915– 30 September 1916	8·0	4·9	17·4	14·0	1·3	1·3
1 October 1916– 30 September 1917	8·5	4·7	17·6	12·3	1·5	1·1
1 October 1917– 30 September 1918	6·9	4·0	17·1	13·9	3·4	3·4
1 October 1918	1·0	1·1	3·3	2·2	0·1	0·1

Source. J. M. Winter, 'Britain's "Lost generation" of the First World War', *Population Studies*, 31, 3, 1977, table 7, p. 458.

reason. This was the case with the 10th West Yorkshire Regiment, which had to replace its original complement of junior officers six times over.[92]

One explanation behind the relatively high casualty figures for infantry officers is that at least until the last six months of the war the average British infantry battalion would go into the line with twenty-five officers, compared to a German battalion with eight or nine officers. The Germans had learnt by 1916 to conserve their officers and made greater use of NCOs. Hanbury-Sparrow recognised this fact and believed that the problem of the supply of junior officers was directly related to the quality of the rank and file and junior NCOs. 'Here was the secret of the British Army's weakness vis-à-vis the Germans. The latter could use NCOs where we had to use officers, and thousands of promising young officers were killed doing lance-corporals' work, simply because section commanders had not it in them to exercise sufficient authority to carry out their task.'[93] From 4 August 1914 to 30 September 1919 33,337 officers were killed, died of wounds and died, 74,082 were wounded and 9,362 were missing or had become p.o.w.s.[94] As some 229,316 combatant commissions were awarded during the war, an officer stood approximately a one in six chance of being killed and a one in three chance of being wounded.

By November 1918 the officer strength was 164,255, the majority with temporary commissions.[95] Over the next eighteen months the army rapidly demobilised and slowly began to shrink to its pre-war strength, despite occupation duties, hostilities in Ireland and labour disputes in Britain. The number of officers demobilised up to 20 May 1920, including the RAF and the army, was 188,767. The War Office return on demobilisation by industrial groups indicates the occupational background of these officers.[96] Approximately one-third of all officers demobilised from the army and the RAF were from the professional classes, commercial and clerical, and students and teachers. Engineers and those employed with the building trade also formed an important group. Other major groups were associated with industry, commerce, agriculture and trade. It is not possible to establish whether these men were managers or employees, but the overwhelming majority came from a different social and education background to the pre-war regular officer class. This is complemented by the fact that by 1917 the candidates for regular commissions passing through Sandhurst and Woolwich reflected an increase in lower middle-class parental backgrounds.

During the First World War the officer class expanded from 28,060 to over 229,316. Although commissions were initially awarded to those candidates possessing similar social and educational background to the pre-war officer class, this soon changed because of the increase in officer casualties and the rapid expansion of the army. A large number of commissions were awarded from the ranks, and eventually this method became the only route to a commission apart from those candidates for a regular commission attending Sandhurst and Woolwich. The regular officer class attempted to socialise the temporary officers and inculcate professionalism and a traditional cult of leadership. Certainly the majority of temporary officers who had volunteered before 1916 enthusiastically adapted to many of the social and professional requirements of the regular officer class. C. E. Bean, the official historian of the Australian army, believed that in the case of the British the traditional respect of a soldier for his officer was based partly on class distinction.[97]

A consensus of opinion emerges from contemporary sources that the quality of new officers deteriorated after 1916. This criticism was made by both regular and temporary officers commissioned before that date, and relates to a combination of social and professional factors. Many officers believed that there was direct correlation between social and educational background and military leadership. After 1916 the majority of new officers were drawn from a different social and educational background from the regular officer class and the early temporary officers and thus they were unable to lead men in battle with the same degree of confidence. This generalised subjective view is partly supported by the need to establish Officer Cadet Battalions which effectively 'taught' leadership, and by the fact that in 1917 and 1918 the army faced major problems in morale on the western front and during the German spring offensive in 1918 and this can partly be related to officer leadership. But contradicting this generalisation is the fact that although the army had suffered heavy casualties in 1916 and 1917, and morale in France had been badly affected by Third Ypres, it suffered no major act of mutiny as did the French in 1917. That is not to say that throughout the war there were not numerous individual and collective acts of disobedience and indiscipline, the mutiny at the base camp at Étaples in 1917 being the most infamous.[98] But the army managed to contain these outbreaks, survived the disaster of March 1918, and returned to a successful offensive in the summer and autumn of 1918. If the quality of junior officers had been so bad it is unlikely the army could have survived this traumatic period – which is not to say that the British army in France was not having to struggle to keep up the momentum by October 1918.

It would be wrong to assume that as a result of the war many civilians who had served as temporary officers were critical of the regular officer class and the high command. Criticism is usually associated with the war poets and writers such as Wilfred Owen, Siegfried Sassoon and Robert Graves. These three all served as temporary officers, and Graves and Sassoon were to display in their writing quite ambivalent attitudes. Both Graves and Sassoon were good regimental soldiers, and Sassoon took a great delight in the physical side of trench warfare.[99] Many young temporary officers looked back on their time in the army as the most exciting and stimulating of their lives.[100] Although the nature of battle in the First World War did much to 'destroy neo-feudal myths about the unique compatability of officering with gentlemanly status'[101] it lingered on, survived in the post-war army and could be found in the Second World War.

For the regimental officer, the First World War meant acquiring new specialised skills in such areas as signalling, mortars, machine guns and transport. Specialised schools and courses had to be organised to enable officers to familiarise themselves with them. The technical and logistical corps were greatly expanded, affecting the officer strength of the army and reflecting the industrialisation of war. Both the Army Service Corps and the Army Ordnance Corps were expanded to meet the new requirements. The Royal Engineers increased in officer strength some fifteenfold and the Royal Artillery some sevenfold. This increase was due to the siege nature of the war and a greater requirement for what the infantry referred to as 'the plumbers' of the battlefield. Perhaps the most dramatic expansion came with the RFC, reflecting the importance of air power, and the political decision to establish an independent air force in April 1918.

Two new arms, the Machine Gun Corps, and an offshoot from it, the Tank Corps, show a steady increase during the last two years of the war. Reflecting the need to maximise all manpower, and because of political pressure, the Women's Army Auxiliary Corps was established in March 1917. There were no military ranks in the WAAC; instead of officers there were controllers and administrators. It was believed that only men

Table 3.6. *Officer strength by arm of service, 1914–18*

	Infantry	Cavalry	RA
August 1914	10,351	876	3,331
1915	49,056	1,891	10,332
1916	55,685	1,834	13,390
1917	64,436	2,517	16,791
1918	67,689	4,007	21,651
	RE	ASC	AOC
August 1914	1,565	819	233
1915	4,317	4,751	912
1916	9,026	6,772	1,406
1917	10,909	9,680	1,770
1918	16,371	11,456	2,102
	RFC	MGC	Tank Corps
August 1914	103		
1915	702		
1916	3,476	1,080	181
1917	9,268	4,969	1,247
1918	18,286 (March)	6,507	2,887

Source. Statistics of the Military Effort of the British Empire, pp. 207–27.

could hold the king's commission. The infantry officer strength shows a steady increase by sixfold during the war, and even the cavalry, with its more limited role, at least on the western front, expanded over fourfold.

But the post-war army quickly reverted in size, organisation and ethos to that of pre-war days. There were, of course, a number of changes, because the impact of the conflict could not be ignored totally. Organisation, weapons and equipment had changed, but, despite these factors, the army of 1924 looked remarkably similar to that of 1914. The increase in the importance of the technical and logistical corps, the gunners and sappers, and the establishment of the Tank Corps, were not reflected in the organisation of the post-war army. The Tank Corps survived, but with a restricted establishment, and it faced the hostility of the traditional arms. In practical terms the army remained dominated by the cavalry and infantry. This is partly explained by financial restrictions and the political and military requirements of imperial policing, but it was also a reaction by the regular officer class, and for that matter the regular rank and file, to the horrors of modern war and a determination to get back to 'real soldiering'.

With the reduction of the army from a wartime to a peacetime establishment there was considerable competition for regular commissions, and appointments depended upon substantive rather than temporary or acting rank. Although the pre-war officer class had suffered severe casualties, many regular officers had been promoted to temporary command and staff appointments, and there had been a steady influx of junior regular officers as well as those temporary officers who had been awarded a regular commission. Thus, in the post-war army, far from there being shortage of regular officers there was an embarrassing surplus. It was to increase with the amalgamation of some regiments in 1922 and the disbandment of the southern Irish ones. The War Office and regimental colonels could pick and choose whom they wanted as regular officers in receipt of full pay. Lord Russell of Liverpool had converted his territorial commission in the 5th King's (Liverpool) Regiment to a regular one during the war. He found after the armistice, like so many officers, that promotion was likely to be a slow business. In the 1st Battalion:

There was a plethora of senior officers who had come from appointments all over the world. Although our C.O. was, of course, the senior substantive lieutenant-colonel, at least two of the company commanders were his senior in the Army, being brevet colonels. I, with the exalted rank of lieutenant, commanded my platoon and it was five years before I got my company. It seemed rather a come-down after having commanded a company on active service for over two years, finally ending up as a major and second-in-command.[102]

The parental background of entrants to Sandhurst and Woolwich shows that between 1920 and 1930 the percentage of 'gentlemen' declined dramatically, whilst the percentage of military professionals rose substantially. So the war was responsible for considerably reducing the 'gentlemanly' intake into the officer class, which became more middle-class and self-recruited. However, it would be wrong to conclude

Table 3.7. *Occupations of fathers of entrants to Sandhurst and Woolwich, 1910–30 (%)*

Year[a]		'Gentle-men', etc.	Business-men and managers	Military profes-sionals	Civilian profes-sionals	All others
1910	S	20·5	9·3	43·8	23·0	3·4
	W	12·9	12·2	35·3	36·0	3·6
1917[b]	S	9·2	23·7	20·1	35·7	11·3
	W	9·5	22·6	17·9	41·7	8·3
1920	S	17·6	8·1	37·6	30·6	6·1
	W	8·5	8·5	41·9	36·4	4·6
1930	S	9·1	12·0	50·8	23·9	4·2
	W	1·7	11·1	62·4	23·9	0·9

Note: header spanning — 'Gentle-men', etc. / Business-men and managers / Military profes-sionals / Civilian profes-sionals / All others are under "Father's occupation".

Notes
[a] S Sandhurst, W Woolwich.
[b] Second intake only.

Source. C. B. Otley, 'The social origins of British army officers', *Sociological Review*, 18, 2, July 1970, tables V and VI, pp. 213–40.

that the ethos and perceptions of the officer class were substantially changed by the experience of the First World War. In many ways the officer class became more introverted and isolated from civil society, and the life style of many officers became one of 'shabby gentility'. These middle-class officers were still imbued with the 'gentlemanly' concept of soldiering and in a small volunteer army were able to continue traditions for which the experience of the First World War was merely an unusual aberration.[123] It was to take another world war to effect a substantial change in the officer class; even then the ghost of the 'gentlemanly' concept of soldiering survived and can be found today haunting the officers' messes of the socially elite regiments.

Notes

1 C. B. Otley, 'The Origins and Recruitment of the British Army Elite, 1870–1939', unpub. Ph.D., Hull, 1965, p. 7.
2 *Statistics of the Military Effort of the British Empire, 1914–1920*, HMSO, 1922, pp. 234–5. It should be noted that statistics relating to officers during the First World War are only approximate, as even the official ones were admitted to be inaccurate.
3 There is no satisfactory collective noun for officers which explains the subtle social and professional differences between the regiments and corps. Philip Mason has written in his book on the Indian Army, 'Not quite a caste, something more than a class, not exactly a military order – the officers of the Victorian Army were a society set apart' (*A Matter of Honour*, London, 1974, p. 370). The term 'corps', meaning a body of persons engaged in the same activity, does not apply, because although all officers were in theory commissioned soldiers their functions varied considerably. This author has preferred to use the term 'class' when referring collectively to British officers.
4 Otley, 'Origins and Recruitment', pp. 83–95, particularly, table 12.
5 The links between the public schools and the officer class have been well established. See Brian Simon and Ian Bradley (eds.), *The Victorian Public School*, Macmillan, London, 1975; Ian Worthington, 'Antecendent education and officer recruitment: the origins and early development of the public school–army relationship', *Military Affairs*, December 1977, pp. 183–9; and for a study of the officers of one regiment, the 2nd Cameronians, John Baynes, *Morale*, Cassell, London, 1967.
6 For the development of 'leadership' qualities at public schools see Rupert Wilkinson, *The Prefects*, Oxford, 1964.
7 William Robertson's own autobiography, *From Private to Field-Marshal*, Constable, London, 1921, is very revealing on these points.
8 For a contemporary view of officers' pay and allowances see J. K. Trotter, 'The submerged subaltern', *Nineteenth Century*, April 1912, pp. 706–18.
9 See John Keegan, 'Regimental ideology', in G. Best and A. Wheatcroft (eds.), *War, Economy and the Military Mind*, Croom Helm, London, 1976, pp 3–18. One pre-war regular subaltern in the Gloucestershire Regiment has commented, 'Socially, regiments varied enormously. I think it would be generally true to say that those recruited from the heavily industrialised areas accepted perhaps a lower standard (or it may have been a different standard) from many of the County Regiments, but this did not necessarily affect their fighting values.' Brigadier A. L. W. Newth in reply to the

author's questionnaire, 17 February 1977. Since 1976 the author has received over 200 sets of answers to detailed questionnaires he compiled for regular, temporary and territorial officers who served in the First World War. The author would like to acknowledge the generous assistance he received with this project from Mr Roderick Suddaby and his staff, Department of Documents, Imperial War Museum. References to this source will hereafter be referred to as KRS Q.

10 Although written in the last decade of the nineteenth century, the chapter 'Which branch of the service to join?' in *The Queen's Commission* by Captain G. J. Younghusband, John Murray, 1891, is an instructive and illuminating guide to this subject. Baynes also refers to it with reference to the 2nd Cameronians in *Morale*, pp. 31–2.

11 Keegan, 'Regimental ideology', p. 5, and Maurice Garnier, 'Social Class and Military Socialisation: a Study of the Royal Military Academy, Sandhurst', unpub. Ph.D., California, 1964.

12 KRS Q, Major-General E. G. W. Harrison, 21 May 1978.

13 KRS Q, Colonel P. R. Mundy, 27 October 1976.

14 KRS Q, Lieutenant-Colonel H. D. Thwaytes, 20 February 1977.

15 KRS Q, Brigadier W. J. Jervois, pre-war regular officer of the 1st Northamptonshire Regiment, 1 November 1976.

16 John Lucy, *There's a Devil in the Drum*, Faber and Faber, London, 1938, p. 95.

17 KRS Q, Major-General R. C. Money, 13 January 1977.

18 Colonel W. N. Nicholson, *Behind the Lines*, Jonathan Cape, London, 1939, pp. 137–9.

19 Brigadier J. E. Edmonds, *Military Operations, France and Belgium, 1914*, II, Macmillan, London, 1925, p. 467.

20 Alan Shepperd, *Sandhurst*, Country Life Books, London, 1980, pp. 118–24.

21 *Statistics of the Military Effort*, p. 234.

22 C. E. Hudson, a temporary captain in a service battalion of the Sherwood Foresters, was offered a permanent commission in the regular army during the winter of 1916–17. Brigadier C. E. Hudson, VC, unpublished autobiography, p. 221, Sandhurst collection.

23 C. B. Otley, 'The social origins of British army officers', *Sociological Review*, 18, 2 July 1970, pp. 225–6.

24 Ibid, pp. 222 and 237.

25 The Territorials were to remain the 'poor relation' of both the regular and service battalions for some time to come. But their importance can be seen by the fact that the number of Territorial officers was 9,563 on 4 August 1914, and from that date until the end of the war 60,044 commissions in the Territorial Force were granted. *Statistics of the Military Effort* p. 235.

26 Brigadier E. A. James, *British Regiments, 1914–1918*, Samson Books, London, 1978, appendix II to Part II.

27 A good general account of the supply of officers for the New Armies can be found in Captain Basil Williams, *Raising and Training the New Armies*, Constable, London, 1918, pp. 57–70.

28 The experiences of one such junior regular officer of the 1st Royal Berkshire Regiment can be found in A. A. Hanbury-Sparrow, *The Land-locked Lake*, Arthur Barker, London, 1932, pp. 124–30.

29 Williams, *Raising and Training*, p. 63.

30 Captain Alan Haig-Brown, *The OTC and the Great War*, London, 1915, p. 99.

31 Williams, *Raising and Training*, p. 65.

32 *History of the Corps of Royal Engineers*, V, Chatham, 1952, p. 31.

33 R. C. Sherriff 'The English public schools in the war', in George A. Panichas (ed.), *Promise of Greatness* Cassell, London, 1968, p. 136.

34 Clement Attlee, *As it Happened*, Heinemann, London, 1954, p. 38.

35 Harold Macmillan, *Winds of Change, 1914–1939*, Macmillan, London, p. 61.

36 Bryan Cooper, *The Tenth (Irish) Division in Gallipoli*, Herbert Jenkins, London, 1928, pp. 1–11.

37 *History of the 50th Infantry Brigade, 1914–1919*, privately printed, 1919, p. 8.

38 Quoted in Martin Middlebrook, *The First Day on the Somme*, Allen Lane, London, 1971, p. 17.

39 Guy Chapman, *A Passionate Prodigality*, MacGibbon & Kee, London, 1965, p. 14.

40 KRS Q, H. W. Yoxall, 8 November 1977.

41 *History of the Corps of Royal Engineers*, pp. 32 and 140–51.

42 Hanbury-Sparrow, *Land-locked Lake*, p. 127, and John Terraine (ed.), *General Jack's Diary 1914–1918*, Eyre and Spottiswoode, London, 1964, p. 107.

43 IWM, J. Jack, *The War Diary of Captain James Jack 1915–1916*, II, p. 67.

44 KRS Q, Brigadier C. A. F. Drummond, 18 February 1978.

45 KRS Q, Brigadier I. M. Stewart, 1 August 1977.

46 Hanbury-Sparrow, *Land-locked Lake*, p. 216.

47 Siegfried Sassoon, *Memoirs of a Fox-hunting Man*, Faber and Faber, London, 1955, p. 264.

48 *Ibid*, p. 274.

49 Arthur Osburn, *Unwilling Passenger*, Faber and Faber, London, 1932, p. 250.

50 *Customs of the Army: Guide for Cadets and Young Officers*, by Regular, Harrison, 1917, pp. 10–15.

51 C.N., *The Making of an Officer*, Hodder and Stoughton, London, 1916, p. 26; *A General's Letters to his Son on obtaining his Commission*, Cassell, London, 1917, pp. 32–5.

52 *Notes for Young Officers*, HMSO, 1917, p. 68.

53 *Customs of the Army*, pp. 7–8.

54 KRS Q, Harold Knee, 10 April 1978.

55 Captain Owen Rutter, *The Song of Tiadatha*, Fisher Unwin, London, 1920, p. 15.

56 Charles Carrington, *Soldier from the Wars Returning*, Hutchinson, London, 1965, p. 86.

57 Macmillan, *Winds of Change*, pp. 64–7.

58 *Ibid.*, pp. 98–9.

59 Robert Graves, *Goodbye to all that*, Harmondsworth, London, 1961, pp. 105–7.

60 *General Jack's Diary*, p. 13.

61 Philip Gibbs, *Realities of War*, Heinemann, London, 1920, p. 57.

62 *History of the Corps of Royal Engineers*, V, p. 32.

63 The overwhelming majority of former officers, regular, temporary and territorial, who replied to the author's questionnaire all agreed on this point.

64 Williams, *Raising and Training*, p. 101.

65 James, *British Regiments*, p. 119.

66 *Statistics of the Military Effort*, p. 235.

67 *General Jack's Diary*, p. 247.

68 Graves, *Goodbye to all that*, p. 196.

69 Chapman, *Passionate Prodigality*, p. 180.
70 F. P. Crozier, *Impressions and Recollections*, Werner Laurie, London, 1930, p. 193.
71 Attlee, *As it Happened*, p. 43.
72 KRS Q, Captain Leonard Humphreys, 21 August 1978.
73 *Ibid.*
74 Nicholson, *Behind the Lines*, pp. 223–4; KRS Q, Lieutenant-Colonel W. G. Taylor. Taylor served in the ranks of the HAC 1914–15, and was then commissioned into the 13th Royal Fusiliers. He served as an instructor at No. 5 Officer Cadet Battalion at Cambridge from October 1916. Frank Richards, *Old Soldiers never die*, Faber and Faber, London, 1933, p. 239.
75 See *Statistics of the Military Effort*, II, Estimated Strength of the Forces Abroad and at Home. For comments of front-line officers about the overmanning of home service battalions and the staff see Carrington, *Soldier from the Wars Returning*, p. 250, and Lieutenant-Colonel S. G. Hutchison, *Warrior*, Hutchinson, London, 1932, p. 277. The question of the proportion of 'teeth to tail' in armies is a recurring one and not unique to the British. For an analysis of the problem for the British and American armies in the Second World War see John Ellis, *The Sharp End of War*, David and Charles, Newton Abbot, 1980.
76 Hanbury-Sparrow, *Land-locked Lake*, p. 293.
77 *General Jack's Diary*, p. 256.
78 See D. S. W. Fosten and R. J. Marrion, *The British Army 1914–1918*, Osprey, London, 1978, and John Mollo, *Military Fashion*, Barrie and Jenkins, London, 1972.
79 Macmillan, *Winds of Change*, p. 80.
80 Graham Greenwell, *An Infant in Arms*, Dickson and Thompson, London, 1936, p. 192.
81 Chapman, *Passionate Prodigality*, p. 84.
82 Hanbury-Sparrow, *Land-locked Lake*, pp. 211 and 202–4.
83 Carrington, *Soldier from the Wars Returning*, p. 244.
84 Richards, *Old Soldiers never Die*, p. 98.
85 Lucy, *There's a Devil in the Drum*, p. 95.
86 A. P. Wavell, *Other Men's Flowers*, Cape, London, 1958, p. 131.
87 A random selection would include Chapman, *Passionate Prodigality*, pp. 141–42; Hanbury-Sparrow, *Land-locked Lake*, p. 190; Richards, *Old Soldiers never die*, pp. 92 and 168–70; Mark Severn, *The Gambardier*, Ernest Benn, London, 1930 pp. 73–7; and J. F. C. Fuller, *Memoirs of an Unconventional Soldier*, Nicholson and Watson, London, 1936, pp. 137–42.
88 See, for example, Alan Clark, *The Donkeys*, Hutchinson, London, 1963.
89 Tim Travers, 'The hidden army: structural problems in the British officer corps, 1900–1918', *Journal of Contemporary History*, 17, 1982, pp. 523–44.
90 The majority of British generals killed were on the western front. The casualties break down by year to: 1914, four; 1915, nineteen, 1916, thirteen; 1917, seventeen, and 1918, seventeen.
91 J. M. Winter, 'Britain's "lost generation" of the First World War', *Population Studies*, 31, 3, 1977, pp. 449–66.
92 *History of the 50th Infantry Brigade*, Calculated from the list detailing officers service during the war.
93 On officer strength in British and German battalions see *General Jack's Diary*, p. 127; and on the role of the junior British officer, Hanbury-Sparrow, *Land-locked Lake*, p. 212.
94 *General Annual Reports of the British Army, 1 October 1913 to 30 September 1919*, pp. 71–2.

 95 *Statistics of the Military Effort*, p. 234.
 96 *Ibid.*, p. 707.
 97 C. E. W. Bean, *Official History of Australia in the War, 1914–1918. The Australian Imperial Force in France 1916*, III, Angus and Robertson, London, pp. 53–4.
 98 See Douglas Gill and Gloden Dallas, 'Mutiny at Etaples base in 1917; *Past and Present*, November 1975, pp. 88–112.
 99 See the comments of Vivian de la Pinto, who served as a junior officer under Sassoon in the 25th Royal Welsh Fusiliers in June 1918 'My first war', *Promise of Greatness*, pp. 80–1.
100 See, for example, Greenwell, *Infant in Arms, passim*.
101 Otley, 'Origins and Recruitment, p. 7.
102 Lord Russell of Liverpool, *That Reminds Me*, Cassell, London, 1959, p. 59.
103 See the excellent chapter 2 of Brian Bond, *British Military Policy between two World Wars*, Clarendon Press, 1980, pp. 35–71.

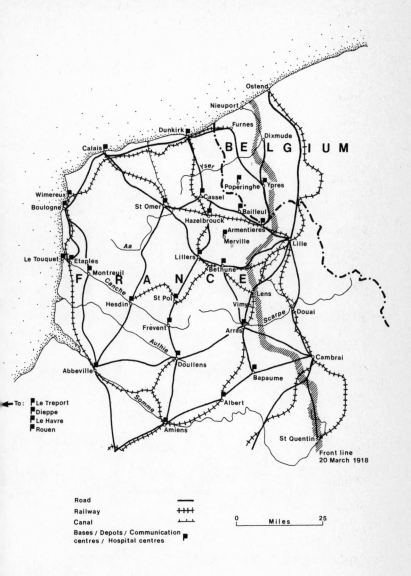

The administrative infra-structure of the BEF in France and Flanders.

Clive Hughes 4

The New Armies

The earliest propagandists for the New Army painted a picture of eager and united effort by all classes of men, requiring only the spur of patriotism to enlist and serve against a common enemy. This chapter seeks to demonstrate that social considerations could play a prominent part in enlistment for, and in the raising of, New Army units. It also examines the reactions of the volunteers to army life, and professional attitudes to the new force. It concludes with a case study of a brigade of the 38th Division.

I

Lord Kitchener accepted the post of Secretary of State for War on 5 August 1914, and two days later issued his 'call to arms' for 100,000 men. He anticipated a three-year conflict and a need for more men than the 500,000 suggested by the government; this force, separate from the Territorials, undertook automatically to serve overseas. Infantry battalions would become 'Service' formations of existing regiments.

The First New Army was divided into six divisions, each raised by an Army Command area. This was achieved by the end of August, but reliance on voluntary enlistment meant that statistics were subject to periodic fluctuation, and recruitment had already slackened before it was given a fresh impetus by the announcment of a second New Army and news of the first battles from France. The newer force admitted married men and others up to thirty-five years of age, and since the regular depots were already glutted these concessions ensured that the ranks filled by 4 September. The pressure of volunteers, however, increased and threatened to overwhelm the recruiting system. A call for 500,000 men on 10 September was premature, but the Third New Army tightened height standards and coincided with a decline brought about by tales of squalid conditions in makeshift camps, and by delays in paying allowances to wives.

Though these ills were remedied in October and November by lower height and raised age standards, the peak had been passed, and during 1915 the decline became more noticeable despite occasional increases due to news of further fighting, and the desperate resort to a 'Bantam' height of 5 ft. Appeals continued to be made until May 1915, when the coalition government realised the necessity of manpower regulation. Voluntary recruitment took another year to die, Lord Derby's Scheme of October to December 1915 being the last attempt to save the system, attracting, as expected, insufficient response. Kitchener, having accepted the need for compulsion, was drowned at sea only days after its full implementation in May 1916.

From late August 1914 recruitment was co-ordinated at a national level by the Parliamentary Recruiting Committee. Composed mainly of

representatives from each political party, it encouraged local meetings
to stimulate enthusiasm and used party agents to organise door-to-door
canvassing. It also published two million posters and twenty million
leaflets by March 1915,[1] but was unable to maintain an adequate flow of
volunteers. It acted as a War Office control, especially when sanction
was given to raise troops at local level.

It is impossible to quantify accurately the reasons impelling
individual enlistment. Patriotism certainly motivated some volunteers,
even though some of the better educated were aware of the economic
rivalry underlying the conflict with Germany. For many, boyhood
recollections of heroic imperial unity during the South African War
assisted in the decision, though by no means everyone was eager to do so
precipitately. Indeed, among the earliest to volunteer were those seizing
the chance to escape the dull routine of a city office or the wearying
labour of the mines and factories.

To such men the war offered a brief respite, an exciting and
adventurous opportunity that some did not seriously consider would
involve them in fighting overseas. Others feared missing active service
before hostilities terminated, declined to wait even a few days until
overworked recruiters could cope with them, and sought less crowded
units. P. G. Heath enlisted in the Territorials in 1914 because he
believed the New Armies would not be ready before the war ended.[2]

Conversely, many waited until they were convinced of the need to
join, and enlisted only after their affairs were properly settled. These
men were responsible for September's boom figures: Germains's
'superior type of citizen' of the Second and Third New Armies.[3]
Reactions varied from George Coppard's impetuous enlistment on
hearing a military band in Croydon[4] to Morgan Watcyn-Williams's days
of internal conflict before deciding to volunteer. Convinced that war
was evil, he was ultimately prepared to fight in order to restore peace.[5] A
desire to retain the respect of social equals or to emulate the actions of
relatives provided many with sufficient motivation. The 'Pals' system,
which encouraged coteries of workmates or friends to volunteer, played
on this, besides offering group support to ease the transition to army life.

Economic pressures also assisted recruitment. The war had brought
some industries to a virtual standstill, making the army a welcome
change from unemployment or a three-day week. Labour exchanges
actively encouraged enlistment, and even the chronicler Donald Hankey
could not deny that 'fear of starvation' impelled some to volunteer.[6] For
those in employment there was encouragement by some firms in the
form of promises to keep volunteers' places open, or of supplementing
army pay with sums designed to remedy the disparity with civilian pay.
Such offers were often made in anticipation of a short war.

When the North Eastern Railway Company decided to raise its own battalion in September 1914, 2,000 employees had already enlisted. Assurances of welfare assistance for dependants, job security after the war, and contributions to superannuation and pensions funds helped 3,000 more to offer their services.[7] This could backfire: on 5 September 1914 the Cardiff Railway Company circularised employees offering various inducements to enlist. Four days later it retracted, despite an excellent response, fearing drastic undermanning.[8] The railways, the civil service, the General Post Office and other 'essential' employers subsequently pressurised men not to enlist, treating defiant volunteers as having resigned.

Less benevolent employers, especially the wealthier servant-keeping classes, were capable of more browbeating than encouragement. A stark choice of enlistment or dismissal was sometimes offered to servants or tenants. When Alfred Mansfield journeyed to his depot in 1914 he was accompanied by eight servants of a peer who had felt that younger members of his staff ought to volunteer.[9] Winter states that 'duty' and 'obligation' as reasons for enlistment occur mainly in lower-class accounts.[10]

Some parts of the country produced proportionately more recruits than others. Rural districts were unable to compete in numerical terms with populous areas. Even within the latter, where war industries flourished fewer men were enlisting than in areas where loss of overseas trade induced a slump, though vital concerns such as steel or coal suffered from an exodus of workers into the army. These shortages were remedied by the unemployed and unfit, but ultimately the loss of skilled men had to be checked. By January 1915 10,000 skilled engineers had enlisted; also 16 per cent of the 920,000 building trades workers; and a similar proportion of the 999,474 coal miners nationwide.[11]

The New Armies also revealed a grim inheritance from late Victorian and Edwardian society. Years of malnutrition, squalid housing and industrial disease showed up in breakdowns under the strains of service. Many accounts refer to cursory medical examinations on attestation; some doctors hurried batches of recruits through because until May 1915 they were paid 2s 6d per man,[12] while others were simply overworked, and by the winter of 1914–15 discharges on medical grounds were rife in some units. In fairness, there are also many accounts of thorough examinations, but as the need for men grew, standards were officially relaxed. During the Derby Scheme 16 per cent of married and 24 per cent of single men were rejected on attestation.[13] Early in 1916 the 40th Division was reduced by two-thirds when thorough examinations revealed a high proportion of unfit men,[14] and that March it was hinted in Parliament that 200,000 medical discharges had occurred in the previous twelve months.[15]

Other problems were caused by volunteers over or under the official age limit. This was exacerbated by the recruiter's entitlement to at least 2*s* 6*d* bounty per man;[16] the reduction to 1*s* from October 1914 had no significant effect, though some recruiters conscientiously turned away those too young or too old. Discovery could result in a discharge, though by 1915 some units preferred to pass under-age men to reserve formations, where they stayed until they reached the official age for overseas service.

Family pressures were also important in considering enlistment. The army's allowances for wives and children did not go far, and delays in tracing and paying those entitled discouraged married men in the early months. Only after spring 1915 were mothers or other dependants catered for, though common-law wives were not discriminated against in this respect.

It will therefore be seen that the popular conception of a 'rush to the colours' is inaccurate. Rather, it was those without strong commitments who usually went first, to be followed by those impelled by socio-economic factors. The battalions they filled were also subsequently eroded by ill health, discharges of the under-aged, and combing out of skilled men for munitions work.

The First and Second New Armies were raised by the War Office, one division of each to be created by the six Commands into which the country was militarily divided. Usually, recruits were sent to the depot of their chosen regiment, where at first a small cadre of regulars was available to help a battalion form. These soon filled to overflowing, so that Second New Army units were easily raised in many cases. War Office control at this stage is demonstrated by the utilisation of New Army recruits by the Special Reserve who ran the depots, to fill the regular battalions.

By the time the Third New Army was announced, some Commands were still struggling to fill their ranks, while others were over-full, owing to the disparities of population and industrial reaction mentioned earlier. From now on, therefore, new armies were created semi-independently of the Commands, though individual units might still be War Office-raised. Some Second New Army units were still half empty as late as April 1915. The rural 9th Battalion, Devonshire Regiment, attracted only eighty local men and was forced to fill up with Londoners and Midlanders.[17] The 8th Battalion, East Surrey Regiment, conversely, was formed out of one huge trainload of recruits, though most were from Suffolk or South Wales.[18] The authorities were clearly able to detach blocks of manpower from crowded depots to create or fill other units.

As towns and individuals began to be permitted to raise formations commensurate with local enthusiasm, the War Office in November 1914 concentrated on a reserve Fourth New Army. This was achieved by waiting until the depots reached a strength of 2,700, then hiving off sufficient men to form a New Army battalion as a reserve for earlier units. This army was disbanded in April 1915 and its title taken by the mainly locally raised Fourth and Fifth New Armies.

War Office-controlled units often differed from others in their social composition. New Army accounts portray an egalitarian mixture of occupations or classes. While some middle or upper-class volunteers were prepared to soldier cheek-by-jowl with the working-class majority, many more were not. Germains delicately suggests that the First New Army, the earliest to volunteer, was generally 'of the same class as the average run of Regular recruit'.[19] Certainly, in predominantly lower-class units a sprinkling of socially elevated recruits would stand out, but proportionately there may not have been very many more than in pre-war days. J. H. M. Staniforth, educated at Oxford, enlisted about September 1914 in the Connaught Rangers. At the depot his companions were 'blind drunk ... about a dozen seedy, ragged, lousy, unshaven tramps, who ... lay on their cots smoking, spitting, quarrelling, making water all over the room ... hiccuping and vomiting'. Even when he reached the 6th Battalion he noted, 'There are only three decent men in C Company ... The rest are quite indescribable villains', and by the end of October his officers were pressing him to take a commission to escape his surroundings.[20]

This can be contrasted with the Cameron Highlanders, who had a Glasgow Stock Exchange company in their 5th Battalion and a Glasgow University company in the overflow 6th Battalion. The 'social tone' of the Second and Third New Armies pleased Germains,[21] and many of their units contained a more diverse mixture of occupations, possibly owing to indiscriminate shuttling of men from depots to needy battalions. Thus the author of *The New Army in the Making* commanded a battalion comprising East Anglian agricultural labourers, London clerks, Lancashire mill workers and Welsh miners.[22] The later 13th Battalion, Rifle Brigade, of the Fifth New Army contained notable groups of professional footballers and golfers, Welsh civil sevants, gamekeepers, members of the Boys' Brigade, twenty-two expatriate South Africans, and a lower-class contingent from south-east London.[23]

The War Office raised some units at 'local' level without entirely devolving control. The 11th Battalion, Liverpool Regiment, was assisted by Lord Derby and became the first complete New Army formation on 24 August 1914. The Legion of Frontiersmen sponsored the 25th Battalion, Royal Fusiliers, an eclectic mixture including a millionaire, former officers and men from several British units, the merchant and Royal Navies, the United States army and the French Foreign Legion, an ex-colonel of the Honduras army, clowns, cowboys, musicians, seal trappers, publicans, a Scots lighthouse keeper, a Buckingham Palace servant and a convict gold miner.[24]

In September 1915 Northern Command used a Territorial officer, Lord Feversham, to recruit countrymen for the 21st Battalion, King's Royal Rifle Corps (Yeoman Rifles). By November, however, the unit was accepting many college students and others paradoxically superior to the intended standard.[25] This sort of formation was more successfully raised by 'local' recruitment, the extent of which shows how far the War Office was forced to relinquish total control in order to cope.

Since most towns possessed a drill hall, there was local interest in recruiting from the very beginning. The Territorials benefited from this local link, and were often preferred to distant and socially less desirable regular depots. It was in the larger municipalities that agitation to raise localised Service units first appeared, the mayors and corporations of London, Manchester and Birmingham first receiving authority to do so.

The Lord Mayor of London was the very first, on 21 August 1914, and he demonstrated the value of the idea by filling the 10th Battalion, Royal Fusiliers, in four days, only hours after the first War Office unit to be completed. Local government reforms in the late nineteenth century offered independence from the counties in public health, highways and education, fostering an increased local consciousness which was expressed during the South African War in civic rewards for those who had fought in that conflict. The situation in 1914 offered an opportunity to boost communal enthusiasm by channelling efforts into a local formation.

Corporations were not the only interested bodies. Several Territorial Force Associations raised 'local' Service units, and by the end of September 1914 authority had also been issued to three MPs, two peers, the West Yorkshire Coal Owners' Association, the Church Lads' Brigade, the British Empire Agency and sundry others. Some of these operated within a distinct geographical area, but others cast their net wide and aimed at a particular type of individual, appealing to many who hesitated at joining working-class Special Reserve or Territorial formations.

Raisers of 'local' formations were often keen to encourage this 'better sort' of recruit. The 10th Royal Fusiliers were the 'Stockbrokers' battalion, while the Liverpool 'Pals' at first carefully segregated applicants into occupational groups such as 'Cotton Association', 'Banks and Insurance', 'Provision Trade' or 'Law Society and Chartered Accountants', and raised three battalions in a week.[26] At Manchester an entire brigade of clerks, warehousemen and local authority employees was similarly raised in two weeks.[27] There was careful selection of units not only by the upper classes but also by the lower middle and working classes, the attraction being that of serving with friends and workmates.

Nationwide, distinctive formations began to take shape: the 'Grimsby Chums', the 'Oldham Comrades', the 'Glasgow Corporation Tramways' battalion. Among the most socially exclusive were the 16th Battalion, Middlesex Regiment, raised in August 1914 as the 'Public Schools Battalion', shortly followed by the Royal Fusiliers' 'University and Public Schools Brigade'. Response for the latter was swift, over 5,000 men by 12 September.[28] Being, by virtue of their composition, full of 'officer material', a constant stream of men subsequently left the UPS units. When Lancelot Spicer considered enlisting in such a battalion, T. McKinnon Wood, the Secretary of State for Scotland, dissuaded him on the grounds that Kitchener was anxious at the number of young gentlemen entering the ranks who would be better employed as officers.[29]

Despite their attractiveness, some battalions took longer to form than expected, or compromised and lowered their standards. The 'Manchester Scottish' seem to have failed and been incorporated in the 15th Battalion, Royal Scots (1st Edinburgh City).[30] Mrs E. Cunliffe-Owen raised the 23rd Battalion, Royal Fusiliers (1st Sportsman's), for 'upper and middle-class men' in four weeks but ultimately accepted chauffeurs, sailors and mechanics.[31] The Northumberland Fusiliers' 'Tyneside Scottish' and 'Tyneside Irish' brigades were sanctioned on 14 October 1914, but the former's acceptance of non-Scots recruits enabled them to fill by mid-November, two months ahead of their more fastidious rivals.

In all, 115 Service battalions were raised 'locally', of which eighty-three were begun during 1914. During 1915 the main effort seems to have gone into smaller formations: Hull was alone in raising two garrison artillery batteries by January 1915, but from then until January 1916 localised effort created forty-three brigades of field artillery, eleven divisional ammunition columns, twenty-eight batteries of garrison artillery and forty-eight field, signals or army troops companies of engineers.[32]

By area, the north was most successful, Lancashire and Cheshire producing twenty-four 'local' battalions, Yorkshire fifteen, the north-east fifteen and Cumbria one. The London area raised twenty-three battalions, though many were UPS or similar formations appealing nationwide. The south of England raised thirteen, the Midlands seven, Scotland seven, Wales and the border countries five, the West Country three and East Anglia two 'local' battalions. Among the ancillary formations London raised the most artillery units and Yorkshire the most engineers.[33]

Lord Derby was the most successful individual raiser and co-ordinator. Besides five Liverpool and one St Helens battalions, he created eight brigades of field and two batteries of garrison artillery with two divisional ammunition columns, and assisted other formations in Manchester and Wales, in addition to his efforts as chairman of the West Lancashire Territorial Force Association.

Ireland and Wales attempted the most ambitious formations, though Kitchener mistrusted the divisive effects of nationalistic bodies within his 'national force'. He approached Sir Edward Carson as early as 7 August 1914, seeking to utilise the thousands of men in the Ulster Volunteer Force. Carson eventually agreed, and the UVF formed the 36th (Ulster) Division. Farther south, John Redmond tried to raise an 'Irish Brigade' in September, but such units as the 10th and 16th (Irish) Divisions were not combined as a corps. The Commander-in-Chief Ireland also unnecessarily obstructed appointments of Roman Catholic chaplains, commissioned only Protestants, and refused distinctive badges. The movement collapsed by February 1915.[34]

The Welsh Army Corps, the brainchild of Lloyd George, achieved moderate success. Deft political in-fighting at Cabinet level ensured the unhampered establishment of the force, and Lloyd George also secured adequate Nonconformist chaplains and the commanders of his choice. A representative Welsh National Executive Committee raised fifteen new Service battalions, together with ancillary formations for the 38th (Welsh) Division. Further development was discouraged by the War Office in the summer of 1915, and surplus troops were formed into reserves or posted to non-Welsh formations.

In conclusion, Kitchener's insight into the likely nature and duration of the conflict was balanced by inability to control recruiting. Few of his measures proved durable in maintaining an adequate flow of volunteers, even when powers were devolved to local level. Some 557 service and reserve battalions of the New Army were raised, compared to 568 Territorial formations:[35] three million men in all before the introduction of conscription.

II

The war brought a release from the socio-economic tensions of later Edwardian Britain, promoting inter-class unity, and resulting in a reversal of opinion regarding the status of soldiers. Even so, propagandists stressed the social acceptability of the New Armies: Germains lauded the 'decent self-respecting, industrious working men'[36] who composed them, and Kipling naively thought that the possibly corrupting influence of 'old soldiers' had been transferred to the Special Reserve.[37] Ian Hay's chronicle includes a scene where a pre-war 'bad hat' is summarily dismissed,[38] while 'An Officer' insisted that his Second New Army unit differed greatly from the peacetime social standard.[39]

In reality it was impossible to keep ex-soldiers out of service units; indeed, they were encouraged to join both as instructors and as leaven for the untrained mass. Nor could it be said that the lower-class volunteers left all their civilian habits behind on enlistment. The propagandists assured readers that there were few crimes or cases of drunkenness. A tendency arose where men were away from home, especially for the first time, to drink or misbehave. The brigade major of the 120th Brigade noted sourly in April 1915 'a good deal of drunkenness' in the 18th Battalion, Middlesex Regiment (1st Public Works Pioneers), and many bad conduct sheets in the allegedly superior '1st Sportsman's Battalion'.[40] Staniforth found theft rife in the 6th Connaught Rangers,[41] as did W. F. Pressey in an artillery depot at Portsmouth,[42] while the miners of the 9th Battalion, Northumberland Fusiliers, stole apples to sell and cups from public houses.[43] Dennis's assertion of no theft in the 'Yeoman Rifles' can be ascribed to their socially elevated composition.[44]

Volunteers often found army life shockingly different, especially in socially inferior or mixed units. Men of the higher classes missed their home comforts, and Hankey admitted that 'gentlemen' were often ill at ease.[45] Foul language, night urinal buckets, unappetising food and the personal habits of the lower working class put sensitive recruits through a purgatorial existence. Watcyn-Williams found himself annoyed by obscenity even in a 'public schools' battalion, and resented the total dominance of army authority in all matters.[46] The only solution was to 'pal up' with an equal, be first in the meal queues, and acquire some of the less savoury habits of service life as self-defence.

Reactions to the army were not helped at first by a breakdown in arrangements for feeding and housing recruits. Army food, if superior to that available at the lowest social levels, often left much to be desired. Greasy stews nauseated many but were better than no food at all, frequently the case where new camps were being hurriedly set up. Pressley, on enlistment, was warned to bring his own food when joining next day,[47] though others had money to supplement inadequate rations. Those volunteering for depot-raised units had to put up with overcrowding even at new camps, where rotten tents and verminous blankets were often the only alternative to sleeping in the open. Local assistance could ease these problems by the provision of billets or other premises. Municipally raised units were often housed locally, with parks made available for training.

Surprisingly, disturbances in the New Army were comparatively few, generally spontaneous, resulting mainly from the inadequacies of the early days. Poor hutting at Codford led to mass meetings and refusals to parade by units of the 25th Division.[48] Staniforth at Fermoy in late October 1914 helped quell armed riots by drunken soldiers in which two men died.[49] and even the '4th Public Schools' battalion was capable of disobeying orders as a protest against rotten food.[50] Among other examples South Wales miners at Preston in September 1914 marched through the town advertising their grievances against boredom and lack of pay or food.[51] Most such disputes were tactfully handled, and the source of trouble was usually removed.

This was possible because the men were often keen to improve their military skills and would put up with discomforts. Service life may not have been the enthusiastic crusade depicted by propagandists, but it certainly included off-duty reading of drill and signalling manuals in Dennis's case,[52] while some men of the 8th Battalion, Norfolk Regiment, asked their officers for extra parades.[53]

There existed a feeling among some that they would not be expected to serve overseas. This may, in part, account for home service enlistments in the Territorials, but elements of the New Armies were by no means convinced of the serious nature of the obligation they had undertaken as late as 1916. Dennis thought his unit would never be sent to France, and even Hankey saw fighting as 'a great game ... We don't believe in it really,'[54] while to the miners of the 6th Battalion, Yorkshire Regiment, army life was a fine holiday.[55]

Acceptance of the role of soldier was frequently delayed by shortages of uniforms at the start of the conflict. In the period before the woollen industry was capable of clothing the crowds of volunteers in khaki, recruits either had to remain in civil garb or accept a substitute. Dishevelled and ragged after weeks or sometimes months of training in their old clothes, it was impossible for men to feel any pride in their appearance. The use of obsolete scarlet uniforms assisted marginally but the principal stop-gap was 'Kitchener Blue', which Kipling was moved to denounce as 'indescribable ... blue slops', devoid even of brass buttons.[56] The garb had to some the appearance of convict uniform,[57] while Mansfield was mistaken by one lady for a Belgian refugee.[58]

'Kitchener Blue' was, nevertheless, widely used from late September 1914 to mid-1915, except by some 'local' battalions whose raisers could purchase alternatives. The 11th Battalion, Border Regiment (Lonsdale), and the Welsh Army Corps were outfitted in grey, while the 11th Battalion, Welsh Regiment (Cardiff Commercials), were clad in brown uniforms which earned them the nickname 'chocolate soldiers'.[59] All these were discarded on the arrival of khaki – an event which Hankey significantly terms 'the formal beginning of a new life'.[60]

The foul-mouthed, bullying type of NCO was all too common and gave many recruits their first painful introduction to military authority. Much resentment could build up while men were forced to stand still and be insulted, though this was an effective initiation into army *mores*, to be accepted or copied before any successful transition to soldierhood.

New formations were stocked with serving or recalled NCOs if possible, but employed some curious criteria for appointments to junior non commissioned rank. Teachers used to drilling children were encouraged to enlist in order to instruct recruits, and given corporal's status. The selection by men of their own NCOs was not unknown, and preference in socially mixed units was often given to the better dressed or educated. Staniforth became a corporal because he was not afraid of the 'blackguards' in his company.[61]

For those to whom army life did not appeal there was the alternative of desertion. Some repeatedly fled before actual attestation, after securing their 'king's shilling' and a day's allowance of 1s 9d. Others simply walked away from the depot or during the journey to the training centre and could not be traced in the confusion of the early days. Pressey noted that men frequently absconded when drafts were due for France,[62] and one corrupt recruiter actually made a trade of encouraging men of the 12th Battalion, East Surrey Regiment (Bermondsey), to enlist, then desert with their kit, which he sold.[63]

Those who stayed began preparing for their avowed role. Route marching was simply organised, as was basic drill, but the shortage of weapons was a headache which many units did not overcome until embarkation was imminent. The original six-month period allocated for training in the New Army was insufficient, yet it was reduced to four months in 1915, so desperate was the need at the front. The scattered units of the Fourth and Fifth New Armies had to wait until earlier formations left Salisbury Plain and other exercising grounds before carrying out divisional manoeuvres.

The 'dug-out' officers and NCOs did their best, but their open warfare training was not really what was required, nor did it help when they regressed to obsolete tactics or terminology. With the arrival in France of the 9th (Scottish) Division in May 1915, the New Army formations came under the critical gaze of the regulars, and began at last to show whether Kitchener's experiment would be successful.

III

Initially, and perhaps inevitably, feeling in the regular army was solidly against the raising of new bodies of troops. Aside from any doubts regarding their value as soldiers, there was a feeling at first that New Army formations should be slotted into undermanned units of the BEF rather than wait until they could fight as independent formations. Field Marshal Sir John French pressed Kitchener in 1914 to halt all further expansion of the new force and break it up as reinforcements, not foreseeing the longer-term necessity of increasing the British presence on the western front.[64] His subordinate, Major-General Sir Henry

Wilson, was even more scathing about Kitchener's 'ridiculous and preposterous army', declaring it a waste of manpower, since in his view 'these mobs' could not be ready for action within two years.[65] In a curious echo, Brigadier-General J. E. Caunter, in early advice to the Welsh National Executive Committee, warned, 'Don't raise artillery . . . you won't have them ready for two years'.[66]

From the beginning, regulars felt that no worthwhile force could be produced in the time allowed for training. The question of discipline in New Army units worried many both before and after their arrival at the front, and their fears were not entirely baseless. It was all very well for Hankey to insist that trust between officers and men overcame class barriers,[67] but the result could be the over-familiarity which enabled the 'Yeoman Rifles' to call men by their Christian names on parade.[68] The retired or reassigned regular officers and senior NCOs did not always provide inspired leadership. Depot commanders were often appointed to lead new battalions, and the move was for many a promotion they might never otherwise have received. Some 'dug-out' officers and senior NCOs did not prove equal to adapting to new theories of warfare or to the more intelligent type of recruit.

'An Officer' pointed out the difficulty of recalled staff in this respect, and urged the new junior NCO to 'most tactfully but definitely abandon his old relations with the men . . . not to be too intimate . . . not to show favouritism . . . and extract unquestioning obedience . . .'[69] In Hankey's view this had to be tempered with tact, since adverse comments by recruits could affect recruitment, an unusual situation which he admits put a strain on the NCOs.[70] No such inhibitions affected the veterans who enlisted with their employers of the mercantile and professional classes in the 12th Battalion, Gloucestershire Regiment (Bristol). Initial deference on the drill ground gave way to harrying, the reversal of roles being marked by the issue of khaki and the move to the training camp.[71] Kipling and others maintained that in matters of common discipline the men exerted their own control;[72] Germains preferred to believe that their willingness to learn made strict regulation unnecessary.[73]

The hostility of regulars is well displayed by accounts from the 2nd Battalion, Royal Welsh Fusiliers. Robert Graves in particular paints a picture of patronising contempt for the New Army at first, only gradually modified as these units showed they were capable of maintaining the good name of the regiment in action. The allegedly poor leadership of New Army battalions was, with inexperience, their main handicap against acceptance.[74] When the 2nd RWF were transferred to the 38th (Welsh) Division in February 1918 very few old soldiers remained, yet the colonel still felt obliged to remind his unit of its 'regular' status,[75] only weeks after receiving large drafts of men from two disbanded Service battalions, one formerly of the same division.[76] As

late as August 1918 'duration' men were banned from membership of the
regimental old comrades' association.[77]

In 1915 a subaltern in the 2nd Battalion, Worcestershire Regiment,
expressed resentment at the very keenness of the New Army when he
wrote, 'There are some of K's army near here ... K's think they are
going to end the war in a fortnight.'[78] Much adverse comment seemed to
have centred on the UPS battalions of the 33rd Division. By April 1916
three of the four battalions in France were disbanded and most of their
personnel returned home for training as officers. The remaining unit,
the 20th Battalion, Royal Fusiliers, was allegedly composed of those
unsuitable for such training, but by virtue of their social make-up also
poor fighting men. Graves castigates the unit as inefficient and
unreliable in action,[79] a view apparently shared by medical officer
Dunn[80] and ranker Frank Richards,[81] both of the 2nd RWF.
Watcyn-Williams of the 21st Battalion, Royal Fusiliers, on the other
hand, states that his unit worked well with the regulars before its
disbandment.[82]

Other New Army formations periodically suffered from prejudice. The
'Bantams' were never entirely accepted; the 40th Division was the last
New Army formation to reach France, in June 1916, and with its fellow
35th Division engendered a spate of mostly contemptuous comment. A
draft sent to the 2nd Battalion, Suffolk Regiment, in July 1916 was
'from the Bantams of all people, tiny little fellows they are too, no
discipline at all'.[83] Frank Richards found men drafted from the 19th
Battalion RWF good fighters in 1918, but that was after the debacle at
Cambrai in December 1917, where the performance of other 'Bantam'
units led to wholesale disbandments.

There were many other regulars who came to respect and admire the
New Armies. General Gough's opinion was that Major-General Sir Ivor
Maxse's 18th Division was one of the best in the entire army.[84] Much of
this was due to Maxse's positive and flexible attitude to training: P. G.
Heath recalled how he would solve a tactical problem after the textbook
fashion, then tell his audience to forget the official solution,
demonstrating some new and better way to achieve the same end.[85]
Ranker John F. Lucy of the 2nd Battalion, Royal Irish Rifles, resented at
first the untidy and inefficient new soldiers of the 25th Division to which
his unit was transferred in October 1915, feeling that over-earnestness
did not make up for the sort of battalion pride ingrained in the
regulars.[86]

Lucy's account is particularly interesting because it shows the
progression of a regular soldier's attitude from initial contempt to
eventual acceptance. His unit found the New Army men despondent
over a few losses in a quiet sector, their trenches inadequate, their policy
towards the enemy one of *laissez faire*. The aggressive, efficient methods

of the Royal Irish Rifles soon altered matters, with the keen newer units copying their style and performing creditably. In fact the regulars eventually came to admire the way in which New Army officers were willing to listen to their advice and improve on textbook methods of fighting.[87]

H. E. Trevor, a regular major of the 2nd Battalion, King's Own Yorkshire Light Infantry, served in France from August to November 1914, when he took up a staff appointment with the Territorial 47th Division. In October 1915 he became lieutenant-colonel commanding the 8th Battalion of his regiment – 'an uncommonly fine battalion'. In April 1916 he saw his old regular unit in France, and was moved to remark, 'It isn't such a good battalion as this one nowadays.' His opinion of the New Army remained high after his appointment as brigadier-general of the 103rd (Tyneside Irish) Brigade in July 1916, and there is no unfavourable comparison with the regulars throughout his correspondence.[88]

The first major test of the new formations came at Loos in September 1915. Though, on the whole, the New Army did as well – or fared as badly – as the regular and Territorial forces involved, one main incident has been taken by Graves and others to show their inadequacy. On the second day of fighting the 21st and 24th Divisions were thrown in, but under heavy fire fell back *en masse*. These formations had no front-line experience whatsoever, having landed in France only two to four weeks previously. They had been on the move for some days, latterly on heavily congested roads and without hot food. Some regulars were only too eager to capitalise on their misfortune: Lieutenant-General Haking, their commander, blamed poor march discipline but ignored the delays met with *en route* to the battlefield.[89] Graves gives the impression that the eventual retirement was more precipitate than was in fact the case, formations being enfiladed and facing unbroken barbed wire.[90] It seemed as though the earlier adverse opinions were well founded.

On the other hand, even the men whom Haking helped to rally stated that they were willing to continue the fight, while the official history devotes much space to refuting the suggestion that the divisions had fled and let the New Army down.[91] Germains throws the blame entirely on faulty staff work.[92] Nevertheless, Sir John French's despatch a few weeks later seemed to many to lay the failure of the main attack squarely on the two divisions, and was resented by Spicer and other survivors.[93] This judgement was confirmed about the same time by the exchange of regular for New Army units in the 21st, 24th and five other New Army divisions. The regulars were intended to 'stiffen' the new formations, and, while there might have been some success in Lucy's case, generally it had little effect in the long term.

The same is true of the post-Somme period, when gaps were filled with recruits from areas other than those in which the often close-knit local battalions were raised. Whether this was a deliberate ploy to reduce heavy concentrations of casualties from small areas in an attempt to forestall adverse public reaction and consequent political pressure is unimportant. From September 1916 the reclassification of the New Army reserves in the UK as 'Training Reserve' battalions, shorn of regimental connections, disrupted any strong local link by sending drafts from what was effectively a common pool of conscript manpower. The distinctiveness of the New Army, and also much of the old regular aloofness, can be said to have ended at about this time, and the army at the front became essentially the 'national force' envisaged by Kitchener at the beginning.

IV

The 113th Brigade was part of the Welsh Army Corps. Originally known in October 1914 as the 1st or North Wales Brigade, it became the 128th Brigade of the 43rd Division between December 1914 and April 1915, when the dispersal of the reserve Fourth New Army led to its retitling as a unit of the 38th (Welsh) Division.

The six counties of North Wales had not been a fertile recruiting ground before 1914. The initial response in August 1914 was slow: only seventeen volunteers in the first five days of the war, though figures soon increased.[94] The first New Army units were War Office-raised at the Wrexham depot, drawing on the coal and steel communities of the populous north-east. Farther west the rural and slate quarrying areas maintained an overwhelming preference for the Territorials until the advent of the Welsh Army Corps in late September.

Authorised on 10 October, the new movement was permitted to incorporate several partly formed and unallocated battalions. One of these was the 13th Battalion, Royal Welsh Fusiliers, or 'North Wales Pals', originally sanctioned on 3 September and 'locally' raised by the Denbighshire and Flintshire Territorial Force Association at Rhyl. A higher social standard than the Wrexham units may account for the fact that the unit grew only slowly. In early September a 'University of Wales Battalion' began to form at Bangor and Aberystwyth. Open to past and present students, teachers and others who had received higher or secondary education in Wales, it attracted some 350 volunteers.[95] Both units merged at the end of September, but there were apparently still 650 vacancies a month later.[96]

The '1st Brigade' as originally conceived would have comprised the University Battalion and three Welsh battalions raised in Liverpool, London and Manchester. In London a meeting on 16 September launched the 'London Welsh Battalion'. The project was not favourably regarded, and official sanction was delayed until 29 October, by which time some men had enlisted elsewhere.[97] The Liverpool aspect was so unpalatable to Lord Derby that the scheme collapsed, as did the one in Manchester.

A brigade commander was appointed on 30 October in the person of Brigadier-General Owen Thomas, a former Volunteer Force officer from Anglesey who had raised a Welsh colonial unit in the South African War. His promotion was a concession wrung from Kitchener by Lloyd George, who needed this popular Welsh-speaker as a figurehead for local recruiting. Early in November he set up his headquarters at Llandudno, which with other recession-stricken North Welsh resorts was used to billet the Welsh Army Corps that winter.

The brigade gathered itself together slowly. The 13th RWF moved from Rhyl on 18 November, by now so over strength that it began to form the 16th Battalion from the surplus, though it was December before its identity was officially recognised. In the meantime the London Welsh were entitled the 15th Battalion, and moved from London to Llandudno on 5 December. A 14th Battalion was also begun on 2 November, under the title 'Carnarvonshire and Anglesey'.

The latter unit was one of the few in Wales raised by a county recruiting committee. Anglesey, early in September, had organised a network of thirty local committees to hold meetings, but no sanction was given for a county battalion, and enthusiasm consequently waned.[98] In Caernarfonshire a durable committee was formed in November, but only after pressurising a Lord Lieutenant hostile to the New Army. Elsewhere in North Wales the system was not applied until the Derby Scheme, though Montgomeryshire and east Denbighshire organised Territorial recruiting drives and censuses of manpower at an earlier period.

Canvassing was carried out in Caernarfonshire by teachers, chapel elders, doctors, shopkeepers and others who had local knowledge and influence. More recruits were gained by this than from meetings: forty-three in Anglesey produced a negligible response by early October 1914.[99] Other methods included route marches by men of the brigade through unresponsive areas of Gwynedd during the winter of 1914–15. Where no civilian committees existed, the Welsh National Executive Committee left recruiting in the hands of brigade commanders.

From December 1914 the Welsh Army Corps began to fill rapidly. In January 1915 fifty men a day were reportedly joining at Llandudno,[100] though in the same month battalions increased their establishments from 1,007 all ranks to 1,368 to incorporate reserves. The brigade had been 2,132 strong on 23 November, reaching 3,000 by mid-December, 3,880 by 9 January and 5,030 men by 1 February.[101] All the battalions showed a steady progression, except the 14th RWF, which by early

January was hardly half full when the others were over establishment. Three weeks later this battalion was over 1,300 strong – a startling rise which can be explained only by its having accepted large drafts from outside Caernarfonshire and Anglesey; perhaps these were necessary owing to local apathy, perhaps to the inadequacy of the civilian recruiting committee.

The movement's only other county committee-raised unit, the 15th Battalion, Welsh Regiment (Carmarthenshire), attracted even fewer local men and filled with Lancashire volunteers.[102] The 14th RWF typifies the 'local' battalion which lowered its standards to fill its ranks. When it embarked for France that December only 24 per cent of its personnel came from Caernarfonshire, 9 per cent from Anglesey, 26 per cent from other areas of North Wales, 20 per cent from South Wales and 21 per cent from England. There were also two Irishmen and two Americans in its ranks.[103] This can be compared with the 1/6th (Carnarvonshire and Anglesey) Battalion, RWF Territorials, where 95 per cent of Gallipoli casualties were local.[104]

On 2 February 1915 a 17th Battalion RWF began forming at Llandudno under the title '2nd North Wales', though Emlyn Davies states that many of its recruits were from Lancashire and Staffordshire, light-heartedly attracted by the idea of a seaside sojourn.[105] Also associated with the brigade were the 18th Battalion (2nd London Welsh) and the 19th Battalion, a 'Bantam' unit which again included many volunteers from Liverpool, Manchester and the Midlands.[106] None of these units remained for long: the 17th RWF was transferred to the 114th Brigade in July; the 18th RWF became a reserve formation; and the 19th RWF joined other 'Bantams' in the 119th Brigade in May.

The War Office discouraged the formation of new battalions after February but, when it took over recruiting from the Welsh National Executive Committee in August, made no effort to form surplus and reserve troops into the basis of a second division. New recruits were in fact directed via the Special Reserve at Litherland, who thereafter took first choice. In November 1915 the 'dug-out' Owen Thomas was replaced by Brigadier-General Ll. A. E. Price-Davies, a Shropshire-born regular who successfully commanded the 113th Brigade in France until 1917.

Thomas had been vital in the projection of the brigade as socially acceptable in a local context. 'Class' counted for less, perhaps, than nationality and religion in an area which was a bastion of Welsh Nonconformity. Soldiering had always been frowned upon, and denominational newspapers certainly reflect no notable pro-war stance until September 1914. Lloyd George's championing of the Welsh Army Corps boosted the movement in the eyes of many, as did his persuasion of Kitchener to provide more Nonconformist chaplains. Certain influential ministers in North Wales overturned previous attitudes by making fervent appeals for volunteers even from chapel pulpits.

Though some resented their pastors acting as recruiters, the proportion of Nonconformists in Welsh units rose. In E Company of the 16th RWF in October 1915, 54 per cent of the men were Church of England, 6 per cent Roman Catholic, and the remaining 40 per cent was made up by no fewer than ten Nonconformist denominations.[107] Under the Derby Scheme the Nonconformist proportion rose to 49 per cent.[108] Nobody had taken up an earlier suggestion to raise a Merioneth 'Pals' battalion from 'religious young men',[109] but the brigade was certainly being advertised as 'well behaved' at recruiting meetings in January 1915.[110] Not surprisingly, therefore, Emlyn Davies found that his sergeant-major did not swear,[111] and at Llandudno chapel services, Sunday schools and Bible classes were well attended by soldiers.

There was an exception. The London Welsh, many of whose men had no strong Welsh connections, had at first been amazed at the size of the Great Orme's Head under which Llandudno lay, but were soon enjoying the delights of the resort. Harold Diffey has recorded the consequent thefts of shop produce and vending machines, and how pay nights proved busy for the regimental police.[112] The London Welsh battalions also produced 110 deserters out of 273 from the entire Welsh Army Corps dismounted troops by July 1915.[113]

The movement projected a strongly nationalistic image, and the promise of Welsh officers was used as a recruiting ploy. In August 1915 some 195 out of 302 officers of the brigade were of 'Welsh nationality', the remainder being connected by birth, parentage or residence.[114] Like some other New Army formations, the brigade drew heavily on its own ranks for officer material. The strong university element in the 13th and 16th RWF was made use of, one company of each battalion being set aside as an 'OTC'. In August it was stated that, of 302 officers, 138 were former rankers of the brigade, eighty-four officers had come from OTCs and outside formations, and sixty more rankers had been commissioned into other units.[115] P. Aubrey Roberts, for example, enlisted in the 16th RWF late in 1914 and had risen to sergeant before receiving a commission in his own battalion in March 1915.[116]

The use of influence to secure commissions was rife in the Welsh Army Corps, and especially in the 113th Brigade. Owen Thomas nepotistically ensured that his three sons became officers in the formation in December 1914, and it was no coincidence that both Lloyd George's sons furthered their commissioned careers under Thomas.

The 113th Brigade, like many New Army formations, suffered medical problems. North Wales had few industrial slums, but overcrowded artisans' dwellings in towns, insanitary cottages in the slate quarrying areas and the neglected accommodation of agricultural labourers bred unhealthy men in quantity. One result was short height and one Anglesey recruiter seriously believed that the original 5 ft 6 in standard would bar up to 70 per cent of the county's manpower.[11] Special efforts were made to prevent too many Welsh enlisting in the 15th Battalion, Cheshire Regiment (Birkenhead 'Bantams'), in November 1914. In February 1915 the War Office allowed a concessionary Welsh infantry standard of 5 ft 2 in., and lowered it an inch in May.

The proportion of medical discharges was also high. Thomas told the Caernarfonshire recruiting committee in May that one of his battalions alone had lost 119 men,[118] while the problem was being exacerbated by the re-enlistment of discharged soldiers. It was suggested that many discharges were due to some commanders scrupulously 'weeding' the less fit, while others were disinclined to oppose the opinion of over-zealous medical officers.[119] Many volunteers were rejected before enlistment: of 1,739 Anglesey men who offered their services under the Derby Scheme, nearly 20 per cent were rejected before attestation.[120]

Such losses drained battalions' strength and efficiency. Up to the end of June 1915 the Welsh Army Corps had lost 20 per cent of all enlisted men by transfer, death, desertion or discharge. This can be broken down by unit for the 113th Brigade.[121]

By the time they proceeded overseas units had, therefore, lost many of the men who gave them their 'local' character. The 14th RWF was allocated by the regimental record office a block of 1,500 individual soldiers' identification numbers. Only 60 per cent of the men with these numbers embarked with the unit, the rest presumably having transferred or gone out of the army.[122]

It is possible that the brigade may have had many under-age enlistments. In E Company, 16th RWF, 21 per cent of all volunteers claimed to be nineteen years old on enlistment, the minimum for overseas service. By comparison, less than one per cent admitted to being eighteen, and less than 8 per cent were aged twenty years. Thirty-three per cent were aged between twenty and twenty-five; 43 per cent between twenty-six and forty; and 2 per cent up to forty-nine years of age. The proportion of alleged nineteen-year-olds remained high during the Derby Scheme, 80 per cent of recruits being under twenty-six years old.[123] Marital status was also recorded: 63 per cent before October 1915 were single men, rising to 94 per cent under the Derby Scheme.

The social composition of the company can also be gauged from occupations stated on enlistment. It is worth noting the contrast in heavier manual trades represented before and after the Derby Scheme. Twenty-two per cent of recruits in the earlier period were miners, only per cent of those enlisting after October 1915. As many of the coal, steel agricultural and other trades became 'essential' at this time, the

Table 4.1. Total losses of units associated with the 113th Brigade up to 30 June 1915

RWF battalion	Total enlisted	Transfers	Deaths	Desertions	Discharges	Total losses
13th	1,833	607	1	1	120	729
14th	1,532	105	2	6	224	337
15th	1,575	20	0	53	284	357
16th	1,660	119	0	4	131	254
17th	1,324	72	1	6	96	175
18th	1,417	11	1	67	138	217
Totals	9,341	934	5	137	993	2,069
Welsh Army Corps totals (dismounted troops)	27,836	2,049	21	273	2,908	5,251

Table 4.2. *Civilian occupations of (a) soldiers in E Company, 16th Battalion RWF, October 1915, and of (b) Derby Scheme volunteers in D Company, 20th Battalion RWF, January 1916*

Occupational groups	% of total	
	(a)	(b)
Heavier manual workers	51	24
Manufacturing, transport and other workers	20	21
Clerks, salesmen and servants	18	31
Shopkeepers	4	10
Professional classes	4	10
Miscellaneous	3	4

reduction is hardly surprising. A corresponding increase in the proportion of non-manual workers can also be seen. Before October 1915 only some 8 per cent of recruits were of the middle class or on its fringes, and this subsequently rose to about 20 per cent. In October 1915 most of the NCOs were either re-enlisted men in their forties or the better educated clerks.[124]

Slate quarrymen in Gwynedd exemplify the reaction of local industry to enlistment. Trade had slumped on the outbreak of war, but many of the workers preferred not to enlist. In January 1915 it was calculated that, of 8,400 quarrymen in July 1914, only 700 were in nearly full-time employment, with 4,900 others working a three or four-day week. Some 400 men were redundant, 1,200 had enlisted, and 1,200 had left the area to seek other work. Even those still working had often accepted a pay cut.[125] Apathy was blamed on Nonconformist teaching, family ties and hostility towards quarry owners such as Lord Penrhyn, who in August 1914 promised to keep open the places of the quarrymen who enlisted.[126] Men at some quarries were allegedly threatened with dismissal if they did not.[127] An increasing number, therefore, left to fill posts vacated by volunteers from the railways, docks and coal mines.

For those who did volunteer for the 113th Brigade, training continued at Llandudno until August 1915. Winter billets in the lodging houses of the resort were adequate, and no resulting disturbances have been recorded. The 38th (Welsh) Division then moved to Winchester to complete its training, which apparently resulted in its being 'upgraded' from the Fifth to the Fourth New Army.[128] Though training was predictably for open warfare, some instruction was given prior to embarkation in December by experienced officers and NCOs on trench tactics.

Regular army reaction to the division was hostile, and more lasting than for other New Army formations. Apart from the way in which Lloyd George had forced his corps on Kitchener, and doubts about the quality of leadership and training, regulars professed disgust at the blatantly political character of the movement. Two brigade commanders were Liberal MPs, and another commanded the 14th RWF. When Brigadier-General Ivor Philipps, MP, was promoted to major-general commanding the division in January 1915, seniority-minded regulars saw him only as a jumped-up ex-Indian Army major who had no right to a divisional command.[129] His attachment to Lloyd George's Ministry of Munitions from July to December 1915 can hardly have improved his standing.

As with other late New Army formations, experienced officers were lacking. The 113th Brigade battalions possessed only three retired regulars, three former Volunteer or ex-Territorial officers, and four attached Territorials in August 1915. Among the eight RWF battalions of the division, only six officers out of 326 are shown by the Army List to have seen previous active service.[130] An attached regular staff officer, Major H. C. Rees, found standards of training inadequate and persuaded Philipps to replace two brigade commanders (including Thomas) and nine battalion commanders. In the 113th Brigade one was promoted to the staff, one remained in his command, and two were shunted to reserve battalions. Rees also maintained that Philipps was an excellent administrator and valued his service with the division.[131]

During 7–11 July 1916 the 38th (Welsh) Division took part in its first major action at Mametz Wood, on the Somme. The battle has been studied by Colin Hughes in his work *Mametz*, from which it is clear that after some initial confusion the Welshmen fought hard and well under trying conditions. The failure of the first assaults, however, gave the XV Corps commander an excuse to remove Philipps on 9 July, and created a stigma which resulted in the division being downgraded to line-holding troops and sent from the Somme. A year later the division fought splendidly at the opening of the third battle of Ypres, only to be again removed elsewhere. Indeed, excepting these two actions and a minor (if costly) operation at Bouzincourt in April 1918, the division's potential was not fully realised until the final advance of September – November 1918.

Hughes has quoted, with effect, an attached regular officer who was severely critical of the politically oriented officering.[132] While neither Robert Graves nor Frank Richards condemn, Dunn's account at the time his battalion joined the division in 1918 confirms the regular dislike of the 'political' label which persisted, and hints strongly that neither the War Office nor GHQ ever forgave the formation its connection with Lloyd George.

The Welsh Army Corps may have sacrificed military efficiency to political expediency, but the strength of regular prejudice seems unnecessary considering the further purge of officers carried out after Mametz Wood, and the increasing proportion of non-Welshmen in the ranks. The Welsh National Executive Committee had decided as early as December 1914 that, except for recruiting purposes, the use of 'local' battalion titles would be avoided. It can be argued that this began the ultimate breakdown of 'local' identity, which was accelerated under active service conditions, but only became noticeable after major actions. Emlyn Davies summarises the views of the survivors and epitomises the fate of the New Army when he says, 'We never again recovered the spirit which had hitherto pressed us on . . . Men unknown to us stepped forward, and we continued forward, near incommunicado.'[133]

Notes

1   R. Douglas, 'Voluntary enlistment in the First World War and the work of the Parliamentary Recruiting Committee', *Journal of Modern History*, 42, 4, 1970, p. 568.
2   I(mperial) W(ar) M(useum), unpub. memoirs of P. G. Heath.
3   V. W. Germains, *The Kitchener Armies*, Peter Davies, London, 1930, p. 116.
4   G. Coppard, *With a Machine Gun to Cambrai*, HMSO, London, 1976, p. 1.
5   M. Watcyn-Williams, *From Khaki to Cloth*, Caernarfon, 1949, pp. 44, 62.
6   D. Hankey, *A Student in Arms*, Melrose, London, 1916, p. 19.
7   J. Shakespear, *A Record of the 17th and 32nd Service Battalions, Northumberland Fusiliers (NER) Pioneers, 1914–1919*, Northumberland Press, Newcastle upon Tyne, 1926, pp. 1–2.
8   IWM, recruiting literature K.44699, Cardiff Railway Company circulars dated 5 and 9 September 1914.
9   IWM, unpublished memoirs of Second Lieutenant A. Mansfield.
10 D. Winter, *Death's Men*, Allen Lane, London, 1978, p. 33.
11 Germains, *Kitchener Armies*, p. 146.
12 N(ational) L(ibrary) of W(ales), Welsh Army Corps papers, recruiting orders (No. 4 Recruiting District), Nos. 155 of 11 December, 1914, and 284 of 10 May 1915.
13 Douglas, 'Voluntary enlistment', p. 582.
14 F. E. Whitton, *History of the 40th Division*, Gale and Polden, Aldershot, 1926, pp. 8–9.
15 *The Times*, 16 March 1916.
16 War Office, *Royal Warrant for the Pay, Appointment, Promotion and Non-effective Pay of the Army, 1914*, London, 1914, Section XIII, articles 1260–4.
17 C. T. Atkinson, *The Devonshire Regiment, 1914–1918*, Eland, Exeter, 1926, pp. 54–5.
18 IWM, P. G. Heath, Mss.
19 Germains, *Kitchener Armies*, p. 66.
20 IWM, letters of Captain J. H. M. Staniforth, 18 October and 1 November 1914. I am most grateful to the Rev. J. H. M. Staniforth for permission to quote from this material.
21 Germains, *Kitchener Armies*, p. 134.
22 'An Officer', *The New Army in the Making*, London, 1915, pp. 16–18.
23 L. Macdonald, *Somme*, Michael Joseph, London, 1983, pp. 22–4.
24 R. Meinertzhagen, *Army Diary, 1899–1926*, Oliver and Boyd, London, 1960, pp. 130–1.

25 IWM, unpublished memoirs of G. V. Dennis.
26 F. C. Stanley, *The History of the 89th Brigade, 1914–1918*, Daily Post, Liverpool, 1919, p. 11.
27 F. Kempster and H. C. E. Westropp (eds.), *Manchester City Battalions Book of Honour*, Manchester, 1917, pp. xi–xviii.
28 *The History of the Royal Fusiliers 'U.P.S.' University and Public Schools Brigade*, The Times, London, 1917, p. 31.
29 L. D. Spicer, *Letters from France, 1915–1918*, Robert York, London, 1979, p. xi.
30 J. Ewing, *The Royal Scots, 1914–1919*, I, Oliver and Boyd, Edinburgh, 1925, p. 9.
31 Germains, *Kitchener Armies*, pp. 76–8.
32 PRO, Kitchener Papers, 30/57/73, list of locally raised units, August 1916.
33 *Loc. cit.*
34 D. Gwynn, *The Life of John Redmond*, n.p. 1932, pp. 389–408.
35 E. A. James, *Historical Records of British Infantry Regiments in the Great War, 1914–1918*, Samson, London, 1976; totals extrapolated from listed formations.
36 Germains, *Kitchener Armies*, p. 41.
37 R. Kipling, *The New Army in Training*, London, 1915, p. 12.
38 I. Hay, *The First Hundred Thousand*, Edinburgh, 1915, pp. 35–6.
39 'An Officer', *New Army in the Making*, p. 14.
40 IWM, diary of Major C. H. Wolff, 7 and 12 April 1915.
41 IWM, Staniforth, Mss.
42 IWM, unpublished memoirs of W. F. Pressey.
43 IWM, letters of A. Thompson, 14 September 1914.
44 IWM, Dennis, Mss.
45 Hankey, *Student in Arms*, pp. 20, 26–7.
46 Watcyn-Williams, *Khaki to Cloth*, pp. 51, 53.
47 IWM, Pressey, Mss.
48 W. de B. Wood, *The History of the King's Shropshire Light Infantry in the Great War, 1914–1918*, Medici Society, London, 1925, pp. 207–8.
49 IWM, Staniforth, Mss., 24 October and 1 November 1914.
50 Watcyn-Williams, *Khaki to Cloth*, p. 50.
51 H. Cartmell, *For Remembrance*, Preston, 1919, pp. 33–5. I am most grateful to my colleague Peter Simkins for his kindness in permitting me to examine the draft of his forthcoming book on the Kitchener armies, which mentions various disciplinary problems, and also for the helpful suggestions of J. J. Putkowski in this matter.
52 IWM, Dennis, Mss.
53 IWM, papers of Major C. F. Ashdown, account by Major H. P. M. Berney-Ficklin.
54 Hankey, *Student in Arms*, p. 21.
55 H. C. Wylly, *The Green Howards in the Great War*, Richmond, 1926, p. 170.
56 Kipling, *New Army Training*, p. 5.
57 'An Officer,' *New Army in the Making*, pp. 26–7.
58 IWM, Mansfield, Mss.
59 A. C. Whitehorne and T. O. Marden, *The History of the Welsh Regiment*, Western Mail and Echo, Cardiff, 1932, p. 284.
60 Hankey, *Student in Arms*, p. 28.
61 IWM, Staniforth, Mss., 18 October 1914.
62 IWM, Pressey, Mss.
63 J. Aston and L. M. Duggan, *The History of the 12th (Bermondsey)*

Battalion, East Surrey Regiment, London, 1936, pp. 4–5.

64 G. H. Cassar, *Kitchener: Architect of Victory*, William Kimber, London, 1977, p. 205.

65 Sir C. E. Callwell, *Field Marshal Sir Henry Wilson, his Life and Diaries*, I, Cassell, London, 1927, p. 178.

66 NLW, Welsh Army Corps Papers, file 'Memoranda', Caunter to WNEC, *c.* October 1914.

67 Hankey, *Student in Arms*, p. 80.

68 IWM, Dennis, Mss.

69 'An Officer', *New Army in the Making*, pp. 21, 62.

70 Hankey, *Student in Arms*, p. 44.

71 Macdonald, *Somme*, pp. 246–8.

72 Kipling, *New Army in Training*, p. 10.

73 Germains, *Kitchener Armies*, p. 135.

74 Robert Graves, *Goodbye to all that*, Cape, London, 1976, pp. 75–6, 95, 152.

75 (J. C. Dunn), *The War the Infantry knew, 1914–1919*, London, 1938, p. 161.

76 Frank Richards, *Old Soldiers never Die*, Faber and Faber, London, 1964, p. 272.

77 Dunn, *War the Infantry Knew*, p. 509.

78 IWM, letters of Lieutenant-Colonel E. C. Barton, undated letter *c.* June – August 1915. I am most grateful to Mrs. G. Barton for permission to quote from these letters.

79 Graves, *Goodbye*, pp. 178, 180, 185.

80 Dunn, *War the Infantry Knew*, p. 168.

81 Richards, *Old Soldiers*, pp. 154, 212–13.

82 Watcyn-Williams, *Khaki to Cloth*, p. 61.

83 IWM, Lieutenant-Colonel E. C. Barton, Mss., letter from Lieutenant R. F. Barton, 30 July 1916.

84 Sir H. Gough, *Soldiering on*, Arthur Barker, London, 1954, pp. 131–2.

85 IWM, P. G. Heath, Mss.

86 John F. Lucy, *There's a Devil in the Drum*, London, 1938, p. 342.

87 *Ibid.*, pp. 338–43.

88 IWM, letters of Brigader-General H. E. Trevor, especially 8 November 1915, 17 April 1916.

89 Sir J. E. Edmonds, *History of the Great War: Military Operations France and Belgium, 1915* II, HMSO, London, 1928, p. 277.

90 Graves, *Goodbye*, p. 135.

91 Edmonds, *Military Operations*, pp. 335, 342–5.

92 Germains, *Kitchener Armies*, pp. 189–90, 202–4.

93 Spicer, *Letters from France*, pp. 14–15.

94 PRO, Ministry of National Service papers, NATS 1/84, daily recruiting statistics for 23rd Recruiting Area.

95 *North Wales Chronicle*, 2 October 1914.

96 NLW, WAC papers, file 'R/90 Recruiting (General)', Lieutenant Colonel T. A. Wynne-Edwards to Sir Ivor Herbert, 27 October 1914.

97 J. E. Munby (ed.), *A History of the 38th (Welsh) Division*, London, 1920, p. 2.

98 NLW, WAC papers, file 'Lt. Hugh Pritchard', Pritchard to Secretary, WNEC, 28 September 1914.

99 *Ibid.*, file 'R 90 County Meetings (Anglesey)', Anglesey County Council to WNEC, 7 October 1914.

100 *Ibid.*, file '68', memorandum dated January 1915.

101 *Ibid.*, files '160', '30–113 Brigade HQ', 'Memoranda'; periodic strengths 23 November 1914 to 1 February 1915. The brigade was some 300 under

establishment on 1 February.

102 Munby, *38th Division*, pp. 3–4.
103 U(niversity) C(ollege) of N(orth) W(ales), Bangor, Ms 7060, 'Nominal Roll of NCO's and Men . . . who embarked with the Battalion on December 1st 1915'.
104 UCNW, Welsh Library, ID 141, 'Statement of Casualties reported to the Anglesey and Caernarfonshire Territorial Force Associations up to 31 October 1915'.
105 E. Davies, *Taffy went to War*, privately published, Knutsford, 1974, p. 3.
106 E. B. Davies, *Ar Orwel Pell*, Grwasg Gromer, Llandysul, 1965, p. 26.
107 NLW, Ms 6080a, figures extrapolated from the roll book of E. Company, 16th RWF, October 1915. This was retitled D Company, 20th RWF, in November 1915.
108 NLW, Ms 6079a, figures extrapolated from the roll book of D Company, 20th RWF, January 1916.
109 *The North Wales Observer and Gazette*, 18 September 1914.
110 *Y Genedl Gymreig*, 19 January 1915.
111 Davies, *Taffy went to War*, p. 2.
112 H. Diffey, 'Memoirs of the 1914–18 war', *Y Ddraig Goch*, XXII, 1, 1979, p. 62.
113 NLW, WAC papers, file 'Memoranda', statements of unit losses up to 30 June 1915.
114 *The Caernarvon Herald*, 20 August 1915.
115 *Ibid.*
116 G. D. Roberts, *Witness these Letters*, Denbigh, 1983, p. 10.
117 NLW, WAC papers, file 'Lt. Hugh Pritchard'.
118 *Y Genedl Gymreig*, 1 June 1915.
119 NLW, WAC papers, file 'K', Lieutenant-Colonel Wilkie (17th Battalion, Welsh Regiment) to the Secretary, WNEC, 29 July 1915.
120 *Y Genedl Gymreig*, 11 January 1916.
121 NLW, WAC papers, file 'Memoranda', statements of unit losses up to 30 June 1915.
122 UCNW, Bangor, Ms 7060.
123 NLW, Mss 6080a, 6079a.
124 *Ibid.*
125 Gwynedd Archives, XNWQU/188, North Wales Quarrymen's Union to the President, Cabinet Committee, 4 January 1915.
126 UCNW, Bangor, Ms 3192, 'Bethesda during the War', account of recruiting meeting on 28 August 1914.
127 *Y Genedl Gymreig*, 8 September 1914 and 8 June 1915.
128 Munby, *38th Division*, p. 13.
129 IWM, Air Vice-Marshal Sir Philip Game papers, Game to his wife, 2 August 1916.
130 War Office, *The Army List for September, 1915*, London, 1915, col. 1124–24j.
131 IWM, unpub. memoirs of Brigadier-General H. C. Rees, vol. 1915–17, pp. 80–1, 86.
132 C. Hughes, *Mametz*, Orion Press, Gerrards Cross, 1982, pp. 123–4.
133 E. Davies, *Taffy went to War*, p. 39. I am most grateful to Emlyn Davies for permission to quote from this account.

Ian Beckett 5

The Territorial Force

In the creation of the Territorial Force, as with his army reforms generally, Haldane was forced to settle for a lowest denominator of practical political attainment rather than the grander design. The original concept of a 'real national army' was thus considerably modified in the course of its evolution between 1906 and 1908, and the resulting structure of the Territorials reflected crucial compromises. These were not only to have serious repercussions on the force's role during the Great War but were to cast a shadow over the inter-war years as well.

The nature of the compromises on such fundamental issues as the composition of the county associations that were to administer the Territorial Force and the promotion of military values in schools and among youths is well known.[1] The most significant was the change that took shape in the actual role Territorials were supposed to fulfil. The auxiliary forces that the Territorials replaced (Militia, Yeomanry and Volunteers) had been judged by the Norfolk Commission in 1904 incapable of taking the field against regular troops and inadequate as a means of expanding the army in war. By contrast, it was intended that Territorials should both support and expand the army. Initially they would provide for the defence of Britain against raids, invasion being deemed impossible by the Committee of Imperial Defence (CID) enquiries in both 1903 and 1907/8. After six months' training upon mobilisation, however, the force would be ready for overseas service. It was not at first clear how sufficient drafts would be found for the regular army while the Territorials trained, although the transformation of the Militia into the Special Reserve partially solved this problem. The whole justification of the training period as a necessary preliminary to expanding the army was then made a nonsense by Haldane's concession to possible political opposition of switching the emphasis of the Territorials between February and March 1907 from overseas service to home defence.

At a third of the original planned strength, the Territorial Force came into existence on 1 April 1908 with an establishment of 302,199 men organised in fourteen infantry divisions and fourteen cavalry brigades. Although it initially failed to attract more than 183,000 of the 200,000 Volunteers and Yeomanry Haldane had expected to transfer, recruiting was stimulated by an invasion scare in 1909 and by Haldane's extensive speaking tours and the interest of King Edward VII in the force. But by the close of 1910 the apparent boom was over. Service in the Territorials, with a four-year term of engagement, statutory drills and a fifteen-day summer camp, was no more adequately remunerated than service in the auxiliaries. There was frustration at delays in finding accommodation and ranges and in securing separation allowances for all married men at camp, while the attitudes of employers remained as crucially ambivalent for the Territorials as for Volunteers in the past. Understandably, there was much apprehension at the end of the first four years' term of enlistment and, as feared, increasing numbers declined to re-engage.[2]

From a peak of 270,041 officers and men in 1909 the force declined to 245,779 by September 1913. Wastage ran at 12·5 per cent compared to only seven per cent in the regular army and, compared to auxiliaries who had represented 3·6 per cent of the male population in 1903, Territorials represented only 0·63 per cent of the male population in April 1913. The problem was accentuated by the wide disparity in the distribution of the force over the country. Overall, the force was 66,000 men short of establishment in 1913, with 80 per cent having served for less than four years, and with 40,000 men under the age of nineteen. Increasing numbers were failing to attend camp, and by September 1913 only 18,878 officers and men, or not much more than 7 per cent, had taken the Imperial Service obligation committing them in advance to overseas service. Haldane had anticipated that between a sixth and a quarter might do so. A Territorial Reserve had been established but by 1913 was pronounced a failure, with only 1,669 former Territorials. A 'Veteran' or National Reserve launched in 1910 was more successful in providing a facility for filling Territorial vacancies in the event of war.[3]

The failure of the Territorials to match Haldane's optimistic manpower targets increased criticism of the force which, in turn, only generated more disillusionment. Regulars had had little confidence in the auxiliaries, and the Territorials had equally few friends in the military establishment. The efficiency of Territorial artillery provoked a major controversy in 1908, and the standard of training, attendance at camp and attainment of musketry requirements all received critical scrutiny in later years. No proper mobilisation scheme existed for the Territorials as late as 1912 and, in any case, priority was accorded to the BEF, since the value of expending resources on troops with no liability to foreign service was questioned. In 1914 Territorial infantry still lacked the modern short Lee Enfield rifle and the artillery was still armed with obsolete fifteen-pounders and 5 in. howitzers.[4]

Military criticism, however, rested upon more than narrow professional judgement, since many of the attacks upon the Territorials emanated from those who favoured conscription. Haldane had advertised the force as a 'practical test of the voluntary system', so that its very existence could be interpreted as an obstacle to compulsion. The National Service League had become openly hostile to the Territorials by 1913, while the Army Council came out in favour of conscription in April 1913. Even Territorials themselves became sufficiently despondent to advocate its introduction, ten associations having declared for compulsion by April 1913, and seventeen backing a thinly veiled recommendation for compulsion proposed by Essex in the Council of County Territorial Associations the same month. In the Commons, Territorial MPs often criticised their own force, while one of the most damaging attacks in the columns of the conscriptionist *National Review* in September 1910 had been penned by Lord Esher, chairman of the County of London Association. Much of the press ridiculed the force.

It was thus more a measure of the doubts concerning its efficiency than the possibility of invasion that prompted an official invasion enquiry by the CID in October 1908 to recommend that two of the six regular divisions should be retained in Britain after mobilisation, a recommendation reiterated by the next inquiry in April 1914. Even youth organisations had fought shy of the Territorials when Haldane offered affiliation in 1910. The severe pressure on the force as a whole was not improved by Haldane's tendency to concentrate his efforts on successful rather than unsuccessful recruiting areas while his successor, J. E. B. Seely, proved either unable or unwilling to arrest the apparent lack of interest by the government in the Territorials.[5]

By 1 July 1914 the Territorial Force stood at 268,777 officers and men, of whom 18,683 had taken the Imperial Service obligation. But whatever the expectations of the Territorials at the approach of war, all were to be set aside by the appointment of Kitchener as Secretary of State for War on 5 August 1914. Recently it has been suggested that there was more purpose to Kitchener's strategic decisions than has sometimes been apparent. Equally, it has been argued that his neglect of the potential of the existing Territorial machinery was a sound decision, although his specific reasons for doing so at the time are somewhat obscure.[6] Few associations had prepared plans for expansion but, although they varied in size and efficiency, they were not as depleted in staff as later suggested. The Territorial Reserve was certainly insignificant, but there was the National Reserve, which Kitchener confused with the Special Reserve, and the subsequent return of former Territorials to serve in the force demonstrated that there was a reserve capability.

That Kitchener was a great magnet for recruiting is undeniable, but if his 'New Armies' attracted more recruits than the Territorials it should be borne in mind that restrictions were placed on the ability of the force to recruit, and its very neglect militated against its recruiting. Kitchener, it has been claimed, believed that associations would be swamped if they were responsible for all recruiting and that the Territorials could not expand and train simultaneously. But this was equally true of the New Armies, while the Adjutant-General's department proved little better at coping with the rush of recruits. Kitchener did refer to the Territorials as a 'Town Clerks' army', and he probably distrusted the measure of independence the associations enjoyed and the opportunities for local nepotism in appointments. There were occasional charges of this as in Oxfordshire in October 1914 but the New Armies were not entirely free of nepotism either. The Territorials were certainly not fit for immediate service but were further handicapped by the removal of the majority of their regular adjutants and instructors to staff the New Armies, either immediately or after six months. Thus, although some Territorials went abroad almost immediately and the average length of time required to prepare first-line units for overseas service was just over eight months, compared with over nine months for New Army units, the second-line Territorial formations took an average of twenty-seven months to train.[7]

The pre-war Territorial could, of course, claim far more acquaintance with military knowledge than new recruits, but Kitchener preferred men with no knowledge to those with 'a smattering of the wrong thing'. This undoubtedly comes close to the military reasoning that lay at the heart of his decision. Many contemporaries have recorded his distrust of 'amateurs', based upon his experience of Chanzy's army in the Franco-Prussian War and of irregulars in South Africa. The Territorials were, of course, not liable to overseas service, and Esher noted that Kitchener was reluctant to pressure married men into volunteering to go abroad. More significant perhaps was the fact that the Territorials were responsible for home defence, and it is clear that invasion 'preoccupied and alarmed' the Secretary of State. Use of the Territorials to expand the BEF would disorganise the force for its home defence role, as indeed its division into overseas and home service units was judged to have done in September 1914, although it must also be said that Kitchener's scrapping of existing defence plans did not materially contribute to home defence organisation either.[8] The overrriding impression is that Kitchener's decision to ignore the Territorials was an instinctive one for a regular soldier who, moreover, knew nothing of the home army. On the morning he took over the War Office, Kitchener told Sir Charles Harris that 'he could take no account of anything but regular soldiers'. None of the many who criticised the decision could change his mind thereafter.[9]

It has been argued that Kitchener's reservations concerning Territorials were rapidly dispelled, since he told Esher on 13 August that he would be prepared to utilise those who volunteered for foreign service. The Army Council had already agreed that complete units could proceed overseas, the original idea being that they would be transferred to the New Armies. It has also been argued that the despatch of the first Territorial units abroad in September also indicated Kitchener's willingness to afford them due opportunity. There is little evidence to suggest his view had significantly changed.

The majority of the formations sent overseas were specifically to release regulars in imperial garrisons. The 42nd (East Lancashire)

Division sailed for Egypt on 10 September 1914; the 43rd (Wessex) for India on 9 October, followed by the 44th (Home Counties) and 45th (2nd Wessex) in December. The 1/7th and 1/8th Middlesex went to Gibraltar; the 1/1st Brecknockshire Battalion to Aden; half the 1/8th Manchesters to Cyprus, and the 1st London Brigade to Malta. The first two units sent to France – 1/14th London (London Scottish) and 1/1st Queen's Own Oxfordshire Hussars on 16 and 22 September respectively – were intended solely as line of communications troops. Esher later claimed that Kitchener was only reluctantly persuaded to send more Territorials to 'fill the gap' in France and Flanders. With additional pressure from Sir John French seven Yeomanry, three engineer, one medical and twenty-two infantry units were in France by the end of December 1914. The total of infantry battalions rose to forty-eight by February 1915 and the first complete division – 46th (North Midland) – arrived in the same month, with the first Territorial brigade – 149th Brigade of 50th (Northumbrian) Division – going into action in April 1915.[10]

In numerical terms the Territorials were not neglected, since associations were authorised on 15 August 1914 to raise new units to replace those volunteering for overseas service. Successive orders on 21 and 31 August, reiterated in concise form on 21 September 1914, authorised the general duplication of the 'first line' with a 'second line'. A 'third line' was established in November 1914 when first-line units proceeded overseas, and this was extended to cover all associations in March 1915.

The original designation of 'Imperial Service', '1st Reserve' and '2nd Reserve' units was changed in February 1915 to '1st', '2nd' and '3rd Line' units. The nomenclature to indicate the lines, viz. 1/1st, 2/1st and 3/1st was prescribed a month earlier, while the original 'territorial' designations of higher Territorial formations were discontinued in May 1915 and numbers substituted. Thus the East Lancashire Division became 42nd (East Lancashire) Division and the Lancashire Fusiliers, East Lancashire and Manchester Brigades became the 125th, 126th and 127th Brigades respectively.

By 1918 a total of 692 Territorial battalions had existed, compared to 267 regular or reserve and 557 New Army battalions. Territorials formed twenty-nine infantry and five mounted divisions, while the New Army formed thirty infantry divisions.

In terms of overseas service some 318 Territorial battalions, twenty-three Territorial infantry divisions and two mounted divisions served abroad, compared to 404 New Army battalions and thirty New Army divisions. The Territorials thus contributed as much to the overall war effort as the New Armies. There is little doubt that the creation of the latter led to an unnecessary duplication of effort that damaged both organisations, and that Territorial associations could probably have been made an adequate basis for expansion. The evidence is inconclusive, although the experience of New Zealand suggests that the Territorials could have been used more constructively in 1914.[11] There were admittedly difficulties pertaining to the employment of Territorials abroad under existing legislation which might have been resolved through a sympathetic approach. Unfortunately, the military authorities treated these problems in such a way that the Territorials emerged from the war with a deep sense of grievance.

The first of the legislative difficulties – the Imperial Service obligation – has already been briefly mentioned. Prior to 1914 only five complete Territorial units indicated a willingness to serve overseas when required. An invitation was therefore extended on 10 August 1914 for complete units to volunteer for Imperial Service. On 21 August units where at least 80 per cent had volunteered were authorised to recruit to war establishment, while two or more units with less than the required percentage could combine to produce service units. The latter proved unsatisfactory and from 31 August second-line units could be raised where 60 per cent of the first line had volunteered, enabling the first line to complete from the second and to return their own home service men to the second line as a nucleus. It is not uncommon to find units where 80 per cent or 90 per cent of the first line volunteered immediately, such as the 1/9th London (Queen Victoria's Rifles), the 1/4th Gloucesters or the 1/8th Scottish Rifles. In the latter case, however, the other units in the Scottish Rifle brigade of the 52nd (Lowland) Division did not show anything like the same enthusiasm. In other instances commanding officers made commitments on behalf of their men which proved somewhat optimistic, as in the 51st (Highland) Division, where a 75 per cent acceptance was officially recorded, only for it to fall significantly when individuals had to signify their assent personally and on paper. One brigade that 'had volunteered to a man' subsequently opted for home service. The later requirement for only 60 per cent to offer to serve abroad was clearly more realistic.[12]

In some units there could be initial reluctance, and some pressure could be applied, but this was not always the case. Equally, the way in which home servicemen were then treated could vary considerably from unit to unit. Even within a single unit there could be wide discrepancies, as in the 1/10th Middlesex, where a company recruited from Battersea College responded to a far greater extent than the others, or the 1/4th Royal Scots, where 90 per cent of an artisan company volunteered but only 15–20 per cent of a 'bankers' company'.[13]

The response of the artisans of the 1/4th Royal Scots was thought to be particularly praiseworthy, as the company contained the largest proportion of married men in the battalion. Kitchener and others like Churchill and French rightly recognised that many pre-war Territorials were older and had more responsibilities than war time recruits, and this was certainly significant in many individual decisions to choose foreign or home service. Ironically, many of those opting to remain at home achieved faster promotion, since they were more experienced than newer recruits. Again, many Territorials were too young for foreign service, nineteen years of age being the minimum, although it was not uncommon for boys to lie about their age. In some units there was a belief that foreign service might lead to transfer to other formations, as in the 1/1st City of London Yeomanry and the 1/5th Scottish Rifles, where resistance was such that officers were accused before a divisional enquiry of sabotaging the appeal for volunteers.[14]

Another crucial factor could be fitness for service. About 20 per cent of the 1/6th West Yorkshire, 19 per cent of the 2/8th Sherwood Foresters and 15 per cent of the 1/1st Montgomeryshire Yeomanry were declared unfit, while the 1/6th Royal Welsh Fusiliers were passed for overseas service only after multiple teeth extractions and the promise of dentures, which failed to materialise for another year. The 42nd Division was at almost full establishment on mobilisation but was considerably reduced by medical inspection. When it arrived in Egypt in September 1914 the GOC there, Sir John Maxwell, found 100 men blind, 1,500 'swarming with lice', one dying of Bright's disease and 'hundreds ... so badly vaccinated that they could hardly move'. One officer believed the division had 'picked up any loafer or corner boy they could find to make up their numbers'. The hospitals at both Cairo and Alexandria were badly congested by November 1914, and a medical officer estimated that at least a further 200 men would need repatriation.[15]

Those Territorials who did volunteer for overseas service subsequently believed that their sacrifice had been insufficiently recognised. In the case of those going to imperial garrisons, there was a feeling that they had actually been penalised for early readiness. Most dissatisfaction was associated with India. Kitchener had categorically and unnecessarily promised that those sent there would, after completing their training, be replaced by less well trained men and brought back to France. Other grievances included the poorer scale of rations in the subcontinent, pecuniary disadvantages arising from poorer allowances, inferior equipment and frequent movements which disrupted training, as did the removal of specialists for administrative duties elsewhere. When the matter was raised in the War Council in March 1915 Kitchener dismissed the complaints, but pressure continued, as in the case of the commanding officer of the 1/6th Hampshires, who urged his association in September 1916 to get the War Office to redeem its promise.

Individual battalions did eventually reach France, while others saw service in Mesopotamia or supplied drafts there from March 1915. For the rest, the government could only offer the hope in November 1916 that they would be granted favourable consideration for early demobilisation, but the majority were still there in 1919 facing a fifth hot season. Indeed, the outbreak of the Third Afghan War in May 1919 resulted in Territorials awaiting transportation home being hastily sent north in *ad hoc* service units. There was discontent amounting to near mutiny in some units, and others were reluctant to close with the enemy, although some did well. In 1920 Territorials still in India were complaining that they had been denied the opportunity of securing civilian employment. Not unexpectedly, those counties from which the original three divisions had been drawn faced great difficulties in recruiting when the Territorial Force was reconstituted in 1920.[16]

A second major difficulty connected with the use of Territorials was that the ability to enlist for home rather than imperial service continued to be sanctioned until March 1915. There is some evidence to suggest that, until eliminated, home service could be an attractive option for new recruits. At Caernarfon, for example, incomplete recruiting figures between 18 September and 8 December 1914 suggest a ratio of home to foreign service enlistments of four to one, while the recruiting officer at Stafford complained in December 1914 that the 2/1st Staffordshire Yeomanry, designated for home service, was attracting all available recruits. The fact that there were sufficient home service Territorials to form sixty-eight new provisional battalions in April 1915 is also significant. Their creation, however, did not eradicate all home service in the force, and in August 1915 some 82,588 home servicemen were still borne on Territorial returns. The position of these men and all those enlisted for home service was not finally extinguished until the passing of the Military Service Acts of January and May 1916. Under the first, all Territorials under forty-one were given until 2 March 1916 to take the Imperial Service obligation or be forced to resign (officers) or be discharged (other ranks) and thus made liable to conscription.[17]

Similarly, the Acts also eliminated that provision of the Territorial and Reserve Forces Act which enabled pre-war Territorials to seek their discharge at the end of their term of engagement. Some 159,388 pre-war Territorials would have been entitled to discharge under normal peacetime conditions between 1914/15 and 1916/17, although the four-year term was automatically extended by one year in war. It is impossible to say how many took advantage of their right rather than accept a month's furlough and bounty upon re-engagement for another four years or the duration. Many certainly preferred to take the furlough rather than leave their existing units, but there are instances of men taking a chance on discharge, as in the 1/4th Black Watch, 1/6th King's and 1/1st Staffordshire Yeomanry. Those whose services were compulsorily retained were offered a furlough where possible, and a bounty, but the War Office refused to bring back retained time-expired men from India to complete service at home.[18]

Another difficulty for the War Office was the integrity of Territorial units and the theoretical illegality of transferring Territorials or amalgamating or disbanding their units. No other issue generated as much controversy; it was a measure of the seriousness of the grievance that the War Office felt obliged to issue a defence of its action in 1919.[19] Most volunteering for service in 1914 did so on the understanding that they would be kept together. The standard form, E624, upon which individuals signified their assent, clearly stated that a man would remain with his own unit. But the casualties suffered by the regulars in autumn 1914 necessitated the provision of more reinforcements than could be supplied by the Army or Special Reserves. With the New Armies as yet untrained, only the Territorials were available. In January 1915 associations were asked to seek volunteers willing to transfer to the Army Reserve, while, in February, attention was focused on the possibility of amending the 1907 Act. A draft Bill was discussed in April but aroused considerable opposition. Sir John Simon suggested simply announcing that 'preference must be given to those who are willing, in case of need, to serve with units other than their own'. Instead, a new form, E624A, was issued in May on which those who had already volunteered as well as new recruits were required additionally to agree to possible transfer. There was increasing pressure to drop the form, the Earl of Derby claiming that it was 'murdering recruiting', and on 5 July 1915 Kitchener reluctantly withdrew the stipulation that all must sign both forms. In fact Territorial legislation did not restrict the power of 'attachment' but the idea of new legislation was again revived in April 1916. In the event it was not required, as clauses were included in the second Military Service Act to enable transfers to take place between Territorial and other units.[20]

A related problem was that of maintaining Territorial units at the front, this also reaching a critical stage in early 1915. Even reinforcing the handful of Territorial battalions in France was sufficiently difficult for Kitchener and the Adjutant-General to warn that they might have to be withdrawn from the front, and three were pulled back in May. In March 1915 the responsibility of supplying drafts to first-line units passed from the second line to the third, but the numbers of trained men required were not available and in June 'exceptional' measures were instituted by which all trained men in the second line battalions in excess of a total strength of 700 were to be available for drafting to the first line, half being replaced from the third. In July the number of men to be retained in the second line was reduced to 600, with no replacement.

The constant loss of trained men undoubtedly damaged the efficiency of the second line units. Even first line formations suffered, the failure of the 53rd (Welsh) and 54th (East Anglian) divisions at Suvla Bay in August 1915 being attributed to their previous role as 'sucked oranges' for Territorial units in France. Second line formations generally had an often unjustified poor reputation in view of their particular problems in this respect. The 2/18th London (London Irish) was described as a 'shadow' of its original by the summer of 1915. When the 178th Brigade of 59th (2nd North Midland) Division was sent to Ireland to assist in the suppression of the Easter Rising in April 1916 so many trained men had been sent to France that most of the remainder had had only three months' training and some had not yet fired a full-sized rifle. In August 1916 each battalion of the brigade lost a further 200 men, the commanding officer describing this as 'heartbreaking as it meant masses of new recruits, beginning training all over again and many months before the Brigade would be fit for service'.[21]

Such difficulties might have been more readily accepted had it not been for the fact that the drafting system in France and Flanders appeared to have completely broken down at an early stage. The process often seemed quite arbitrary, as when 200 men of the 2/4th City of London were allocated to the 1/13th London (Kensingtons) while a draft of Kensingtons went elsewhere at a time of no apparent pressure on the system at all. Criticism of such drafting surfaced in the Commons as early as November 1914 and reached a crescendo in March and April 1916.[22]

After 11 December 1915 no more direct recruiting was permitted into the Territorial Force, except for a few specified units, and all recruits under the Derby Scheme and subsequent Military Service Acts were recruited for general service and allocated as required. Not surprisingly, drafting became more and more haphazard, particularly with the heavy casualties on the Somme. Thus the 3/10th King's (Liverpool Irish) supplied drafts to three Territorial and two Kitchener battalions that summer, one draft arriving in the 13th King's still in Liverpool Irish kilts. One recruit to the 3/25th London (Cyclists) was transferred to the 3/10th London just before being posted to France in November 1916 but on arrival at Le Havre was sent, still wearing his 3/25th badges, to the 1/7th London. The 1/16th London (Queen's Westminster Rifles) was said to have had men from seventeen different regiments, including kilted units, in their ranks at one point during the Somme campaign, and the London battalions in particular appear to have felt the blow to *esprit de corps* keenly. The County of London Association had tried to extract a promise from the War Office that 'class corps' at least would be maintained, but this was not always possible.[23]

Increasingly there was the possibility that Territorial units would be amalgamated or even disbanded. Temporary amalgamations took place in the wake of heavy casualties in early 1915, as in the case of the 1/1st, 1/2nd and 1/3rd Monmouthshire battalions between May and July 1915. Amalgamation became more permanent in the course of 1916, such as that between the 1/4th and the 1/5th Black Watch. There was an air of fatalism about the associations which bred insularity, and an attempt in the spring of 1916 by the City of Glasgow and other Scottish associations to fight battlefield amalgamation received sympathy but no practical support from others that had yet to experience the problem. There was also general acceptance in April 1916 for the transfer of Territorial ASC personnel to the regular army for the duration. In January 1918 the second line Territorial units took the brunt of the reductions consequent on the reorganisation of the BEF, with the War Office refusing to give any guarantee that disbanded units would be reconstituted after the war. Subsequently the War Office was forced to accept the 'Pledge' of Territorial integrity in return for the force becoming generally available for imperial service upon reconstitution in 1920.[24]

The powerlessness of associations to determine the fate of their own units reflected declining influence generally as the War Office gradually subsumed more of their formal responsibilities. Associations had faced difficulties from the very beginning in raising, equipping and maintaining their formations. They competed directly with the War Office as well as with corporations and individuals in securing war supplies in 1914. Hampshire resorted to sending an officer to London who filled three taxi cabs with mobilisation equipment, and similar difficulties were experienced elsewhere. Oxfordshire had to find 181,600 separate articles and, with costs inflated by scarcity, spent £48,972 1s on mobilisation, while the West Riding had spent £349,902 by April 1915. It had not been anticipated that expenditure would be so large, nor that the numbers of men handled would be so great. East Lancashire, with a pre-war establishment of 18,000, was administering 49,000 after seven months, while the County of London Association had clothed 100,000 men by June 1915. There were also increasing numbers of wives and dependants to whom separation allowances were paid. At the peak, Gloucestershire was supporting 13,042 dependants, Worcestershire 14,550, Warwickshire 16,000, east Lancashire 60,000 and London some 78,000. With new claims averaging 159 per week in the North Riding in 1916 it was small wonder that the number of staff required to constantly adjust existing or verify new claims rose accordingly. In west Lancashire, for example, the number of clerks increased from twenty in 1914 to 128 by 1918.[25]

Initially, it appeared that associations might also be required to help raise the New Armies. On 7 August 1914 Kitchener had merely requested co-operation but by 4 September the pressure of recruits resulted in responsibility for housing and preliminary training being handed over to a new committee headed by Lord Midleton. Midleton immediately turned to the associations, but on 11 September his committee was relieved of its duties and the invitations to associations rescinded. The War Office announced that assistance would not now be required, but the associations were again being asked for help with accommodation in December. In fact Cambridgeshire and the Isle of Ely, Denbighshire and Flint, and the East Riding were responsible for raising eleven New Army units. Generally, however, recruitment for the New Armies and the Territorials was kept separate and distinct.[26]

Territorial recruiting undoubtedly suffered by comparison with the New Armies, which were believed to be more likely to go abroad, and the 'bringing money' for Territorials was also lower, although Territorials maintained lower age limits and height requirements than the New Armies. In London it was found that mayors were promoting the New Armies rather than the Territorials on whose associations they sat, but there is at least one example – from Heywood in Lancashire – of Territorials disrupting a New Army recruiting meeting. Successive War Office restrictions on particular categories of Territorial recruiting were also detrimental, such as the stop put on new artillery batteries in late 1914 and the cessation of Yeomanry recruiting between June and September 1915. There had been discussion of passing the surplus of the Third New Army to the Territorials, but in November 1914 Territorial 'waiting lists' were abolished and the residue passed to the New Armies. In Wales at least, Territorials did better than the Welsh Army Corps, since the latter's organisers were required to help complete Territorial units first, but here too Territorial recruiting ultimately declined. Transfers and amalgamations were also believed to have an effect on Territorial recruiting. Isolated events like the 'charge' of the 1/14th London Scottish at Messines in November 1914 could provide a temporary stimulus, as did a major Territorial recruiting campaign in spring and summer 1915 modelled on the formula of Derby's 'Whirlwind Campaigns' in west Lancashire which had netted 16,000 Territorial recruits in three months. But, led by Staffordshire in April 1915, associations increasingly pressed for conscription. When voluntary direct enlistment in the Territorials ceased in December 1915 some 725,842 men had enlisted in the force, or approximately half the number enlisted in the New Armies during the same period.[27]

The end of Territorial recruiting naturally reduced the role of the associations but further responsibilities were stripped away so that they soon ceased to resemble the miniature War Offices depicted by Esher in September 1914. Clothing was taken over by the War Office in early 1915, although associations remained distributing agents, and in 1916 control was lost over the Territorial ASC and the National Reserve. In

November 1916 some of the responsibilities of the Director-General of
the Territorial Force were transferred to the Military Secretary.
Alarmed by rumours that the post would be abolished altogether, and
by fears of other statutory powers being removed, association
representatives met Derby, now Secretary of State for War, in January
1917.

Derby denied that any powers would be curtailed without
parliamentary approval, but in March 1917 the War Office announced
the centralisation of depots and the closure of many Territorial ones.
Territorial record offices were also closed in 1917 and all men passing to
Territorial units allocated regular numbers so that they and any
Territorials subsequently transferred would lose Territorial identity. In
September 1917 the Council of County Territorial Associations met for
the first time in three years to protest against the 'whittling away' of
responsibilities and the 'gradual extinction' of the force, especially as it
now seemed the administration of separation allowances would also be
removed. Another delegation met Derby in October; the allowances
were saved and depots given a stay of execution in January 1918,
although associations were urged to cut staffing levels. Derby had held
out a possible major role in demobilisation, but it did not materialise,
and the only additional responsibility assumed during the war proved to
be the unpopular administration of the new Volunteer Force.[28]

Further Territorial grievances resulted from the relationship with
regulars. As far as the other ranks were concerned, there appears to have
been little or no animosity between the first Territorials to arrive in
France and the regulars who assisted in their familiarisation. Not only
did the Territorials receive a warm welcome but there was considerable
mutual admiration, although the social quality of the early Territorials
should not be overlooked.[29] By contrast, when Territorials later assisted
the New Armies in familiarisation there appears to have been friction on
occasions, although one Yeomanry officer believed that Territorials were
probably 'kinder' than regulars might have proved. There had certainly
been resentment among Territorials in England in December 1914 that
the New Armies received more Christmas leave and, when in France,
that the New Armies had better equipment. Many Territorials arrived
in France with the old long Lee Enfield rifle, the celebrated attack of the
London Scottish at Messines being undertaken with rifles incapable of
rapid fire. The 1/6th West Yorkshires bitterly resented an attempt to
deprive them of modern rifles after Neuve Chapelle in order to equip
Kitchener units, while in the 49th (West Riding) Division generally the
disparity in artillery equipment with regular and New Army formations
was adversely remarked.[30]

If there was little friction between Territorials and regulars at lower
levels, it clearly existed among commissioned ranks. When brigades had

first been organised in the old Volunteer Force in 1888 both Volunteers
and regulars had commanded, although the number of Volunteers was
progressively reduced. Haldane, too, had promised that suitably
qualified Territorials would be given higher commands. In 1914,
however, no Territorial had commanded a division and there were only
three Territorial infantry brigade commanders – the first, Noel Lee, who
was killed at Gallipoli, having been appointed only in 1911.

The absence of successors to these pioneers was raised in the
Commons in October 1916 without result, but in February 1917 the
Under-Secretary of State for War, Ian Macpherson, stated that eighteen
Territorials had risen above the rank of lieutenant-colonel at the front
and three at home. In March Macpherson claimed that the percentage
of candidates from the New Armies and Territorials (19·6 and 15·7 per
cent respectively) taking up places on staff courses now collectively
exceeded that of regular and overseas candidates (31·3 and 33·3 per cent
respectively). It was remarked that this was not encouraging if the
declining numbers of regular officers were taken into account, and in
January 1918 Derby was forced to defend the War Office in a speech at
the Aldwych Club. He argued that no men of talent were overlooked and
that since 1914 a total of 1,973 Territorial or New Army officers had held
AQ or QM staff appointments, compared to 4,651 regulars, with the
proportion of the former rising all the time. Four Territorials had
commanded divisions and fifty-two had commanded brigades, while
sixty-one Territorials below the rank of lieutenant in 1914 had achieved
that of lieutenant-colonel. What Derby did not indicate was that many
of the Territorial appointments had been only temporary, and in
February 1918 Macpherson revealed that there were currently only ten
Territorials commanding brigades and that, throughout the entire war,
only three had become GSO1s.

Territorials, then, might hold an increasing number of appointments,
but rarely on a long-term basis, and rarely those that mattered. In 1918,
for example, the only three regular officers in the 53rd Division included
the GOC, GSO1 and one of three brigadier-generals. Of 286 officers who
passed through the three battalions of the 24th London (the Queen's)
during the war, only five reached the rank of lieutenant-colonel, and
none rose higher. Similarly, in India, Territorials were denied staff
appointments, although they were more welcome on transfer to the
Indian Army than newly commissioned civilians. To some extent the
passing over of experienced Territorials was possibly due to their
generally higher age than surviving regulars, but rather more significant
was the prejudice against 'amateurs' which had been a long-standing
feature of regular attitudes towards auxiliaries.

One regular staff officer wrote to Henry Spenser Wilkinson in
February 1915 that naturally his 'chiefs' preferred regulars if they were

available, while one Yeomanry officer later recalled a wartime divisional conference in which battalion command appointments were discussed. The only Territorial present joked that no one in his battalion could be a candidate, as they were all Territorials. 'No jest ever fell flatter, for no one in the room regarded the statement as other than a perfectly natural statement of fact.' The officers of the 184th Brigade of 61st (2nd South Midland) Division believed that the failure of their first major operation in July 1916 was used as an excuse to remove the last remaining Territorials in brigade and divisional appointments, while the regular staff of the division were said to have 'gloried in their contempt' for Territorials.[31]

The attitude of regular officers generally was at best patronising. General Sir Aylmer Hunter-Weston of VIII Corps remarked to officers of one Territorial battalion in 1917 that 'temporary officers, not being accustomed to valets in private life, did not know how to make use of their servants in the Army'. They found this insulting 'when a large number of officers of all Regiments had risen from the ranks'. A newly appointed wartime officer of the Special Reserve like Robert Graves found it fashionable to sneer at Territorials, while two Territorials who later became well known, Dennis Wheatley and Lord Reith, both had unpleasant experiences with regular officers in their units. Other examples abound, and there were allegedly cases in which Territorials removed the Ts from their uniform because they were 'made to consider it a badge of inferiority'. In one such case a 'court martial' sentenced the officer who had succumbed to the temptation to have his head shaved in the shape of a T.[32]

Adding to the sense of grievance was the pre-war regulation whereby Territorials were automatically junior in precedence to regulars of the same rank. In fact the system of promotion in the Territorial Force itself had many anomalies due to the existence of both temporary and substantive rank, which was marked most frequently by the seniority problems involved when new officers came out to the front senior to those who had preceded them there. This internal difficulty was not satisfactorily resolved until 1917, but of more concern was that the pre-war convention also made experienced Territorials junior to newly commissioned officers in the New Armies.[33]

The irony was that the Territorials provided large numbers of candidates for commission to the army as a whole. Initially the War Office had refused to contemplate any form of commission for Territorials in regular units, although they could take New Army commissions. By November 1914, however, casualties among regular officers reached such proportions that French asked the 1/28th London (Artists' Rifles) to provide fifty subalterns for immediate employment with 7th Division. A total of fifty-two were selected for the 'Suicide

Club', given elementary hints on leadership and sent off with pips on their private's uniforms. In all some 10,256 men of the Artists received commissions during the war. Similarly, the Inns of Court OTC, which provided 11,000 new officers, was also nominally a Territorial unit. Some 60,863 Territorial commissions were issued between 4 August 1914 and 1 April 1920, although only 335 Territorials were granted permanent regular commissions.[34]

The 'craft unionism' of regulars was also apparent in military criticism of the Territorials' performance. Many regulars clearly expected little from the latter – such as Ralph Creyke of the Scots Guards, who, while acknowleding that some 'are pretty good and others fair', felt that 'the main body must be pretty useless'. Sir Ian Hamilton failed to appreciate the problems of Territorials at Gallipoli, the regular who commanded 52nd Division at the time complaining that his 156th Brigade had not received artillery support while attached to 29th Division. Accordingly its losses at Suvla on 28 June 1915 of 70 per cent among officers and 50 per cent among other ranks would have tried even the best regulars, a fact duly acknowledged after the war. Significantly, Hamilton had been highly critical of auxiliaries as a young officer, and, although Macready as Adjutant-General was an exception, those regulars who had served as adjutants with auxiliaries generally tended to be more sympathetic.

French, who had been a Yeomanry adjutant, had a high opinion of the potential of the Territorials. He was satisfied with their performance in France and was subsequently to praise them for 'filling the gap'. Reservations about the ability of the 46th Division to take the place of the regular 29th in France in March 1915 did not detract from his overall view, and he had contemplated using fifty Territorial battalions in his projected Zeebrugge operation. Haig also favoured the employment of Territorials at an early stage, while Sir Henry Rawlinson's first impression of the 49th Division in early 1915 was also favourable.[35] Still other regulars who had initial doubts concerning the efficiency of Territorials were converted by their performance in the field, such as Brigadier-General F. J. Duncan of 165th Brigade, whose opinion of 'mere civilians' changed during his tenure of command, or Major-General W. E. Peyton, whose experience commanding the 2nd (Yeomanry) Mounted Division made him 'hot to think of the half-hearted recognition these same officers (i.e. Yeomanry officers) received at all our hands; I mean from officers of the Regular Army, before they had an opportunity of showing themselves'. There are many similar examples, and indeed the OC of 18th Brigade considered a draft joining the 1/16th London (Queen's Westminster Rifles) far superior in physique, breeding, appearance and morale to a regular draft that arrived at the same time.

Objective reports on Territorials in France and India in December 1914 and April 1915 respectively both concluded that they had no sense of interior economy, while that from France found them slow to move and insufficiently instructed in keeping correct distance, maintaining communications and entrenching. It was generally believed that Territorials had less recuperative power than regulars, and after the war the Kirke Committee suggested that Territorials and New Army formations alike were better in static positions than in mobile operations but that their greater intelligence enabled them to overcome training deficiencies. In fact Territorials in India did remarkably well in the rigorous 'Kitchener tests' during the war. Naturally the efficiency of units or formations varied greatly but it was generally held that, by 1918, there was little to differentiate Territorials, regular and New Army units.[36]

The most often criticised aspect of the Territorial Force was its allegedly lax discipline, even though there was invariably less crime in Territorial units.[37] To a large extent such criticism derived from failure to understand its different ethos. The recurrent phrase in Territorial histories is 'family', with the idea that, since officers and men might well be social equals in civilian life, discipline must be based upon something other than a rigid code. This is seen most clearly in London 'class corps' such as the HAC, where 'there was a dull indifference to discipline, yet a wonderful loyalty to duty'. Several accounts from the 1/5th London (London Rifle Brigade) emphasise a 'club' atmosphere, while the three London Scottish battalions were run along 'public school lines'. This feeling was not confined to London, and there is similar emphasis on self-discipline in units like the 1/6th West Yorkshire and 1/7th and 1/8th West Yorkshire (Leeds Rifles). Life therefore appeared more relaxed in Territorial units, and on occasion this was a source of some pride.[38]

This is not to suggest that Territorial units were free of social problems. Indeed, the very closeness of some units could cause difficulty for newcomers, one Liverpool officer of the 1/4th East Lancs being regarded as a 'foreigner' in a battalion recruited from Blackburn. Others experienced similar problems on joining Territorial units later in the war, when there appeared to be something of a caste system operating, at least initially, between 'veterans' and new arrivals. In 164th Brigade one battalion's 'Festubert men' enjoyed considerable deference on the part of later arrivals. A handful of accounts also record rivalry between men of the first and second lines when drafted to each other's units. This was understandable in that any large drafts of relatively experienced men, especially if a unit was disbanded or amalgamated, would have to be assimilated into its host and the not inconsiderable problems of seniority resolved. There had been some early problems in first-line units when Yeomanry regiments were reduced from four peacetime to three wartime squadrons and infantry battalions from eight to four companies, a process not completed in all cases until January 1915.[39]

It is also a misapprehension to suppose that the Territorials consisted primarily of 'class corps' in terms of social composition. Figures available for some London units do indicate a preponderance of middle-class members but 'class corps' were a small percentage of the whole and the Territorials, like the Volunteers before them, were overwhelmingly a working-class movement. The 1/8th Royal Scots and 1/8th Scottish Rifles were thus both described as 'slum' battalions. Officers of the 1/2nd County of London Yeomanry (Westminster Dragoons) found their journey to Egypt aboard the same vessel as the 1/9th Manchesters particularly trying, since the latter were inclined to spit and swear and were 'gifted with a badger's qualities'. Similarly, the arrival of the 51st Division in Bedford in autumn 1914 wreaked havoc with the town's sewage and drainage systems, since few men had experience of modern sanitation. Other essentially working-class formations included both the 59th and 62nd divisions. Some 76 per cent of the 1/7th and 1/8th West Yorks were manual workers and almost all in the second-line battalions. Still other units were a mixture of classes and occupations, like the 1/1st Cambridgeshire, with its town/country profile, while others had elements drawn from particular industrial concerns or even educational establishments. Even the Yeomanry was far less dependent upon the farming community than might be supposed. Thus the 1/1st Royal Wiltshire Yeomanry contained railwaymen, the 1/1st Derbyshire Yeomanry comprised 25 per cent colliers and 30 per cent tradesmen and clerks, and the 2/1st Royal Bucks Hussars recruited both London policemen and employees of the *Daily Telegraph*.[40]

Territorial officers did tend to be largely middle-class. Dennis Wheatley divided them into three broad categories —— the 'hearty huntin', shootin' and fishin' type' from country units who were popular but brainless; the rare men of real ability in country and city units; and the 'great majority' in city units who 'held inferior positions in civil life and had become Territorial officers as one of the few means open to them of ordering other people about'.

Rather more objectively, those units for which detailed analysis is available do indicate a likely preponderence of professional or businessmen, such as the 1/8th London (Post Office Rifles) or 1/7th and 1/8th West Yorks. Initially commanding officers would have considerable influence over the choice of new officers, and pre-war standards would be maintained, but this could not endure war wastage. Most infantry battalions would have between twenty and thirty officers at a time, but the actual number who passed through a battalion would be far greater. The 1/5th Seaforth Highlanders, for example, had 221

officers during the war; the 1/5th Beds and Herts had 231; and the 1/4th
Seaforths had 273 officers. When Captain A. Roberts of the 1/15th
London (Civil Service Rifles) returned in May 1916 from convalescence
he found only one officer who had been with the battalion in 1914, and
Roberts himself was killed in July. Inevitably there was a drop in officer
standards even though, after December 1915, no one could be directly
commissioned into the Territorials without military experience in the
ranks or an appropriate training unit. Undoubtedly misfits still reached
the front, such as the forty-year-old old schoolmaster suffering from
chronic neuritis who reached the 1/4th Oxford and Bucks Light Infantry
in October 1916.[41]

Another officer draft joining the 1/4th Oxford and Bucks the same
month was from the Scottish Rifles, much as a draft of kilted officers
reached the 1/6th Royal Northumberland Fusiliers in late 1915 – an
indication of how far the 'territorial' character of the force declined as
the war progressed. In 1914, of course, many units had that unity born of
close identification with a given locality, like the 1/5th Duke of
Cornwall's Light Infantry, with 948 genuine Cornishmen out of 1,032
officers and men, or the 1/6th Gordons, with only eleven non-Scots
among 867 officers and men. The pace of change would vary
considerably thereafter according to the experience of individual units,
but even from the beginning there were some that lacked territorial
integrity. A dispute over the restriction of the Welsh language in the
2/1st Denbighshire Yeomanry revealed that only 27 per cent were
actually Welsh. The novelist Patrick MacGill claimed that he and the
CO were the only genuine Irishmen in the 1/18th London (London Irish)
in 1914, while paradoxically the 1/6th Royal Welsh Fusiliers had always
had an Irish contingent. Replacement could also begin at once through
filling vacancies on mobilisation, as in the case of the 1st Wessex RFA in
the haste to send it to India in September 1914, or through the transfer
of men or units to France in the autumn of 1914. The 51st Division thus
received a Lancashire brigade in April 1915. The 1/7th Royal Scots were
unfortunate enough to have 227 officers and men killed and 246 injuried
in the worst-ever British railway accident near Gretna Green in May
1915 *en route* to embark for Egypt. Others lost men to commission like
the 961 men of the 15th London (Civil Service) Rifles or the sixty-seven
men of the 2/1st Royal Bucks Hussars commissioned during the war.[42]
The biggest factor for change was, of course, battle casualties.

Clearly much depended upon how soon a unit proceeded on active
service and, once there, on the relative periods spent in quiet or active
sectors or on actual operations. Some Territorial units suffered heavy
casualties almost immediately, such as the 1/14th London Scottish,
which had 34 per cent casualties at Messines in November 1914, only
two days after reaching the front line. The 1/4th Royal Scots was

'gutted' at Gallipoli; the 1/4th Hampshires 'played out' by September 1915 after service in Mesopotamia; the 1/13th London (Kensingtons) savaged at Neuve Chapelle and Aubers Ridge; the 1/4th Duke of Wellington's effectively 'disbanded' at Ypres in December 1915, and so on. Even greater changes took place as a result of the Somme battles in the summer and autumn of 1916, in which the Territorials suffered 83,696 casualties. A further 83,678 were suffered by Territorial units during Third Ypres in 1917, and 160,939 between 21 March 1918 and the armistice. Table 5.1 gives an approximate illustration of the kind of change overcoming Territorial battalions by analysing data on the place of birth and/or enlistment of those killed or died of wounds or other causes. Naturally, it cannot be a precise survey, since losses may have fallen disproportionately on sections within a unit, but it is persuasive in its indication of how 'territorial' character was steadily lost.[43]

On occasions drafts might fortuitously strengthen the territorial element, but increasingly men returning to a unit would find strangers – 'Derbyites' or middle-aged conscripts and, by 1918, eighteen-and-a-half-year-olds. The 1/7th Sherwood Foresters had only eleven of its original members still serving in January 1918, while the 1/4th Oxford and Bucks had twenty-five of its original men left by the end of the war. Later drafts were often not only lacking in intelligence and more resistant to discipline but also of declining physique. The 1/13th London received a draft of Bantams in 1916, while in 1918 units such as the 1/5th Cheshires and 1/5th DCLI and the 59th Division as a whole were receiving B category men 'entirely untrained for hard active service conditions'.[44] The serious manpower situation in the spring 1918 forced the ultimate betrayal of the Territorial principle. Thus 50th Division was reduced to cadre strength after its horrific losses during the German offensive and reconstituted in July 1918 without a single original unit and only one Territorial battalion. Similarly, 53rd, 60th and 75th Divisions, serving in

Table 5.1. *Percentage of those killed in action, died of wounds or other causes in seven Territorial units, born or residing in the unit's original recruiting area*

Unit (and recruiting area)	1915	1916	1917	1918
1/8th Scottish Rifles (Glasgow)	79	66	45	40
1/6th West Yorkshire (Bradford)	68	66	31	17
1/6th and 2/6th South Staffordshire (Wolverhampton and Staffordshire)	85	85	65	54
1/1st Buckinghamshire Battalion (Buckinghamshire)	65	70	34	38
2/1st Buckinghamshire Battalion (Buckinghamshire)	–	68	43	45
1/1st Royal Buckinghamshire Hussars (Buckinghamshire)	53	22	41	–

Palestine, were completely reorganised between May and August 1918 when all but one battalion from each brigade was despatched to France and replaced by Indian Army battalions.[45]

The problems of the Territorials in the Great War can perhaps be put into clearer perspective by considering one county association and its units in more detail: Buckinghamshire and, in particular, its infantry battalions. The county had a strong amateur military tradition prior to 1908 on which the association could build in raising a Yeomanry and an infantry regiment as well as an ASC unit and a mounted field ambulance. The Royal Bucks Hussars had always been heavily dependent upon the agricultural community for recruits. By contrast, the Volunteer Battalion had come to reply upon the employees of the chair-making industry at High Wycombe and the London & North Western Railway's carriage works at Wolverton. Railway communications within the county were poor, and as the most favoured camping season was at Easter or in August, the new Bucks Battalion would be equally reliant upon the towns.

Of those other ranks constituting the new battalion in April 1908, a total of nine were professional men; twenty-seven were tradesmen; twenty-seven were clerks or employed in similar capacities; three were of unknown occupation; 279 were manual workers and a further 147 were employees of the LNWR. Some 454 out of the total 492 had served in the Volunteers, with an average length of service of just over five years and an average age of twenty-six. The continuing dependence upon urban manual workers thereafter can be illustrated by figures for recruits to D (Aylesbury) Company and its (from 1912) Chesham detachment between 1909 and May 1914, which reveal a total of seven professional men; twenty-three tradesmen; thirty-six clerks or similar; one unknown and 198 manual workers as having enlisted. A majority of the manual workers were employees of the Aylesbury printers Hazell Watson & Viney and, indeed, over 100 Hazell's men were with the 1/1st Bucks in March 1915. Officers were overwhelmingly middle-class and oriented towards business or the professions. Dependent as it was 'on others' employees, the association not unexpectedly joined others in pressing for more concessions to employers prior to the war. The Territorial Reserve was also a failure in Buckinghamshire, with only six officers and one man enlisted by 1914, although the National Reserve stood at sixty-four officers and 1,660 men and there was also a small corps of guides, raised in 1912. On the eve of war first-line units were at 83 per cent of establishment.[46]

The first duty in August 1914 was naturally to mobilise and equip first-line units and, in due course, the 2/1st Royal Bucks Hussars and 2/1st Bucks Battalion, which were constituted on 14 and 26 September respectively. The process went reasonably smoothly, and some pride was taken in the unequal comparison between the uniforms and equipment of the 2/1st Bucks and the plain clothes and dummy rifles of local New Army recruits. There was, however, recruiting competition with the latter, and the association later expressed the view that Territorials had suffered accordingly. Nevertheless, the association was ready to help the War Office find alternative accommodation to relieve the pressure on the regular depot at Oxford in September 1914, although it was also quick to criticise what was regarded as incompetence there.

Thus on 14 November 1914 the depot commander, Sir Charles Cuyler, was asked to explain a report that recruits from Buckinghamshire were being sent to the Wiltshire Regiment. Cuyler promised to try and fit every Bucks man in where he wished to go, while the association's recruiting sub-committee resolved that all recruits should be given the option of joining regulars or Territorials without undue pressure being applied. In fact between 4 August 1914 and 20 June 1915 the association recruited not only 3,291 men for the Territorials but also some 2,640 regulars in addition to any recruited by regular recruiting officers or those who had independently joined other corps in London or elsewhere.[47] The introduction of conscription ended formal involvement in recruiting, although the association's county recruiting officer was simply translated into a War Office recruiting agent, handling tribunals and reporting frequently to the association. In all, the county found some 19,450 men for the armed forces prior to the introduction of compulsion.[48]

Thereafter the association's main concern was ensuring that Bucks men continued to reach Bucks units, a task in which it was reduced to virtual impotence. In April 1916 the association protested at rumoured battlefield amalgamation, while in October it complained that an attempt was being made to force Oxford and Bucks Light Infantry badges on the 3/1st Bucks Battalion. In October 1917 it opposed the closure of its depot on the grounds 'of the unique position of this County in respect to the Buckinghamshire Battalion, which alone of the battalions of the Oxford and Bucks Light Infantry is a representative Buckinghamshire corps'. In March 1918 there was disquiet at the disbandment of the 2/1st Bucks Battalion, and the association extracted a promise from the Adjutant-General that no similar fate would befall the 1/1st Bucks. Not surprisingly, in 1919 the association was demanding a separate regular regiment for the county and a special letter officially recognising the services of the 2/1st Bucks.[49]

The 1/1st and 2/1st Bucks themselves showed all those characteristics already outlined. The *Bucks Free Press* claimed in August 1914 that between 60 and 70 per cent of the 1/1st Bucks had immediately volunteered for overseas service. In reality, upon the first request on 11 August, only 533 men had volunteered. The numbers were unequally distributed, with seventy out of seventy-five men in the Aylesbury Company and twenty-four out of thirty-two of the Chesham detachment volunteering but none of the twenty-seven members of the band. By the following day acceptance had risen to 600. Those opting for home service were then deprived of equipment, labelled 'Never Dies' by the CO and made to camp apart. Some 240 men, many of whom were older NCOs or men with families, were sent back to form the nucleus of the 2/1st Bucks. Not surprisingly, they resented their treatment, and there was persistent emnity between the battalions even after the war. The 2/1st's subsequent refusal to send experienced NCOs to the first line in March 1915 in return for men left behind when the 1/1st went overseas further accentuated the division. When the 2/1st, in turn, was asked to volunteer in April 1915 the greater understanding born of experience resulted in all but 140 men, mostly elderly or unfit, volunteering, including all but one of the band that had refused in 1914. The 2/1st sent this contingent to the 3/1st, but it contained some whom officers had not 'pressed' to volunteer, and these were promptly sent back in the first draft. Ironically, the association had opposed the introduction of a special badge for Imperial Service men in 1910 on the grounds that it would create invidious distinctions within the force.[50] By comparison, the Royal Bucks Hussars appear to have had few problems in finding the necessary quota, but there was still animosity between first and second line officers and men over seniority problems when the latter were drafted to the former.[51]

As indicated in Table 51, Bucks units suffered the common decline in 'territorial' character during the war. There were instances of men declining to re-engage in both the 1/1st Bucks Battalion and the 1/1st Royal Bucks Hussars, but, of course, the greatest factor in change was the rate of casualties. In the case of the two infantry battalions it was uneven, since both suffered the bulk of their casualties in just two major operations. The 1/1st Bucks held such a quiet sector of the line around Hebuterne for twelve months from June 1915 that they had a trench cow, but between 21 and 24 July 1916 they lost 242 casualties around Ovillers on the Somme. The next major operation, around Saint-Julien on 16 August 1917, cost 291 casualties. Similarly, the 2/1st Bucks suffered 322 casualties in its first action on 18/19 July 1916 within three months of arriving in France, while its second major attack on 22 August 1917 resulted in 349 casualties. Inevitably the scale of these losses resulted in major change.

In the wake of their first attack the 1/1st Battalion received its first draft of 'strangers' from 1/1st Hunts Cyclists, while that in 1917 brought fifteen new officers alone. After their first attack the 2/1st battalion received drafts from northern Territorial units who had volunteered for service on the understanding that they would serve in their own units and thus reached the 2/1st in 'bad humour'. Officers were drafted in from four different regiments and the battalion had a 'rocky' time for some months. Almost inevitably, both battalions discovered that drafts declined in quality throughout the war. Discipline was noticeably slacker in the 1/1st Bucks after its transfer to the less demanding Italian front with the rest of the 48th (South Midland) Division in November 1917, while a draft reaching the 2/1st in July 1917, just before its second major attack, was apparently 'swept up from many places' and low in both efficiency and physique.

The decline of officer quality was especially felt. Of the thirty officers who embarked with the 1/1st Bucks in March 1915 only two remained with the battalion throughout the war. Of the remainder four were killed; two died of wounds; twelve were wounded (of whom eight returned at various stages); two were invalided out and eight moved to other duties. When the second-in-command of the 2/1st Bucks, Geoffry Christie-Miller, returned to England to attend a staff course in January 1918 he was the only original officer remaining. Desite these problems, the 1/1st in particular had a fine reputation and was the representative Territorial battalion granted one of seven medals awarded to the British army by the king of Italy in 1920. The 2/1st was unfortunate enough to be one of the battalions of 61st Division chosen for disbandment in 1918.[52]

The Territorial Force as a whole began to be disembodied in December 1918, the Army Council resolving that no special decoration would be awarded those who had originally taken the Imperial Service obligation in 1914. It appears to have been assumed that disembodied Territorials would automatically receive any pensions due, but the Ministry of Pensions had not actually been consulted in advance and hastily authorised disembodiment as the equivalent of discharge for pension purposes. It was not unrepresentative of the thoughtlessness that had characterised official attitudes towards the force since 1914.

The Territorials did not fit easily into the War Office's perceptions of the post-war military situation, since there seemed little likelihood of invasion, and part-time soldiers were unsuited to a garrison role in the newly expanded empire. A role was envisaged in medium-scale wars falling short of those for which conscription might be reintroduced, but Territorials were wary of undertaking obligations without firm guarantees of the future integrity of their units. The subsequent 'pledge' was the price of Territorial agreement to a general liability for overseas service but one still qualified by legislative requirements in the event of war. It was to bedevil the relationship between War Office and Territorials throughout the inter-war years. The War Office continued to regard the Territorial Army, as the force was restyled after 1921, as the most expendable part of the army at a time of retrenchment.

Adequate compensation for the Territorials' sacrifices was still denied, while the army continued to exhibit its worst prejudices against Territorials in command and staff appointments until the late 1930s.

Imperfect though it may have been as a means of expansion in 1914, the Territorial Force made a considerable contribution to the British army in the Great War, suffering 577,016 casualties in all theatres, its officers and men winning seventy-one VCs. That its reward was so lacking was regrettable but only in keeping with the pattern of the amateur military tradition in Britain.[53]

Notes

Crown copyright material from the Public Record Office appears by permission of Her Majesty's Stationery Office. The author also gratefully acknowledges the generosity of the following in allowing him to consult and utilise archives in their possession: the Trustees of the Imperial War Museum; the Trustees of the Liddell Hart Centre for Military Archives; the National Army Museum; the Guildhall Library; the Ministry of Defence Library (old War Office); the Council of Territorial, Auxiliary and Volunteer Reserve Associations; the Army Museums Ogilby Trust 2nd Battalion, the Mercian Volunteers; the Board of Trustees of the Inns of Court and City Yeomanry, and the county record offices of Berkshire, Hampshire, Oxfordshire, Staffordshire, Surrey and Hereford and Worcester. E. D. Kingsley and W. Ward-Jackson kindly gave permission to quote copyright material in the IWM. For Buckinghamshire material thanks go to the Buckinghamshire County Record Office, the Rt Hon. Lord Burnham, Colonel John Christie-Miller, Major Elliot Viney and all those former members of the 48th Division and Bucks units whom the author has interviewed or corresponded with over the years.

1   The creation of the Territorial Force and its subsequent progress to 1914 is examined in Edward M. Spiers, *Haldane: an Army Reformer*, Edinburgh University Press, 1980, pp. 92–115, 161–86. Spiers also covers the wider aspects of Haldane's reforms both in his biography of Haldane and in his *Army and Society, 1815–1914*, Longman, London, 1980, pp. 265–87, as does John Gooch, 'Mr. Haldane's Army', in John Gooch (ed.), *The Prospect of War*, Frank Cass, London, 1981, pp. 92–115, and 'Haldane and the National Army', in Ian F. W. Beckett and John Gooch (eds.), *Politicians and Defence: Studies in the Formulation of British Defence Policy, 1840–1970*, Manchester University Press, 1980, pp. 69–86.

2   Evidence of the perennial concerns of Territorial associations can be found in a nation-wide response to a War Office request for recommendations for improving recruitment in October 1911 in PRO, WO 32/6602, and in the minutes of the Council of County Territorial Associations retained at the Duke of York's headquarters, Chelsea, London. This culminated in a major discussion of proposals by the Essex Association at the CCTA annual meeting on 14 April 1913 and a deputation to Asquith and Seely on 26 November 1913 at which most of the usual arguments were rehearsed. An account of the deputation can also be found in Surrey RO, Minutes of Surrey C(ounty) T(erritorial) A(ssociation), 1913–22, and L. Magnus, *The West Riding Territorials in the Great War*, Kegan Paul, London, 1920, pp. 10–12. For the situations of individual counties see, for example, Guildhall Library Mss, 12613, Minutes of the Recruiting Committee, 1908–13; Hants. RO,

37M69/3, Minutes of the Hampshire CTA, 1912–17; Oxon. RO, Report upon the Administration of the County Territorial Association, 1908–13; F. H. Reynard, *A Brief History of the Territorial Association of the County of York (North Riding), 1908–19*, Joseph Walker, Northallerton, 1919, p. 16; PRO, WO 32/11242, for the state of recruiting in Edinburgh, 1913.

3　Statistics are culled from the minutes of the annual meeting of the CCTA, 14 April 1913, and its National Reserve Advisory Committee, 10 September 1913; Cd 7254 (1914), *The Annual Return of the Territorial Force for the year 1913, passim*. I. F. W. Beckett, *Riflemen Form: a Study of the Rifle Volunteer Movement, 1859–1908*, Ogilby Trusts, Aldershot, 1982, p. 85. Evidence of disparity in the popularity of the force can also be found in contrasting Manchester and Birmingham and other parts of the country; see M. D. Blanch, 'Imperialism, nationalism, and organised youth' in J. Clarke, C. Critcher and R. Johnson (eds.), *Working Class Culture*, Hutchinson, London, 1979, pp. 103–20.

4　MOD, Old War Office Library (hereafter WOL), 'Reports of GOC's on the Physical Capacity of Territorial Force Troops to carry out the Work and endure the Hardships which were incidental to the manoeuvres, 1910'; PRO, WO 32/9192, for discussion of 1911 inspection reports; *ibid.* WO 32/5451, Report of the Committee on Musketry Training for the Territorial Force, 1914; *ibid.* WO 32/7110, DRO to DMT, 24 April 1912; I(mperial) W(ar) M(useum), 79/54/1, Mss of C. J. Low, p. 3; S. Bidwell and D. Graham, *Fire-power*, Allen and Unwin, London, 1982, pp. 50–4; *Official History of the Great War* (hereafter OFH), *Military Operations in France and Belgium, 1914*, II, Macmillan, London, 1925, pp. 300 n. 71, 350.

5　Gooch, 'National Army', pp. 69–86; Howard Moon, 'The Invasion of the United Kingdom: Public Controversy and Official Planning, 1888–1918', unpub. Ph.D., London, 1968, II, p. 413; Michael Allison, 'The National Service Issue, 1899–1914, unpub. Ph.D., London, 1975, pp. 202–6; T. C. Kennedy, *The Hound of Conscience*, University of Arkansas Press, Fayetteville, 1981, p. 18; Spiers, *Haldane*, p. 185; Hugh Cunningham, *The Volunteer Force*, Croom Helm, London, p. 148; J. O. Springhall, *Youth, Empire and Society*, Croom Helm, London, 1977, pp. 29–30, 40, 56, 128 n. 23; Surrey RO, Proceedings of a deputation to the Prime Minister, 26 November 1913 for Seely and Asquith's bland response to Territorial grievances.

6　G. Cassar, *Kitchener: Architect of Victory*, William Kimber, London, 1977, pp. 195–212; K. Neilson, 'Kitchener: a reputation refurbished', *Canadian Journal of History* 15, 2, 1980, pp. 207–27; Peter Simkins, 'Kitchener and the expansion of the army', in Beckett and Gooch (eds.), *Politicians*, pp. 87–109; David French, *British Economic and Strategic Planning, 1905–1915*, Allen and Unwin, London, 1982, pp. 124–37; F. W. Perry, 'Manpower and Organisational Problems in the Expansion of the British and other Commonwealth Armies during the two World Wars', unpub. Ph.D., London, 1982, pp. 35–42, 72–4.

7　C. A. C. Keeson, *The History and Records of the Queen Victoria's Rifles, 1792–1922*, Constable, London, 1922, p. 481; Sir Charles Harris, 'Kitchener and the Territorials: first hours at the War Office', *The Times*, 28 August 1928, p. 13; WOL, TF1, *A Chronological Summary of the Principal Changes in the Organisation and Administration of the Territorial Force since Mobilisation*, 1918, pp. 1–3; General Sir Ivor Maxse, 'The Territorial Army', *Journal of the Royal United Service Institution*, LXXI, 484, 1926, pp. 661–76; Lord Grey, *Twenty-five Years, 1892–1916*, Hodder and Stoughton, London, 1925, II, p. 68; Oxon. RO, Minutes of CTA, 31 October 1914 and 12 December 1914; Colin Hughes, *Mametz: Lloyd George's Welsh Army at the*

Battle of the Somme, Orion Press, Gerrards Cross, 1979, pp. 21–2, 124–5; Perry. 'Manpower', p. 73.

8   Violet Bonham-Carter, *Winston Churchill as I knew him*, Eyre and Spottiswoode, London, 1965, p. 319; Winston S. Churchill, *The World Crisis*, Thornton Butterworth, London, 1931, p. 150; L. S. Amery, *My Political Life: War and Peace*, Hutchinson, London, 1953, II, p. 25; Earl of Midleton, *Records and Reactions, 1859–1939*, John Murray, London, 1939, p. 278; J. A. Spender and C. Asquith, *The Life of H. H. Asquith, Lord Oxford and Asquith*, Hutchinson, London, II, p. 132; Esher Mss, 2/13, diary entry for 13 August 1914 and 7/27, Esher to Brett, 13 August 1914; M. and E. Brock (eds.), *H. H. Asquith: Letters to Venetia Stanley*, Oxford University Press, 1982, pp. 166–9; H. H. Asquith, *Memories and Reflections*, Cassell, London, 1928, II, p. 55; PRO, WO 32/5266, Douglas to Kitchener, 29 September 1914; John Gooch, 'The bolt from the blue', in Gooch, *Prospect of War*, pp. 1–34.

9   Sir John Dunlop, 'The Territorial Army in the early years', *Army Quarterly*, XCIV, 1967, pp. 53–5; Harris, *The Times*, 28 August 1928; Sir Philip Magnus, *Kitchener: Portrait of an Imperialist*, London, Harmondsworth, 1968, p. 347; R. B. Haldane, *An Autobiography*, Hodder and Stoughton, London, 1929, pp. 278–80; A(rmy) M(useum) O(gilby) T(rust), Spenser Wilkinson Papers, OTP 13/36/2, Wilkinson to Asquith, 24 August 1914.

10 Simkins, 'Kitchener', pp. 87–109; M. V. Brett, *The Journals and Letters of Lord Esher*, Nicholson and Watson, London, 1934–38, III, pp. 177–8; PRO, WO 163/21, Minutes of Army Council, 9 August 1914; WOL, TF2, *Miscellaneous Letters during the War Period, July 1914–June 1915*, No. 26, n.d. (7–10 August 1914) note to Needham; No. 230, Note by TF1, 19 October 1914; E. David (ed.), *Inside Asquith's Cabinet*, John Murray, London, 1977, p. 189; PRO, WO 159/3, Memorandum by Kitchener on 'The War', 31 May 1915; IWM, Henry Wilson Mss, Box 73/1/13, File 34A/18, Esher to Duncannon, 24 August 1918 (I owe this reference to Dr Keith Jeffery); PRO, WO 158/931, Memorandum by MT1 7 November 1914; Brock, *Asquith*, p. 261; *OFH, France and Belgium, 1914*, II, pp. 7–8, 486–7; *OFH, Order of Battle of Divisions*, HMSO, London, 1936, IIa, *passim*.

11 WOL, *Chronological Summary*, pp. 1–5; E. A. James, *British Regiments, 1914–18*, Samson, London, 1978, pp. 122–32; Perry, 'Manpower', pp. 72–4, 329–36, 391–6.

12 Dunlop. 'The TA', pp. 53–5; WOL, *Chronological Summary*, pp. 1–5; *ibid., Miscellaneous Letters*, No. 32, Bethune to GOC's, 10 August 1914, and No. 77, note of 31 August 1914; A. A. Taylor (ed.), *From Ypres to Cambrai*, Elmfield Press, Morley, 1974, p. 7; IWM, V. G. Ricketts Mss, p. 9; J. M. Findlay, *With the 8th Scottish Rifles, 1914–18*, Blackie, London and Glasgow, 1926, p. 5; W. N. Nicholson, *Behind the Lines*, Cape, London, 1939, p. 19; PRO, WO 161/104, Oughterson and Mansbridge to Williams, 14 June 1916.

13 IWM, P.246, P. H. Jones Mss, pp. 2–4, quoting diary entries of 11 and 17 August 1914; P. G. Bales, *The History of the 1/4th Duke of Wellington's Regiment, 1914–19*, Edward Mortimer, London and Halifax, 1920, p. 4; IWM, 77/5/1, S. E. Gordon Mss, p. 23; Henry Williamson (ed.), *A Soldier's Diary of the Great War*, Faber and Gwyer, London, 1929, p. 15; PRO, WO 32/5266, Douglas to Kitchener, 29 September 1914; IWM, 79/15/1, W. H. Saunders Mss, p. 13; *ibid.*, L. R. Grant Mss, p. 7.

14 Field Marshal Lord French, *1914*, Constable, London, 1919, p. 293; Martin Gilbert, *Winston S. Churchill*, Heinemann, London, 1971, III, p. 57; IWM, 82/38/1, R. W. F. Johnston Mss, p. 1; *ibid.*, 79/54/1 C. J. Low Mss, letter to Aunt Bell', 8 August 1915; *ibid.*, 77/5/1, S. E. Gordon Mss, p. 22; Oxon. RO,

Minutes of CTA, 12 September 1914, IWM, V. G. Ricketts Mss, p. 16; A. S. Hamilton, *The City of London Yeomanry (Roughriders)*, Hamilton Press, London, 1936, p. 14; John Reith, *Wearing Spurs*, Hutchinson, London, 1966, pp. 26–8.

15 E. V. Tempest, *History of the 1/6th Battalion, the West Yorkshire Regiment*, Lund Humphries, London and Bradford, 1921, p. 5; W. C. Oates, *The Sherwood Foresters in the Great War: the 2/8th Battalion*, J. and H. Bell, Nottingham, 1920, p. 23; R. W. W. Wynn and W. H. Stable, *The Historical Records of the Montgomeryshire Yeomanry, 1909–19*, 1926, II, p. 28; Lord Silsoe, *Sixty Years a Welsh Territorial*, Gomer Press, Llandysul, 1976, pp. 27–8; PRO, WO 161/112, Winder to Williams, 17 October 1917; *ibid.*, Kitchener Papers, 30/57/45, 0047, Maxwell to Fitzgerald, 11 October 1914; IWM, PP/MCR/77, Mss of E. B. Cook, EBC/1, Pitt to Cook, 16 September 1914; Guildhall Library Mss, 17685, Cane to Errington, 12 November 1914.

16 F. P. Gibbons, *The 42nd (East Lancashire) Division*, George Newnes, London, 1920, p. 15; *OFH, Mespotamia Campaign*, HMSO, London, 1923, I, p. 90, 160, 188, 338; WOL, *Miscellaneous Letters*, No. 822, Donald to Wolfe Murray, 6 April 1915; IWM, 79/15/1, W. H. Saunders Mss, I, pp. 38, 46, 52–3, 78; II, pp. 20; Major-General N. Woodyatt, 'The Territorials (Infantry) in India, 1914–20', *Journal of the Royal United Service Institution*, LXVII, 1922, pp. 717–37; Lieutenant-General W. D. S. Brownrigg, 'The development of the Territorial Army', *JRUSI*, LXXXIII, 1938, pp. 485–99; PRO, Cab. 42/2 (also Cab. 22/1), Minutes of War Council, 19 March 1915; Hants. RO, 37M69/3, Minutes of CTA, 15 September 1916; *Hansard*, Fifth Ser., LXXXVI, 1855, Forster, 2 November 1916; T. A. Heathcote, *The Afghan Wars, 1838–1919*, Osprey, London, 1980, pp. 175–6, 189–92, 195–6; General Sir G. Barrow, *The Life of General Sir Charles Monro*, Hutchinson, London, 1931, pp. 230–1; Surrey RO, Minutes of CTA, 7 April 1919; *ibid.*, Minutes of General Purposes Committee, 19 April 1920; Peter Dennis, 'The reconstitution of the Territorial Force, 1918–20', in A. Preston and P. Dennis (eds.), *Swords and Covenants*, Croom Helm, London, 1976, pp. 190–215.

17 *Hansard*, Fifth Ser., LXXIII, 2292, Tennant, 28 July 1915; Clive Hughes, 'Army Recruiting in Gwynedd, 1914–1916', unpub. M.A., Wales, 1983, p. 166; Staffs. RO, Ingestre Estate Papers, D240/E/R/3/85, Molyneaux Seel to Green, 11 December 1914; Surrey RO, Minutes of CTA, 18 October 1915; Perry, 'Manpower', p. 41; WOL, *Miscellaneous Letters*, No. 785, Memorandum of 24 April 1915; *ibid.*, *Chronological Summary*, pp. 12–13; PRO, WO 162/6, 'History of the Development and Work of the Directorate of Organisation, 1914–18', p. 88; WOL, *Returns of the Territorial Force at Home*, 30 August 1915; *The Times*, 16 February 1916, p. 5, and 18 February 1915, p. 3; *Hansard*, Fifth Ser., LXXX, 1340, Tennant, 7 March 1916.

18 *Hansard*, Fifth Ser., LXXXVII, 1446–7, Tennant, 11 January 1916; *ibid.*, LXXX, 1521, Tennant, 8 March 1916; *ibid.*, LXXXII, 644, Tennant, 10 May 1916; *ibid.*, LXXXIII, 1672, Tennant, 6 July 1916; A. K. McGilchrist, *The Liverpool Scottish, 1900–1916*, Young, Liverpool, 1930, p. 160; IWM, PP/MCR/146, A. S. Benbow Mss, p. 19; *ibid.*, 77/5/1, S. E. Gordon Mss, p. 162; W. L. Andrews, *Haunting Years*, Hutchinson, London, n.d., p. 180; R. R. Thompson, *The 52nd (Lowland) Division, 1914–18*, Maclehose Jackson, Glasgow, 1923, p. 246; IWM, V. G. Ricketts Mss, p. 37; *ibid.*, PP/MCR/86, A. G. Williams Mss., p. 199; Staffs. RO, D1300/1/9, Orderly Book of 1/1st Staffs. Yeomanry; *Hansard*, Fifth Ser., LXXXIV, 533 and 820, Forster, 13 and 18 July 1916.

19 Worcs. RO, 004.6, BA 5204/5, Minutes of CTA General Purposes Committee, 1 March 1919, reprints the statement by Army Council dated 21 February

1919.
20 J. H. Lindsay, *The London Scottish in the Great War*, Regimental
Headquarters, London, 1925, pp. 19–20; A. F. L. Bacon, *The Wanderings of a
Temporary Warrior*, Witherby, London, 1922, pp. 32, 47; PRO, Cab.
41/36/19, Asquith to the King, 29 April 1915; *ibid.*, WO 32/5452, Simon to
Kitchener, 29 April 1915; *ibid.*, Derby to Sclater, 2 July 1915; Randolph S.
Churchill, *Lord Derby: King of Lancashire*, Heinemann, London, 1959, pp.
185–6; *Hansard*, Fifth Ser., XIX, 182–199, House of Lords, 1 July 1915; *ibid.*,
347, Heneage and Newton, 8 July 1915; *ibid.*, LXXIII, 350, Cecil and
Tennant, 7 July 1915; *ibid.*, LXXVIII, 1071, Prothero and Tennant, January
1916.
21 PRO, Cab. 22/1, Minutes of War Council, 8 January 1915; *OFH, France and
Belgium, 1914*, I, p. 340; WOL, *Miscellaneous Letters*, No. 489, AG to GOCs,
4 January 1915; *ibid.*, Chronological Summary, pp. 49–54; *ibid.*, *Circular
Instructions affecting the Territorial Force*, HMSO, London, June 1915 and
July 1915, *passim; OFH, Military Operations, Gallipoli*, Heinemann,
London, 1932, II, p. 314; C. H. Dudley-Ward, *History of the 53rd (Welsh)
Division, 1914–18*, Western Mail, Cardiff, 1927, p. 12; P. H. Dalbiac, *History
of the 60th Division*, Allen and Unwin, London, 1927, p. 33; E. May, *Signal
Corporal*, Johnson, London, 1972, p. 19; Oates, *Sherwood Foresters*, pp.
24–25; N(ational) A(rmy) M(useum), 7908–62–2, E. W. S. K. Maconchy
Mss, pp. 439, 448–9, 461; E. U. Bradbridge, *The 59th Division, 1915–18*,
Wilfrid Edmunds, Chesterfield, 1928, p. 6.
22 O. F. Bailey and H. M. Hollier, *The Kensingtons: 13 London Regiment*,
Regimental Old Comrades' Association, London, 1935, pp. 67–8; *Hansard*,
Fifth Ser., LXVIII, 202–3, Hunt and Tennant, 16 November 1914; *ibid.*,
LXXXI, 584–5, Tennant, King and Nield, 28 March 1916; 924–5, Tennant
and Nield, 30 March 1916; 756, Tennant, Needham and Snowden, 29 March
1916; 1367–8, Radford and Tennant, 6 April 1916; 1597, Crooks and Tennant,
11 April 1916; 1789, Markham and Tennant, 12 April 1916; 1977–78, Nield
and Tennant, 13 April 1916; 2092–4, Tennant, 17 April 1916; 2294, Needham
and Tennant, 19 April 1916.
23 WOL, *Chronological Summary*, p. 51; McGilchrist, *Liverpool Scottish*, pp.
261–2; R. H. Haigh and P. W. Turner (eds.), *The Long Carry*, Pergamon,
Oxford, 1970, p. 7; J. Q. Henriques, *The War History of 1st Battalion,
Queen's Westminster Rifles*, Medici Society, London, 1923, pp. 108–9; A.
Rifleman (A. M. Bowes-Smith), *Four Years on the Western Front*, Odhams,
London, 1922, p. 153; IWM, PP/MCR/86, A. G. Williams Mss, p. 316;
Guildhall Library Mss, 12613, 2, Minutes of London CTA, 25 November
1915; Lindsay, *London Scottish*, pp. 345, 381–2; A. S. Dolden, *Cannon
Fodder*, Blandford, Poole, 1980, p. 149.
24 *Hansard*, Fifth Ser., LXXII, 1474, Rolleston and Tennant, 28 June 1915;
LXXIII, 994–5, MacCullum and Tennant, 15 July 1915; LXXXI, 315, Bryce
and Long, 22 March 1916; XCIV, 626, Allen and Macpherson, 11 June 1917;
G. A. Brett, *A History of the 2nd Battalion, the Monmouthshire Regiment*,
Hughes, Pontypool, 1933, pp. 44–5; A. G. Wauchope, *A History of the Black
Watch in the Great War*, Medici Society, London, 1926, II, p. 67; Oxon. RO,
Minutes of CTA, 26 June 1915; Hants. RO, 37M69/3, Minutes of CTA, 16
June 1916; Surrey. RO, Minutes of CTA, General Purposes Committee, 10
April 1916; Worcs. RO, 004.6, BA 5204/5, Minutes CTA, General Purposes
Committee, 8 April 1916; Guildhall Library, Mss, 12613, 2, Minutes of
London CTA, 13 April 1916; PRO, WO 162/6, p. 148; *Hansard*, Fifth Ser.,
107, 1554, Yate and Macpherson; Peter Dennis, 'Reconstitution', pp.
190–215; Peter Dennis, 'The County Associations and the Territorial Army',

Army Quarterly and Defence Journal, 109, 2, 1979, pp. 210–19.

25 NAM, AF Gloucs. 12031, 'Secretary's Report on the Administrative Work of the Gloucestershire CTA during the War', 15 March 1920, p. 35; *OFH, France and Belgium, 1914*, II, pp. 6–7; Hants. RO, 37M69/3, Minutes of CTA, 14 August 1914; Oxon. RO, Minutes of CTA, 30 October 1915 and 27 January 1916; Magnus, *West Riding*, p. 40; NAM, 7209-1-1, Papers of Caernarvon CTA, 1908–36, Ransome to Cookson, 16 December 1914; *ibid.*, Gloucester 'Report', p. 7; PRO, WO 161/104, 'Report on the Work of the County of London Territorial Association', February 1916; NAM, Gloucs. 'Report', pp. 26–34; Worcs. RO, 004.6, BA 5204/5, Minutes of CTA, 26 January 1918; PRO, WO 161/112, Hardis to Williams, 20 February 1918; *ibid.*, Winder to Williams, 17 October 1917; *ibid.*, WO 161/104, 'Report', February 1916; Reynard, *North Riding*, p. 18; PRO, WO 161/112, Parkes to Williams, 16 May 1918.

26 PRO, WO 32/11341, Kitchener to Lords Lieutenant and Chairmen of CTAs, 7 August 1914; French, *British Economic and Strategic Planning*, p. 131; PRO, WO 159/18; Oxon. RO, Minutes of CTA, 12 September and 31 October 1914; Hants. RO, 37M69/3, Minutes of CTA, 18 September 1914; WOL, *Chronological Summary*, p. 53; *ibid.*, *Miscellaneous Letters*, Nos. 20, 51, 96, 116; PRO, Kitchener papers, 30/57/73, WS 59, List of locally raised units; J. M. Osborne, *The Voluntary Recruiting Movement in Britain, 1914–1916*, Garland, New York and London, 1982, p. 113.

27 A. Aiken, *Courage Past*, privately published, Glasgow, 1971, pp. 3–4; W. Sorley Brown, *The War Record of the 4th Battalion, King's Own Scottish Borderers and the Lothian and Border Horse*, John McQueen, Galashiels, 1920, pp. 207–8; AMOT, Spenser Wilkinson Papers, OTP 13/36/4, Wilkinson to Asquith, 18 September 1914; Hansard, Fifth Ser., LXVI, 975, Tennant, 17 September 1914; PRO, WO 161/104, Oughterson and Mansbridge to Williams, 14 June 1916; *ibid.*, Cab. 45/207 (i), Stewart to Vesey, 18 December 1914; Hants. RO, 37M69/3, Minutes of CTA, 18 December 1914; WOL, *Chronological Summary*, p. 19; PRO, WO 159/18, Memorandum, 17 September 1914; Hughes, 'Recruiting', pp. 170–1; Lindsay, *London Scottish*, p. 227; PRO, WO 161/112, Raworth to Williams, 5 October 1917; *ibid.*, Winder to Williams, 17 October 1917; *ibid.*, Parkes to Williams, 16 May 1918; WOL, *Miscellaneous Letters*, No. 997, Memorandum of Director of Recruiting, 19 July 1915; Worcs. RO, 004.6, BA 5204/5, Minutes of CTA, 24 July 1915; Staffs. RO, D797/2/2, Blizzard Scrapbooks, for recruiting drives of 3/5th North Staffs; Hants. RO, 37M69/3, Minutes of CTA, 21 May 1915; Surrey RO, Minutes of CTA, 28 May 1915, and Minutes of General Purposes Committee, 19 April and 10 May 1915; *Statistics of the Military Effort of the British Empire, 1914–1920*, HMSO, London, 1922, pp. 365–6; PRO, NATS 1/399.

28 PRO, Kitchener Papers, 30/57/59, W1/10, Esher to Kitchener, 10 September 1914; *ibid.*, WO 161/104, 'Report'; Reynard, *North Riding*, pp. 22–3; NAM, Gloucs. 'Report', p. 12, WOL, *Miscellaneous Letters*, No. 13, Note for Secretary of State, 5 August 1914; PRO, WO 163/21, Minutes of Army Council, 30 October and 21 November 1916; *The Times*, 27 January 1917, p. 7; Oxon. RO, Minutes of CTA, 27 January 1917; Guildhall Library Mss, 12613, 2, Minutes of London CTA, 20 February 1917; PRO, WO 161/110, WO Order, 29 March 1917; Hants. RO, 37M69/3, Minutes of CTA, 16 March and 19 April 1917; *ibid.*, 37M69/4, Minutes of CTA, 21 December 1917 and 23 January 1918; Minutes of CCTA, 17 September, 4 October and 7 November 1917 and 9 January 1918; PRO, WO 162/6, p. 68; Guildhall Library Mss, 12613, 2, Minutes of CTA, 15 November 1917; Worcs. RO 004.6, BA 5204/5,

Minutes of CTA, General Purposes Committee, 20 October 1917; Oxon. RO, Minutes of CTA, 27 October 1917; WOL, *Chronological Summary*, pp. 6–11, 53–5, 59–61, 62a; Reynard, *North Riding*, p. 31; Surrey RO, Minutes of CTA, 23 April 1917.

29 Andrews, *Haunting Years*, p. 98; IWM, V. G. Ricketts Mss, p. 16; *ibid.*, PP/MCR/86, A. G. Williams Mss, p. 86; E. H. G. Roberts, *The Story of the 1/9th King's in France*, Northern Publishing, Liverpool, 1922, p. 34; A. Behrend, *Make me a Soldier*, Eyre and Spottiswoode, London, 1961, p. 114; Taylor, *Ypres to Cambrai*, pp. 81–3; Rifleman, *Four Years*, p. 25. The 1/13th London (Kensingtons) became unpopular with regular units when a letter from a former journalist in their ranks claiming that they alone had reached objectives at Festubert was printed in *The Times* in July 1915, PRO, WO 32/4893. French to Kitchener, 9 August 1915, quoted in C. J. Lovelace, 'Control and Censorship of the Press during the 1st World War', unpub. Ph.D., London, 1982, pp. 81–2.

30 Nicholson, *Behind the Lines*, p. 207; E. Riddell and M. C. Clayton, *The Cambridgeshires, 1914–18*, Bowes and Bowes, Cambridge, 1934, p. 30; V. F. Eberle, *My Sapper Venture*, Pitman, London, 1973, p. 34; IWM, 79/54/1, C. J. Low Mss, letter to wife, 25 August 1915; *ibid.*, 78/22/1, C. L. A. Ward-Jackson Mss, letters of 1 May, 13 October and 21 October 1915; *ibid.*, 77/5/1, S. E. Gordon Mss, p. 53; *ibid.*, DS/MISC/26, E. Marchant Mss, letter of 22 December 1914; *OFH, France and Belgium, 1914*, II, p. 300, n. 71; R. F. K. Goldsmith, 'Territorial vanguard: a London Scottish diary', *Army Quarterly and Defence Journal*, 103, 2, 1976, pp. 230–8; IWM, R. W. F. Johnston Mss, Johnston to Suddaby, July 1983; F. W. Bewsher, *The History of the 51st (Highland) Division, 1914–18*, Blackwood, Edinburgh and London, 1921, p. 30; Tempest, *1/6th West Yorks*, p. 34; N. Tennant, 'A Yorkshire Terrier', *Stand to*, 9, 1983, pp. 10–12.

31 Beckett, *Riflemen Form*, pp. 135, 186–7, 225, 246; Brian Bond, 'The Territorial Army in peace and war', *History Today*, XVI, 3 March 1966, pp. 157–66; Howard Green, *The British Army in the First World War*, privately published, London, 1968, pp. 36–45; *Hansard*, Fifth Ser., LXXXVI, 833, Ashley and Forster, 19 October 1916; *ibid.*, XC, 1313, Blake and Macpherson, 21 February 1917; *ibid.*, 2197 and 2229–31, Tennant and Macpherson, 1 March 1917; *ibid.*, XCI, 78, Croft and Macpherson, 5 March 1917; *The Times*, 30 January 1918, p. 10; *Hansard*, Fifth Ser., CIII, 936–7, Croft and Macpherson, February 1918; G. H. Barnett, *With the 48th Division in Italy*, Blackwood, London and Edinburgh, 1923, p. x; Silsoe, *Sixty Years*, pp. 20, 49, 76; J. M. A. Tamplin, *The Lambeth and Southwark Volunteers*, Regimental Historical Fund, 1965, pp. 211–380; Surrey RO, Minutes of CTA, 7 April 1919; IWM, W. H. Saunders Mss, III, pp. 30–1; T. Ashworth, *Trench Warfare, 1914–18: the Live and Let Live System*, Macmillan, London, 1980, p. 87; AMOT, Spenser Wilkinson Papers, OTP 13/24, Hamilton of Dalzell to Wilkinson, 3 February 1915; Lieutenant Colonel the Hon. S. Peel, MP, 'The Territorial Force', *Army Quarterly*, I, 1, 1920–21, 36–54; IWM, 80/32/2, Christie-Miller Mss, pp. 112, 122–4, 189, 364–5.

32 IWM, 80/32/2, Christie-Miller Mss, pp. 341–2; *ibid.*, 82/38/1, R. W. F. Johnston Mss, answer to questionnaire, pp. 2–4; Robert Graves, *Goodbye to all that*, Cape, London, 1929, pp. 123–5; Dennis Wheatley, *Officer and Temporary Gentleman, 1914–19*, Hutchinson, London, 1978, pp. 123–28; Reith, *Wearing Spurs*, *passim*; IWM, 79/3/1, I. L. Meo diaries, entry for 14 July 1915; A. Behrend, *As from Kemmel Hill*, Eyre and Spottiswoode, London, 1963; p. 24; IWM, 78/22/1, C. L. A. Ward-Jackson Mss, letter of 1

May 1915; C. M. Slack, *Grandfather's Adventures in the Great War, 1914–18*, A. H. Stockwell, Ilfracombe, 1977, pp. 74–5.

33 AMOT, Spenser Wilkinson Papers, OTP 13/36/6, Wilkinson to Asquith, 27 September 1914, and Wilkinson to Kitchener, 25 September 1914; WOL, *Chronological Summary*, p. 69; IWM, 79/54/1, C. J. Low Mss, letters of 22 February and 14 March 1915; Cd 8642 (1917), Report of the Committee on the Promotion of Officers in the Special Reserve, New Armies and Territorial Force, 9 May 1917; M. M. Haldane, *A History of the 4th Battalion, the Seaforth Highlanders*, H. F. and G. Witherby, London, 1927, p. 325. See also CCTA Minutes for 11 September and 23 October 1918 for a dispute on the precedence of New Army and Territorial units in the *Army List* and official *Gazette*.

34 *Hansard*, Fifth Ser., LXVI, 563, Newman and Tennant, 9 September 1914; WOL, *Miscellaneous Letters*, No. 155, Bethune to Military Secretary, 28 September 1914; H. A. R. May, *Memories of the Artists Rifles*, Howlett, London, 1929, p. 143–44; *Regimental Roll of Honour and War Record of the Artists Rifles*, Howlett, London, 1922, p. xviii; IWM, W. T. Colyer Mss, I, pp. 395–6, 404; II, p. 7; AMOT, Regimental Files, file of the 27th London (Inns of Court) OTC: *Statistics of the Military Effort*, pp. 234–5.

35 Remark by General Sir E. C. Bethune at RUSI, 11 October 1922, *JRUSI*, LXVII, 1922, p. 735; IWM, P391T, Creyke to Bacon, 20 December 1914 and 26 January 1915; R. Hamilton, *The War Diary of the Master of Belhaven, 1914–18*, John Murray, London, 1924, pp. 173, 179, *OFH, Gallipoli*, II, p. 320; PRO, Cab. 45/249, Diary of Major General Egerton, pp. 28–9, 31, 56, 58, 78–80; *ibid.*, WO 32/3116, Report of the Committee on the Lessons of the Great War, October 1932, pp. 35–7, 51; Beckett, *Riflemen Form*, p. 181; PRO, WO 32/5048, Notes on a Conference on Volunteer Policy, 4 September 1917, for remarks by Macready; *ibid.*, Cab. 22/1, Minutes of War Council, 7, 8 and 13 January 1915; *ibid.*, Kitchener Papers, 30/57/50, WA77, French to Kitchener, 7 March 1915; *The Times*, 9 January 1917, p. 3; Richard Holmes, *The Little Field Marshal: Sir John French*, Cape, London, 1981, p. 256; Liddell-Hart Centre for Military Archives, Kiggell Papers, I/38, Haig to Kiggell, 4 October 1914, and I/39 Haig to Kiggell, 12 October 1914; PRO, Kitchener Papers, 30/57/51, WB19a, Rawlinson to Kitchener, 21 April 1915.

36 IWM, A. D. Talbot Mss, 16, Talbot to Slingsby, 30 May 1915; *ibid.*, 77/5/1 S. E. Gordon Mss, p. 265; *ibid.*, P229, H. E. Trevor Mss, HET/1, Trevor to Parker, 24 December 1914, and HET/3, Trevor to Parker, 21 March 1915, Berks. RO, D/EBy 013, Peyton to Henderson, 13 October 1915; J. Brent Wilson, 'The Morale and Discipline of the BEF, 1914–1918', unpub. M.A., New Brunswick, 1978, pp. 85–6; WOL, *Miscellaneous Letters*, No. 452, 'Report' by DMT, 21 December 1914; *ibid.*, No. 516, Order of C-in-C, 11 January 1915; *ibid.*, No. 822, Donald to Wolfe Murray, 6 April 1915; Woodyatt, 'Territorials in India', pp. 717–37; PRO, Cab. 45/249, Egerton diary, p. 94; Cd 1734 (1922), Report of the War Office Committee of Enquiry into Shell Shock, 1922, pp. 45–6, evidence of J. G. Burnett; *ibid.*, WO 32/3116, Kirke Report, pp. 35–7.

37 Brent Wilson, 'Morale and discipline', pp. 191–9, for comparison of 46th and 56th divisions on the Somme; IWM, X/WFS/1/6, W. F. Scott Mss, 10 May 1915; Bewsher, *51st Division*, pp. 3–4, 411; *ibid.*, P229, H. E. Trevor Mss, HET/3, letter of 21 March 1915; C. Messenger, *Terriers in the Trenches: the History of the Post Office Rifles*, Picton, Chippenham, 1982, p. 129; Staffs. RO, D1300/1/9, shows only twenty-four men of the 1/1st Staffordshire Yeomanry on field punishment No. 2 and none on field punishment No. 1 between 12 December 1915 and 12 February 1916; *ibid.*, D1300/3/13, shows

seven men absent without leave from December 1914 to August 1915; IWM, 80/32/2, Christie-Miller Mss, p. 85–6.

38 A. French, *Gone for a Soldier*, Roundwood Press, Kineton, 1972, p. 29; Eberle, *Sapper*, p. 102; Haldane, *4th Seaforths*, p. 143; Hughes, 'Recruiting', p. 164, referring to 1/4th RWF; IWM, E. D. Kingsley Mss, pp. 19–20; W. H. A. Groom, *Poor Bloody Infantry*, William Kimber, London, 1976, p. 45; B. Latham, *A Territorial Soldier's War*, Gale and Polden, Aldershot, 1967, p. 23; Rifleman, *Four Years*, pp. 92–3, 247; IWM, PP/MCR/86, A. G. Williams Mss, p. 63; M. Brown, *Tommy goes to War*, Dent, London, 1978, p. 39; Lindsay, *London Scottish*, pp. 382–3; Tempest, *1/6th West Yorks*, pp. 44–5; Pat M. Morris, 'The Leeds Rifles and the First World War', paper read at RMA, Sandhurst, November 1978 (Mrs Morris's doctoral thesis, 'Leeds and the Amateur Military Tradition: the Leeds Rifles and its antecedents, 1815–1918', unpub. Ph.D., Leeds, 1983, will be available shortly); IWM, PP/MCR/137, E. Scullin Mss, p. 155; *ibid.*, 48/15, sound records transcript of interview with General Sir Philip Neame, VC, p. 9; Green, *British Army*, pp. 36–45; IWM, 82/38/1, R. W. F. Johnston Mss, pp. 70–1; A. F. Barnes, *The Story of 2/5th Battalion, the Gloucestershire Regiment, 1914–18*, Crypt House Press, Gloucester, 1930, pp. 42, 85; M. Moynihan, *A Place called Armageddon*, David and Charles, Newton Abbot, 1975, pp. 120–1; J. Nettleton, *The Anger of the Guns*, William Kimber, London, 1979, pp. 16–22; IWM, PP/MCR/175, E. C. Palmer Mss, pp. 16–18; Hughes, 'Recruiting', pp. 172–3.

39 Behrend, *Make me a Soldier*, pp. 25–6; N. Gladden, *The Somme, 1916*, William Kimber, London, 1974, pp. 100–6; N. Gladden, *Ypres, 1917*, William Kimber, London, 1967, pp. 16–17; F. A. J. Taylor, *The Bottom of the Barrel*, Regency Press, London and New York, 1978, p. 47; Nettleton, *Anger of Guns*, p. 30; W. V. Tilsley, *Other Ranks*, Cobden-Sanderson, London, 1931, p. 173 and *passim*; IWM, L. R. Grant Mss, p. 15; Wheatley, *Temporary Gentleman*, p. 76; E. G. Godfrey, *The Cast Iron Sixth: a History of the 6th Battalion, London Regiment*, F. S. Stapleton, London, 1938, pp. 180–2; G. A. Strutt, *The Derbyshire Yeomanry War History, 1914–19*, Bemrose, Derby and London, n.d., pp. 90–1; M. L. Melville, *The Story of the Lovat Scouts, 1900–1980*, St Andrew Press, Edinburgh, 1981, p. 26; Peel, 'Territorial Force', pp. 36–54; Perry, 'Manpower', p. 25.

40 R. Pound, *The Lost Generation*, Constable, London, 1964, p. 72; IWM, DS/MISC/75, J. K. Stanford Mss, p. 20–2; W. R. Kingham, *London Gunners*, Methuen, London, 1919, p. xiii; Wheatley, *Temporary Gentleman*, p. 55; Beckett, *Riflemen Form*, pp. 39–90; PRO, Cab. 45/249, Egerton diary, pp. 28–9, 117; IWM, P.430, H. E. Politzer Mss, unsigned letters from RMS *Aragon*, 10, 13 and 14 September 1914; *ibid.*, PP/MCR/77, E. B. Cook Mss, EBC/3, Pitt to Cook, 16 September 1914; Nicholson, *Behind the Lines*, pp. 9, 40–1; Silsoe, *Sixty Years*, p. 17; Gladden, *Somme*, p. 24; IWM, PP/MCR/175, E. C. Palmer Mss, p. 7; Taylor, *Bottom of Barrel*, p. 34; Bradbridge, *59th Division*, pp. 5–6; E. Wyrall, *The History of the 62nd (West Riding) Division, 1914–1918*, Bodley Head, London, n.d., pp. 3–4; Morris, 'Leeds Rifles'; Tempest, *1/6th West Yorks*, pp. 4–5; Roberts, *1/9th King's*, p. 8; Thompson, *52nd Division*, pp. 6–10; Riddell and Clayton, *Cambridgeshires*, pp. 1–2; R. Palmer, *Letters from Mesopotamia*, Women's Printing Society, London, n.d., p. 20; G. Harbottle, *Civilian Soldier*, privately published, Newcastle, 1983, p. 10; C. E. Carrington, *Soldier from the Wars Returning*, Hutchinson, London, 1965, p. 101; J. F. Tucker, *Johnny get your Gun*, William Kimber, London, 1978, pp. 16–19; IWM, 79/15/1, W. H. Saunders Mss, p. 4; Oxon. RO, Minutes of CTA, 31 October 1914; Denis

Winter, *Death's Men*, Allen Lane, London, 1978, p. 156; C. W. Thompson, *Records of the Dorset Yeomanry, 1914–19*, Bennett, Sherborne, 1921, p. 121; Moynihan, *Armageddon*, p. 107; Strutt, *Derbyshire Yeomanry*, p. 8; author interviews with Mr L. Burnham (16 June 1980), Captain C. H. Perkins (18 June 1980), Mr. C. E. Pitcher (9 July 1980), Messrs J. and S. Lawrence (22 May 1981); Burnham Papers, Mss, History of 2/1st Royal Bucks Hussars. Lord Burnham, honorary colonel of the Royal Bucks Hussars, was criticised by the War Office for offering illegal bonuses to estate workers to enlist – see Osborne, *Voluntary Recruiting*, pp. 24–6.

41 Wheatley, *Temporary Gentleman*, pp. 53–4; A. H. Maude (ed.), *The 47th (London) Division, 1914–19*, Amalgamated Press, London, 1922, pp. 6–7; Morris, 'Leeds Rifles'; Brett, *2nd Monmouthshire*, p. 34; D. Sutherland, *War Diary of the 5th Seaforth Highlanders*, Bodley Head, London, 1920, p. 3; F. A. M. Webster, *The History of the 5th Battalion, Beds. and Herts. (T.A.)*, Frederick Warne, London, 1930, p. 247; Haldane, *4th Seaforths*, p. 309; Tempest, *1/6th West Yorks*, pp. 280–1; IWM, A. Roberts Mss, Roberts to Burleigh, 17 May 1916; S. F. Hatton, *The Yarn of a Yeoman*, Hutchinson, London, n.d., p. 87; IWM, H. M. Allen Mss, letters of 7, 8, 9 and 10 November 1916; WOL, *Circular Instructions*, December 1915; Guildhall Library Mss, 17686, Inns of Court OTC, Press cuttings on recruiting, 1915–18; G. Greenwell, *An Infant in Arms*, Allen Lane, second edition, London, 1972, pp. 143–5 (the letters are now in IWM). For examples of 'misfits' as officers see the self-revealing E. Campion Vaughan, *Some Desperate Glory*, Frederick Warne, London, 1981, *passim*, and IWM, I. L. Meo diaries, *passim*.

42 Greenwell, *Infant in Arms*, pp. 144–5; Harbottle, *Civilian Soldier*, p. 47; E. C. Matthews, *With the Cornwall Territorials on the Western Front*, W. P. Spalding, Cambridge, 1921, pp. 1–2; D. Mackenzie, *The 6th Gordons in France and Flanders*, Rosemount Press, Aberdeen, 1921, pp. 226–36; Hughes, 'Recruiting', p. 197; P. Macgill, *The Amateur Army*, Herbert Jenkins, London, 1915, p. 15; Silsoe, *Sixty Years*, pp. 18–19; Hants. RO, 37M69/3, Minutes of CTA, 18 December 1914; Bewsher, *51st Division*, pp. 6–7; Dudley-Ward, *53rd Division*, p. 13; PRO, Cab. 45/249, Egerton diary, pp. 29–30; James, *British Regiments*, p. 43; *A History of the Prince of Wales' Own Civil Service Rifles*, Wyman, London, 1921, pp. 394–5; IWM, 79/54/1 C. J. Low Mss, letter of 14 August 1915; *ibid.*, E. K. Foreman Mss, letter of 20 September 1915; Worcs. RO, 705:198, BA 5334/1, letter of J. S. Preeece to mother, 24 October 1915; Burnham Papers, Mss, History of 2/1st Royal Bucks Hussars. Territorial artillery units changed formations so frequently that 'sometimes we did not know ourselves what division we were with': P. J. Campbell, *The Ebb and Flow of Battle*, Hamish Hamilton, London, 1977, p. 107.

43 French, *1914*, pp. 262–4; C. R. M. F. Cruttwell, *The War Service of the 1/4th Royal Berks. (TF)*, Blackwell, Oxford, 1922, pp. 47, 99; PRO, Cab. 45/249, Egerton diary, pp. 28–9; IWM, PP/MCR/86, A. G. Williams Mss; Palmer, *Letters from Mesopotamia*, pp. 41–2, 47; Tucker, *Johnny*, p. 21; Haldane, *1/4th Seaforths*, p. 142; *The War History of the 6th Battalion. South Staffordshire Regiment*, Heinemann, London, 1924, pp. 75, 221–41; Bales, *1/4th DWR*, p. 38; *Statistics of the Military Effort*, pp. 324–8; Tempest, *1/6th West Yorks*, pp. 311–45; Findlay, *With the 8th Scottish Rifles*, pp. 226–37; Major-General Swann, *The 2nd Bucks Battalion*, Bucks CTA, Aylesbury, 1930, pp. 30–8; *Soldiers Died in the Great War*, HMSO, London, I, pp. 75–6; *ibid.*, 47, pp. 53–63.

44 Carrington, *Soldier from the Wars Returning*, pp. 199–229; Greenwell, *Infant*

in Arms, pp. 139, 156; Latham, *Territorial Soldier's War*, p. 59; Andrews, *Haunting Years*, p. 213; Rifleman, *Four Years*, pp. 153, 332; Groom, *Poor Bloody Infantry*, p. 45; Martin Middlebrook, *The Kaiser's Battle*, Allen Lane, London, 1978, pp. 88, 91; Graham Greenwell to author, 19 March 1979; C. E. Wurtzburg, *The History of 2/6th Battalion, the King's (Liverpool) Regiment*, Gale and Polden, Aldershot, 1920, pp. 2, 13; Tempest, *1/6th West Yorks*, pp. 280–1; Haldane, *4th Seaforths*, pp. 321–3; Thompson, *Dorset Yeomanry*, p. 132; IWM, P246, P. H. Jones Mss, pp. 175–7, 211, *ibid.*, 79/15/1, W. H. Saunders Mss, II, pp. 51–3; Messenger, *Terriers*, p. 114; R. H. Haigh and P. W. Turner, 'The German breakthrough, March 1918', in R. H. Haigh and P. W. Turner, *World War One and the Serving British Soldier*, MA/AH Publishing, Kansas State University, 1979, POL/8/77, p. 33; Tucker, *Johnny*, p. 60; W. A. V. Churton, *The War Record of the 1/5th Battalion, the Cheshire Regiment*, Phillipson and Golder, Chester, 1920, p. 102; Matthew, *Cornwall Territorials*, pp. 114–16; Bradbridge, *59th Division*, pp. 171–2.

45 A. L. Raines, *The 5th Battalion, Durham Light Infantry, 1914–18*, privately published, 1931, p. 175; E. Wyrall, *The History of the 50th Division, 1914–19*, Lund Humphries, London, 1939, pp. 349–53; Dudley-Ward, *53rd Division*, p. 214; Dalbiac, *60th Division*, pp. 219–23; Silsoe, *Sixty Years*, pp. 105–10. The fate of the 50th, 53rd and 60th divisions invalidates the notion of Martin Middlebrook in *The First Day on the Somme*, Allen Lane, London, 1977, p. 39, and repeated in *The Kaiser's Battle*, p. 90, that Territorial divisions remained exclusive throughout the war.

46 I. F. W. Beckett, 'The amateur military tradition in England: a case study of Victorian Buckinghamshire', *Journal of the Society for Army Historical Research*, LIX, 238 and 239, 1981, pp. 91–110, 161–70; author interview with Messrs A. and H. Wootton (9 June 1982); interview of Mr J. C. Pemberton, University of Buckingham, with Mr Hedges, 18 March 1974; J. B. Clark to author, 9 June 1980; Bucks. RO, T/A, 1/60, Draft of 'Citizen Soldiers', pp. 71, 85, 90–1; *ibid.*, T/A, 1/26, Correspondence file, Fremantle to Barnett, 16 October 1908; *ibid.*, Fremantle to Crouch, 21 September 1908; *ibid.*, Fremantle to Christie-Miller, 1 June 1909; *ibid.*, Fremantle to Cave, 19 October 1909; *ibid.*, Fremantle to Mosley, 18 December 1908; *ibid.*, Fremantle Mss, D/FR/A/78, Cuyler to Fremantle, 2 September 1908; *ibid.*, Williams to Fremantle, 9 May 1908; *ibid.*, Williams to Fremantle, 14 October 1909; *ibid.*, D/FR/A/79, Christie-Miller to Fremantle, 21 May 1909; *ibid.*, T/A, 6/1, Muster Rolls of 1st Bucks. Batallion, 1908, and T/A, 6/2, Aylesbury Company, 1909–14; Oscar Viney, 'Reminiscences', typescript, 1960, p. 71; PRO, W032/6602: Bucks. RO, T/A, 1/1 Minutes of CTA, 7 March 1912: *ibid.*, T/A, 1/4, Minutes of General Purposes Committee, 14 November 1913; Minutes of CCTA, 15 May 1913; Bucks. RO, T/A, 1/22, Annual Report, 1913/14.

47 Bucks. RO, T/A, 1/6, Minutes of CTA, Finance Committee, 3 September 1914; Swann, *2nd Bucks*, p. 4; Bucks. RO, T/A, 1/1, Minutes of CTA, 12 September 1914 and 13 March 1925; *ibid.*, T/A, 1/13, Minutes of CTA, Emergency Committee, 5 September, 14 November 1914; *ibid.*, T/A, 7/1 'Recruiting File', Campbell to Buckinghamshire, 28 December 1914; *ibid.*, T/A, 1/13, Minutes of CTA, Recruiting Committee, 5 November 1914 and 18 January 1915; *ibid.*, T/A, 1/4, Minutes of General Purposes Committee, 3 September 1914; *ibid.*, T/A, 1/22, Annual Report, 1914–15; WOL, *Miscellaneous Letters*, No. 576, memorandum of 3 February 1915; Major General J. C. Swann, *Citizen Soldiers of Bucks, 1795–1926*, Hazell Watson and Viney, Aylesbury, 1930, pp. 52–3.

48 Bucks. RO, T/A, 1/13, Minutes of CTA, Recruiting Committee, 4 November 1914, 18 January, 10 May, 12 August, 21 October and 17 November 1915; *ibid.*, T/A, 7/1, 'Recruiting'; *ibid.*, T/A, 7/17, *passim*, for reports by Green, and T/A, 7/18, 'National Service' file on tribunal statistics; PRO, WO 159/3, memorandum on 'The War', 31 May 1915; *Bucks Herald*, 5 January 1918; Bucks RO, T/A, 1/4, Minutes of CTA, General Purposes Committee, 5 January 1918.

49 Bucks RO, T/A, 1/4, Minutes of CTA, General Purposes Committee, 6 April, 4 and 5 October 1916, 4 October 1917, 2 January and 6 February 1919; *ibid.*, T/A, 1/1, Minutes of CTA, 2 March 1916 and 7 March 1918; *ibid.*, T/A, 1/22, Annual Report, 1914/1915; IWM, 80/32/1, Christie-Miller Papers, WO to Bucks. CTA, 23 January 1919. For details of the Bucks Volunteers between 1914 and 1918, see I. F. W. Beckett, 'The local community and the Great War: aspects of military participation', *Records of Bucks*, XX, 4, 1978, pp. 503–15.

50 *Bucks Free Press*, 21 August 1914; L. W. Crouch, *Duty and Service: Letters from the Front*, privately published, Aylesbury, 1917, pp. 24–5; Viney, 'Reminiscences', pp. 70–4, IWM, 80/32/2, Christie-Miller Mss, pp. 28–9, 66–8, 79; Bucks. RO, D/X, 780/29, Diary of C. P. Phipps, 28 May 1915; author interview with Messrs J. Stammers, A. Seymour and J. Tranter (25 November 1980); Bucks. RO, T/A, 1/1, Minutes of CTA, 7 April 1910. Not all men of the 1/1st Bucks with family responsibilities opted for home service – see IWM, P.329T, Gilbert Nash Mss, letters of a married man with three children, who died of wounds on 9 May 1915.

51 F. H. Cripps, *Life's a Gamble*, Odhams, London, 1957, pp. 97, 114–15; author interview with Mr L. Burnham (16 June 1980), Captain C. H. Perkins (18 June 1980), Mr C. E. Pitcher (9 July 1980) and Messrs J. and S. Lawrence (22 May 1981); Bucks. RO, T/A, 3/25, Order Book of 3/1st Royal Bucks. Hussars, 1915; Burnham Papers, Mss, History of 2/1st Royal Bucks Hussars; *ibid.*, Frederick Lawson to W. A. W. Lawson of 6 November 1915 and 11 January 1916; *ibid.*, 'Elephant' to W. A. W. Lawson, 16 January 1916; Bucks. RO, T/A, 1/1, Minutes of CTA, 5 July 1917; PRO, W095/4293, War Diary of 1/1st Royal Bucks. Hussars; *ibid.*, WO 95/4506, War Diary of 1/1st Royal Bucks. Hussars.

52 Crouch, *Duty and Service*, p. 84; Burnham Papers, Frederick Lawson to H. L. W. Lawson, 19 February 1916 and 24 July 1917; Swann, *Citizen Soldiers*, pp. 58–77; P. L. Wright, *The First Bucks. Battalion*, Hazel Watson and Viney, Aylesbury and London, 1920, pp. 16–17, 36, 43, 83, 215–16; IWM, 74/136/1, L. L. C. Reynolds Correspondence Books, entries for 11 April 1917, 23 June, 15 and 27 July, 20 September, 22 December 1917, 24 and 30 March, 6 April, 7 and 8 May, 9 September 1918, for comments on officer quality and discipline in 1/1st Bucks; Ashworth, *Trench Warfare*, p. 131; Bucks. RO, T/A, 6/11–14, 'Casualty' Books for 1/1st Bucks, 1915–18, *passim*; author interview with Lieutenant-Colonel Howard Green, 22 February 1980; Graham Greenwell to author, 13 February 1979; C. E. Carrington to author, 20 January 1977; Swann, *2nd Bucks. Battalion*, pp. 15, 23, 25; IWM, 80/32/2, Christie-Miller Mss, pp. 125–9, 174, 198, 206, 211–12, 374; PRO, WO 95/2763, War Diary of 1/1st Bucks.; *ibid.*, WO 95/3066, War Diary of 2nd Bucks.

53 PRO, WO 163/23, Minutes of Army Council, 11 December 1918; *The Times*, 28 December 1918, p. 3, and 30 December 1918, p. 5; PRO, PIN 15/205; *Statistics of the Military Effort*, p. 238. For post-war developments see Dennis, 'Reconstitution', pp. 190–215; Dennis, 'County Associations', pp. 210–19; Peter Dennis, 'The Territorial Army in aid of the civil power in Britain, 1919–26', *Journal of Contemporary History*, 16, 1981, pp. 705–24.

Peter Simkins **6**

Soldiers and civilians:
billeting in Britain and France

One of the biggest problems caused by the rapid expansion of the army in 1914 was that of housing the enormous numbers of volunteers who flocked to the recruiting offices in the early months of the war. At the beginning of August there was only enough accommodation in barracks for 174,800 single men,[1] yet during that month alone 298,923 men joined the army, and in the first week of September some 30,000 recruits were daily being attested, a figure which represented the average *yearly* intake before the war. By the end of September the number of enlistments since the start of hostilities had risen to 761,824, and on 31 December the total stood at 1,186,357.[2]

I

The War Office had, in fact, wasted little time in trying to tackle the accommodation problem. On 9 August 1914, two days after the publication of Kitchener's initial appeal for volunteers, the Military Members of the Army Council agreed that a scheme should be prepared at once for the quartering of the New Expeditionary Force, as the First New Army was then called. They also recommended that recruits should stay at the regimental depots for about a week before being sent to training centres, where the barracks being vacated by units of the original British Expeditionary Force could be used to house the new formations.[3] Over the next few days specific training centres were selected for the six divisions of the First New Army. The 9th (Scottish) and 14th (Light) Divisions were to be concentrated in and around Aldershot, with the 10th (Irish) Division at Dublin and the Curragh and the 12th (Eastern) Division at Colchester.[4] To avoid overcrowding at Colchester, some units of the 12th Division would go to Shorncliffe in Kent and the Purfleet area in Essex, the troops at Purfleet being housed in tents pending the construction of huts.[5] The 11th (Northern) Division would be quartered at Belton Park, near Grantham, while Tidworth, on Salisbury Plain, was chosen as the training centre for the 13th (Western) Division, although at least one of its three infantry brigades would have to go under canvas until huts had been erected at Chiseldon, near Swindon.[6] Contracts for a divisional hutment at Grantham and a brigade hutment were issued as early as 23 August.

In the meantime, the design branch of the Directorate of Fortification and Works had produced a complete set of drawings for a standard hutted camp to house one infantry battalion at war strength. These plans, which were intended to serve as a model for any future construction programme, received Army Council approval by 17 August.[7] Nine days later, on the 26th, an attempt was made to streamline the machinery for the quartering of troops. The old Directorate of Supplies and Quartering in the Quartermaster General's

Department was split into two distinct branches, and Major-General C. E. Heath was appointed Director of Quartering and given a strengthened staff, including an experienced engineer officer from the retired list as Assistant Director.[8] However, as the recruiting figures continued to climb it became clear that the scale of the task had been seriously underestimated. What made matters worse was that, in failing to impose some sort of ceiling upon enlistments until the depots and training centres were able to cope with the flow of recruits, Kitchener undermined the work of the Quartering Directorate as it strove to keep its planning in step with the actual rate of expansion of the army.

Not surprisingly, the regimental depots were overwhelmed by the massive influx of men who, in the last week of August and the first half of September 1914, were pouring in much faster than the depot staffs could process them and post them to training centres. Returns submitted to the War Office on 29 August revealed that many depots, designed to house between 250 and 500 men in peacetime, were bursting at the seams. Fifteen depots contained well over 1,000 recruits, and one, the depot of the South Staffordshire Regiment at Lichfield, was crammed with 2,408 men. On 30 August depot commanders were instructed to dispatch recruits to training centres without delay, whether they had received uniforms or not, but by 12 September the total for all arms at depots was a staggering 312,000 and six infantry depots now contained more than 2,000 recruits each. The Cheshire Regiment's depot at Chester had as many as 3,052.[9]

With every inch of space taken up and with thousands of men sleeping in the open, depot staffs turned to local authorities, Church organisations and private citizens for assistance in housing the overflow of recruits. At Preston, where Fulwood Barracks was the depot for both the East Lancashire and Loyal North Lancashire Regiments, the mayor, Alderman H. Cartmell, noted that men asked for permission to sleep in suburban gardens, 'declining the offer of a bed, but not too proud to accept a certain breakfast there rather than an uncertain one at the barracks'. When the weather deteriorated, the people of Preston welcomed soldiers into their homes, transformed schools and clubs into dormitories and provided entertainments and hotpot suppers for the men. These gestures were repeated in towns and cities throughout the country. Householders in Inverness allowed recruits of the Cameron Highlanders to write letters and air clothes in their sitting rooms, an arrangement which was greatly appreciated, as a large number of men were obliged to sleep on the stone floor of a local distillery, where there were no heating or drying facilities.[10]

Such hospitality did not always alleviate the difficulties. For example, at Richmond in Yorkshire, where at one stage 5,000 recruits of the Green Howards were housed in barracks and billets, the local gentry, farmers and townspeople furnished blankets and straw, opened recreation rooms and supplied free meals, but the town was so congested that 500 men from Middlesbrough and Sunderland had to be sent home on extended leave. Moreover, despite all the efforts of the inhabitants of Preston to relieve the pressure on the depot there, some 250 Welsh recruits left Fulwood Barracks on 11 September and headed for the railway station, carrying a banner which read 'No Food, No Shelter, No Money'. Only after a police inspector, a Member of Parliament and the mayor had agreed in turn to investigate their complaints were the men persuaded to go back to the depot.[11]

In the opening weeks of the war, when patriotic enthusiasm was at its height, the kindness shown to recruits by the public at large undoubtedly did much to stifle discontent and to ensure that incidents of this type remained isolated. Private Harold Hunt of the 1/7th (City of London) Battalion, the London Regiment, discerned a marked change in public attitudes towards young people and soldiers. 'Up to the war', he recalled 'we youths had counted but little in the scheme of things. We were regarded as decadent by our elders but now we had become knights in shining armour and I must confess I for one revelled in it all.'[12] In Salford, where a committee headed by Montague Barlow, MP, had begun to raise a brigade for the Lancashire Fusiliers, the Corporation provided free transport and baths for the men. Reginald Cockburn, training in London with the Inns of Court OTC, found free travel on buses and trams 'a novel and exhilarating experience'. Rifleman Percy Jones was equally impressed by the reception given to the 1/16th London Regiment (Queen's Westminster Rifles) when the battalion marched to St Albans in August:

The people along the line of route showered things on us and refused to take any money. A gentleman in Watford bought out a whole fruit stall as it stood and told the lucky coster to give us the lot. When we halted people rushed out of their houses to distribute food and drink.[13]

The creation of the Second and Third New Armies immediately threw an added strain upon public generosity and upon the resources and imagination of the Quartering Directorate, but by the time these formations officially came into existence, on 11 and 13 September respectively, their training centres had already been allocated. In the Second New Army, the 15th (Scottish) Division and a brigade of the 20th (Light) Division would camp in the vicinity of barracks at Aldershot, with the other two brigades of the 20th Division at Blackdown and Bordon. The 16th (Irish) Division would go to Tipperary and Fermoy, the 17th (Northern) Division to Wool, Wareham and Lulworth in Dorset, the 18th (Eastern) Division to Shorncliffe and Purfleet, and the 19th (Western) Division to Bulford, Tidworth and Swindon.[14] Even though married quarters were taken over and the allowance of space per man was reduced from 600 to 400 cubic feet, accommodation in barracks was still only sufficient for up to 262,000 recruits, so over two-thirds of the Second New Army had to be placed under canvas at the outset. For the Third New Army it was necessary to find a whole series of previously unexploited sites. It was decided that the 21st Division would be stationed at Halton Park, between Tring and Wendover, the 22nd Division at Seaford in Sussex and the 23rd at Frensham in Surrey, though men of the 21st and 22nd Divisions would be housed in billets at Tring and Lewes while their camps were being prepared. Another site in Sussex, at Shoreham, was chosen for the 24th Division, and the 25th and 26th Divisions were to go to camps west of Salisbury, the former around Codford and the latter at Sherrington, Stockton and Wylye.[15]

The instructions to depot commanders to process recruits as quickly as possible did not solve the basic problem, merely transferring the congestion from depots to the training centres. Severe overcrowding was the principal hardship for units housed in existing barracks at Aldershot. Salamanca Barracks, considered full in peacetime with 800 men, housed 2,000 in September 1914, and both here and at Maida Barracks, where the 5th Cameron Highlanders and 8th Black Watch shared quarters intended for a single battalion, beds and furniture were moved out so that the men could be packed in side-by-side on the floor.[16] Men sent to the new training centres fared even worse. On 12 September 700 men of the 8th Royal West Kents, a battalion of the 24th Division, reached Shoreham in a downpour to discover that no arrangements had been made to receive them. They were marched from the station to a field and told to stay under some trees to keep dry until bell tents were pitched and damp blankets issued. At Wareham, in Dorset, the camping ground allotted to the 7th Green Howards consisted of two fields by the side of a road. Initially there were only enough tents to hold half the battalion, the unlucky ones being obliged to wander into the town at night in search of shelter.[17]

Whereas most regimental depots were in or near large towns, the newest training camps were often some miles away from major population centres and, without a cushion of civilian help close at hand, many troops virtually had to fend for themselves. Inevitably some took the law into their own hands. At Bovington, also in Dorset, men of the 10th Lancashire Fusiliers threatened to pull down the tents of their officers, while Private Alexander Thompson of the 9th Northumberland Fusiliers wrote of growing indiscipline among miners in his battalion:

The pitmen here have been looting for all they were worth. They met a cart filled with apples. They took every apple and sold what they did not eat to others. They have also been stealing cups etc from pubs! They cannot be blamed really because we all came unprepared for what awaited us and the pitmen have very little cash to buy food.[18]

The formation of the Second and Third New Armies spurred the War Office to revise and greatly enlarge its previous hutting programme. On 17 September H. J. Tennant, the Under-Secretary of State for War, declared in the Commons that ten new training camps had been opened and hutments for 490,000 men had been ordered, although it was unlikely that all would be completed before the end of November.[19] Indeed, the programme announced by Tennant was no more than a partial solution to the problem. Quarters had to be found too for the Special Reserve battalions at their coast defence stations; for the reserve battalions of the first three New Armies; for the first-line Territorial units still at home, including those with an anti-invasion role which were now being concentrated in East Anglia and Kent as part of the Central Force; and for the 'Pals' battalions and other units being raised by local authorities and which would ultimately comprise the bulk of the Fourth and Fifth New Armies. The billeting of many Territorial units in schools, hired buildings and private houses from August onwards went some way towards easing the pressure, as did Kitchener's decision that the raisers of 'Pals' battalions must make their own arrangments to house their recruits during the winter months. Even so, the task remained immense and the War Office was forced to expand the hutting programme yet again, this time to meet the needs of 850,000 men.[20]

Unfortunately for the men under canvas, a period of almost incessant rain began in mid-October, revealing that inadequate care had been exercised in picking the sites for some new training centres. The camp of the 11th Cameronians (Scottish Rifles) at Codford was situated in a field bounded by a stream on three sides, despite warnings from a local resident that the field was frequently flooded and used for skating in winter. The November rains quickly turned the camp into a morass. At Chiseldon the fields in which the 4th South Wales Borderers were encamped actually contained the source of a stream, which, when it overflowed, transformed the site into a lake, making it uninhabitable.[21] The conditions at these and other camps were soon reflected in an increase of sickness in the New Armies. According to figures quoted by Tennant in the House of Commons, 1,508 cases of pneumonia were recorded among British troops training in the United Kingdom up to 31 January 1915 and, of these, 301 had died.[22]

Things might not have been so bad had the War Office been able to stick to its hutting programme, but by mid-November the wet weather, labour disputes, unscrupulous contractors, shortages of materials – particularly seasoned timber – and the lack of skilled workers due to unrestricted enlistment, all conspired to cause severe delays at several of the more important sites.[23] An attempt by the War Office to move troops into the huts available, even when they were only half finished and before proper roads and paths had been laid, did not improve the situation. Men of the 6th Buffs (East Kent Regiment) at Sandling Camp, near Shorncliffe, actually had to put up tents inside their huts to keep dry, and at Seaford recruits of the 11th Welsh Regiment, who lived under canvas by day and slept in unfinished huts at night, had to cross a mile or so of thick mud to get from one to the other. As Private I. P. James of that battalion recalled, 'We were by now really browned off and while we expected these conditions in France we did not see why someone else's mistakes should cause us to be treated as a lot of numbers.'[24]

Those prepared to endure poor treatment in the first flush of enthusiasm after enlistment had become less tolerant after two or three months of continuing hardship, and November 1914 was marked by a wave of unrest in the units of the first three New Armies. Mass meetings and demonstrations took place at Codford, where whole companies in the 25th Division refused to go on parade. There were also strikes at Seaford, especially in a brigade of the 22nd Division, which was composed chiefly of Welsh miners.[25] With discontent mounting in the training camps, the War Office sought an alternative short-term solution to the accommodation problem. As noted above, many Territorial and Special Reserve battalions had been billeted in private houses and other buildings since August, but the policy was now extended to include a large proportion of the first three New Armies. Thus some 800,000 troops, or the equivalent of the combined populations of Edinburgh and Leeds at that time, were billeted on the civilian population of Britain in the winter of 1914–15, bringing the nation face to face with its army to an unprecedented degree.[26]

II

Billeting, once the cause of a great deal of protest, not least from the keepers of inns and alehouses upon whom soldiers were traditionally lodged, had declined in importance as a method of quartering troops with the increase in barrack accommodation in the early nineteenth century. Immediately prior to the First World War billeting on a large scale was practically unknown, and was confined mainly to troops on the march to manoeuvres or exercise camps. Consequently the regulations in force in 1914 were not geared to the accommodation crisis which arose that autumn, and the whole system had to be revised after careful inspection in all parts of the country and much correspondence with the Home Commands. For instance, the business of handling complaints and claims for damages required a considerable organisation in itself, and experience convinced Sir John Cowans, the Quartermaster General, that this task, as well as the selection of suitable billets, was best carried out at local level. All the Home Commands were therefore divided into specific quartering areas, for each of which an Area Quartering Committee, under a Permanent President, was formed to co-ordinate the arrangements for housing troops other than in barracks or hutments. These committees were in turn subdivided so that billeting in every district could be supervised. The Permanent Presidents, who had War Office valuers attached to them, were responsible for the assessment of rent and damages and for the periodic inspection of the premises involved.[27]

The revised regulations, issued in late November 1914 and refined the following year, decreed that it lay with the local chief officer of police not only to select the persons on whom billeting notices should be served but also to prepare lists of accommodation available. Unoccupied buildings were to be hired, whenever possible, in preference to billeting soldiers in occupied private dwellings. If the latter could not be avoided, then the homes of 'substantial householders' should be utilised before dwellings in poorer districts. Licensed premises were now deemed undesirable as billets. In the case of private houses, the numbers billeted should not exceed one man to every two rooms. It was also advised that, unless the full consent of the occupants was forthcoming, soldiers should not be quartered in houses where only women, with or without children, were living. Billets for officers were not to be in the same buildings as those for the men, but should be conveniently close.[28] Since billeting was expensive, the authorities concerned did their utmost to ensure that public buildings were used. Thus when the 10th Black Watch moved from Codford to Bristol, two companies were quartered in the Colston Hall, one at the Victoria Gallery and the fourth at a skating rink.[29] In practice, however, most soldiers were billeted in occupied private dwellings and the regulations were ignored or circumvented as frequently as they were observed.

Once an area had been allocated to a particular unit, a small party was sent on ahead, armed with the lists supplied by the police, to secure billets for the main body. This was usually done by knocking at each house and asking the occupants how many soldiers there were willing or able to accept. Depending on the reply, the number of men to be quartered in the house was chalked on the wall or door. The process could be exhausting for billeting parties, as Arthur Macgregor, a sergeant in the 2/14th London (London Scottish), discovered at Watford:

I was given a list of about 250 billets – and today I visited 100 of them. Just think of that, 100 frowsy women in the slummiest part of Watford – 100 stairs to climb, steep and dark – 100 times to say the same thing and answer the same questions. By gum, I was fed up by the time 6 o'clock came round.[30]

Not all billeting parties met with a friendly reception, for, as Rifleman Norman Ellison of the 1/6th King's (Liverpool) Regiment noted,

'Patriotism undergoes an acid test when there comes a knock at your door and, without warning, you are asked to provide a billet for the strange soldiers.' The landlady of a boarding house in Folkestone, when told by an officer of the 7th Royal Sussex Regiment that he was going to billet men there, retorted, 'Young man, you will do nothing of the sort!' and shut the door in his face. Such reactions showed that long-held views about the 'brutal and licentious soldiery' had not totally evaporated. On arriving in Epsom in 1914, David Kelly and a fellow recruit of the University and Public Schools Brigade of the Royal Fusiliers encountered what Kelly described as 'the complete aloofness mingled with fear which the old middle class felt for our professional Army'. Told by the lady of a house to go away, as they were not wanted, Kelly and his companion nevertheless forced their way in and installed themselves in her kitchen, where their 'hostess' reluctantly produced some bread and onions:

... the lady, who had been regarding us with suspicion and hostility changing to bewilderment, suddenly broke in with 'Are you volunteers?' We agreed. 'Oh' (with intense relief), 'I thought you were common soldiers!'[31]

Even those who had formerly served in the army sometimes failed to grasp that its social composition had now radically changed. A retired army surgeon in Whitstable said that he would have soldiers in his home 'provided they are clean men who will not spit upon the wallpaper'. As Norman Ellison commented, 'The war was still young and the idea of educated civilian soldiers unknown to him.' The unfortunate Ellison was the victim of another incident at Canterbury, where he and one of his comrades found the bolts of their rifles covered with jam and suspected that their unfriendly billet landlady had committed the deed. 'She said her child had done it. We wondered, but were moved to another house.'[32]

Communities, as well as individuals, had difficulty in concealing their anxieties about the effects of billeting. When the Leeds Bantams (17th West Yorkshire Regiment) moved into billets in nearby Ilkley in February 1915, Lance Corporal Ernest Sheard recorded that 'the Ilkley people, especially the mothers, had formed a League, its object being to keep the girls away from the soldiers'. Private John Tucker, of the 2/13th London Regiment, noted that the inhabitants of Saffron Walden also kept their daughters out of sight. 'We hardly saw a young girl all the time we were there,' he recalled. An officer of the 9th Royal Welsh Fusiliers, arranging billets in Weston-super-Mare in January 1915, became aware that the residents of one area regarded all Welsh regiments 'as composed of wild and undesirable Welsh miners of whose unruliness they had been wont to have taste in the summer seasons'. At Colchester in 1916 Private Arthur Winstanley of the 2/5th Manchesters, a battalion mostly composed of men from Wigan, was billeted on a watch repairer who 'expressed surprise that we could speak without using the dialect, and that we had good table manners'. Scottish regiments too were viewed with considerable apprehension at first. Describing his battalion's stay in Bedford, Alex Runcie, then a private in the 1/6th Gordon Highlanders, observed that local people 'had visions of all kinds of savages armed with claymores descending on them', and added:

One girl asked me if I didn't feel the cold at night, on the hills with only my plaid to cover me while sleeping. Another, knowing the house we were quartered in, remarked that the bath in it would be a great surprise for us, never having seen one before. As the said bath had no water laid on and was upstairs, so that hot water had to be carried from the basement to the bath, this was quite a laugh.[33]

The evidence of men like Runcie acts as a reminder of the underlying parochialism and immobility of a substantial proportion of the British population in 1914, for all the advances in education and public transport and the growth of mass-circulation newspapers. Clearly this parochialism by no means disappeared with the coming of war and the creation of a huge citizen army.

Money, however, helped to overcome ignorance and prejudice. It was estimated that, in towns the size of Bournemouth, between £10,000 and £20,000 a week was spent by troops in the winter of 1914–15.[34] An allowance of up to 3s 4½d per man per day was paid to householders. This included a basic sum of 9d a night for lodging, 7½d for breakfast, 1s 7½d for dinner and 4½d for supper. The rate for officers was 3s per night, but they had to pay separately for their own food.[35] There were, of course, variations in this scale, according to local circumstances. In some cases only a room and bed were required, with the troops being fed in centralised messes on army rations. In others the landlady was asked to feed the men out of the billeting allowance. A third method was to deliver army rations to the billets, leaving the lady of the house to prepare the meals.

Whichever course was adopted, there were many people only too ready to take advantage of the system. Troops of the 3rd (Special Reserve) Battalion of the East Lancashire Regiment noticed that the inhabitants of Plymouth grumbled much less as soon as details of the billeting allowances were known. Stanley Casson, an officer in the battalion, relates that some householders accepted as many as ten men, the soldiers often having to sleep on the floor. 'We were besieged by prospective landladies who begged us to let them take the "dear boys" in and cherish them. Cherishing was a popular entertainment in those days.' Private W. J. Wood of the 1/5th Gloucestershire Regiment was billeted on a lady of 'the shark type' at Chelmsford, complaining that 'Every weekend we were "bled" for extras, imaginary or otherwise.'[36]

Men who were unlucky enough to meet unfriendly or unscrupulous householders were quick to express their anger. Noting in his diary that few people in Boxmoor, Hertfordshire, had welcomed his men, Second Lieutenant P. H. Pilditch of the 7th London Brigade, Royal Field Artillery, wrote, 'It made me absolutely wild. I wished a few of them could experience the hardships of an invasion, and go through what these poor fellows will have, before long, to go through for them.' At Wimborne, in Dorset, Alexander Thompson was just as critical of his 'hosts'. 'This species of animal rather makes one feel as though one wished one hadn't joined the Army . . . They are of no use to the nation as far as I can see. Dirty, lazy and caring for no one but themselves.' On the other hand, criticism was not the prerogative of soldiers alone, for, although the conduct of a majority of troops was exemplary, the anti-social behaviour of others seemed to justify the fears harboured by civilians. Pilditch wrote in February 1915 that men of his unit had been stealing coal from a house. 'It's this sort of thing that makes it so hard to answer those people who won't put themselves out to billet men and horses.'[37]

Drinking was perhaps the most common cause for complaints from civilians. A lady in Hampshire had sixty-one men, mainly from Liverpool, billeted in her stables in May 1915. A lot of them were 'the worse for drink though not incapable', she told her brother. 'I felt I must sit up till I saw all light out – so I did not see much of my bed that night!' The following month she wrote again in a similar vein. 'We have had a terrible time with billeted Regts . . . but I am sure it helps a little if the village people see one doing all one can, and putting up with inconveniences.' A Dorset man recalled that, before he left home to enlist, men of the 12th Manchester Regiment were billeted on his family at Ferndown, describing them as 'a beery lot' who were rather unpleasant. 'I had a sister there, you see, and she used to bring in the coffee and that at night for them and if they were partly drunk they'd throw a cup of coffee at her . . . My mother didn't think a great deal of it because of the destruction that they caused.'[38]

Soldiers also succumbed to temptations other than petty theft. Billeting threw together large numbers of men and women under circumstances which greatly increased the opportunities for sexual adventure. Men living away from home, many for the first time ever, felt free from some of the social and moral conventions imposed by their family, neighbourhood and class. By the same token, women whose husbands or fathers had left home to join up were sometimes unable to ward off the young soldiers billeted on them. Charles Cain of the 2/5th Manchesters confessed that he learned much about 'the wine, women and song bit' when billeted at Southport in the first winter of the war:

The men I was with were rough with women, boasted of their conquests, many of whom were actually raped, but there were no prosecutions to my knowledge.

Suffice it to say that ten soldiers were billeted on one woman who had three teenage daughters, and the mother and all the daughters finished up in the family way.

Cain admits that not all sexual advances ended in conquest, relating how one ex-miner in his billet was in the habit of walking around the house naked. 'He called this advertising, but as far as I know it had the opposite effect to what he wanted, for she [the landlady] locked herself in the kitchen, and her complaints landed Charlie in the guard room.'[39] Women were, of course, constrained by far more than the risk of gossip. In April 1915 Ronald McNeill, Conservative MP for the St Augustine Division of Kent, wrote to the *Morning Post* that, in districts where many troops had been quartered, 'a great number of girls' were about to become unmarried mothers. The illegitimate birth rate in 1915 was, in fact, exceptionally low, suggesting that McNeill was exaggerating the current situation, although cases were numerous enough to provoke widespread discussion and correspondence in the press.[40] The wives of soldiers were no doubt often deterred from extra-marital affairs by the possibility that all allowances and pensions could be withdrawn following 'gross misconduct' on their part.[41] Soldiers too were very conscious of the dangers facing their womenfolk. Private Gilbert Nash of the 1/1st Buckinghamshire Battalion, writing from a billet in Chelmsford, realised that billeting money would 'come in handy' but told his wife in High Wycombe not to take in troops. 'It is all chance work,' he warned, 'for there is a lot of rough ones about just now, so if you can do without I would sooner you did not have any.'[42] Nevertheless, in spite of all the deterrents, the illegitimate birth rate did rise in 1916, one reason being, as the Registrar General commented, 'the freedom from home restraints of large numbers of young persons of both sexes'.[43]

It must be pointed out that most soldiers later looked back on the time they spent in billets in the United Kingdom as the happiest part of their military service, a period when they could at least enjoy the comparative luxuries of a soft bed and regular home-cooked meals. The 15th Royal Welsh Fusiliers, for example, were quartered in boarding houses and hotels at Llandudno in the winter of 1914–15 and were received like holiday visitors, occupying bedrooms and being catered for by the hotel waitresses and staff.[44] Having got to know his hosts better, Arthur Winstanley of the 2/5th Manchesters had similarly fond memories of his billet at Colchester:

This family did all in their power to make us happy and comfortable . . . We lads never went out at night; after a day's work under the NCOs and officers of various types, we thought of nothing, only getting into a light pair of slippers, and gathering together with the family in the drawing room . . . The parting from the Cooper family was just as poignant as leaving home. They had grown to love us; after all, we were only in our twentieth year, and full of the spirits and moods that elderly people like to see in lads.[45]

It should also be emphasised that a significant proportion of the locally raised Pals battalions were spared the worst of the accommodation problems suffered by units of the first three New Armies. In many cases the Pals were permitted to live at home on a subsistence allowance or were housed in buildings or tented camps in or near their place of origin while their own hutments were being built. Recruits of the Sheffield City Battalion (12th York and Lancaster Regiment) and the 1st Bradford Pals (16th West Yorkshire Regiment) were billeted at home for some three months after formation. The Hull Commercials (10th East Yorkshire Regiment), raised early in September 1914, did not move to Hornsea until 17 November 1914, and the 1st Salford Battalion (15th Lancashire Fusiliers) stayed in and around Salford until the end of December. The Accrington Pals (11th East Lancashire Regiment), who were at full strength by 24 September, left for billets in Wales as late as February 1915. Moreover the hutted camps constructed for Pals units were generally finished sooner, and were of a considerably higher standard, than those provided for the first three New Armies under direct War Office contracts. This was largely because the raisers of Pals battalions could make extensive use of local government machinery to expedite matters and, with their knowledge of local conditions and contractors, could more easily monitor the progress of the work involved.

Apart from the social problems which it both caused and reflected, billeting had adverse effects on training, for it took time to assemble the men each morning before marching them off to an open space for drill and field exercises, while the length of the day's training was further reduced by the need to get recruits back to billets for the evening meal. With men scattered throughout a town or village, it was also difficult to foster *esprit de corps* above platoon or company level. The concentration of units for brigade and divisional work was likewise delayed, making it harder for the War Office and the regional Commands to achieve consistency in the training of the larger formations. Consequently, performance tended to vary, with some divisions reaching the desired standard of efficiency more rapidly than others. All the same, but for the enormous help civilians gave the army in the winter of 1914–15, the incidence of sickness and discontent in the ranks of the New Armies would almost certainly have been higher during those critical months, thereby constituting an even greater threat to the training programme. In this way, billeting, as a practical expression of civilian support, was a key element in the gigantic act of national improvisation which produced Britain's first mass army.

Despite all the hold-ups resulting from bad weather, shortages and labour troubles, most New Army units were able to move out of billets into huts in the spring of 1915. By the autumn of 1915 there were sufficient huts for 850,000 men and several of the camps had grown to immense size. One of the biggest complexes was at Catterick in Yorkshire, where the two camps of Hipswell and Scotton could together accommodate 40,000 men, the equivalent of two divisions.[46] The overall accommodation problem at home therefore became much less severe in the latter half of 1915, particularly as the early New Army units were then going overseas, enabling the War Office to move the later formations into the camps and training centres they had vacated. The practice of billeting soldiers in private houses in Britain continued, to some extent, for the remainder of the war, although it never again approached the scale of the first winter.

III

By contrast, the gradual strengthening of the British Expeditionary Force across the Channel inevitably led to a massive increase in the amount of accommodation required for troops when they were out of the line. The size of the BEF, including dominion contingents, grew from 269,711 officers and other ranks in December 1914 to 986,189 in December 1915 and 1,029,642 by 1 February 1916. The peak figure was reached on 1 August 1917, when there were an estimated 2,044,627 officers and men serving with the British armies in France and Belgium.[47]

Within the BEF, of course, no unit – not even a front-line infantry battalion – stayed in the trenches all the time. The arrangements varied in detail from formation to formation and sector to sector but, in the middle years of the war, a British infantry division in the fighting zone would usually have two of its three infantry brigades in the line and one in reserve at any given moment. Each of the brigades in the line would, in turn, have two battalions in the front trenches, with a third in close support and the fourth in rest billets behind the lines where it could, if called upon, act as a local reserve.[48] This meant that, in the normal routine of trench warfare, approximately half the infantry strength of a division would be at rest or in reserve and, according to the system of rotation employed in his unit, an infantryman might therefore expect to spend something between a quarter and half of his time in rest billets during any tour of duty in the forward area. These rest billets might be some three to five miles back from the line, the distance being determined by factors such as the nature of the terrain, the availability of accommodation and the degree of observation enjoyed by the enemy artillery. Periodically the entire division would be withdrawn some twenty miles farther to the rear for a longer rest of three weeks or more to enable it to reorganise and to train fresh drafts sent out from England. Charles Carrington has recorded that in 1916, when he was serving as an officer in the 1/5th Royal Warwickshires, he spent 101 days in the front-line trenches and in close support positions, with 120 days in reserve and seventy-three out in rest. The remainder of his time that year was taken up by leave, travelling, courses and a spell in hospital.[49]

Since the BEF was on foreign soil and in a region where there was little, if any, barrack accommodation which it could utilise, it was again necessary to pursue alternative methods of housing troops from the very start. With the stabilisation of the front after the autumn of 1914, greater attention was devoted to the possibility of providing hutted camps for the units in France and Belgium, but the sectional huts then in use proved too bulky for rapid shipment and it was not until 1916 that the Engineer-in-Chief in France adopted a design proposed by Captain P. N. Nissen for a semicircular hut, built of corrugated iron sheets on a wooden foundation, which could be transported on a lorry and erected by six men in half a day. An order for 27,000 Nissen huts, each capable of holding 40 men, was placed at the end of 1916 and another for 20,000 more a few months later. The first order was completed by the autumn of 1917, though the second was delayed until 1918 and the rate of supply fell far short of the demand.[50] Thus on the western front, as in Britain, the billeting of large numbers of men on the civilian population could not be avoided. The effect, as R. H. Mottram has pointed out, was rather like having two or three million Frenchmen, many of whom could not speak English, living for four years in Cheshire, Lancashire and Cumberland in order to help repel an invasion of Scotland.[51]

In many respects, British billeting methods in France and Belgium closely resembled those employed at home. When a unit was coming out of the line or moving to another sector an advance party, containing at least one officer and NCO, proceeded ahead of the main body to the billeting area designated by the army, divisional or brigade staff. Wherever possible, billets were arranged in consultation with the local civil authority, either through the resident British Town Major or by contacting the mayor of the town, village or commune concerned, from whom a list of inhabitants likely to provide quarters would be obtained. The next step was for the billeting officer to negotiate direct with the people themselves in the hope of securing sufficient accommodation by the time the main body arrived. The billeting rates were fixed at three francs per head per night for Generals, two francs for lieutenant-colonels and majors and one franc for captains and subalterns. Twenty centimes a night was paid for each NCO and private provided with a bed or straw, and five centimes for shelter only if no straw was supplied. On leaving the billets the commanding officer of the unit, again in consultation with the mayor or his representative, signed a certificate which stated the total amount owed for accommodation, payment subsequently being made by the branch requisition office of the appropriate army headquarters.[52]

The constant rotation of units in and out of the line and from sector to sector ensured that any soldier spending more than a few weeks in France would occupy a variety of billets during his period of active service. These might range from large public buildings in towns like Armentières and Béthune to tiny miners' cottages in the area around Loos and Vermelles or isolated farms near the battle zone. In successive spells of rest at Armentières between 1 August and 25 October 1915 Sergeant E. W. Cotton of the 1/5th Northumberland Fusiliers was billeted in a factory, a school, a lunatic asylum, a weaving exchange, a hospital and a convent.[53] The level of comfort enjoyed by both officers and men could also vary considerably in the space of a few days or even within the boundaries of a relatively small village. Writing from one such village near Givenchy in November 1915, Captain Alfred Bland of the 22nd Manchesters (7th City Battalion) informed his wife that men of C company were occupying a big house which had bedrooms, central heating and Turkish carpets while A company was billeted in draughty peasant cottages with brick floors and no heating apart from a kitchen stove. On 5 December he recorded that the battalion was now lodged in the 'loveliest of lovely billets', with the whole of his company accommodated in one house which afforded 'heaps and heaps of room'. He added, 'We five officers occupy three bedrooms with real beds in them and two sitting rooms with fires in fireplaces, easy chairs, sofas, tables, curtains and sumptuous upholstery.' Yet the next day the battalion moved nine miles to a place which Bland called 'an arid inhospitable cess-pool'.[54]

Most frequently, however, units out on rest were accommodated in farms which, in northern France and Belgium, were constructed on a more or less standard pattern. The farm buildings generally formed a square, with the farmhouse itself on one side and stables and barns for livestock and straw on the other three. In the centre of the square there was invariably an enormous and foul-smelling midden or dungheap. Officers were usually lodged in the farmhouse with the farmer and his family. 'We are billeted in a farm three or four miles behind the firing line, and are really pretty comfortable considering,' Second Lieutenant T. A. Brown of the 6th Dragoon Guards confided to his aunt on Christmas Eve, 1914. 'We share the kitchen, in which we have our meals, with a family of thirteen, but one gets used to the din after a bit.'[55] NCOs and men had to make do with the surrounding barns and stables, as Alexander Gillespie, an officer in the 2nd Argyll and Sutherland Highlanders, told his family in March 1915. 'They lie down in the stalls beside the cows, climb up hen-ladders to roost in the lofts and curl up in any corner where they can put a bundle of straw.'[5] Sometimes the condtions in rest billets were not much of an improvement on those in the trenches. At Monchaux in March 191

Rifleman Percy Jones of the 1st Queen's Westminster Rifles commented, 'We have got a miserable billet for our platoon this time. The barn is dirty, the roof leaks, and the walls are pitted with holes, so it is pretty cold.'[57] Private Archie Surfleet of the 13th East Yorkshire Regiment fared just as badly at Prouville in July 1916:

This billet is the worst yet! The roof is negligible; the floor-covering consists of dirty straw on the damp earth and there are some horses in the better half of the shed; we are separated only by a dilapidated, wooden barrier. In fact, it is such a rotten show, Smith and I have decided to bivouac outside in a broken-down wagon in the orchard. What a life![58]

Merely by bringing them into close and regular proximity to each other, billeting increased the chances of friction between soldiers and civilians, and, in France and Belgium, differences in language, custom and environment added to the social problems which the system had already encouraged at home. Every British soldier crossing to France received a printed message from Lord Kitchener reminding him that it was his duty 'to maintain the most friendly relations' with French and Belgian citizens, that he should always be 'courteous, considerate and kind' and must never do anything likely to injure or destroy property. 'In this new experience,' the message concluded, 'you may find temptations both in wine and women. You must entirely resist both temptations, and while treating all women with perfect courtesy you should avoid any intimacy.'[59] In a war lasting more than four years and in an army numbering millions of men it is scarcely surprising that not all lived up to these ideals or that the reserves of goodwill on both sides were often stretched to the limit.

For his part the average Tommy found much to criticise in his new hosts. Some men were shocked by the scant regard paid to basic hygiene by the folk in rural areas. Referring, in April 1915, to Flemish peasants near Hill 60, Ellison remarked, 'The people have as much idea of the general rules of sanitation as a gargoyle and are filthy and untidy in dress and everything else.' Lieutenant H. A. Munro of the 1/8th Argyll and Sutherland Highlanders noted that the inhabitants of Robecq drank from a ditch covered with green scum. 'One afternoon I saw our billettee wash her hands and face in the ditch, then a pair of stockings and other garments, and finally fill a pail of drinking water at the same spot.' Rifleman R. Preston, a labourer from Huddersfield who served in the 8th King's Royal Rifle Corps, wrote that, in Belgium, it was nothing 'to see a married couple arm in arm walking down a country lane, for the man to stop to relieve himself with her not bothering to unlink her arm'. A farmer's wife on whom Percy Jones was billeted in 1916 told him that the English 'are weak and feeble because they wash all the strength out of their bodies. She sees no harm in a bath once or twice during the summer but certainly not every week thro' the winter!'[60]

The mercenary outlook of many civilians was a particular source of annoyance to British troops. Captain Lionel Crouch of the 1/1st Buckinghamshire Battalion observed in July 1915 that villagers near the line at Hébuterne were charging the equivalent of a private's weekly pay for a tin of milk, while Lieutenant L. D. Spicer of the 9th King's own Yorkshire Light Infantry complained, the following year, that the French were asking three times the normal price for cigarettes. If inflated prices might be expected near the battle zone, where the few surviving shopkeepers had trouble replenishing stocks, they were perhaps less excusable elsewhere. 'Taking the people of these villages all through,' wrote Second Lieutenant J. H. Mahon of the 1/8th King's (Liverpool) Regiment, 'they seem to be a money-grubbing lot and don't appear to appreciate a bit that it is very much to their benefit to have English soldiers over here.' An officer of the 15th Cheshire Regiment (1st Birkenhead Bantams) described the inhabitants of one village as 'the most miserable vultures I have met. Out to rob the men and not the least bit obliging.' Archie Surfleet reflected sourly in 1917 that the better-paid Canadians unwittingly spoiled things for their British comrades. 'As soon as they appear in a place everything goes up in price and we hate to follow them into billets.'[61]

Men who had volunteered for the army in the belief that they would be helping to deliver beleaguered France and Belgium were understandably bitter when they were made to feel unwelcome. 'The old people were surly and inclined to treat us as intruders,' wrote Private Albert Conn of the 8th Devonshire Regiment.[62] In May 1915 one French farmer spread manure throughout an orchard in an effort to stop the 2nd Argyll and Sutherland Highlanders digging practice trenches, and David Kelly recalled that peasants on the Somme would not make a room available to officers of the 110th Brigade for a conference on the eve of the 1916 offensive.[63] Disputes over water supplies were common in villages behind the lines, where local inhabitants removed ropes and buckets from wells and took the handles from pumps to prevent British soldiers from using them.[64] Billeting parties were rarely sure how they would be received. Captain Reginald Cockburn of the 10th King's Royal Rifle Corps discovered that in some villages 'it seemed to be the recognised custom to refuse the overtures of all officers who requested rooms in which to sleep'. After a while he evolved a set plan to be used when negotiating for billets:

1. Say good morning, politely, and salute. 2. Ask if you can see the officer's room please. If trouble occurred, then the discussion continued on these lines: 3. Say that there was no other room, and offer to pay. 4. Say that you are very sorry, but you must sleep somewhere. 5. Must you sleep in the field, without any cover over your head? You plead that after all you are a poor British officer, and have noticed 'with surprise' the difficulties encountered when seeking hospitality from the French people. You cannot understand it . . . 6. You are fighting for her

country, and how would she like it if the *sales Boches* were there? She would get no consideration from them, ... 7. You jolly well wish that the Boches would come, and you are disgusted with her. 8. Walk away in high dudgeon, saying that you will go straight to the Mayor. Number 8 sometimes took effect, and I have observed that these people can be as pleasant as possible afterwards ... As a rule, all they wanted was money; the Belgians were worse in that respect. They robbed the soldier even more unscrupulously than did the French, who themselves were bad enough in all conscience.[65]

It cannot be denied that French and Belgian civilians had good cause to resent the presence of British soldiers. Even if, as R. H. Mottram claims, the enormous British force in France and Flanders was one of the most docile and good-natured armies in history, widespread damage to property and massive inconvenience to civilians were the inescapable by-products of its having to fight a modern industrialised war in a heavily populated and civilised country. The exigencies of war dictated that crops would be trampled, gaps cut through hedges and vast areas of land requisitioned for camps, dumps and training grounds. Conversely, the French could hardly be blamed for losing patience when, month after month, they were required to billet foreign troops who spread mud and lice through their homes, stole their poultry and made indecent advances to their women.[66] Gillespie conceded that the men of his battalion did not always behave themselves, adding that 'the finest officers and training couldn't make saints of men straight from Falkirk High Street and the south side of Glasgow'.[67] Private Clifford Carter of the 10th East Yorkshire Regiment (Hull Commercials) accepted that French people who refused to share their water were sometimes simply taking revenge on soldiers who had soiled the wells or pinched buckets. He also confessed that men of his unit had stolen spoons and cups from cafés and *estaminets* for use in their billets. 'This was undoubtedly one of the reasons for the attitude of suspicion shown by the country folk in many places – an attitude which was most strongly condemned by the very men who caused it.'[68]

Divisional commanders were empowered to pay civilians compensation for minor damages up to a value of 125 francs, but hard-pressed divisional staffs were unable to investigate all cases thoroughly and the system was clearly liable to abuse at this level.[69] When the proprietors of a hop field alleged, in the winter of 1917–18, that men of the 4th North Staffordshire Regiment had been pilfering hop poles for use as fuel Major H. D. Myer wondered how many claims had been submitted for the same missing items.[70] More serious cases, however, were referred to a Claims Commission which was set up at the Boulogne base early in the war and which was soon dealing with thousands of cases a month.[71]

The written evidence left by the soldiers themselves indicates that countless acts of petty theft and looting went unpunished. T. P. Marks, who served in the Gloucestershire Regiment, suggests that almost every soldier on the western front laid himself open, at one time or another, to the charge of looting.[72] Albert Conn narrowly escaped being caught taking eggs from a farm in December 1915 and was again fortunate when the farmer failed to pick him out of an identity parade next morning.[73] In March 1918 Bombardier William Shaw of the 151st Siege Battery was horrified to see British gunners drinking communion wine and stealing candlesticks from a church, the officers being too preoccupied with the problems of the retreat to take any disciplinary action.[74] Private R. D. Fisher of the 1/24th London Regiment frankly admitted stealing wine from a cellar in a deserted village near Aveluy on 26 March 1918, and an officer of the 1/1st Hertfordshire Regiment cheerfully recorded that their mess cook, a Scot, secured enough crockery during this period 'to have stocked up half a dozen messes ... but Jock was never brought to book'.[75]

The word 'looting' was, of course, capable of wide interpretation. In the main, soldiers resisted the temptation to take really valuable objects or, indeed, anything which they might afterwards have to carry on a long march. Most men probably restricted themselves to the petty pilfering of eggs, chickens and fuel or removing useful domestic articles from empty or ruined buildings near the lines – the sort of 'scrounging' that has long been an acknowledged part of the soldier's trade and which few officers and NCOs felt inclined to punish. Carrington has argued that the farther away from one's own group the victim belonged, the less was the moral blame attached to the theft, and William Linton Andrews, an NCO in the 1/4th Black Watch, declared that, in his unit, looting was seen as just retribution for profiteering civilians.[76] By the strict letter of military law a soldier on active service who was found guilty of breaking 'into any house or other place in search of plunder' could be sentenced to death, but in fact no one paid the supreme penalty for this offence in France and Belgium.[77] The extent to which officers were prepared to connive at looting is illustrated by an extract from the diary of Captain Lionel Ferguson of the 13th Cheshire Regiment with reference to the situation near Hazebrouck in mid-April 1918:

The troops are having the time of their lives, living on ducks, chickens, and pigs etc., which have all been left in the farms. The country is well covered with villages, market towns and farms, now a picture of silence. One can walk into any house or shop and take what is required. It is hard to stop this looting, although it is best not to be caught in the act of taking anything.[78]

On the whole British soldiers were reasonably courteous towards French and Belgian women. Surfleet claimed that he 'never saw any girl molested in any way; they were invariably treated with the utmost respect by most of the troops'.[79] This did not mean that all men took heed of Kitchener's advice to 'avoid any intimacy'. On the contrary, they were quick to grasp that the French were far less inhibited than themselves in physical matters and, conscription having removed most French males from the areas in which they were billeted, the more determined soldiers could find opportunities for casual sex. Indeed, Gerald Brenan, an officer in the 1/5th Gloucestershire Regiment, slept with a peasant girl at Merris only three days after arriving in France in 1915.[80] Others, no doubt conditioned by family background, education and religious and moral scruples, declined to do more than engage in crude banter with girls they passed in the street or indulge in a little mild flirtation. In April 1918 Second Lieutenant Harold Knee of the 1/1st Hertfordshire Regiment was billeted on a family who had two pretty young daughters. 'We used to gather round the big table and play "Tip it"; the women folk enjoyed this game immensely, and so did we for we were able to hold hands, and even knees, under the table.' Later in the year he fell in love with a girl in a draper's shop, though their relationship remained purely platonic. 'I never overstepped the bounds of decorum,' Knee wrote, 'never transgressed in any way, never sought to kiss her.'[81]

Men seeking more full-blooded encounters could, if all else failed, resort to the brothels or 'red lamp' establishments in the bigger towns and cities. In August 1917 the writer Dennis Wheatley, then an officer with a divisional ammunition column, patronised a luxurious brothel in Amiens, where he spent the night with an attractive blonde in a room entirely covered with mirrors; the following morning he was given a breakfast of omelettes, melon and champagne.[82] Most, however, could only frequent the seedier establishments in towns like Béthune and Saint-Omer. Some, like Alexander Runcie, who visited a 'red lamp' at Béthune in 1915 largely 'out of curiosity', were discouraged from further adventure by their general tawdriness. 'The girls ... were an unhealthy-looking lot, a dull sickly colour, no beauties either in face or form. Their clothes, what little they wore, didn't look too clean. If this was a house of joy, I had been sadly misinformed.'[83]

According to Surfleet, the warnings issued to men about the risks of venereal disease were 'good enough to deter the vast majority of overseas soldiers and those who "caught a dose" suffered so much in so many ways, their misery killed the "urge" and discretion usually triumphed'.[84] Nevertheless the numbers of men who contracted VD was high enough to cause the British military authorities considerable concern. Statistics show that, from 1914 to 1918, 153,531 British and dominion troops in France and Belgium were admitted to hospital suffering from gonorrhoea, syphilis or other forms of venereal disease. In 1916 such cases represented 19·24 per cent of all admissions.[85] Various steps were taken in an attempt to halt the upward trend of the figures.

In January 1917 it was laid down that any officer or soldier contracting VD would not be eligible for leave for a year after leaving hospital, and, in April 1918, even the licensed brothels, or *maisons de tolérance*, which were regularly inspected by medical officers, were placed out of bounds to all troops as a result of public pressure in the United Kingdom.[86] Despite these measures, the figures reached a peak in 1918, when 60,099 British and dominion troops were treated for VD in France, an average of thirty-two out of every 1,000 men on the ration strength of the forces under Haig. The incidence of VD was, in fact, highest in the dominion units. For example, the ratio of known cases among Australians in France in 1917 was eighty-five out of every 1,000 men. The seriousness of the problem may also be judged from the fact that in 1917 twice as many men were admitted to hospital with VD as were admitted with pneumonia, frostbite and trench foot combined.[87]

All these problems notwithstanding, both soldiers and civilians emerged from prolonged exposure to each other with a great deal of credit. The letters, diaries and memoirs of British soldiers contain innumerable references to acts of kindness and generosity by the French and Belgians, often recorded by the very men who had complained most bitterly about their lack of hospitality. In a letter to his wife in December 1915 Captain Alfred Bland declared, 'We have struck homely little cottages where all are only too happy to do us any service. They make us coffee at odd times; we use their stoves for our own cooking; they pass round sweets; we share our cigarettes. *C'est une véritable entente cordiale!*'[88] Percy Jones, writing in February 1916, stated that the woman at the farm where he was billeted 'has proved a rare friend to us. She will do anything we ask of her, and it is difficult to persuade her to take money for the fresh butter, milk, eggs and apples we get.'[89] Private Clifford Carter of the Hull Commercials confirmed that those men who 'took the trouble to mix with the people in their homes and chat with them, proved them to be, with few exceptions, most friendly and lovable'.[90] British soldiers were also full of admiration for the stoicism of peasants who clung to their farms and cottages near the line and appreciated that their own presence sometimes added to the tribulations of the civilians. In the words of Reginald Cockburn, 'I often wondered whether, if our country were swarming with foreigners, our poor peasant and country folk would not, even if they were making money out of them, sooner grow tired and impatient of their harassing guests. At times one has felt such an intolerable nuisance, and able to do so little.'[91]

For soldiers coming tired and dispirited from the horrors of the trenches, periods in rest billets were of incalculable worth. 'We don't need much, now, to make us happy,' wrote Archie Surfleet in December 1916: 'a pile of clean straw, a clean shirt, ten francs, an *estaminet* out of

Jerry's range and we are as happy as sandboys.'[92] An officer who served in the 15th Royal Irish Rifles remembered the difference in the mood of his battalion after a spell of rest: 'Everybody to our surprise had become so polite and pleasant and good-humoured. Looking back we realised that in the trenches . . . we had been scratchy and quarrelsome, always ready to speak roughly and to return an unpleasant answer.'[93] Another officer, Second Lieutenant H. R. Bate of the 2/6th Manchesters, aptly summarised the therapeutic effects of a few days in domestic billets. 'Returning to unspoiled countryside, where the grass was green and flowers grew, was bliss. Mixing again with ordinary men and women in civilian clothes walking about the lanes and streets, was a welcome reminder that stability still remained in a world at war.'[94]

In the final analysis it is doubtful whether the billeting system, either in Britain or in France, produced any lasting changes in social attitudes. It may have helped to break down some of the worst aspects of pre-war parochialism and chauvinism but probably contributed much less in this regard than, for example, the growth of mass communications and universal popular culture later in the century. At home, traditional attitudes to the army certainly altered but, again, this process owed far more to the fact that so many civilians had donned uniform than to contacts through billeting. What billeting did achieve was to make the lives of millions of soldiers just a little easier during one of the most frightful wars in history, and for that reason, if for no other, the expedient may be counted a success.

Notes

1 'Supply services during the war, Part I, Quartering', note by General Sir John Cowans, Quartermaster-General to the Forces, *Statistics of the Military Effort of the British Empire during the Great War, 1914–1920*, HMSO, London, 1922, p. 833.
2 Daily recruiting returns submitted to the Adjutant-General for the period 4 August to 27 December 1914, Adjutant-General's papers, PRO, WO 162/3; monthly recruiting figures, August 1914 to 11 November 1918, *Statistics of the Military Effort of the British Empire* p. 364.
3 Minutes of meeting of the Military Members of the Army Council, 9 August 1914, PRO, WO 163/44.
4 Minutes of Proceedings of the Army Council, 1914: 11 August 1914, PRO, WO 163/21.
5 Minutes of meeting of the Military Members of the Army Council, 12 August 1914, PRO, WO 163/44.
6 *Ibid.*, 17 and 20 August, PRO, WO 163/44.
7 Major-General H. L. Pritchard (ed.), *History of the Corps of Royal Engineers*, V, Institution of Royal Engineers, Chatham, 1952, pp. 69–70; Major D. Chapman-Huston and Major Owen Rutter, *General Sir John Cowans: the Quartermaster General of the Great War*, Hutchinson, London, 1924, II, p. 21.
8 Account by Major-General Sir George Scott-Moncrieff, quoted in Chapman-Huston and Rutter, *General Sir John Cowans*, II, p. 22;

Major-General H. L. Pritchard (ed.), *History of the Corps of Royal Engineers*, V, p. 69.

9   Note on the strengths of infantry depots, from returns submitted to the Adjutant-General's Department, 29 August 1914, PRO WO 162/4; Circular from Adjutant-General's Department to GOCs-in-C of Commands, 30 August 1914, PRO, WO 162/3; Statement showing the strengths of infantry depots, 12 September 1914, PRO, WO 162/24.

10 H. Cartmell, *For Remembrance: an Account of some Fateful Years*, Toulmin, Preston, 1919, p. 13; *Historical Records of the Queen's Own Cameron Highlanders*, IV, Blackwood, Edinburgh, 1931, p. 273.

11 Colonel H. C. Wylly, *The Green Howards in the Great War*, privately published, Richmond, 1926, p. 384; H. Cartmell, *For Remembrance*, pp. 34–5.

12 H. E. Hunt, 'The Saga of a Citizen Soldier', unpub. account, 1973, IWM, P. 268.

13 Sir C. A. Montague Barlow (ed.), *The Lancashire Fusiliers: the Roll of Honour of the Salford Brigade*, Sherratt and Hughes, Manchester, 1920, pp. 41–4; Major R. S. Cockburn, 'First World War Diary and Recollections', unpub. account, 1965, IWM, P. 258; P. H. Jones, unpub. account, 1919, IWM, P. 246.

14 Army Order XII of 11 September 1914 (AO 382 of 1914).

15 General Sir John Cowans, 'Supply services', p. 833; Minutes of meetings of the Military Members of the Army Council, 3 and 10 September 1914, PRO, WO 163/44; Army Order XVIII of 13 September 1914 (AO 388 of 1914), appendix B.

16 *Historical Records of the Queen's Own Cameron Highlanders*, IV, p. 274; Lieutenant-Colonel Norman MacLeod (ed.), *War History of the 6th (Service) Battalion, Queen's Own Cameron Highlanders*, Blackwood, Edinburgh, 1934, p. 2; Major-General A. G. Wauchope (ed.), *A History of the Black Watch (Royal Highlanders) in the Great War, 1914–18*, III, *New Army*, Medici Society, London, 1926, p. 3.

17 Lieutenant-Colonel H. J. Wenyon and Major H. S. Brown (eds.), *The History of the Eighth Battalion, the Queen's Own Royal West Kent Regiment*, Hazell Watson and Viney, London, 1921, p. 2; Lieutenant-Colonel Ronald Fife, *Mosaic of Memories*, Heath Cranton, London, 1943, pp. 61–2.

18 M. J. H. Drummond, unpub. account, *c.* 1963, IWM, DS/MISC/29; Alexander Thompson to his mother, 14 September 1914, IWM, 79/55/1.

19 *Parliamentary Debates, House of Commons, 1914*, LXVI, col. 983.

20 Telegram from Adjutant-General's Department to GOCs-in-C of Commands, 4 September 1914, PRO, WO 159/18; Minutes of meeting of the Military Members of the Army Council, 12 September 1914, PRO, WO 163/44; Cowans, 'Supply services', p. 834.

21 Colonel H. H. Story, *History of the Cameronians (Scottish Rifles), 1910–1933*, Hazell Watson and Viney, Aylesbury, 1961, p. 241; C. T. Atkinson, *The History of the South Wales Borderers, 1914–1918*, Medici Society, London, 1931, p. 61.

22 *Parliamentary Debates, House of Commons, 1914–15*, LXIX, cols. 901–2.

23 S. Higenbottam, *Our Society's History*, Amalgamated Society of Woodworkers, Manchester, 1939, pp. 191–2; Major-General Sir George Scott-Moncrieff, 'The hutting problem in the war', *Royal Engineers Journal*, XXXVIII, 1924, p. 368.

24 Colonel R. S. H. Moody, *Historical Records of the Buffs (East Kent Regiment), 1914–1919*, Medici Society, London, 1922, p. 70; I. P. James,

letter, n.d., *c.* July 1963, BBC Great War series correspondence, IWM, BBC/GW.

25 Major W. de B. Wood (ed.), *The History of the King's Shropshire Light Infantry in the Great War, 1914–1918*, Medici Society, London, 1925, pp. 207–8; Arthur Crookenden, *The History of the Cheshire Regiment in the Great War*, Evans, Chester, n.d., p. 345; Oswald Sturdy, letter, n.d., *c.* July 1963, BBC Great War series correspondence, IWM, BBC/GW; Sir Charles Woolley, letter to the author, 17 November 1978. The late Sir Charles Woolley was an officer in the 8th South Wales Borderers at Seaford in 1914.

26 Cowans, 'Supply services', p. 833; Chapman-Huston and Rutter, *Cowans*, p. 26.

27 Cowans, 'Supply services', p. 833; Chapman-Huston and Rutter, *Cowans*, p. 25; Pritchard, *Royal Engineers*, V, p. 74.

28 Army Orders, December 1914 (AO 518 of 1914); 'Rules for Billeting', issued with Army Orders dated 1 June 1915, paras. 1–22.

29 Wauchope (ed.), *Black Watch*, III, p. 205.

30 Arthur Macgregor to Dulcie Newling, 17 March 1915, IWM, CON/AEM.

31 Norman Ellison, War Diary, 1914–19, IWM, DS/MISC/49; account by Lieutenant C. D. Jay, quoted in Major Owen Rutter (ed.), *The History of the Seventh (Service) Battalion, the Royal Sussex Regiment, 1914–19*, Times Publishing Company, London, 1934, p. 8; Sir David Kelly, *The Ruling Few*, Hollis and Carter, London, 1952, p. 89.

32 Ellison, War Diary, IWM, DS/MISC/49.

33 Ernest Sheard, 'My Great Adventure: the Great War, 1914–1918,' unpub. account, n.d., IWM,PP/MCR/133; John F. Tucker, *Johnny get your Gun: a personal narrative of the Somme, Ypres and Arras*, William Kimber, London, 1978, p. 17; H. Lloyd Williams, *Personal Experiences during the Years of the European War*, unpub. account, 1927, IWM 73/148/1; Arthur Winstanley, *My Recollections of the War,* unpub. account, 1928, IWM, P. 157; Alex Runcie, 'Territorial Mob', unpub. account, c. 1960, IWM, P. 185.

34 Chapman-Huston and Rutter, *Cowans*, p. 26.

35 Army Order 289 of 4 August 1914; Army Order VII of 23 April 1915 (AO 164 of 1915).

36 Stanley Casson, *Steady Drummer*, Bell, London, 1935, p. 36; W. J. Wood, 'With the 5th Gloucesters at home and overseas', *The Back Badge* (journal of the Gloucestershire Regiment), 1936, p. 105.

37 P. H. Pilditch, *The War Diary of an Artillery Officer, 1914–1919*, entries for 14 December 1914 and 6 February 1915, IWM, CON/PHP; Alexander Thompson to his mother, 15 April 1915, IWM, 79/55/1.

38 Lavinia Williams-Freeman to Sir Henry Cunynghame, *c.* 10 May and 6 June 1915, IWM, 84/31/1; interview with Perry Webb, IWM, Department of Sound Records, 000578/08.

39 C. A. Cain, 'The Footsloggers', unpub. account, 1967, IWM, PP/MCR/48.

40 *Morning Post*, 17 April 1915; *Daily Mail*, 17 April 1915; *Observer*, 18 and 25 April 1915; *Sunday Pictorial*, 18 April 1915; *Annual Report of the Registrar-General for 1915*, Parliamentary Papers, 1917–1918, V, Cd 8484, p. vii.

41 *Parliamentary Debates, House of Commons, 1914–15*, LXX, col. 268.

42 Gilbert Nash to his wife, 12 October 1914, IWM, P. 329.

43 Annual Report of the Registrar-General for 1916, PP, 1917–1918, V, Cd 8869, p. xix.

44 W. A. Tucker, *The Lousier War*, New English Library, London, 1974, p. 13.

45 Winstanley, 'My Recollections of the War', IWM, P. 157.

46 Lieutenant-Colonel Howard N. Cole, *The Story of Catterick Camp,*

1915–1972, Forces Press, Aldershot, 1972, pp. 13–15.

47   Estimated strengths of the Expeditionary Forces by months since December 1914, *Statistics of the Military Effort of the British Empire*, facing p. 64.

48   See, for example, Major-General Sir Arthur Scott and P. Middleton Brumwell, *History of the 12th (Eastern) Division in the Great War, 1914–1919*, Nisbet, London, 1923, p. 11; Lieutenant-Colonel H. R. Sandilands, *The 23rd Division, 1914–1919*, Blackwood, Edinburgh, 1925, p. 26; Cyril Falls, *The History of the 36th (Ulster) Division*, M'Caw Stevenson and Orr, Belfast, 1922, p. 31.

49   Charles Edmonds (Charles Carrington), *A Subaltern's War*, Peter Davies, London, 1929, p. 120.

50   Pritchard, *Royal Engineers*, pp. 80, 164; Captain Wilfrid Miles, *Military Operations, France and Belgium, 1916*, Macmillan, London, 1938, II, p. 540.

51   R. H. Mottram, *Through the Menin Gate*, Chatto and Windus, London, 1932, p. 143.

52   General Routine Order No. 1547, 29 April 1916, 'Instructions for Requisitioning and Billeting in France and Belgium', see *Extracts from General Routine Orders issued to the British Army in the Field, II, Quartermaster General's Branch*, GHQ, France, and HMSO, London, 1918, pp. 201–3, 254–6.

53   First World War diary of E. W. Cotton, April–October 1915, IWM, P. 262.

54   Alfred Bland to his wife, 23 November, 5 and 6 December 1915, IWM, 80/1/1.

55   T. A. Brown, *A Year in the Salient, and other letters*, printed for private circulation, 1918, p. 30; for descriptions of typical farm billets see H. D. Myer, 'Soldiering of Sorts', unpub. account, n.d., IWM, 79/17/1; Ellison, War Diary, IWM, DS/MISC/49; A. D. Gillespie, *Letters from Flanders*, Smith and Elder, London, 1916, pp. 56–7; Lancelot Spicer, *Letters from France, 1915–1918*, Robert York, London, 1979, pp. 37–8.

56   Gillespie, *Letters from Flanders*, p. 56.

57   P. H. Jones, unpub. account, 1919, IWM, P. 246.

58   A. Surfleet, 'Blue Chevrons: an Infantry Private's Great War Diary', unpub. account completed *c.* 1962 and based on a diary which the author kept in 1916 and 1917, IWM, P. 126.

59   A copy of this message is held by the Imperial War Museum's Department of Printed Books, K.2129.

60   Ellison, War Diary, IWM, DS/MISC/49; First World War diary of H. A. Munro, 1 May–22 September 1915, IWM, P. 374; R. Preston, unpub. account, *c.* 1980, IWM, P. 438; P. H. Jones, unpub. account, IWM, p. 246.

61   L. W. Crouch, *Duty and Service: Letters from the Front*, Hazell Watson and Viney, Aylesbury, 1917, p. 62; Spicer, *Letters from France*, p. 4; First World War diary of J. H. Mahon, IWM, 78/22/1; Lieutenant-Colonel Harrison Johnston, *Extracts from an Officer's Diary, 1914–18*, Falkner, Manchester, 1919, p. 16; Surfleet, 'Blue Chevrons', IWM, P. 126.

62   A. V. Conn, 'A Worm's Eye View of the Great War', unpub. account, n.d., IWM, 81/41/1.

63   Gillespie, *Letters from Flanders*, pp. 151–2; D. V. Kelly (Sir David Kelly), *39 Months: with the 'Tigers', 1915–1918*, Benn, London, 1930, p. 27.

64   See T. A. Bickerton, 'The Wartime Experiences of an Ordinary Tommy', unpub. account, 1964, IWM, 80/43/1; T. P. Bovingdon, unpub. account, n.d., IWM, 83/34/1; Emlyn Davies, *Taffy went to War*, privately published, *c.* 1969, p. 24; First World War diary of S. A. Newman, IWM, 77/83/1; J. W. Stephenson, 'With the Dukes in Flanders', unpub. account, n.d., IWM, 78/36/1.

65   Cockburn, 'First World War Diary and Recollections', IWM, P. 258.

66 Mottram, *Through the Menin Gate*, pp. 141–5; 'Ex-private X' (A. M. Burrage), *War is War*, Gollancz, London, 1930, p. 47.
67 Gillespie, *Letters from Flanders*, p. 57.
68 First World War journal of Clifford Carter, based on contemporary diaries, I, 1914–1917, unpub. account, n.d., IWM, P. 428.
69 General Routine Order No 632, 11 February 1915, GRO No. 634, 11 February 1915, GRO No. 763, 7 April 1915, GRO No. 1239, 31 October 1915, GRO No. 2540, 19 August 1917, see *Extracts from General Routine Orders, II, Quartermaster General's Branch*, 1918, pp. 17–18, 21–4.
70 Myer, 'Soldiering of Sorts', IWM, 79/17/1.
71 'Notes on the Work of the Claims Commission', see *Extracts from General Routine Orders*, II, appendix V, pp. 257–9.
72 Thomas Penrose Marks, *The Laughter goes from Life; in the Trenches of the First World War*, William Kimber, London, 1977, pp. 25–6.
73 Conn, 'A Worm's Eye View', IWM, 81/41/1.
74 William Shaw, *Call the Roll: Memories of a Flag Wagger*, n.d. n.p. (possibly Canada, 1979), p. 87.
75 R. D. Fisher, 'A Story of the 1914–18 War', unpub. account, n.d., IWM, 76/54/1; H. J. Knee, 'War Memoirs: October 1916 to April 1919', unpub. account, n.d., IWM, 77/8/1.
76 Charles Carrington, *Soldier from the Wars Returning*, Hutchinson, London, 1965, pp. 183–4; William Linton Andrews, *Haunting Years: the Commentaries of a War Territorial*, Hutchinson, London, n.d. p. 216.
77 Army (Annual) Act, 1913, Part I, para. 6 (g), see *Manual of Military Law*, 1914, p. 381; *Statistics of the Military Effort of the British Empire*, p. 648; Anthony Babington, *For the Sake of Example*, Leo Cooper, London, 1983, appendix, 'Traceable executions in the British army, 1914–1920', pp. 228–31.
78 L. I. L. Ferguson, 'War Diary, 1914–1919', unpub. account, n.d., IWM, 77/166/1.
79 Surfleet, 'Blue Chevons', IWM, P. 126.
80 Gerald Brenan, *A Life of One's Own*, Hamish Hamilton, London, 1962, p. 214.
81 Knee, 'War Memoirs', IWM, 77/8/1.
82 Dennis Wheatley, *Officer and Temporary Gentleman, 1914–1919*, Hutchinson, London, 1978, p. 153.
83 Runcie, 'Territorial Mob', IWM, P. 185.
84 Surfleet, 'Blue Chevons', IWM, P. 126.
85 Major T. J. Mitchell and Miss G. M. Smith, *Medical Services: Casualties and Medical Statistics of the Great War*, HMSO, London, 1931, pp. 77, 131, 144–5, 155, 164 and 174.
86 Major-General Sir W. G. Macpherson (ed.), *Medical Services: Diseases of the War*, HMSO, London, 1923, II, pp. 123–5.
87 Mitchell and Smith, *Medical Services: Casualties*, pp. 164, 174; Macpherson (ed.), *Medical Services: Diseases*, II, p. 118.
88 Alfred Bland to his wife, 8 December 1915, IWM, 80/1/1.
89 Jones, unpub. account, IWM, P. 246.
90 Clifford Carter, First World War Journal, IWM, P. 428.
91 Cockburn, 'First World War Diary and Recollections', IWM, P. 258.
92 Surfleet, 'Blue Chevons', IWM, P. 126.
93 J. L. Stewart-Moore, 'Random Recollections', II, 'The Great War, 1914–1918', unpub. account, 1976, IWM, 77/39/1.
94 Canon H. R. Bate, 'Sixty Years After: Some Memories of a Platoon Commander', unpub. account, 1974, IWM, P. 430.

SPECIMENS OF MEN IN EACH OF THE FOUR GRADES.

GRADE I.   GRADE II.   GRADE III.   GRADE IV.

7 Jay Winter

Army and society:
the demographic context

When working men joined the army during the First World War they did not cease to be members of the working class. Thus the history of the rank and file in the war forms an important though neglected chapter in the history of the working class. Similarly, the ways in which officers perceived the war, and were enduringly affected by it, are incomprehensible without reference to the unspoken assumptions[1] of their class and its fortunes in the pre-war period. In this chapter I shall point to some ways in which the war service of six million men from Britain and Ireland needs to be seen in a context that includes the history of the communities and society they came from.

I

One of the most striking features of pre-war society is the way it was pervaded by class sentiments, with all their complexities, ambiguities and nuances. The men who joined Kitchener's armies in 1914–15 or who were conscripted in the later years of the war lived in what was probably the most class-conscious nation in Europe. This reflected both Britain's early industrialisation and the long history of industrial strife which was inextricably bound up with it. If anywhere in Europe before 1914 there was a proletariat, it was in Britain. Compared to France and Germany, a higher proportion of the labour force was concentrated in capital-intensive production in engineering and mining. Conversely a lower proportion of the industrial labour force was located in the more scattered forms of production associated with the clothing and food trades.[2] The decline of agriculture and the concomitant urbanisation of the population had gone further than elsewhere. Growth in the service sector and in transport in the late nineteenth century had helped to reduce regional variations in prices and wages sufficiently to establish a national market for labour and other goods and services which did not exist to the same extent in France or Germany. While there were still important divisions within the working class in 1900, they paled in comparison with the gap in living conditions, disposable income, and mental outlook which increasingly separated those who earned their living through manual labour and those who did not.[3]

The world of work bore the imprint of Britain's head start in the process of economic growth in another way. Trade-union association among British workers had begun earlier than on the Continent, and, while never representing more than a minority of workers, trade unionists had a longer cumulative experience of industrial disputes and bargaining than had either their French or German counterparts. The language of class, which had been created in the first half of the nineteenth century, made sense of such conflicts and of the enormous disparities of income and power that lay behind them. A rhetoric of inequality based on adversary relations at work between employers and employees and on separate cultures outside work appeared on the eve of the Great War to capture the special features of social stratification in Britain.

Such class awareness, and its expression in solidarity or in suspicion, was not without foundation, being based as well on a realistic assessment of significant differences in life expectation that accrued to men and women of different social strata by accident of birth. A working-class child born in late Victorian or Edwardian Britain had an uphill struggle for survival, much more hazardous than that faced by its middle-class or upper-class contemporaries. The more prosperous had fewer children, and those they bore were more resistant to viral and bacterial infection than children of poorer families. A glance at infant mortality figures (deaths before age one per 1,000 live births annually) should suffice to suggest the extent of pre-war deprivation in working-class areas. At the turn of the century, for example, approximately 200 per 1,000 infants failed to survive the first year of life in the following county boroughs: Birmingham, Blackburn, Bootle, Burnley, Dudley, Great Yarmouth, Preston, Salford, Sheffield, Stockport, Wakefield, Wolverhampton and York. The names read as if taken from a Baedeker guide to industrial England. In contrast, infant mortality rates in more prosperous areas were well below the national average. In the metropolitan borough of Hampstead, for example, in 1910, sixty per 1,000 infants died in the first year of life; in England and Wales as a whole the infant mortality rate was 105. Over the years 1910–12 children of unskilled workers were subject to an infant mortality rate twice that of children of professional men and women.[5] In such contrasts we can see most clearly the demographic meaning of class in pre-war Britain.

National statistics reflect working-class mortality experience more than that of the more prosperous simply because of the numerical preponderance of the labouring population, estimated to be roughly 80 per cent of the population in 1910. To set the aggregate demographic position of Edwardian Britain in historical perspective, we may note that the infant mortality rate in 1911 was twice that of Egypt in 1972 or of non-white South Africans in 1975. In the years 1910–12 life expectation at birth for men in England was 51·5 years. This figure is slightly higher than that registered for Ecuadorian males in 1961–63, and about the same as that registered for Iraqi males in the more recent period 1970–75.[6] It is therefore not an exaggeration to suggest that in large parts of working-class Britain, though not among the middle class, there were before 1914 conditions of poverty and ill health which today we associate with countries of the Third World.

In the last two generations, expectation of life at birth in England and

Wales has risen approximately twenty years, largely owing to the eradication of certain infectious diseases; the infant mortality rate is now only fourteen infants per 1,000. It is sobering to consider how recent is the assumption, which people of all classes now take for granted, that children will survive the first months of life. In at least this respect, working-class men who went to war knew untimely death more frequently and experienced bereavement perhaps with a greater degree of fatalism than we do today.

They were also intimately acquainted with hard labour, dreary conditions – both at home and at work – long hours, in many cases subsistence wages, estimated in the title of one contemporary book of social observation as 'round about a pound a week'.[7] Theirs was an environment of 'normal' deprivation; it was especially marked among the families of semi-skilled and unskilled workers, even when they were in regular work. The fact that such conditions were commonplace may help us to understand how ordinary men could cope with army life during the 1914–18 war. Factory production required a discipline, and at times involved dangers, not very far removed from those of military exercises. Men who had worked for years in a cotton mill, in a forge or on the land could tell any soldier all he needed to know about monotony and drudgery.

For many, army food was more substantial, and probably more nutritious, than what they had been able to buy on pre-war wages. Alcohol may have been weaker and harder to come by during the war, but in other respects, such as the provision of boots and clothing, many were decidedly better-off in uniform than they had been before. Away from the front line, their accommodation was often no more overcrowded than what they had been used to at home. To take only one pre-war example, more than three-quarters of the families in the Scottish industrial burgh of Coatbridge lived in dwellings of two rooms or less.[8] The crush was not quite so marked in many English cities; but contemporary photographs of Manchester or parts of London show the appalling extent of pre-war urban squalor. Despite the protest of a garden here and an allotment there, the face of working-class Britain before the Great War was disfigured by tenements and factories which amply deserve the title of 'classic slum'.[9]

What is most remarkable about the world of labouring men and their families in this period of mass deprivation is the stubborn survival and elaboration of distinctive forms of working-class culture. Pub life, football enthusiasm and music hall entertainment all gave expression to it. In addition, by 1914 the cinema was emerging as a key leisure industry and a major vehicle for the expression of popular images and beliefs. In the period of the war it would have been only a slight exaggeration to claim that whoever said cinema said Charlie Chaplin. It was only in the 1920s that his characterisation of 'the little guy' was fully formed, but, as one historian has perceptively noted,[10] even earlier he had developed a style which helped to make him the archetypal figure of pre-war working-class culture: decent, sentimental, doggedly preserving, constantly at sea in a storm not of his own creation. Frequently he is the victim of forces he does not understand or control, but somehow manages to survive. His is a world largely without politics. It is a world with a stable class system in which ordinary folk largely accept their place and obey rules that only add burdens to their lives. Through his sheer capacity to outwit snobs, villains and other superior creatures, his resignation in the face of poverty, and his commitment to simple loyalties and emotions, Chaplin embodied a number of beliefs that were widely held in pre-war Britain. Among them was a mixture of deference, respectability, chauvinism and swagger which (in addition to illusions of escape from workaday reality) contributed much to the flood of volunteering that swept a fifth of the industrial labour force into the army in the first year of the war.[11]

Unemployment did not fill the ranks of Kitchener's armies: popular sentiment did. The protection of 'little Belgium', the defence of the empire, the need to be seen to be doing one's military duty alongside the men of one's district or village: these may sound like outworn clichés today, but in 1914 they had force and substance in the minds of ordinary people. Such symbols of collective identity were deeply embedded in working-class culture, and existed without any contradiction alongside notions of class solidarity. Industrial militancy and patriotism were complementary and not antagonistic sentiments, and to understand their compatibility is to begin to see why so many men whose lives were stunted and constrained by a system of class subordination chose to fight in a cause which preserved and perpetuated it, though in a modified form.

The reasons why so many men from the more privileged classes enlisted at the outbreak of war are not difficult to ascertain. Theirs was an interest well worth protecting. Even the so-called 'Great Depression' of the 1870s and 1880s had not seriously undermined the enormous wealth that had been accumulated during the third quarter of the nineteenth century. A stable currency and booming export trade helped produce additional income in the form of substantial returns from overseas investment in the pre-war decades. Despite tremors associated with a building slump, the pre-war period was distinctly prosperous, as many of the well-to-do demonstrated conspicuously. There was a division with the middle class between London-based commercial wealth, and manufacturing wealth located principally in the provinces.[12] This distinction, however, was never sharply drawn, and interlocking directorates and alliances by marriage made certain that no interest was excluded from social position and political influence. Until 1914 landed society set the tone and formed the backdrop for political developments in both major parties. The Conservative Party was still that of Balfour rather than of Bonar Law and Baldwin, as it was soon to become. There were decidedly more 'new men' in the Liberal Party, but most of them, like Campbell-Bannerman and Asquith, were integrated remarkably well into the social world regulated by the traditional aristocracy.[13] With the possible exception of Ramsay MacDonald, the pre-war Labour Party had little or no connection with the aristocracy – it was too insignificant to earn the compliment of co-optation or to cause great alarm in either major party.

The other parliamentary group, the Irish Nationalists, caused little disturbance in British politics, for the simple reason that they sat in Westminster solely for the purpose of legislating themselves out of existence. There was thus much reason for the pre-war belief that British political institutions were inherently stable and also intrinsically superior to other nations'. Such confidence, not to say smugness, informed discussions about how well society could withstand the shocks of the war, which was at first viewed as a struggle that would be of short duration. A few people shared Sir Edward Grey's fears about bread queues forming in wartime London's streets; but enthusiasm for the war effort in 1914 was overwhelming. It was reinforced by an understandable – though in hindsight frightening – degree of ignorance about the nature of mechanised warfare between industrialised nations. No sombre thoughts of trenches and gas masks troubled the clerks and greengrocers, teachers and farmers, manufacturers and publicans who joined up by the thousand in the first months of the war.

None of this analysis of the forces of order and consciousness of stability and inequality on the eve of war is meant to suggest that there was no social conflict in Edwardian Britain; on the contrary. Beginning in 1910, there was a wave of crippling strikes by dockers, miners and, for a brief period, railwaymen, which threatened to bring the whole economy to a halt. Much of the trouble was due to many employers' stubborn refusal to recognise trade unions at all and to their persistence in this attitude at a time when real wages were declining and unemployment rates were low. Other disputes arose because coal owners and others opposed the principle of a minimum wage, described by the government's chief industrial conciliator during the 1912 coal strike as a revolutionary measure. These struggles generated considerable tension at the time, but they did not contain a revolutionary message or potential. The wave of strikes was checked, if not ended, after 1912, and aside from a minimum wage for miners, the outcome was pretty much a draw. But one of its prime results was to reinforce a structure of industrial relations where the State acted as a third party in disputes, thereby helping to regulate and contain similar conflicts in the future.[14]

Trade unions came in for as much calumny and social ridicule then as they do now; but middle-class social observers felt they had less to fear from the regularly employed and dues-paying members of the Amalgamated Society of Engineers or the Amalgamated Society of Railway Servants than from what in a European context would have been called the lumpenproletariat: the outcasts and deviants of the great industrial and commercial cities, those at the bottom of the working-class heap. Numerous writers conjured up the spectre of a host of misfits – the feeble-minded, the 'epileptic, the insane and mentally unstable, the criminal, the chronic pauper and unemployable classes'[15] – whose control was draining the resources of the solid citizenry and whose proliferation, if left unchecked, would threaten the stability of the country.

It would be a mistake to locate such statements about the supposedly hereditary character of social disability and ability solely on the lunatic fringe. A glance at the scientific and literary journalism of the period will show how endemic were such fears of what was termed race suicide. Social observers were alarmed by a dual process: first the phenomenon of 'population decline', which was shorthand for recognising that although the population was growing, its rate of growth was dwindling rapidly; and secondly, 'fertility decline', the differential features of which alarmed middle-class people whose average family size was substantially smaller than that of the working class in general and of the unskilled in particular.[16] This belief in Britain's biological decline compared to rapidly growing countries like Germany or in the decline in the birth rate of the privileged classes which provided the nation's leaders indicates some unease about the future among sections of the privileged population, frightened at the possibility of losing the stability on which their prosperity rested. These eugenic ideas were based less on an accurate observation of current realities than on fears passed down from several generations of Victorians concerned about the destructive potential of urban concentrations of working people.[17] But they are also important evidence about the extent to which contemporary middle-class observers were aware of the important variations within the working class. Many of these writers described and deplored the perpetuation of a sector of society, estimated to number three or four million,[18] who lived on the margins of subsistence. But they came to no consensus about what measures could be taken to relieve the plight of the desperately poor – until the First World War did it for them.

II

The physical reality of class inequality was apparent to the recruiting

officers who had to find new recruits to maintain the strength of
regiments whose numbers were severely depleted during the great
offensives of 1916 and 1917. The ways in which social deprivation
compounded their difficulties can be seen in the reports of the National
Service Medical Boards, whose doctors examined over two million men
in the twelve months following November 1917. The Parliamentary
Paper on their work has a pictorial frontispiece which forcefully
captures the meaning of class inequality in pre-war Britain. It presents
four men, naked except for loincloths, whose cases exemplified the four
categories used to classify degrees of fitness for military service during
the First World War. Grades I and II were eligible for overseas combat
duty, since they included men either with no disability or with a 'slight
disability' consistent with exposure to 'considerable physical exertion.'
Grade III men had 'marked physical disabilities' which precluded their
direct participation in combat but still permitted them to serve in
clerical units. Grade IV men were unfit to serve in any capacity.

This manner of classification could have been used to describe the
physical differences between upper and middle-class men (grades I–II),
skilled workers (grades II–III), and unskilled workers (grades III–IV).
(The exceptions were miners and agricultural labourers, whose work
made them physically the fittest members of the working class). There
were, of course, men of all social classes in all four grades, but the
correspondence between class, stature and overall health was too
striking for the medical service boards to miss. They applied a standard
devised by the noted anatomist Sir Arthur Keith to describe the relative
fitness of men from different localities and occupational groups. Sir
Arthur's optimal cohort was formed by 1,000 Cambridge
undergraduates, whose fitness varied as follows: 700 in grade I; 200 in
grade II; Seventy-five in grade III; and twenty-five in grade IV. If this
distribution had described the fitness of the eligible male population of
Britain in 1917, seventy per cent of all recruits would have been placed
in grade I. Instead, there were only thirty-four per cent nationally in
grade I, and this figure is only the national average. Some areas yielded
a considerably lower percentage of combat-fit men, and a
disproportionately high percentage of men in grades III and IV. Not
surprisingly, these were the same areas which registered infant
mortality rates above 200 per 1,000 live births at the turn of the
century.[19]

What we see in the ranks of the British army in the Great War are the
results of pre-war deprivation. In this context the stamina and
recuperative powers of the forces during the 1914–18 war were even more
remarkable than may have been appreciated at the time. The question
remains, though, as to the long-term effects of active military service on
the health of ex-soldiers. Nearly 50 per cent of the men who served in the

forces in the First World War became casualties – over 700,000 men died
or were killed, and over 1,600,000 were wounded or fell ill in uniform. In
the years between the two world wars, hundreds of deaths due to war
wounds were recorded in successive reports of the Registrars-General of
Scotland and of England and Wales. Even so, these statistics almost
certainly underestimate the extent to which military service caused
deaths indirectly throughout the post-war years by impairing
ex-soldiers' health or otherwise lowering their resistance to infectious
diseases. The Ministry of Pensions frequently denied a wife's
application for a widow's pension if there was any doubt that her
husband's death was attributable to war-related causes.

Three examples will suffice to illustrate the difficulty of measuring
the full extent of war-related disability in the post war period. A gunner
in the Royal Field Artillery contracted bronchitis in May 1916 while on
active duty, and was invalided out of the army. Seven years later he
died of chronic bronchitis at the age of forty-three, but since a
substantial period had elapsed since his discharge his widow's
application for a pension was denied. The reason given was that doubt
existed as to the link between the cause of his discharge and the cause of
his death. Precisely the opposite decision was taken in the case of a
private in the Labour Corps who was gassed during the war, and died at
the age of forty-two of pulmonary tuberculosis five years after the
armistice. His widow and her four children were granted a pension. The
third case concerned a sapper in the Royal Engineers who was not
wounded during the war but who drowned himself in 1922 at the age of
forty-four. Who could say with certainty that he was a casualty of war?
In this case, as in hundreds like it, a pension was denied because (a) he
'was not removed from duty during the war on account of the disease of
which he died'; and/or (b) he had 'died of a disability of which a
continuous medical history has not been shown from the termination of
his active service in the war and which cannot be certified as
attributable to or aggravated by such service'.[20]

In the 1930s the British Legion launched a campaign to bring to
public attention the problem of 'prematurely aged ex-servicemen'
suffering from 'latent results of service'.

Many men were, for years, subjected to a degree of mental and nervous strain,
living under insanitary and unfavourable conditions never experienced before,
and their loss of earning capacity and industrial value is due in no small measure
to these war experiences, combined with difficulties of rehabilitation in civil life,
directly consequent upon service during the War years.

Such men who bore 'the intangible results of War service' ought, the
British Legion argued, to be granted a pension even if no medical link
could be established between their current disabilities and their war
records. The Legion believed upwards of 100,000 ex-soldiers to be in this

category but failed to convince the Prime Minister, Neville Chamberlain of its case. Chamberlain, who had been Minister of National Service in the 1914–18 war, was sympathetic, but saw no way round the difficulty where no medical proof existed 'to substantiate the claim that a particular condition of ill-health is due to war service'.[21] He was right. A precise answer, either medical or statistical, will never be found to the question of how long and how painfully men bore the burden of military service in the Great War.

III

When we turn to the effect of war on the health of the civilian population, we encounter an entirely different situation. The history of civilian health in wartime pointed to the country's future just as much as the physical profile of her soldiers reflected her immediate past. Here infant mortality data are useful indicators of important social trends that were accelerated during the Great War. These statistics also suggest, astonishingly, that the impact of war on the civilian population was of at least as great long-term historical significance as its impact on the men who served in uniform.

An examination of infant mortality rates between 1900 and 1930 shows conclusively that, whereas they began to decline in 1900 and continued to do so throughout these decades, the decline was most rapid in the years of the First World War.[22] Tables 7.1 and 7.2 list county boroughs in England and Wales and principal burghs in Scotland rank order of the decline in infant mortality rates during the war. In Scotland as a whole the infant mortality rate dropped from 111 to ninety-five over the years 1913–14 to 1919–21. In England and Wales, the decline was from 107 to eighty-four deaths per 1,000 live births. But throughout Britain substantially greater improvements in infant survival were registered in areas which had been most marked by pre-war uban poverty. Dundee and Glasgow, Wigan and Birmingham, Swansea and Merthyr Tydfil were all well in advance of the national trends.

These death rates dropped so substantially during the war because of the reduced and/or severity of certain infectious diseases, such as diarrhoea and enteritis, bronchitis and measles, which were endemic among infants, particularly those born in families of semi-skilled and unskilled workers. This dramatic improvement was not the result of better obstetrical and post-obstetrical medical care or other changes in medical treatment. Over half the country's doctors were in uniform during the war years and therefore unavailable to the mothers and infants who might have needed their services. Equally we cannot attribute the improvement in infant health to improvements in sanitation or housing, both of which deteriorated in the many areas

Table 7.1. *The decline in infant mortality rates in the First World War, county boroughs of England and Wales, in rank order of decline: deaths per 1,000 live births*

County borough	1913–14*	1919–21	Change
Swansea	135	88	−47
Preston	152	107	−45
Plymouth	124	80	−44
Burnley	166	122	−44
Blackpool	119	76	−43
Stoke	158	115	−43
Dudley	139	97	−42
Bury	134	92	−42
Wigan	160	119	−41
Birmingham	126	85	−41
Stockport	135	95	−40
Rotherham	133	93	−40
Bootle	135	96	−39
Canterbury	94	56	−38
Newport	118	80	−38
Oldham	140	103	−37
St Helens	148	111	−37
Bolton	130	94	−36
Norwich	114	78	−36
Nottingham	138	102	−36
Sheffield	135	100	−35
Merthyr Tydfil	123	89	−34
Great Yarmouth	112	79	−33
Smethwick	119	86	−33
Manchester	129	98	−31
Grimsby	122	92	−30
Oxford	78	48	−30
Walsall	137	107	−30
Wolverhampton	122	92	−30
Ipswich	101	72	−29
Salford	132	103	−29
West Ham	107	78	−29
Carlisle	127	99	−28
Leicester	120	92	−28
Worcester	90	62	−28
Blackburn	132	105	−27
Gateshead	138	111	−27
Liverpool	137	110	−27
Warrington	122	95	−27
Barnsley	149	123	−26
Birkenhead	121	95	−26
Brighton	101	75	−26
Bristol	99	73	−26
Southport	96	71	−25
Hull	124	101	−23
Newcastle	129	106	−23
Portsmouth	89	66	−23
West Bromwich	126	103	−23

Table 7.1. *Continued*

County borough	1913–14*	1919–21	Change
Sunderland	135	113	−22
Leeds	130	109	−21
Southend	77	56	−21
Cardiff	112	91	−21
Chester	101	81	−20
Gloucester	97	77	−20
Reading	85	65	−20
Tynemouth	128	108	−20
Bradford	125	106	−19
Croydon	88	69	−19
York	106	87	−19
Huddersfield	107	89	−18
Wallasey	89	71	−18
West Hartlepool	122	104	−18
Lincoln	99	82	−17
Rochdale	118	101	−17
Southampton	86	69	−17
Derby	97	81	−16
Hastings	74	58	−16
Northampton	90	75	−15
Burton on Trent	92	78	−14
Exeter	93	80	−13
Barrow in Furness	112	100	−12
South Shields	124	112	−12
Dewsbury	123	113	−10
Coventry	89	80	−9
Middlesbrough	140	132	−8
East Ham	71	64	−7
Halifax	102	98	−4
Wakefield	106	103	−3
Eastbourne	66	64	−2
Bournemouth	68	69	+1
Bath	68	71	+3
Darlington	96	109	+13
England and Wales	107	84	−23

* To estimate pre-war infant mortality levels, a two-year average for 1913–14 has been used. This is preferable to a three-year average including 1915, since that year was one of particularly high infant mortality in many areas. Using it as one component of an average for the pre-war figure would exaggerate the degree of wartime decline in infant mortality rates.

Source. J. M. Winter, 'Infant Mortality in Britain during the First World War', SSRC Report HR 5071, 1979.

where war industries sprang up virtually overnight at the expense of domestic housing. The most likely cause was an improvement in the nutrition of mothers and children, especially of those whose husbands and fathers were semi-skilled and unskilled workers. This gain accrued

Table 7.2. *The decline in infant mortality rates in the period of the First World War, principal burghs of Scotland, in rank order of decline: deaths per 1,000 live births*

Principal burgh	1913–14	1919–21	Change
Kirkcaldy	114	80	−34
Clydebank	109	76	−33
Paisley	126	93	−33
Ayr	117	88	−29
Dundee	149	124	−25
Coatbridge	123	98	−25
Glasgow	131	109	−22
Aberdeen	137	116	−21
Hamilton	116	96	−20
Greenock	112	99	−13
Falkirk	97	85	−12
Edinburgh	106	101	−5
Motherwell	101	96	−5
Perth	98	105	+7
Kilmarnock	92	100	+8
Scotland	111	95	−16

Source. J. M. Winter, 'Infant Mortality in Britain during the First World War', SSRC Report HR 5071, 1979.

therefore precisely to those social groups who in pre-war Britain had been most deprived and malnourished. It resulted primarily from a redistribution of food within the family itself, in such a way as to improve women's nutritional levels during pregnancy and thereby to increase their infants' resistance to disease. Not only were more women earning a full wage than ever before, but they also had a greater degree of control over how family earnings were spent and used that control to make sure that their families were adequately fed.

It is ironic that, even during the worst periods of food shortage caused by submarine warfare, what remained was redistributed much more equitably than had been managed in the peacetime economy before 1914. In part this was made possible by a major increase in home agricultural output and by limited but effective controls on consumption. Such steps would not have been successful, though, had there not also been an increase in family incomes during the war such that, for most people, earnings at least kept pace with price rises.

Family income rose in three ways. First, there were frequently more people per family in work for wages, because mothers, unmarried women, and adolescents were recruited by the thousands into the labour force. Secondly, many workers earned more money than ever before because of wage increases, shifts from low-paid to better-paid jobs, piece-work payments, and heavy overtime work. Thirdly, local and national authorities significantly supplemented family incomes and permitted more of it to be spent on food, by means of separation allowances, pensions, school milk and food, goods distributed by child welfare centres and a host of other measures. In consequence of these improvements in disposable income and access to food, mothers and children were sufficiently better fed to precipitate the steep decline in both urban working-class and rural infant mortality rates during the war.

It is possible to suggest, therefore, that one effect of war on the home front was to reduce the economic distance and thus the gap between the life expectancies of classes and of strata within the working class. It is true that there were many groups whose fortunes were adversely affected by the war, but those at the bottom of the social order, who had the least to lose, were not among them. Income gains were greatest, both absolutely and relatively, among the poorest paid and least skilled of the labouring population. Not only did social elites bear a disproportionate share of war losses,[23] but in the aftermath of war many wealthy families, whose sons had staffed the officer corps, were also hit by death duties and by a decline in incomes derived from rent. Many civil servants or retired people, who lived on fixed incomes or savings, were impoverished by wartime inflation. Skilled workers and men in clerical and service jobs did not do well either, and in some cases suffered a decline in real wages. For all these reasons we may speak of a compression of the class structure under the impact of war.

Despite the onset of inter-war austerity in 1920, this process of compression and simplification in the class structure was not reversed completely. Wage differentials widened, but rural and urban porverty did not recur in the same form or to the same extent. One indicator of the irreversibility of these trends is that, even during the worst years of mass unemployment in the early 1930s, public health did not deteriorate significantly.[24] Indeed, this may be one of the long-term demographic gains of the First World War. Improved nutrition during the formative years of infancy and childhood may have made the female babies who were born during the war, and who came of age, married and had children in the 1930s and after better able to carry a pregnancy to full term, to survive childbirth themselves, and to produce an infant healthy enough to last out the first year of life. Of course, many other influences helped reinforce the trend towards improved health among mothers and children. It is my purpose here simply to point to the fortuitous contribution of the war to these important demographic developments.

This leads to the primary conclusion of this brief analysis. It is that, in contrast to elsewhere in Europe, demographic gains for some classes in Britain balanced, and probably outweighed, the purely demographic losses of the Great War. The disappearance of the poverty of those living below or at the subsistence level, the replacement of the 'outcast London' of the Victorian social investigator Edward Booth by the drab but more prosperous metropolis of the inter-war municipal bureaucrat, Herbert Morrison, to take but one example, was made possible in part by the economic exigencies of war. We are thus left with the paradox, equally applicable to the 1939–45 war, that, because of armed conflict, the country came to be a healthier place to live in.

It should thus be apparent why I have stressed the enormous disparities between the consequences of war for military and for civilian populations. In no way does this argument dismiss or diminish the significance of military losses in the social history of Britain. Rather we must appreciate how the experiences ex-soldiers and civilians carried with them of the effects of war were drastically different. How can one reconcile the 'great release' which a sensitive contemporary, Robert Roberts, saw as the end of Victorian patterns of poverty in Salford during the Great War[25] with the great release immortalised in stone throughout the war cemeteries scattered over fields in France and Belgium? While six million men served in an institution which reflected Britain's past and reinforced a sense of traditional hierarchy and obedience to authority, fourteen million civilians participated in a war economy whose demands helped to change the class structure of the Britain of 1914.

IV

We can understand those who went through combat had difficulty in expressing to men and women who could not know what it had been like the complex emotions and fears aroused by battle. Ex-soldiers were all too aware of having what the New Zealand-born writer, Charles Carrington, called the '1916 fixation'. 1916 was the year of slaughter – for the British on the Somme; for the French at Verdun. But there is another problem of perception which an historian of the First World War must confront. We have tried to present some evidence related to the question of the impact of the Great War on Britain's class structure. But class is not a category to be measured solely in material terms. It is also a relationship, something people feel about themselves and about people who earn a living similarly or in a different way. In order to show that class structure changed during the war and because of the war, it is necessary to demonstrate that people's perception of class changed too. And since the home front did not have its Edmund Blunden or Isaac Rosenberg, evidence is scarce on this important question, on which much more work needs to be done.[26]

Perhaps we can find hints of such war-related changes in class sentiment in two disparate sources. The first is the portrait of a Sussex farming community, *Akenfield*, by Robert Blythe. One of the men he interviewed in 1966 was a seventy-one year old farm labourer who had served at Gallipoli. He recalled with the distant clarity of the elderly that 1914 was the end of the world of feudal ties and subsistence wages on the land. By 1920 deference to employers had diminished sufficiently for a branch of the Agricultural Labourers' Union to be formed in the village, a step which would have led to instant dismissal before the war.[27] How representative such feelings were is hard to say, but many other contemporaries believed that the war had reduced workers' tolerance of conditions accepted as 'natural' before it.[28]

The second source is much further afield, but with echoes of developments we have tried to sketch in the British case. It is the moving exchange between two European aristocrats immortalised in Jean Renoir's elegiac film *The Grand Illusion*. Rauffenstein, the Prussian officer, shares these thoughts with his French captive, but social equal, de Boldieu:

Rauffenstein. I do not know who is going to win this war, but I do know one thing: the end of it, whatever it may be, will be the end of the Rauffensteins and the Boldieus.

de Boldieu. But perhaps there is no more need of us.

Rauffenstein. And don't you find that is a pity?

de Boldieu. Perhaps![29]

Notes

1 James Joll, '1914: the unspoken assumptions', in H. W. Koch (ed.), *The Origins of the First World War*, Macmillan, London, 1972, pp. 307–28.

2 For France see A. Fontaine, *French Industry during the War*, New Haven, 1926, appendix II; for Germany, *Statistisches Jahrbuch für das Deutsche Reich*, 42 Berlin, 1921–2, pp. 66–67, as cited in B. Moore, *Injustice*, Macmillan, London, 1978, p. 178; for Britain, *Report of the Board of Trade on the State of Employment in the United Kingdom in February 1915*, Parliamentary Papers (PP) 1914–16, XXI, Cmd 7850, pp. 6–7.

3 E. Hunt, *Regional Wage Variations in Britain*, Oxford University Press, 1970. For France see E. Weber, *Peasants into Frenchmen*, Chatto and Windus, London, 1970; for Germany, Moore, *Injustice*, chapters 2, and J. Kocka, *A Class Society at War*, trans. B. Weinberger, Leamington Spa, 1984.

4 For examples from all social and political groups, see the essays in J. M. Winter (ed.), *The Working Class in Modern British History*, Cambridge University Press, 1983.

5 J. M. Winter, 'The decline of mortality in Britain, 1870–1950', in M. Drake and T. Barker (eds.), *Population and Society*, Batsford, London, 1982, p. 80.

6 *United Nations Demographic Yearbook, 1976*, New York, 1976, table 21.

7 M. R. Pember Reeves, *Round about a Pound a Week*, London, 1913.

8 J. Cunnison and J. D. Scott, *The Industries of the Clyde Valley during the War*, London, 1924, p. 166.

9 Robert Roberts, *The Classic Slum*, Manchester University Press, 1971.

10 G. Steadman Jones, 'Working-class culture and working-class politics in London, 1870–1900: notes on the remaking of a working-class', *Journal of Social History*, 1974, p. 497. Thanks are due to Mary Bernard for help on the development of Chaplin's career.

11 J. M. Winter, 'Britain's lost generation of the First World War', *Population Studies*, 31, 1977, pp. 449–66.

12 W. D. Rubinstein, 'Wealth, elites and the class structure of modern Britain, *Past and Present*, 76, 1977, pp. 99–126.

13 F. M. L. Thompson, 'Britain', in David Spring (ed.), *European Landed Elites in the Nineteenth Century*, Johns Hopkins University Press, Baltimore, 1977, pp. 22 ff.

14 E. H. Phelps Brown, *The Growth of British Industrial Relations*, Macmillan, London, 1960.

15 A. Tredgold, 'The feeble-minded', *Contemporary Review*, 1910, pp. 720–21.

16 J. M. Winter, 'The fear of population decline in western Europe', in R. Hiorns (ed.), *Demographic Patterns in Developed Societies*, Taylor and Francis, London, 1979.

17 See G. Steadman Jones, *Outcast London*, Harmondsworth, London, 1970, and, for similar European developments, L. Chevalier, *Labouring Classes and Dangerous Classes in Paris during the first Half of the Nineteenth Century*, trans. F. Jellinek, Routledge and Kegan Paul, London, 1973.

18 By Sidney Webb, the prominent Fabian, in coversation with R. H. Tawney. See J. M. Winter and D. M. Joslin (eds.), *R. H. Tawney's Commonplace Book*, Cambridge University Press, 1972, p. 80.

19 For a discussion of the nature of this evidence, see J. M. Winter, 'Military fitness and public health in Britain during the First World War', *Journal of Contemporary History*, 15, 1980, pp. 211–44.

20 Citations taken from files which will form part of an archive within the Pensions and National Insurance (PIN) classification at the Public Record Office, Kew.

21 *Copy of Reports made to the Prime Minister by the British Legion regarding the Condition of Ex-servicemen and of his Reply*, PP, 1937–38, X, Cmd 5738, pp. 6, 22.

22 J. M. Winter, 'Aspects of the impact of the First World War on infant mortality in Britain', *Journal of European Economic History*, XI, 1982, pp. 713–38.

23 Winter, 'Lost generation', pp. 449–66.

24 J. M. Winter, 'Unemployment, nutrition and infant mortality in Britain, 1920–1950', in Winter (ed.), *Working Class*, pp. 229–55.

25 Roberts, *Classic Slum*, chapter 4.

26 For a full discussion, see B. Waites, 'The Impact of the First World War on Class and Status in England, 1910–20', unpub. Ph.D., Open University, 1982.

27 R. Blythe, *Akenfield*, Allen Lane, London, 1969, p. 47.

28 See Waites's dissertation for reference (note 26 above).

29 Jean Renoir, *La Grande Illusion*, trans. M. Alexandre and A. Sinclair, Lorrimer, London, 1968, p. 71.

The post-war army

At the end of the First World War there were 3·75 million men in the army, over fifteen times the number in 1914 (see Table 8.1). It is ironic, therefore, that after the armistice one of the most immediate and pressing needs identified by the War Office was for continued recruitment. All compulsory enlistment under the Military Service Acts was suspended at noon on 11 November 1918.[1] Two days later Lord Milner, the Secretary for War, wrote to Lloyd George concerning the future of the army. No clear policy, he said, had been established for the post-war army, and, although 'ample preparations for demobilisation' had been made, nothing had been done about 'recruiting or keeping men'. There was a risk, asserted Milner, of the government being 'without any army at all in 6 months!'[2]

From the military point of view Milner's caution was commendable – Europe was indeed in turmoil – but one of the first demands made on the post-war army by society at large was for rapid and complete demobilisation. 'Send the boys home,' demanded the *Daily Herald* on 7 December 1918. 'Why in the world the delay? The war is not officially "over", but everybody knows in fact it is over.'[3] At the end of the month the *Daily Express* asked, 'Will nothing bring home to the Government the seriousness of the immediate need for demobilisation?' and went on to stress 'the depth of hostile feeling that has been raised among all classes, and particularly among the fighting men, by all this deplorable delay'.[4]

During the war a careful and elaborate scheme had been drawn up by the Ministry of Reconstruction to provide for orderly demobilisation. The chief aim of the government was to avoid mass unemployment. The release of soldiers, therefore, was to be based on the needs of industry, with so-called 'pivotal men' being given priority on the grounds that their speedy return to civil life would help create jobs for other veterans. The selection of these men, however, was left to employers, and this favoured those who had most recently left employment and been called up for military service. In fact the Ministry scheme, the product of clever Whitehall minds, theoretically sensible and administratively convenient, was completely out of touch with reality. In effect it meant 'last in, first out', and that was unacceptable to the longer-serving citizen soldier. There was much confusion about the demobilisation scheme, and the general election which Lloyd George called immediately hostilities ceased merely added to it. Preoccupied with the campaign, government ministers failed to explain the reasons behind the plan. At the same time they assured electors that the whole process (which did not in fact begin until 9 December) would be accelerated. It was, as Rudyard Kipling remarked, 'an insane interval of waiting'.[5]

The widespread public demand for demobilisation was mirrored by unrest among the troops. One of the chief outbreaks occurred at

Folkestone on Friday 3 January 1919, where some 10,000 soldiers in transit camps returning from leave to their units in France demonstrated at the town hall in favour of immediate demobilisation. They refused to travel to France and mounted pickets at the harbour and railway station to encourage other men to join the protest. The authorities responded by allowing all pivotal men who had guaranteed jobs to be released at once, and those who had any complaints were allowed seven days' additional leave in order to pursue their case. The trouble at Folkestone was followed the next day by a similar demonstration of 2,000 men at Dover and a wave of protests at other army camps both at home and abroad.[6]

These were demonstrations of citizen soldiers, understandably anxious to return home, dismayed by the continual delays and by the apparent injustice of the demobilisation scheme. The end of hostilities, too, inevitably led to a relaxation of military discipline – or, at least, a reduced willingness on the part of private soldiers unquestioningly to accept such discipline. 'Men who had been long patient became suddenly impatient,' wrote Sir Philip Gibbs. 'Men who had obeyed all discipline broke into disobedience bordering on mutiny.'[7] There was a widespread feeling that with the end of actual fighting their military obligations had been fulfilled and they were now simply 'civilians in khaki'. A typical incident involved Army Service Corps personnel at Osterley Park camp in west London. On 6 January 150 men, mostly ex-London bus drivers and trade unionists, broke camp and drove three lorries to Whitehall with the intention of calling on Lloyd George. Eventually they were assured by an officer at the Demobilisation Department that there would be accelerated demobilisation from their camp after 8 January.[8]

Army and public disquiet caused the government increasing concern. Searching for a solution to the problem, Lloyd George bullied Milner into resignation. In January 1919 he was replaced by Winston Churchill, who at once began to sort out the mess. By the end of the month he had abandoned the old scheme and replaced it with effectively a 'first in, first out' system. All men who had enlisted before 1916 were to be demobilised at once. Only those under thirty-seven years of age and possessing fewer than three wound stripes were retained. In April Churchill told the House of Commons that men were being released 'at the enormous rate of 13,000 or 14,000 daily.'[9] By the end of 1919 over three million men had been returned to civilian life (see Table 8.1).

The problem which Milner raised with Lloyd George in November 1918 – that of 'recruiting or keeping men' – exercised the War Office just as seriously as the difficulties of demobilisation. The army's first post-war *Annual Report* noted 'the necessity for refilling at an early date the depleted ranks of the old Regular Army'.[10] There was a particular

Table 8.1. *Size of army and recruitment, 1914 and 1918–22*

	Size of army (effective strength)	Recruitment (year ending 30 September)
August 1914	247,432	25,850 (to 3 August, approx.)
November 1918	3,779,825	n.a.
November 1919	888,952	126,693 (from 15 January 1919)
November 1920	431,916	71,447
November 1921	292,860	44,950
November 1922	217,986	40,607

Source. (1) Size of army – monthly returns PRO, W.O. 161/82 and W.O. 73/109, 111, 113, 115, 117. (2) Recruitment – *Annual Reports* for the years in question.

need to keep men for the armies of occupation, which the CIGS (Sir Henry Wilson) estimated would take up to half a million troops. In addition, various contingents were required in Italy, Salonika, Turkey, Russia and the Middle East. 'No machinery,' noted Wilson in December 1918, yet existed for the provision of these forces, 'since it would be unsafe to assume that they will be obtainable on a voluntary basis'.[11] Although a powerful War Office lobby existed in favour of extending conscription, there were strong social and political arguments against such a move. It had been introduced in 1916 as a specifically wartime emergency measure. In the public mind the abolition of compulsory military service went hand-in-hand with rapid demobilisation as a natural consequence of the end of the war. In the face of Britain's immense post-war commitments, however, the War Office pressed hard for continued compulsion, especially to 'tide over the period until we could raise a voluntary army of sufficient size to meet our requirements'.[12]

Lloyd George was distinctly reluctant to reintroduce the measure after the suspension of military call-ups on Armistice Day. In the meantime the army had to secure men by voluntary means as best it could. In December 1918 it offered serving soldiers a bounty of £20, £40 or £50 if they would re-enlist for two, three or four years respectively. Up to the end of the recruiting year in September 1919 this attracted nearly 75,000 men. In January 1919 the Army Council also lowered the minimum age of enlistment on normal engagements from eighteen years to seventeen, which brough in an extra 7,000 recruits.[13] When Churchill took over at the War Office he doubled the rates of military pay, mainly in order to counter discontent about the gap between army and civilian rates, but it also had the welcome effect of retaining some men who would otherwise have left the army. These measures, nevertheless, barely alleviated the problem, and Churchill eventually persuaded the Prime Minister of the vital need to keep some 1,200,000 men.

The Naval, Military and Air Force Service Act, which passed through Parliament during March 1919, provided for compulsory military service to be maintained until 30 April 1920. It enabled the government to hold on to the most recently conscripted men. Churchill eloquently (as always) justified the measure on 'practical and patriotic' grounds. It was a temporary expedient to meet a temporary need. He assured the House of Commons that government policy was 'to create with all possible speed a volunteer Army for the garrisons of our Empire'. He argued that there was 'no necessity for compulsory service for the purpose of a national Army for a great many years to come, because we have an enormous mass of men already trained'. There was no likelihood of the Bill being rejected – the government had a very substantial parliamentary majority – but its passage gave opposition MPs a chance to air their views on military matters. J. H. Thomas was worried that the conscript army might be used for 'industrial purposes'. This was echoed by another Labour member, Benjamin Spoor. 'Whether they be right or wrong,' he said, 'the workers of Great Britain do see in every form of militarism a real menace to their legitimate advance.' Thomas also argued that sufficient volunteers could be obtained by paying soldiers a decent wage. He was supported by Brigadier Henry Page Croft – one of only two MPs in the short-lived centre-right National Party – who sharply criticised 'those kinds of pre-war sweating' which enabled the government 'to get hungry men into the Army in order to defend our shores'. 'That,' he declared, 'is not a true citizenship.'[14]

The government's perception of the post-war army – in so far as the administration had any particular view on the matter – is contained in a pamphlet entitled *The Mission of the British Army*. This was No. 37 in a series of somewhat improving booklets issued by the Ministry of Reconstruction in 1919, with titles such as *Food Production and its Problems* and *Poor Law Reform*. The aim of the pamphlet was to 'educate the ordinary citizen in his conception of what the British Army is and for what it exists, and especially what are the present calls on the Army arising out of the present condition of the world'.[15] Four authors and several drafts were tried before a final version was approved by Churchill and published in August 1919. In terms of government propaganda the pamphlet represented too little too late. A sustained publicity effort to explain both the original demobilisation scheme and the need for a substantial post-war army during the last two months of 1918 might well have eased the men's disquiet.[16] By the late summer of 1919, however, Churchill's policies had effectively taken the steam out of the soldiers' protests.

Stressing that the United Kingdom could 'by no means' be 'looked upon as a Great Power imbued with "militarist" ideals', *The Mission of the British Army* began with the assertion that 'a well-trained national army on a larger scale might have prevented the war'. If Great Britain had been in a position to land half a million men, or even 250,000, in

France in 1914 – instead of the 80,000 who actually comprised the Expeditionary Force – 'the war might never have taken place . . .'

If we judge from the experience of the past five years, it would have been well worth the sacrifice of leisure and money to form a great National Army before 1914; but the inclinations and the views which were held by the majority of the British people did not tend that way . . . We have paid the price for our remissness in the past, and had it not been for the patriotism and military aptitudes of the nation we should have failed to atone for former impolicy.

The lesson was clear. The nation should not be seduced by such catch-phrases as 'the war was a war to end war' or pious hopes of universal disarmament. Only by examining the empire's responsibilities and maintaining armed forces large enough to meet them could future peace and prosperity be assured.

The qualities of the regular army were extolled. It was both a 'nursery of military training' and a national 'standard of physical and mental training'. The author was at pains to emphasise that the soldier's life was not 'vicious'. 'If we come to examine the facts fairly and squarely,' he wrote, judiciously hedging his bets, 'we find that the soldier only represents the tendencies of the classes from which he springs. His sobriety and his morality are no worse and in fact are probably better than those of the manufacturing towns in the Midlands.'

Looking to the future, the continued need for overseas garrisons was noted. It was vital to protect the country's foreign and imperial trade. 'The necessary insurance to maintain that trade . . . will take the shape of our Regular Forces.' Clearly anxious to reassure his readers, the author had a word or two to say about the possible use of the army 'in industrial disputes at home'. He declared that 'armed force has never been used to coerce the orderly striker' and asserted that 'the notion of a body of trained gladiators to stand at the call of Capital is abhorrent from every English instinct'.

The pamphlet concluded by summarising the present position and, in particular, justifying the 1919 Military Service Act – 'forced upon us by the necessity of releasing three-quarters of our armies of 1918' . . . 'Conscription,' added the author, 'is not being retained as such; the term is being erroneously used.' The reader was assured that further compulsion in the future was not being contemplated. The Military Service Act was 'but one link in the chain of our military evolution' currently leading to the creation of a standing regular army and then to some future but unspecified military system which would 'no doubt take into consideration the position created by the establishment of the League of Nations'.[17]

The re-establishment of a standing regular army depended on the recruitment of sufficient suitable manpower. The recruiting process, too, is the point at which the army and society most continuously meet so a study of post-war recruitment will tell us something about the army's place in society. On 15 January 1919 the War Office took over from the wartime Ministry of National Service and resumed recruitment on pre-war lines. By the end of the recruiting year (30 September 1919), in an eight-and-a-half-month period, over 126,000 men had enlisted. Of these just over 50 per cent joined on normal long-service engagements – 'a remarkable response from a Nation which had just emerged from a costly and bitter struggle'. The *Annual Report* explained the recruiting boom at least in part to three factors. In the first place many of the men were ex-soldiers with war experience for whom an additional period of service with the colours – frequently for a short engagement – 'was often entered into as a temporary expedient in order to bridge a period of unsettlement in the industrial world'. A second factor – it was asserted – lay in the attractions of active service in north Russia. 5,344 men volunteered for the Russian Relief Force. Finally there was the financial inducement (a minimum 2s 6d per day extra) of special exhumation duties connected with the centralisation of military cemeteries in France for which there were large numbers of applicants. 15,445 were actually enlisted. It was not entirely a buyer's market, and the army itself changed the recruiting procedure in order to make the process less intimidating. A 'model recruiting Depot calculated to create in the minds of intending recruits an impression of sympathetic welcome to Army life' was established. The 'susceptibilities of the recruit' were 'carefully safeguarded'. Baths and comfortable sleeping accommodation 'in separate cubicles' were provided, 'whilst an excellent restaurant and recreation rooms, amply and suitably furnished, complete the homelike atmosphere which has been introduced'.[18]

Although recruitment did not stay at the unusually high level of 1919 (see Table 8.1 for 1919–20 and 1921–22 figures), for seven years after the war the numbers enlisting exceeded the annual average of 28,800 recorded in the five years prior to the war. Indeed, during the decade following 1919 the annual figure fell only twice (1926–27 and 1928–29) below the pre-war average. The relative buoyancy of recruitment in this period provides little evidence of a general revulsion from warfare or matters military. Yet this clearly worried the author of *The Mission of the British Army*, since he devoted considerable effort to his argument that possessing a large and well prepared army would not necessarily make Britain 'militaristic'. There was, however, undoubtedly some post-war reaction against militarism, if only in the gloomy introspection of those who had lost family and friends. In the early spring of 1919, watching the 'triumphal march' of the Guards, who had suffered over 44,000 casualties, through London, one observer noted 'a great crowd to greet them. The cheering rather subdued: the heavy losses were too much on all our minds.'[19]

The Great War was generally perceived as a unique and mercifully unrepeatable occurrence: the 'war to end war'. As such the remembered horrors of trench warfare did not necessarily act as a constraint on recruitment for the very reason that they could not recur – or so people believed. Paradoxically, too, the commemoration of war dead could even stimulate recruiting. Dignified and disciplined army ceremonial at Cenotaph or local war memorial might encourage those still attracted to the perceived nobility and grandeur of a military career.

Some interesting regional trends are discernible in the post-war recruiting pattern. The London region and Southern Command (that is, virtually the whole southern part of the country, together with most of the Midlands) were consistently above-average recruiting areas. Until 1926–27 London was the best area in Great Britain. By contrast, until the mid-1920s, Northern Command (the north Midlands and north-east), Western Command (Wales and the north-west) and Scotland were all poor recruiting territory. Within each zone, urban areas recruited better than rural. This reflected pre-war trends and the progressive 'urbanisation' of the army from the mid-nineteenth century onwards.[20] But the returns in the *Annual Report* merely indicate where soldiers enlisted. They do not take account of the element of internal migration which certainly occurred (what might be termed the 'Dick Whittington effect'): men who moved to towns in search of civilian jobs before submitting to the 'last resort' of joining the army.[21]

The relatively poor showing of peripheral regions in the recruiting returns is confirmed by the figures showing recruitment by nationality. There is a myth that the army was always full of poor Irish and Scots, driven by economic desperation from subsistence agriculture to take the king's (or queen's) shilling. It is true that in the early nineteenth century the Irish were heavily over-represented in the army – this was never the case with the Scots – but by the beginning of the First World War the proportion (9·1 per cent in 1913) simply reflected Ireland's share of the United Kingdom population (9·7 per cent in the 1911 census). At the same time Scotland was under-represented – 7·6 per cent as against 10·5 per cent of the population. From the statistics the Welsh appear to be singularly unmartial. In 1913 they comprised 1·4 per cent of the army while representing 5·4 per cent of the population. In contrast to these figures, from about the 1890s onwards the proportion of 'English-born' outweighed England's share of the country's population. The British army both before and immediately after World War I was predominantly, and disproportionately, an *English* army. The post-war recruiting statistics bear this out (see Table 8.2).

Following the war the national shares of the United Kingdom population were approximately as follows: England 75 per cent, Wales 6 per cent, Scotland 10 per cent and Ireland 9 per cent.

Table 8.2. *Recruitment by nationality for men on normal engagements, 1912–13 and 1919–20 to 1921–22; recruiting year: 1 October to 30 September (%)*

	English	Welsh	Scottish	Irish
1912–13	79·4	2·4	8·6	9·6
1919–13	79·8	3·0	8·0	9·2
1920–21	78·7	3·7	8·6	9·0
1921–22	81·2	4·8	10·9	3·1

Source. Annual Reports for the years in question.

The proportional over-recruitment of Englishmen is clear. In the post-war years there was a gentle rise in Welsh enlistment, which, joined by extra Scottish recruits in 1921–22, went some way towards compensating for the sharp drop in Irish enlistment following the suspension of all Irish recruitment in December 1921 after the signing of the Anglo-Irish treaty. Recruitment was never resumed in the twenty-six counties which became the Irish Free State in 1922. The fall in the number of Irish soldiers, mostly those from southern Ireland, is reflected by a slight change in the religious composition of the army. Just before the war 15 per cent of the rank and file were Roman Catholic. In 1921 this figure was 14 per cent, but by 1925 it had fallen to 11 per cent. Virtually all the rest were Protestant, the great majority of whom claimed to be Church of England (73 per cent in 1925).

The change in the 'national' complexion of the army – the fall in Irish numbers – was not a direct result of the war. The pressures of war, nevertheless, acted as a catalyst on existing social and political trends. They did much to stimulate the post-war 'troubles', and in Ireland the concept of the 'nation in arms' soon took on a particular local connotation. National and regional variations also came through in the quality of men enlisting. Recruits from Ireland were among the healthiest in the post-war years. Perhaps this was due to the purity of the Irish climate. At the other end of the scale, in 1919–20, 45 per cent of all those who offered their services in the Western Command were rejected for physical reasons. Some of those who were accepted gave rise to complaint. In July 1919 the army command in Delhi drew attention to the low quality of troops which the War Office proposed to draft out to India. A proportion of the personnel, they noted, were 'category B1, in other words, men who were only able to march at least five miles, see to shoot with the aid of glasses and hear *nil*'. This was not the standard which India had been accustomed to accept before the war.[22] In March 1921 Lord Rawlinson, Commander-in-Chief in India, repeated the point that standards had declined in comparison to before the war. In 1913 289 troops under the age of twenty-five years had been invalided home. In 1920 the equivalent figure was 1,558. 'Of course,' he remarked, 'the physical standard to-day is not what it was in '13.'[23]

The Director-General of Recruiting specifically blamed the war for the fall in quality. 'It is generally agreed,' he wrote in 1920, 'that the strict rationing of food supplies during the late War has retarded the development of growing lads.' Another significant factor was that 'a very large number of boys who were 10 or 12 years old in 1914' were absorbed into the munitions industries. 'Owing to the high wages they received and to the absence of their fathers on service, these lads were subject to less parental control, and in many instances acquired habits prejudicial to their physical and moral development.'[24] Physical standards gradually improved. Yet in 1924 it was still maintained that 'the physique of the youth of the nation has not yet recovered from the effects of war and post-war conditions'.[25] In 1926 58 per cent of those applying were rejected. The chief defects identified were underweight, poor chest measurement and bad teeth. The last of these was particularly serious in Scotland. In 1927 as an experimental measure the dental standard was 'slightly lowered for recruits enlisting in Scotland'. The result was gratifying : a 50 per cent increase in enlistments. The experiment was extended to the rest of the United Kingdom.[26]

One persistent worry of the immediate post-war years was that of the army's general 'weakness'. In 1919 Colonel Charles à Court Repington noted that few old regular officers remained, and inferior regimental officers, who had joined since the war, were 'staying on for the greater part because they are not sure of other employment'. There was also a 'paucity of good N.C.O.s'.[27] On a tour of the British Army of the Rhine in March 1920 Sir Henry Wilson found battalions of the Middlesex Regiment and the Black Watch 'all very young, very raw, very untrained'.[28] Robert Graves recalled that drafts from New Army battalions to his unit of the Royal Welsh Fusiliers early in 1919 'were a constant shame to the senior officers. Paternity orders, stumer cheques, and drunkenness on parade grew frequent; not to mention table manners . . .'[29] Commanding the second battalion, Royal Dublin Fusiliers in Constantinople during 1919, Colonel Charles Bonham-Carter wrote that it was 'a mixture of re-enlisted service men with war experience' who, being volunteers (conscription was never applied in Ireland), were 'good fellows', and recruits: 'the latter included with youngsters a number of the worst sort of corner boys from Dublin'. Drunkenness and inefficiency were common when Bonham-Carter took over the unit. During the eleven months they were at Constantinople the battalion suffered three trials for murder and 'many Courts-Martial'.[30]

A particular change resulting from wartime technological developments was an increased need for technically skilled personnel. In the spring of 1919 Sir Henry Wilson drew the Cabinet's attention to a serious deficiency in transport and communication specialists, men 'vital to the efficiency and mobility of the troops'.[31] A year later Sir

Nevil Macready, recently appointed to the Irish Command, reported that, in order merely to bring the numbers of technical troops in his command up to establishment, he required over 600 men, including wireless operators, motor cyclists, telegraphists, cablemen and drivers.[32] The *Annual Report* for 1919–20 noted the increasing difficulty in obtaining skilled tradesmen 'in competition with private employers in the technical labour market of the Nation'. The character of the modern army had been 'revolutionised' by the evolution of the art of war since August 1914. The growing use of the internal combustion engine had produced a considerable demand for skilled mechanics. The 'development of communication by wireless, by telegraph, and by telephone' had markedly increased the numbers of electrically skilled personnel required. Not only was the army in competition with private employers, it was also competing with the newly established Royal Air Force. In October 1920 the Adjutant General also complained about the high rates of pay being offered to artificers and mechanical transport drivers by other government departments, especially the Irish Office. The basic army rate for artificers was £1 4s 6d, per week; the Irish Office was offering £5 6s 6d with a bonus of £25 at the end of each year's service.[33]

Another constraint on the recruitment of skilled men was a widespread apprehension among the tradesmen themselves that service in the army 'might militate against re-entry into their trade on return to civil life'.[34] The Army Council, with limited funds, ran a number of schemes to ensure that as many soldiers as possible were fitted for return to civil life, but for the most part they relied merely on pious exhortations, soliciting 'the co-operation of other Government Departments, of the Trade Unions and of employers of labour in this country to assist them in fulfilling what is undoubtedly a debt of the Nation'.[35]

Even when skilled men did enlist, they tended to do so only for short periods. In 1921 it was reported that an anticipated revival of trade made them diffident about joining up on normal long-service engagements.[36] Since the Treasury refused to countenance any significant increase in their pay, the army's solution to the problem was to train tradesmen themselves. In 1921 a 'Central Trade School for Boys', providing a three-year course for some three hundred boys a year, followed by two years in army workshops, was set up at Blandford in Dorset.[37] By 1924 the experiment was adjudged a success and the *Annual Report* noted that places in the school were oversubscribed.

Army education received a tremendous boost during the war. Before 1914 the only educational provision was elementary. The subsequent development of higher-level work was stimulated by three main factors: the problem of ex-soldier employment, the demands of the men themselves, and the need 'to assist in diverting their minds from the monotony of trench warfare'. The War Office claimed that the problem of civil resettlement was the most important single factor. It was certainly true that in 1919 a very great effort was put into adult education and resettlement training of one sort and another. The Army of the Rhine took over a whole university at Bonn, set up a Commercial College in Cologne, established facilities for technical education and even provided classes for ordinands. At home there was an equally high level of activity. The Irish Command, taken as typical of home commands, reported at the end of 1919 that approximately 4,000 officers and men had passed through courses of technical and agricultural instruction. In addition over a hundred students had taken advanced tuition at the 150 acre Ballyfair Agricultural Training Farm near the Curragh in County Kildare. Each unit was supplied with a standard set of educational books and technical apparatus. Instructional textbooks on basic subjects were included with a library of 250 volumes of works 'by the best authors', covering such subjects as art, botany, travel, philosophy, religion, science and industry.[38]

During 1919, as well, two 'trade schools', at which soldiers spent the whole of the last six months of their service, were set up, at Hounslow and Catterick, in order to assist men to find civilian employment. Although the Comptroller and Auditor General complained in 1921 that the schools had been established without proper authority, the scheme was regarded as such a success that it was retained. Each year the majority of trainees found jobs and in 1926 the Army Council increased the annual numbers at the two 'Vocational Training Centres', with a new one at Aldershot, from 1,140 to 2,390. Reflecting the degree to which the army had now to make military life and conditions attractive to recruits, this expansion was 'fully justified both on the grounds of their [the Army Council's] moral obligation to the non-tradesman soldier and of military expediency'.[39]

The army also extended its educational provision in other ways. In 1919 a Special Army Education Certificate was introduced. It was accepted by the Board of Education for admission to teacher training colleges, by universities as exemption from matriculation examinations and by a variety of professional and learned bodies.[40] Lower-grade Education Certificates (Nos. 1, 2 and 3) were developed especially so as to encourage the study of practical subjects, such as carpentry, glazing, shorthand, commerce and electricity. In 1920 Sir Archibald Williamson, junior minister at the War Office, drew Parliament's attention to the benefits of these developments. 'The Army,' he declared, 'is now a profession which in peace times confers invaluable service in many ways on the men on resuming civil life.' Mixing assertion with intention, he said that military service was 'no longer a blind alley occupation . . . We are endeavouring to make the Army an avenue to success in civil life, and the effect must be to bring the Army and civil life closer together.'[41] Similar sentiments were voiced by Sir Henry Wilson at the opening of the Imperial Education Conference in June 1919. It was, he said, 'essential that in the future education must be woven into the soldier's life as an integral part of his training'. This was especially important for two reasons: the need to keep pace with 'the development of modern scientific invention', and in order 'to safeguard our men from the old reproach that they left the Army ill-fitted to take their place in the professional and industrial life of the country'. The war, he declared, had 'shown us clearly that we must take every means in our power to promote the co-operation of the Army with the general life of the Nation'.[42] Wilson's fulsomeness was echoed by H. A. L. Fisher, President of the Board of Education, who spoke next and somewhat sweepingly proclaimed that the CIGS's recognition of education as an essential part of army training was 'one of those great steps forward in the social progress of the world for which the war has been responsible'.[43]

The co-ordination of education was assisted by the creation of the Army Educational Corps in June 1920. For the first time this provided a proper career structure for those involved in military education. Yet, despite Wilson's rhetoric, education suffered with every other branch of the army in the financial retrenchment of the early 1920s. The corps, which numbered 482 officers and 595 warrant officers and sergeants in December 1920, was reduced to 162 and 474 respectively.[44] Vocational training, moreover, was restricted throughout the inter-war years by lack of funds, although it did have some tangible results. In the 1920s about one-third of those leaving the army were skilled tradesmen with good prospects of civilian employment, one-third had sufficient education to benefit from a spell in the army's own training schools, while the rest remained ill educated and poorly equipped to compete for jobs on the civilian labour market.[45]

The need for some degree of technical training was emphasised by the high proportion of unskilled men attracted to the colours. A comparison of the trades of men offering themselves for enlistment before the war with the figures available for 1920 gives some indication of the army's manpower constituency and suggests that it did not change very much over the war years (see Table 8.3). Nearly half those presenting themselves at recruiting offices were unskilled. Confirming the 'urban' origins of the average recruit, three-quarters of these men came from towns and cities. Less than a quarter of the total number could fully be described as skilled.[46] Naturally changes in the general labour market influenced the proportions of each occupational group in any one year. The *Annual Report* for 1922–23 noted a particular shortage of building tradesmen. In 1924–25 enlistments were low in agricultural areas 'where

Table 8.3. *Trades of men offering themselves for enlistment, 1906–07 to 1912–13 average, and 1 January to 30 September 1920 (%)*

	1906–07 to 1912–13 five-year average	1 January to 30 September 1920
Town casuals	19	19
Agricultural unskilled labour	11	9
Other unskilled labour	17	19
All unskilled labour	47	47
Skilled labour	23	29
Other occupations (semi-skilled)	25	21
Professions, students	1	1
Boys under 17 years	4	2
Total (%)	100	100
Total number	47,763	68,235

Note. The only post-war figures available are those for the first nine months of 1920.
Source. Annual Reports for the years in question.

labour was reported to be scarce and wages were high in consequence'. A perennial War Office grumble concerned unemployment benefit, which, 'whatever its advantages to National well-being in its broader aspects, must, from the nature of the case, considerably counteract the economic incentive to enlist'.[47]

Army pay, of course, is one of the most obvious factors in 'the economic incentive to enlist'. Its level also provides a crude index of society's formal estimation of the army's value to the nation. Before the war the annual earnings of a private soldier amounted to 63 per cent of the average earnings for semi-skilled workers. In 1920 the position had only slightly improved. The unmarried soldier's average pay and allowances of £2 7s a week equalled 65 per cent of average earnings.[48] Even with the extra payments allowed to certain classes of skilled tradesmen, it is no wonder that the army had difficulty in enlisting the types of men it required. Recruitment was certainly sensitive to wage rates. In the 1922–23 *Annual Report* it was claimed that unfounded publicity about a possible reduction in army pay hit recruitment in Scotland (suitably). In October 1925 a $5\frac{1}{4}$ per cent reduction in wages, reflecting an equivalent fall in the cost of living since 1919, resulted in 'a marked decrease in intake during each of the succeeding three months'.[49] In terms of pay, officers fared a little better than other ranks. In 1913–14 their annual average earnings of £170 were 52 per cent of those for the higher professions as a whole. In 1922–24 their £390 represented 67 per cent of the professional average.[50] Yet it remains abundantly clear that soldiers of all ranks were underpaid in terms of equivalent occupations, and it seems that the government relied on either simple patriotism or economic desperation to fill the army's ranks.

Soldiers' allowances saw some improvement over the war years and during the immediately post-war urgent search for recruits. During the war a separation allowance was granted to married soldiers serving away from their wives and families. In 1919 the allowance was also given to men enlisting on short engagements – a break from the traditional reluctance to enlist married men at all. In 1920 an additional allowance was introduced for soldiers attaining the age of twenty-six years who had married after enlistment. This measure was specially calculated 'to attract an intending recruit who means to make his career in the Army'.[51]

There were also improvements in barrack accommodation and, after the Navy, Army and Air Force Institutes (NAAFI) took over from the Navy and Army Canteen Board in 1921, in recreation facilities. From the war onwards army canteens were staffed by women. In response to criticism of this policy, commanding officers were reported to be in favour of retaining them, 'as they helped to give a good tone to the canteen ... and to bring into it an atmosphere of home'. The typical institute included a restaurant and sitting rooms. Some had billiard tables and a small hall for concert parties and amateur dramatics. Their 'homely' atmosphere may have been one factor in the drop in the amount of beer consumed by private soldiers. In 1913 43 per cent of the total turnover in army canteens resulted from sales of beer. By 1921 the proportion had dropped to 14 per cent, and by 1925 to 11.[52]

In addition to improved social facilities, there was an expansion in the army medical services. At the end of 1919 there were over 60 per cent more medical personnel than there had been in 1914. Financial stringency, unattractive salary scales and the restricted professional opportunities of military medicine, however, resulted in the Royal Army Medical Corps remaining chronically short of qualified doctors for most of the inter-war years. Dental hygiene fared rather better. In 1914 not a single dentist had accompanied the Expeditionary Force to France. But the importance of dental health was soon recognised, and by 1918 over 800 dentists were serving at home and abroad. In January 1921 the Army Dental Corps was formally established as an integral part of the Army Medical Service. By contrast, an efficient military ophthalmic service built up during the war was completely dismantled in 1919.[53]

Broad social attitudes towards the army in the post-war period were very much moulded by its perceived duties. During these years the army had four main roles: the pre-war one of imperial defence; intervention in Russia; a domestic role in aid of the civil power; and peacekeeping in Ireland. The first of these was by far the least contentious, comprising as it did a 'traditional' function. Garrisoning India and securing British interests in the Middle East were what the army had done for generations. Even so, for wartime volunteers and conscripts, imperial duties mattered rather less than speedy demobilisation after 11 November 1918. In May 1919 General Allenby wrote from Egypt that unrest in his army verged on mutiny. 'Nothing,' he told Sir Henry Wilson, 'will convince the troops that Military operations did not end on the signing of the Armistice ... I have, as you know, a very large proportion of '14 and '15 men.' 'These men,' he observed acidly, 'would, most of them, have been dead by now – no doubt – if their service had been in France – but they take no comfort in that consideration.'[54] Four months later there was trouble in India, where troops at Poona began to protest against demobilisation delays. 'In these circumstances,' telegraphed the Viceroy, 'we feel that the retention of demobilisable men indefinitely anywhere in India would probably create a more inconvenient and possibly a more dangerous situation than would be caused by a temporary reduction of the British garrison in India.'[55] In this particular instance, therefore, even the Government of India accepted that the demands of citizen soldiers overrode the requirements of imperial defence.

Russia was a different case. British troops had originally been sent to Archangel in 1918 in an attempt to re-establish the eastern front. After the armistice some people hoped, and many feared, that the troops would be used to attack the Russian Bolsheviks.[56] For war-weary British soldiers this raised the unattractive prospect of continued active service a long way from home. Although the *Annual Report* for 1919–20 claimed that service in Russia actually encouraged some enlistments, the available evidence suggests that for most soldiers the reverse was true. Henry Wilson told the Cabinet on 10 January 1919 that within the army 'the prospect of being sent to Russia was immensely unpopular'.[57]

The possibility of service in Russia, together with that of military deployment in Britain both to maintain public order and break strikes, was raised in a secret questionnaire circulated by the Commander-in-Chief of Home Forces to commanding officers throughout Britain during February 1919. The circular specifically asked whether troops would 'respond to orders for assistance to preserve the public peace', assist in strike-breaking and 'parade for draft to overseas, especially to Russia'. Replies from units indicated that troops, who appreciated 'their duty as citizens in repressing disorderly persons', could be relied on to keep order if requested. On the matter of strike-breaking the general feeling was 'that it would not be fair to ask troops to do what they themselves would consider "blackleg" work'. As for the third enquiry, the commanding officers reported that 'troops will parade for drafts overseas with the exception of Russia'. Among the reasons given for this attitude was ignorance of why the government was intervening in Russia at all, reluctance to take part in active warfare against an undefined enemy and fears of demobilisation delays.[58]

The leaking of this foolishly worded questionnaire to the press was undoubtedly embarrassing for the government. The document clearly identified the areas of action about which the military authorities felt uneasy. But the replies were, on the whole, reassuring. Despite occasional fears that soldiers' soviets might be established, there was no real evidence that the war had radicalised the army in any profound way. The demobilisation chaos made citizen soldiers bloody-minded, not revolutionary. For the most part the attitudes revealed by the questionnaire simply reflected the anxieties and uncertainties of men anxious to return to civilian life with the minimum of fuss or interference. The government, for its part, took the point about strike-breaking to heart and, with a number of minor exceptions, did not employ the army on such duties until the General Strike in 1926. Soldiers were deployed during railway and coal strikes in 1919–21, but their principal official function was to preserve public order.[59] The use of troops in 1926, however, did have an effect on recruiting. In cities and urban districts particularly there was a significant drop in the number of men offering their services.[60] It seems clear that the employment of the army in industrial disputes acted as a brake on enlistment within its principal constituency.

Peacekeeping in Ireland raised different problems. It also put the relatively young and only partially trained post-war army under considerable pressure. In July 1920 Sir Nevil Macready warned the Cabinet, 'Don't lean too hard on the Army.' He advised ministers that 'the Army to-day was not the Army of 1913'. The senior officers were 'first rate', but 'below that, many were young and untrained, and if the strain were doubled you would get near the danger limit. The young recruits did not like to use their weapons.' Another officer from the Irish Command, General Strickland, reported that there were 'a good many' deserters from his forces.[61] The army stuck it out in Ireland until the truce in July 1921 which was followed by the Anglo-Irish treaty in December. But the following May, when it seemed possible that active operations might have to be resumed, the CIGS, Lord Cavan, reported that he was 'afraid to order troops to reinforce from this country' because he had 'received such reports about the unpopularity of Irish service'.[62]

The single most serious incident of insubordination in the post-war professional army had an Irish connection. The Connaught Rangers' mutiny in the summer of 1920 illustrates both the particular stresses acting on southern Irish regiments and also some of the general problems besetting the army at the time. The first battalion of the regiment was stationed in the Punjab, and between 28 June and 2 July nearly 600 out of its 800 men mutinied, giving as their reason that they were 'in sympathy with their country' and that they 'would do no more work until the British troops had been removed from Ireland'.[63] Following the outbreak sixty-one men were convicted of mutiny. Fourteen death sentences were passed. One was carried out. There were some extenuating circumstances. The battalion was badly officered, it had few fully experienced NCOs and it contained a substantial number of relatively new recruits. Of the 206 men in the last two drafts out from home, 172 became mutineers.[64] The unit had also been on intensive training during the hottest summer in living memory. The Rangers had not really had time or the opportunity after the war to re-establish a corporate regimental spirit. No doubt this was not a very different situation from that of many other units in the post-war army. But the combination of factors and the men's growing concern with news from home, especially tales of Black and Tan reprisals, was sufficient to push them beyond breaking point.[65] Perhaps, like the protesting troops in early 1919, they simply wanted to go home.

On the periphery of the regular army are part-time soldiers and veterans. The interest and enthusiasm of the former are a useful indication of the position of military affairs in the nation's life. The Territorial Army, which provided a chance for Everyman to participate, remained sadly under-strength following the war. In 1922 it had an effective strength of 134,769 as against an establishment of 179,622. In 1929 the equivalent figures were 136,791 and 178,002. In contrast to the regular army, London was the slowest recruiting area in the country. Although at the end of the war senior Territorials pressed the War Office to re-establish the force as soon as possible in order to exploit the post-war reservoir of recently discharged trained manpower, matters were delayed until February 1920 while the precise function and conditions of the Territorial Army were decided. Before the war it had been raised as a home defence force, not liable for foreign service. But after the armistice the army's principal responsibilities were imperial, and part-time volunteers could hardly be expected to provide much support abroad. In the end the Territorial Army was formally established as a second-line army, liable in emergencies to serve overseas. Churchill promised that the Territorials would go abroad only in units and that they would not be used simply as draft-finding units for regular formations. Another fear concerned their possible employment in domestic industrial disputes. Although the force was never officially used, Territorial drill halls and personnel were heavily involved with the para-military Defence Force and Civil Constabulary Reserve formed in 1921 and 1926 respectively, and this seems to have retarded enlistment among trade unionists.[66]

A novel feature in post-war Britain was the emergence of veterans' pressure groups. Indeed, the development of ex-servicemen's organisations was perhaps the single most lasting legacy of the 'nation in arms'. Never hitherto having had a mass conscript army, the government had never before needed to make any provision for veterans on a large scale. The corollary to conscription was some sort of official veterans' administration to meet the needs and protect the interests of able-bodied and disabled ex-servicemen. Like much else during World War I, the government began dealing with such matters as pensions, rehabilitation and civil resettlement on an *ad hoc* and haphazard basis. During 1916 and 1917 three pressure groups were formed to represent veteran interests: the National Association of Discharged Sailors and Soldiers, the National Federation of Discharged and Demobilised Sailors and Soldiers, and the Comrades of the Great War. The first two of these, the Association and the Federation, were mildly radical in spirit, and had Labour and Liberal political sympathies. The Comrades, on the other hand, were more conservative. They were founded with the encouragement of Lord Derby, Secretary of State for War, in response to the Federation. Derby was alarmed lest 'the movement to encourage soldiers to take part in political questions will be fanned by certain political factions for their own ends'.[67]

Fears of political manipulation increased after the armistice when a number of more extreme groups sprang up, such as the Soldiers', Sailors' and Airmen's Union – one of whose aims was to undermine British intervention in Russia – and two splinter groups from the Federation: the National Union of Ex-servicemen, who favoured an alliance with the Labour Party, and the International Union of Ex-servicemen, who sought to overthrow the capitalist system through revolutionary tactics. The Home Office Directorate of Intelligence took a close interest in these groups, and the grievances of ex-servicemen featured prominently in the weekly 'Report on Revolutionary Organisations in the United Kingdom' which was circulated to the Cabinet. There was certainly much talk of violent action. Many senior politicians and generals feared that trained ex-servicemen, or even slow-to-be-demobilised conscripts, might form the spearhead of a British revolution.

The peak of veteran agitation came in the summer and autumn of 1919. In June there were disturbances among ex-soldiers at Wolverhampton and Epsom, where one policeman died and twelve other people were injured. The nation-wide peace celebrations in July were boycotted by veterans' organisations. Riots broke out in a number of places, most seriously in Luton, where the town hall was gutted by fire.[68] But much of the steam was taken out of ex-servicemen discontent by an increase in pensions during August. This was followed by a package of reforms which made provision for disabled men, gave

veterans preferential treatment at labour exchanges and encouraged
voluntary agencies to assist them. In 1921 the Asssociation, the
Federation and the Comrades amalgamated to form the British Legion.
This marked the 'neutralisation' of the veterans' movement.[69] The
Legion moved away from the role of political pressure group and steadily
developed as an interest group concerned mostly with securing
employment for its members and providing benevolent support for
needy veterans.

The development of ex-servicemen's associations reflected more the
problems of civil resettlement than any direct expression of shared
experience in the armed forces. Some of the groups were positively
antagonistic to the services, and no doubt many veterans shared the
'attitude of apathy towards the Army and military affairs' which the
Annual Report for 1923–24 noted among the civil population. Yet with
the exception, perhaps, of the War Office Directorate of Recruiting an
'attitude of apathy' was for the most part reciprocated by the army
towards the civil community. The professional army, an enclosed,
specialised and inward-looking institution, is by nature cut off from
society at large. The chief desire of most officers in the aftermath of
World War I was simply to return as quickly as possible to 'proper',
traditional soldiering on the pre-war model. Despite the efforts of
radical soldiers like J. F. C. Fuller and Basil Liddell Hart, the lessons of
the Great War were barely studied on an official level. This was
precisely because, as the CIGS, Sir George Milne, told the Chiefs of
Staff in 1926, the war with Germany had been 'abnormal' and was
unlikely to be repeated.[70]

The post-war army itself had much in common with its predecessor
before the war, but it was not entirely free from change either
originating in or just accelerated by the war. The impact of mass citizen
enlistment – 'the people in khaki' as John Burns put it[71] – certainly
modernised the army in a number of ways. Technological advances also
had their effect, even if mechanisation did not go as far as some soldiers
wished. The demand for technical personnel particularly meant that the
army had to become attractive to potential recruits. This was not
perhaps as difficult as might be thought. There was indeed a climate of
vague pacifism and mild anti-militarism during the 1920s and early
1930s. But the sort of people most affected by it were not likely to think
of joining up anyway. The army was not dramatically rejected by society
in reaction to the horrors of trench warfare. In the post-war years social
attitudes towards military affairs were characterised not so much by
antipathy as by apathy. In his memoirs Sir William Robertson observed
that during the war 'nearly every household in the country had at least
one of its members in the army'. He believed that 'the people and the
army had become one and the same thing ... The brick wall that used

to separate them seemed to have been effectively broken down'. 'But,' he lamented, 'no sooner was the war over than the dislike to military uniform reasserted itself, every one who could promptly discarded it.'[72]

Some military traditions, however, did prompt public demands for reform. In 1923 the War Office abolished Field Punishment No. 1 – popularly known as 'crucifixion' – which allowed offenders to be shackled to gun wheels or railings for up to two hours a day. After a and a number of other offences was abolished in 1930.[73] Although wartime living standards had resulted in a generally healthier civilian population, contemporaries believed, as already indicated, that the average potential soldier was paradoxically less healthy than before. But within the post-war army itself the troops were on the whole better housed and educated; recreational facilities had improved and solders drank less. They were not, however, noticeably better paid. The changes that occured were gradual. It is very likely that sooner or later they would have happened in any case. The army only dimly reflected some of the more general changes in society: enhanced social mobility, a degree of political radicalisation, increasing trade unionism and a broadening of democracy.[74] Partly this was due to the army's fundamental irrelevance to domestic society in the 1920s. Partly, no doubt, the army also resisted (and resists) change for the very good reason that many of the military values it expresses are themselves unchanging. Paradoxically, from the perspective of the 1920s, it seemed that the wartime creation of a 'nation in arms' changed society more than it changed the army.

Notes

1 *Annual Report*, 1913–19. Unless otherwise noted, the statistical information in this chapter has been derived from the *General Annual Report[s] on the British Army for year[s] ending 30 September . . . 1913* (1914, Cd 7252), *1914 to 1919* (1920, Cmd 1193), *1920* (1922, Cmd 1610), *1921* (1923, Cmd 1941), *1922* (1924, Cmd 2114), *1923* (1924, Cmd 2272), *1924* (1925, Cmd 2342), *1925* (1926, Cmd 2582), *1926* (1927, Cmd 2806), *1927* (1928, Cmd 3030), *1928* (1929, Cmd 3265, *1929* (1930, Cmd 3498). These are referred to in the notes as *Annual Report*, 1912–13, 1914–19 and so on.
2 House of Lords Record Office, Lloyd George Mss, F/38/4/24, Milner to Lloyd George, 13 November 1918.
3 Quoted in S. R. Graubard, 'Military demobilisation in Great Britain following the First World War', *Journal of Modern History*, XIX, 1947, p. 300. This is the best account of demobilisation.
4 Quoted in Andrew Rothstein, *The Soldiers' Strikes of 1919*, Macmillan, London, 1980, p. 33.
5 Quoted in Robert England, *Discharged: a Commentary on Civil Re-establishment of Veterans in Canada*, Macmillan, Toronto, 1943, p. 22. This book, written by a World War I veteran, is most illuminating about demobilisation and rehabilitation generally in both world wars.
6 Rothstein, *The Soldiers' Strikes*, pp. 37–85. The merit of this book is the author's extensive use of local newspapers. Other accounts of the period are

in Winston S. Churchill, *The Aftermath*, Macmillan edn., London, 1941, pp. 52–69, Robin Higham, *Armed Forces in Peacetime*, Foulis, London, 1962, pp. 9–19, and Dave Lamb, *Mutinies, 1917–1920*, Solidarity, Oxford and London, n.d.

7   Philip Gibbs, *Realities of War*, new and revised edition, Heinemann, London, n.d., p. 344.

8   Rothstein, *The Soldiers' Strikes*, p. 43.

9   *Hansard*, 8 April 1919, 114 H.C. Deb., Fifth Ser., col. 1830.

10 *Annual Report*, 1913–19.

11 PRO, Cab. 24/71 G.T. 6434, memo by CIGS, 5 December 1918. Quotation of Crown copyright material is by permission of the Controller of Her Majesty's Stationery Office.

12 PRO, Cab. 24/73 G.T. 6673, memo by Churchill, 27 January 1919.

13 *Annual Report*, 1913–19.

14 *Hansard*, 6 March 1919, 113 H.C. Deb., Fifth Ser., cols. 691–3, 701–2, 734–5, 737–8.

15 Papers relating to the pamphlet are in PRO, Reco 1/876. I am most grateful to Mr Gerald Spillan of St Antony's College, Oxford, for this reference.

16 An efficient publicity campaign was later organised. See Sir Ernest D. Swinton, *Over my Shoulder*, George Ronald, Oxford, 1951, pp. 213–18.

17 Ministry of Reconstruction, *The Mission of the British Army*, Reconstruction Problems, No. 37, London, 1919. The author was Colonel H. D. De Watteville, who became quite a well known military writer. He was paid a fee of twenty guineas. PRO, Reco 1/876.

18 *Annual Report*, 1919–20.

19 C. à Court Repington, *The First World War*, Constable, London, 1920, II, p. 511.

20 Edward M. Spiers, *The Army and Society, 1815–1914*, Longman, London, 1980, chapter 2, discusses the rank and file. This book, Alan Ramsay Skelly, *The Victorian Army at Home*, Croom Helm, London, 1977, and H. J. Hanham, 'Religion and nationality in the mid-Victorian army', in M. R. D. Foot (ed.), *War and Society*, Paul Elek, London, 1973, pp. 159–81, are the best sources for the social composition of the army before 1914.

21 In the year 1 October 1923 to 30 September 1924 only 119 (38 per cent) of the 310 men who enlisted at the Royal Ulster Rifles' Belfast depot were born in Belfast. RUR Museum, Belfast, Recruiting Register, 1924–31.

22 I(ndia) O(ffice) R(ecords), Chelmsford papers Mss Eur. E.264, vol. II, p. 26, Viceroy to Secretary of State for India, 8 July 1919.

23 I(mperial) W(ar) M(useum), Wilson correspondence 13D/1, Rawlinson to Wilson, 10 March 1921. Material from the Wilson papers is quoted by permission of the Trustees of the Imperial War Museum.

24 *Annual Report*, 1919–20.

25 *Ibid.*, 1923–24.

26 *Ibid.*, 1926–27 and 1927–28.

27 Repington, *The First World War*, II, p. 536.

28 IWM, Wilson diary, 12 March 1920.

29 Robert Graves, *Goodbye to all that*, Harmondsworth, 1960, p. 231.

30 Churchill College, Cambridge, Charles Bonham-Carter, typescript autobiography, chapter 10, pp. 8, 15–16.

31 PRO, Cab. 24/78 G.T. 7182, memo by CIGS, 26 April 1919.

32 PRO, Cab. 23/21/29(20), appendix II, appendix 'Military requirements in Ireland', May 1920.

33 PRO, Cab. 24/114 C.P. 2006, memo by Adjutant-General, 23 October 1920.

34 *Annual Report*, 1920–21.

35   *Ibid.*, 1923–24.

36   *Ibid.*, 1920–21.

37   *Army Estimates for 1921–22*, House of Commons Papers 1921 (99), p. 47.

38   *Report on Educational Training in the British Army*, 1920, Cmd 568. For criticism of army education, see *Hansard*, 22 March 1922, 152 H.C. Deb., Fifth Ser., col. 519–20, 527, 530.

39   *Army Appropriation Accounts for 1920–21* and *1926–27*, House of Commons Papers, 1922 (47), pp. 175, 207; and 1929 (39), p. vii. The training farm in Ireland had also been set up without proper authority and the Treasury refused to allow funds for it. In an enlightened but unique instance of civil resettlement, the army sold the land and stock to the expert who had been in charge and was now demobilised.

40   *Hansard*, 18 March 1919, 113 H.C. Deb., Fifth Ser., col. 1893.

41   *Ibid.*, 23 February 1920, 125 H.C. Deb., Fifth Ser., cols. 1402–3.

42   IWM, Wilson papers, box 73/1/23, correspondence file, No. 293, papers regarding the Imperial Education Conference, 11 and 12 June 1919.

43   Quoted in *Report on Educational Training*, 1920, Cmd 568, p. 15.

44   N. T. St J. Williams, *Tommy Atkins' Children*, HMSO, London, 1971, p. 125 n.

45   Higham, *Armed Forces in Peacetime*, p. 92.

46   Sometimes the proportion of unskilled was much higher. In 1923–24, at the Belfast recruiting office, 82 per cent of the recruits accepted were unskilled. Of the 310 men, 238 were described as 'labourers', and fifteen separately as 'farm labourers'. RUR Museum, Belfast, Recruiting Register, 1924–31.

47   *Annual Report*, 1922–23.

48   These statistics should be treated as only rough estimates. The pre-war figures derive from the Board of Trade's 1906 *Enquiry into Earnings*, as analysed in Guy Routh, *Occupation and Pay in Great Britain, 1906–60*, Cambridge, 1965, pp. 91–3. The post-war figure for average army pay is as given by Sir Archibald Williamson in the House of Commons, 20 February 1920, 125 H.C. Deb., Fifth Ser., col. 1402. The average earnings figure for 1920 was calculated by increasing the 1906 figure in proportion with the index of (manual workers') wage earnings given in C. H. Feinstein, *Statistical Tables of National Income, Expenditure and Output of the U.K., 1855–1965*, Cambridge, 1976, table 65.

49   *Army Estimates for the Financial Year 1926*, House of Commons Papers 1926 (29); *Annual Report*, 1925–26.

50   Routh, *Occupation and Pay*, p. 64.

51   *Annual Report*, 1919–20. See also written answers, *Hansard*, 23 November 1920, 135 H.C. Deb., Fifth Ser., col. 240.

52   *Conditions of Service of Women Staff employed in the Navy, Army and Air Force Institutes*, 1931, Cmd 3769.

53   F. A. E. Crew, *The Army Medical Services*, HMSO, London, 1953 and 1955, I, pp. 3–94, II, pp. 282–6 and 514.

54   IWM, Wilson correspondence 33B/16, Allenby to Wilson, 17 May 1919.

55   IOR, Chemsford Papers, Mdd. Eur. E.264, vol. 11, pp. 289–9, Viceroy to Secretary of State for India, 23 September 1919.

56   Churchill favoured an anti-Bolshevik crusade. For a detailed account of his policy towards Russia, see Martin Gilbert, *Winston S. Churchill*, IV, *1917–1922*, Heinemann, London, 1975, chapters 12–20.

57   PRO, Cab. 23/8 W.C. 515. See also Rothstein, *The Soldiers' Strikes*.

58   The questionnaire was stolen by an NCO employed on clerical duties in one of the Commands. PRO, Cab. 24/96 C.P. 462, Directorate of Intelligence, 'A Survey of Revolutionary Feeling in the Year 1919', p. 9. It was leaked to the

Daily Herald, and the Labour MP, William Adamson, read it out in Parliament. Churchill gave a summary of the replies. *Hansard*, 29 May 1919, 116 H.C. Deb., Fifth Ser., cols. 1469–72, 1513–16.

59 For the use of troops during industrial unrest, see Keith Jeffery and Peter Hennessy, *States of Emergency: British Governments and Strikebreaking since 1919*, Routledge and Kegan Paul, London, 1983.

60 *Annual Report*, 1925–26.

61 Thomas Jones (ed. K. Middlemas), *Whitehall Diary*, III, Oxford University Press, London, 1971, pp. 25–7.

62 Birmingham University Library, Chamberlain Papers, AC 35/1/11, Austen Chamberlain to Winston Churchill, 11 May 1922, quoted by permission of the University of Birmingham.

63 IOR, L/MIL/7/13314, 'Connaught Rangers' Case' enclosure No. 1 to General Despatch No. 105 (Army), 9 December 1920.

64 *Ibid.*, Chelmsford papers, Mss Eur. E.264, vol. 13, p. 39, Viceroy to Secretary of State for India, 9 July 1920.

65 There are general accounts of the mutiny in H. F. N. Jourdain and E. Fraser, *The Connaught Rangers*, I, RUSI, London, 1924, pp. 570–1; T. F. Kilfeather, *The Connaught Rangers*, Dublin 1969, pp. 122–204; and Sam Pollock, *Mutiny for the Cause*, Leo Cooper, London, 1969. There was grumbling discontent in other southern Irish regiments but no actual mutiny.

66 Peter Dennis, 'The reconstitution of the Territorial Force, 1918–1920', in Adrian Preston and Peter Dennis (eds.), *Swords and Covenants*, Croom Helm, London, 1976, pp. 190–215; Peter Dennis, 'The Territorial Army in aid of the civil power in Britain, 1919–1926', *Journal of Contemporary History*, XVI, 1981, pp. 705–24.

67 Quoted in Stephen R. Ward, 'Intelligence surveillance of British ex-servicemen, 1918–1920', *Historical Journal*, XVI, 1973, pp. 179–88. This, together with Ward's own essay on Britain, in Ward (ed.), *The War Generation: Veterans of the First World War*, Kennikat, Port Washington, N.Y., and London, 1975, pp. 10–37, are the main sources for veterans' matters.

68 PRO, Cab. 24/96 C.P. 462, Survey of Revolutionary Feeling, p. 11; Lamb, *Mutinies*, pp. 29–30.

69 Graham Wootton, *The Politics of Influence: British Ex-servicemen, Cabinet Decisions and Cultural Change (1917–57)*, Routledge and Kegan Paul, London, 1963, p. 258.

70 Brian Bond, *British Military Policy between the two World Wars*, Oxford University Press, 1980, p. 36. Chapter 2 of this book brilliantly describes the character and ethos of the inter-war army.

71 Ward, 'Intelligence surveillance', pp. 181–2.

72 Sir William Robertson, *From Private to Field Marshal*, Constable, London, 1921, pp. 382–3.

73 William Moore, *The Thin Yellow Line*, Leo Cooper, London, 1974, pp. 184–216; *Manual of Military Law, 1914*, p. 721, and *1929*, p. 787.

74 Arthur Marwick, *The Deluge: British Society and the First World War*, Harmondsworth, 1967, pp. 323–34.

antry divisions of the British army, 1914–18

No. and designation	Type	Formation authorised	First sent abroad	Theatres of service (excluding (UK)	Notes
ards	Reg.	Aug. 15	Aug. 15	WF	
	Reg.	Pre-war	Aug. 14	WF	
	Reg.	Pre-war	Aug. 14	WF	
	Reg.	Pre-war	Aug. 14	WF	
	Reg.	Pre-war	Aug. 14	WF	
	Reg.	Pre-war	Aug. 14	WF/It	
	Reg.	Pre-war	Sep. 14	WF	
	Reg.	Sep. 14	Oct. 14	WF/It	
	Reg.	Sep. 14	Nov. 14	WF	
(Scottish)	NA	Aug. 14	May 15	WF	
h (Irish)	NA	Aug. 14	July 15	Dar/Sal/Eg	
h (Northern)	NA	Aug. 14	July 15	Dar/Eg/WF	
h (Eastern)	NA	Aug. 14	May 15	WF	
h (Western)	NA	Aug. 14	July 15	Dar/Eg/Mes	
h (Light)	NA	Aug. 14	May 15	WF	Former 8th. R & R 18
h (Scottish)	NA	Sep. 14	July 15	WF	
h (Irish)	NA	Sep. 14	Dec. 15	WF	R & R 18
h (Northern)	NA	Sep. 14	July 15	WF	
h (Eastern)	NA	Sep. 14	July 15	WF	
h (Western)	NA	Sep. 14	July 15	WF	
h (Light)	NA	Sep. 14	July 15	WF	
t	NA	Sep. 14	Sep. 15	WF	
d	NA	Sep. 14	Sep. 15	WF/Sal	
d	NA	Sep. 14	Aug. 15	WF/It	
h	NA	Sep. 14	Aug. 15	WF	
h	NA	Sep. 14	Sep. 15	WF	R & R 18
h	NA	Sep. 14	Sep. 15	WF/Sal	
h	Reg.	Sep. 14	Dec. 14	WF/Sal	
h	Reg.	Sep. 14	Jan. 15	WF/Sal	
h	Reg.	Oct. 14	Mar. 15	Dar/Eg/WF	
h	NA	Dec. 14	Nov. 15	WF	Former 37th R & R 18
t	NA	Dec. 14	Dec. 15	WF	Former 38th
d	NA	Dec. 14	Nov. 15	Eg/WF	Former 39th
d	NA	Dec. 14	Nov. 15	WF	Former 40th
h	NA	Dec. 14	Jan. 16	WF	Former 41st
h	NA	Dec. 14	Jan. 16	WF	Former 42nd
h (Ulster)	NA	Oct. 14	Oct. 15	WF	Former 43rd
h	NA	Mar. 15	July 15	WF	
h (Welsh)	NA	Dec. 14	Dec. 15	WF	
h	NA	Apr. 15	Mar. 16	WF	R & R 18

No. and designation	Type	Formation authorised	First sent abroad	Theatres of service (excluding (UK)	Notes
40th	NA	Apr. 15	Jun. 16	WF	R & R 18
41st	NA	Apr. 15	May 16	WF/It./WF	
42nd (East Lancashire)	TF	Pre-war	Sep. 14	Eg./Dar/Eg./WF	
43rd (Wessex)	TF	Pre-war	Oct. 14	Ind.	
44th (Home Counties)	TF	Pre-war	Oct. 14	Ind.	
45th (2nd Wessex)	TF	Sep. 14	Dec. 14	Ind.	
46th (North Midland)	TF	Pre-war	Feb. 15	Eg./WF	
47th (2nd London)	TF	Pre-war	Mar. 15	WF	
48th (South Midland)	TF	Pre-war	Mar. 15	WF/It.	
49th (West Riding)	TF	Pre-war	Apr. 15	WF	
50th (Northumbrian)	TF	Pre-war	Apr. 15	WF	R & R 18
51st (Highland)	TF	Pre-war	Apr. 15	WF	
52nd (Lowland)	TF	Pre-war	May 15	Dar./Eg./WF	
53rd (Welsh)	TF	Pre-war	July 15	Dar./Eg.	R 18
54th (East Anglian)	TF	Pre-war	July 15	Dar./Eg.	
55th (West Lancashire)	TF	Pre-war	Jan. 16	WF	Formed on WF
56th (1st London)	TF	Pre-war	Feb. 16	WF	Formed on WF
57th (2nd West Lancs)	TF	Sep. 14	Feb. 17	WF	
58th (2/1st London)	TF	Sep. 14	Jan. 17	WF	
59th (2nd North Midland)	TF	Sep. 14	Feb. 17	WF	R & R 18
60th (2/2nd London)	TF	Sep. 14	June 16	WF/Sal./Eg.	R 18
61st (2nd South Midland)	TF	Sep. 14	May 16	WF	
62nd (2nd West Riding)	TF	Sep. 14	Jan. 17	WF	
63rd (2nd Northumbrian)	TF	Sep. 14	–	–	BU 16
63rd (Royal Naval)	–	Sep. 14	Oct. 14	WF/Eg./Dar./WF	Given No. 16
64th (2nd Highland)	TF	Sep. 14	–	–	R
65th (2nd Lowland)	TF	Sep. 14	–	–	BU 18
66th (2nd East Lancs)	TF	Sep. 14	Feb. 17	WF	R & R 18
67th (2nd Home Counties)	TF	Sep. 14	–	–	R 18
68th (2nd Welsh)	TF	Sep. 14	–	–	R18
69th (2nd East Anglian)	TF	Sep. 14	–	–	R 18
70th					No. not allocated
71st	HS	Nov. 16	–	–	BU 18
72nd	HS	Nov. 16	–	–	BU 17
73rd	HS	Nov. 16	–	–	BU 17
74th (Yeomanry)	TF	Feb. 17	Feb. 17	Eg./WF	Formed in Eg.
75th	Mixed	Feb. 17	Feb. 17	Eg.	R 18. Formed in

Key. Reg. Regular, *TF* Territorial, *NA* New Army, *HS* Home Service, *Eg.* Egypt, *WF* Western front, *It.* Italy, *Dar.* Dardanelles, *Sal.* Salonika, *Ind.* India, *Mes.* Mesopotamia, *R & R* Reduced to cadre but reconstituted, *R* Reconstituted, *BU* Broken up.

Note. The original 30–35th divisions were formed in November 1914 and broken up in A 1915.

Appendix II

Cavalry and mounted divisions of the British army, 1914–18

No. and designation	Type	Formation authorised	First sent abroad	Theatres of Service exc. UK	Notes
st Cavalry	Reg.	Pre-war	Aug. 14	WF	
nd Cavalry	Reg.	Sep. 14	Sep. 14	WF	
rd Cavalry	Reg.	Sep. 14	Oct. 14	WF	
st Mounted	TF	Sep. 14	–	–	Later 1st Cyclist. SU 16
nd Mounted	TF	Sep. 14	Apr. 15	Eg./Dar./Eg.	SU 16
/2nd Mounted	TF	Mar. 15	–	–	Later 3rd Mounted later Cyclist
th Mounted	TF	Mar. 15	–	–	Later 2nd Cyclist. SU 16
eomanry, Mounted	TF	June 17	June 17	Eg.	Later 1st Mounted, later 4th Cavalry (incl. Indian units) Formed in Egypt
nd Mounted	Mixed	June 18	June 18	Eg.	Later 5th Cavalry Formed in Egypt.

Key. *Reg.* Regular, *TF* Territorial, *SU* Split up, *WF* Western front, *Dar.* Dardanelles, *Eg.* Egypt.

An annotated bibliography
of the British army, 1914–18

Keith Simpson

This annotated bibliography is based upon one originally compiled for a symposium on the British army and the First World War, held at the Royal Military Academy, Sandhurst, in November 1978. Now expanded and brought up to date, the books, articles and theses referred to represent a personal selection and are not meant to be a comprehensive listing of all the secondary sources available. This bibliography should complement the wide range of secondary sources quoted in the main text of the book. Divisional and regimental histories have not been included, but can be found listed in the bibliographies. It was impossible to include more than a selection from the large number of privately printed memoirs, collections of letters, school and unit histories that were published during and after the war. As far as possible, where it has proved relevant, an author's military rank and the unit he served with have been given.

The most comprehensive collections of books and articles relating to the army and the First World War can be found in the libraries of the Imperial War Museum, London; the Ministry of Defence (Central and Army), London; the British Museum, London; and the Royal Military Academy, Sandhurst, and the Staff College, Camberley. For those wishing to use any of these libraries it is advisable in the first instance to write seeking permission. Smaller collections can be found in other public and private libraries, and a rich source is still available through antiquarian and second-hand bookshops.

Bibliographies

Bray, Arthur T. E., *The Battle of the Somme 1916: a Bibliography*, thesis submitted for Fellowship of the Library Association, 1967. Although somewhat dated, this bibliography is a useful guide to some of the more obscure secondary sources for the battle of the Somme.

Bruce, A. P. C., *An Annotated Bibliography of the British Army, 1660–1914*, Garland Publishing, 1975. A balanced and representative selection of sources available from published official documents, unpublished collections of papers, books and articles on the British army for the period. It is particularly useful for the army in the decade before 1914.

Enser, A. G. S., *A Subject Bibliography of the First World War: Books in English, 1914–1978*, Andre Deutsch, 1979. This bibliography is badly organised and it is necessary to search quite hard to find a book on a specific subject. However, there is quite a good listing of divisional and regimental histories.

Falls, Cyril, *War Books: a Critical Guide*, Peter Davies, 1930. Cyril Falls compiled his critical guide at the height of the post-war boom in war books. Falls divided war books into a number of categories, including history, reminiscence and fiction. He starred each volume according to his personal assessment of its merits, and wrote a brief critique. His guide is still of value for divisional and regimental histories, memoirs and fiction.

Higham, Robin (ed.), *A Guide to the Sources of British Military History*, Routledge and Kegan Paul, 1972. A dozen military historians have compiled lists of sources for a particular period. They vary considerably in style and content, but fortunately the chapter concerning the Army in the First World War is very well compiled. M. J. Williams's 'The First World War on land' provides a good general guide to private papers, official documents, books and articles, and he suggests further areas of research that need to be undertaken. Naturally, since this was published in 1972, it is in need of some amendment.

Mayer, S. L., and Koenig, W. J., *The Two World Wars: a Guide to the Manuscript Collections in the United Kingdom*, Bowker, 1976. The sections on the First World War show just how much material is held in regimental museums and local government archives. However, there are some notable omissions from the collections listed for some of the national museums and archives.

Biographies

Arthur, Sir George, *The Life of Earl Kitchener*, 3 vol., Macmillan, 1920. The first official biography of Kitchener, written within a few years of his death; although it contains some interesting information it leaves many questions unanswered.

Ash, Bernard, *The Lost Dictator: a Biography of Field Marshal Sir Henry Wilson*, Cassell, 1968. The most recent biography, published before the bulk of his private papers were made available. Wilson's career and influence now need fundamental reassessment.

Barker, A. J., *Townshend of Kut*, Cassell, 1967. A competent study of one of the more controversial British generals in Mesopotamia, who surrendered at Kut in 1916.

Blake, Robert (ed.), *The Private Papers of Douglas Haig, 1914–1919*, Eyre and Spottiswoode, 1952. This edited volume of Haig's papers largely consists of extracts from his diaries. Robert Blake has edited the papers carefully and has included an introduction which is also an essay on Haig and civil–military relations during the First World War. For a fuller assessment of Haig, it is advisable to consult the original diaries and papers, particularly the letters Haig wrote to his wife.

Bond, Brian, *Liddell Hart: a Study of his Military Thought*, Cassell, 1977. Although, strictly speaking, not a biography of Liddell Hart, this book does reveal a lot about the man and his life.

Bonham-Carter, Victor, *Soldier True: the Life of Field Marshal Sir William Robertson*, Muller, 1963. A good, solid biography of Robertson based upon his private papers, but it fails to show Robertson's ability to indulge in military politicking.

Callwell, Major-General Sir C. E., *The Life of Sir Stanley Maude*, Constable, 1920. A conventional biography. Maude had the difficult task of picking up the pieces in Mesopotamia after the disaster at Kut. He led the British and Indian troops to victory, only to die of cholera in Baghdad in 1917.

Callwell, Major-General Sir C. E., *Field Marshal Sir Henry Wilson*, 2 vols, Cassell, 1927. Henry Wilson lost what little reputation he retained in the minds of some of his contemporaries following the publication of this biography. Callwell relied upon the detailed diaries which revealed Wilson's acid pen, his love of political intrigue and his frequent lack of judgement. Although this biography is still referred to by scholars, it is advisable to consult the original diaries and papers.

Cassar, G. H., *Kitchener: architect of Victory*, William Kimber, 1977. The most recent biography, which examines Kitchener's life in considerable detail but leaves a number of important questions unanswered.

Charteris, Brigadier-General John, *Field Marshal Earl Haig*, Cassell, 1929. Charteris's military career was made by Haig, who took him away from regimental duty in India before the war. He served on Haig's staff throughout the war until Haig was forced to remove him because of political and military pressure. As a loyal subordinate and personal friend, Charteris was well placed to write a discreet biography of his military master.

Churchill, Randolph, *Lord Derby*, Heinemann, 1960. A competent biography of Lord Derby, one of the great political fixers of the Edwardian and Georgian era, who during the First World War led the great recruiting drive and then became Secretary of State for War.

Cooper, A. Duff, *Haig*, 2 vols. Faber, 1935. A well written biography which fails to analyse the more controversial aspects of Haig's military career.

Farrar-Hockley, Antony, *Goughie: the Life of General Sir Hubert Gough*, Hart-Davis MacGibbon, 1975. Farrar-Hockley was able to use Gough's private papers and those of his personal staff. This is a sympathetic study by a serving military officer who understood the problems of high command.

Fraser, David, *Alanbrooke*, Collins, 1982. The CIGS of the Second World War served as a regimental officer in the Royal Horse Artillery and then on the staff during the First World War. Like many of his regular officer contemporaries, Alanbrooke was greatly influenced by that experience.

French, The Hon. E. G., *The Life of Field Marshal Sir John French, Earl of Ypres*, Cassell, 1931. An unreliable biography which seeks to absolve French of some of the more controversial aspects of his life.

Gardner, Brian, *Allenby*, Cassell, 1965. A rather limp and disappointing biography of one of the most interesting senior officers of the British army during the First World War. Allenby requires a fresh biography examining his role both in France and the Middle East.

Gilbert, Martin, *Winston Churchill*, III, *1914–1916*, Heinemann, 1971. Martin Gilbert's official biography contains a wealth of information about all aspects of the war, particularly on Gallipoli and the debate between the 'westerners' and the 'easterners.' It also covers Churchill's command of a service battalion in France. Unfortunately Gilbert is usually content to narrate events and rarely analyses decisions or controversies.

Gilbert, Martin, *Winston Churchill*, IV, *1917–1922*, Heinemann, 1975. An important volume of the biography, as it covers Churchill's period as Minister of Munitions and then Secretary of State for War.

Hamilton, Ian B. M., *The Happy Warrior: a Life of General Sir Ian Hamilton*, Cassell, 1966. A sympathetic biography of an intellectual general who had a wide range of interests beyond the army. It reveals that Hamilton was probably too sensitive and indecisive to deal with the series of crises at Gallipoli.

Hamilton, Nigel, *Monty: the Making of a General, 1887–1942*, Hamish Hamilton, 1981. The official biography, based upon his private papers. Montgomery served as a regimental and then a staff officer during the First

World War, and that experience influenced his command and methods during the Second.

Harington, General Sir Charles, *Plumer of Messines*, Murray, 1935. General Plumer has been considered one of the most successful of Haig's army commanders. British soldiers were pleased to be under the command of Second Army because it had a reputation for careful planning and not risking the lives of troops needlessly. Plumer's reputation rested largely on his very good staff, and his biographer, Harington, had been his chief of staff. But this slim volume reveals little about either Plumer or the planning of Second Army's operations, because Harington had to work from memory and from scattered notes, since Plumer destroyed all his papers.

Holmes, Richard, *The Little Field Marshal: Sir John French*, Cape, 1981. The most recent scholarly biography, which although it reveals French's personal weaknesses and failures also brings out his better points. It is also excellent on civil–military relations and strategy.

Liddell Hart, B. H., *Foch: Man of Orleans*, Eyre and Spottiswoode, 1931. Liddell Hart's sensitively written and yet effective demolition of Foch's claim to military greatness in the First World War. Foch is important because he was an anglophile and throughout the war had close personal contacts with the British high command, particularly with Henry Wilson.

Mack, John E., *A Prince of our Disorder: the Life of T. E. Lawrence*, Weidenfeld and Nicolson, 1976. Professor Mack believes that the only way to understand the adult behaviour of Lawrence is by examining his family background and childhood. Mack uses the methodology of a psychologist as well as that of a historian with effect in this stimulating biography.

Magnus, Philip, *Kitchener: Portrait of an Imperialist*, Murray, 1958. Magnus delicately skirts round some of the darker aspects of Kitchener's personality, and fails to analyse his period in office as Secretary for War.

Maurice, General Sir Frederick, *The Life of General Lord Rawlinson of Trent*, Cassell, 1928. Rawlinson was a contemporary of Haig, and one of his army commanders in France during two particularly crucial phases of the war in 1916 and 1918. This biography is based on Rawlinson's edited diaries and letters, and does not really address the fundamental questions relating, for instance, to the planning and conduct of operations on the Somme in 1916.

Neilson, K., 'Kitchener: a reputation refurbished', *Canadian Journal of History*, 15, 2, 1980, pp. 207–27. The author claims that many of Kitchener's decisions were affected by his concern to keep Russia in the war.

Nicolson, N., *Alex: the Life of Field Marshal Earl Alexander of Tunis*, Weidenfeld and Nicolson, 1973. Nicolson's biography is very revealing about Alexander as a young pre-war regular officer, and then as a successful wartime regimental officer who ended in command of the 2nd Irish Guards. Alexander enjoyed the war and saw it as a personal and professional challenge.

Spiers, Edward M., *Haldane: an Army Reformer*, Edinburgh University Press, 1980. In this new biography, Spiers shows that political pressures, the legacy of past debates, economic and military constraints and other factors were important in influencing Haldane's army reforms.

Terraine, John, *Douglas Haig: the Educated Soldier*, Hutchinson, 1963. Based on the private papers and diaries of the field marshal, this is a robust defence of Haig's period of command in France. New evidence based upon other collections of papers and a re-examination of the Haig papers will probably provide a much needed reassessment of the army's most controversial general of the First World War.

Trythall, Anthony John, *'Boney' Fuller: the Intellectual General*, Cassell, 1977. A useful biography of a leading advocate of armoured warfare, the unconventional gadfly of the British army. Fuller served on the HQs staff of the Tank Corps in 1916–18.

Wavell, Field Marshal Archibald, *Allenby: a Study in Greatness*, Harrap, 1940. Wavell served on Allenby's staff during the First World War, and this biography, despite the limitations of source material, is still the best available study of Allenby.

Williams, Jeffery, *Byng of Vimy: General and Governor-General*, Leo Cooper at Secker and Warburg, 1983. Based upon private papers, a competent study of his life, and in particular his period as an army commander in France during the First World War.

Civil–military relations

Gooch, John, *The Plans of War: the General Staff and British Military Strategy, 1900–1916*, Routledge and Kegan Paul, 1974. A scholarly study of the development of the general staff and its influence on strategy.

Guinn, Paul, *British Strategy and Politics, 1914–1918*, Oxford, Clarendon Press, 1965. A good study of British strategy which analyses the debate between the 'westerners' and the 'easterners'.

Hunt, B., and Preston, A. (eds.), *War Aims and Strategic Policy in the Great War, 1914–1918*, Croom Helm, 1978. Although these papers are not directly related to the British army, many are relevant to overall war aims and strategy.

Lovelace, C. J., 'Control and Censorship of the Press during the First World War', Ph.D. thesis, University of London, 1982. An excellent study of this important subject which covers the policy of both the War Office and GHQ in France.

Robertson, Field Marshal Sir William, *Soldiers and Statesmen*, 2 vols, Cassell, 1926. A formidable treatise on civil–military relations and the strategy of the 'westerners' by one of its main architects.

Woodward, David, *Lloyd George and the Generals*, Associated University Presses, London and Toronto, 1983. A detailed study of the relationship between Lloyd George and the British military high command during the war, which concentrates on the question of the supply and deployment of military manpower.

Doctrine and tactics

Ashworth, Tony, *Trench Warfare, 1914–1918: the Live and Let Live System*, Macmillan, 1980. This very interesting book, considers the way in which the army organised and controlled trench warfare, and what actually happened in the front line between major battles.

Bidwell, Shelford, and Graham, Dominick, *Fire-power: British Army Weapons and Theories of War, 1904–1945*, Allen and Unwin, 1982. Mainly concerned with examining the development of tactical doctrine by the Royal Artillery. However, in the first part, by Dominick Graham, there is a scholarly analysis of the wider problems of weapon development and tactical doctrine for the army during the First World War. Graham moves away from the sterile debate about military personalities and examines the practical problems the army faced by having to fight a war at the same time as rethinking tactical doctrine.

Graham, Dominick, '*Sans* doctrine: British army tactics in the First World War', in Travers, T. H. E., and Archer, C.(eds.), *Men at War*, Precedent, Chicago, 1982. A good short survey of the problems of tactical doctrine and military operations during the First World War.

Lupfer, Timothy, *The Dynamics of Doctrince: the Changes in German Tactical*

Doctrine during the First World War. Leavenworth Papers, No. 4, Combat Studies Institute, Fort Leavenworth, Kansas, July 1981. Captain Lupfer completed this excellent study whilst he was serving as an instructor at West Point. Lupfer shows that German doctrinal changes during the war were the product of a collective effort which resulted in new ideas and methods being disseminated to units through a remarkable training programme.

Travers, T. H. E., 'The offensive and the problem of innovation in British military thought 1870–1915', *Journal of Contemporary History*, 13, 1978, pp. 531–53. Travers shows the problems the army faced in adapting tactical doctrine to new weapons and the experience of the South African and Russo-Japanese wars.

Travers, T. H. E., 'The hidden army: structural problems in the British officer corps, 1900–1918', *Journal of Contemporary History*, 17, 1982, pp. 523–44. Examines the tensions between the traditional approach to soldiering and warfare and the need for structural and tactical changes within the officer class before and during the war.

Travers, T. H. E., 'Learning and decision-making on the western front, 1915–16; the British example', *Canadian Journal of History*, April 1983, pp. 87–97. A further contribution to the analysis of how the army tried to adapt tactics and doctrine whilst conducting operations. This is a particularly useful article for studying the preparations before the battle of the Somme. Like the other work by Travers, it is based on a meticulous study of official and private papers.

Wynne, G. C., *If Germany Attacks: the Battle in Depth in the West*, Faber and Faber, 1940. After the First World War, Captain G. C. Wynne had been an assistant to the official historian, Brigadier-General J. E. Edmonds. As a result of his research for the volumes of the official history of military operations, France and Belgium, Wynne wrote this important study of German defensive tactics on the western front based on German sources. He effectively refuted many of the arguments about the conduct of operations which had been laid down by the official history.

Dominion and imperial experience

Adam-Smith, Patsy, *The Anzacs*, Hamish Hamilton, 1978. A popular history of the Australian military contribution to the British war effort.

Bean, C. E. W., *The Australians in France: the Official History of Australia in the War of 1914–18*, III–VI, Angus and Robertson, Sydney, 1929–42. A well written and invaluable source. The volumes also contain a lot of information about the British army.

Bean, C. E. W., *The Story of Anzac: the Official History of Australia in the War of 1914–1918*, Angus and Robertson, Sydney, 1941. These two volumes of the Australian official history fill in many of the gaps left by the British official history of Gallipoli.

Fewster, Kevin (ed.), *Gallipoli Correspondent: the Front-line Diary of C. E. W. Bean*, Allen and Unwin, Australia, 1983. Bean accompanied the Australian Imperial Force to Egypt in 1914 as official war correspondent. After the war he became the official historian of the Australian government and wrote an invaluable set of volumes. Whilst he was official war correspondent he kept a detailed diary which has now been edited and complements some of the material to be found in the official history.

Gammage, Bill, *The Broken Years: Australian Soldiers in the Great War*, Australian National University Press, 1974. A useful study based upon the large collection of diaries and letters at the Australian War Memorial. The main criticism is that the author might have been a little more selective with his material, which at times is repetitive.

Heathcote, T. A., *The Indian Army: the Garrison of British Imperial India, 1822–1922*, David and Charles, 1974. T. A. Heathcote's book on the Indian Army was published at the same time as Philip Mason's *A Matter of Honour*, which tended to receive more attention. However, Heathcote's book supplements Mason's with important detail concerning organisation, recruitment and pay.

Mason, Philip, *A Matter of Honour: an Account of the Indian Army, its Officers and Men*, Jonathan Cape, 1974. Philip Mason had already written an excellent study of the Indian civil service under the pseudonym 'Philip Woodruff'. He develops the argument that the British managed to retain the loyalty of their Indian soldiers through war and insurrection because of a concept of honour. Although this may be an exaggerated and romantic view it does help to explain some of the attitudes displayed by Indian soldiers under considerable stress during the First World War.

Nicholson, Colonel G. W. L., *Official History of the Canadian Army in the First World War, Canadian Expeditionary Force, 1914–1919*, Queen's Printer, Ottawa, 1962. The Canadians made a considerable contribution to the British war effort on the western front, and this single-volume official history is a useful source.

Robson, L. L., *The First A.I.F.: a Study of its Recruitment, 1914–1918*, Melbourne University Press, 1970. This study of the recruitment of the Australian Imperial Force demolishes many myths about the Australian soldier and should be taken as a useful check to Bean's official history.

The experience of war

Hutchison, Lieutenant-Colonel Graham Seton, *Warrior*, Hutchison, 1932. This book is based on the author's memoirs, *Footslogger*, but is an attempt at a wider philosophical study of war and battle. Hutchinson had the same obsession with combat as the German writer Ernst Jünger. After the war he flirted with fascism.

Keegan, John, *The Face of Battle*, Cape, 1976. John Keegan is concerned to analyse what actually happens on the battlefield, and what keeps men together in the face of death and mutilation. He examines three battles, including the first day of the Somme, looking at the men, their weapons and the dangers they faced. It is advisable to read the book as a whole rather than merely selecting the chapter on the Somme.

Leed, E. J., *No Man's Land*, Cambridge University Press, 1979. This book advances the thesis that many Europeans went to war in 1914 to escape the pressures of modern industrialised society only to find that the war, far from being a romantic adventure, was in turn industrialised. This leads him on to examine the continuity of front-line experience.

Marwick, Arthur, *The Deluge: British Society and the First World War*, Bodley Head, 1965. Very much in the tradition of the 'war and society' school of history, and some of the generalised conclusions should be treated with caution.

Pound, Reginald, *The Lost Generation*, Constable, 1964. A commonly held belief since the First World War has been that a whole generation of Britain's most able youth had been decimated. *The Lost Generation* does not seriously address this question, but rather provides biographical sketches of a selection of notable young men killed in the war.

Winter, Denis, *Death's Men: Soldiers of the Great War* Allen Lane, 1978. Denis Winter explains how a recruit progressed from training in Britain, through the base areas in France to the front line. He documents the daily life of the soldier and his reactions to combat and fatigue. But the underlying assumption that all soldiers disliked the war and had similar experiences is wrong.

Winter, J. M., 'Britain's "lost Generation" of the First World War', *Population Studies*, 31, 3, 1977, pp. 449–66. Winter uses demographic evidence to analyse the recruitment, strength and casualties of the army in the First World War. He concludes that proportionally the social and educational elite suffered higher casualties than other social groups.

Wohl, Robert, *The Generation of 1914*, Weidenfeld and Nicolson, 1980. A study of those European men who experienced the First World War and wrote about combat and the change in their lives.

General

Allinson, Sidney, *The Bantams: the untold History of World War I*, Howard Baker, 1981. Despite the exaggerated subtitle – the Bantams received a considerable amount of contemporary publicity – this is a reasonable survey of a military oddity.

The Army Quarterly, 1920–   . This journal began publication in 1920, and for the next two decades its pages were dominated by articles and book reviews about the First World War and its impact on the army. It is an invaluable insight into post-war military opinion and debates about controversial issues. A number of articles and book reviews were by 'Archimedes', the pseudonym of the official historian Brigadier-General J. E. Edmonds.

Ascoli, David, *The Mons Star: the British Expeditionary Force, 1914*, Harrap, 1981. Using a wide variety of published and unpublished accounts in 1914, David Ascoli has captured the spirit of the old regular army. Unfortunately some of the contemporary photographs have been wrongly captioned and others taken by the author of physical features are frequently obscure.

Ascoli, David, *A Companion to the British Army, 1660–1983*, Harrap, 1983. A helpful catalogue of orders and precedence, regimental amalgamations and disbandments, battle honours and the historical development of the army as an institution.

Barker, A. J., *The Neglected War: Mesopotamia, 1914–1918*, Faber and Faber, 1967. A solid and rather uninspiring history of the campaign which relies heavily on the official history.

Barnes, Major R. Money, *The British Army, 1914, and its History*, Seeley Service, 1968. A competent guide to organisation and equipment before 1914.

Barnett, Correlli, *Britain and her Army*, Allen Lane, 1970. One of the best modern general histories of the army by an established writer who does not hesitate to be controversial.

Barrie, Alexander, *War Underground*, Frederick Muller, 1962. The siege warfare nature of the western front saw the development of tunnelling by all the conflicting armies. *War Underground* describes the history of tunnelling by the British army and its military significance.

Brophy, John, and Partridge, Eric, *The Long Trail: Soldiers' Songs and Slang, 1914–1918*, Andre Deutsch, 1963. A fasincating book listing the songs and slang of the British army during the First World War.

Brown, Malcolm, *Tommy goes to War*, Dent, 1978. Malcolm Brown is a television documentary producer who has worked on a number of features dealing with the First World War. This book relates the experiences of soldiering through the letters, diaries and photographs of ordinary men.

Bush, Eric, *Gallipoli*, Allen and Unwin, 1975. A brisk history of the campaign by one of the participants, who interviewed a number of veterans.

Clark, Alan, *The Donkeys*, Hutchinson, 1963. A provocative analysis of the high command of the BEF in 1914–15. Alan Clark was determined to show that the senior military commanders spent much of their time intriguing against one another, and were on the whole rather incompetent. The book started a lively debate between the author and John Terraine over the merits of French and Haig. For a more objective view see Richard Holmes, *The Little Field Marshal*.

Coombs, Rose, *Before Endeavours Fade*, Battle of Britain Prints International, 1976. To anybody who has studied the British army and the First World War, Rose Coombs is known as a mine of information. As a result of her frequent visits to the battlefields of Belgium and northern France she has written this guide, which also catalogues military cemeteries. Although well illustrated with maps and photographs, the guide is too large and cumbersome to be conveniently fitted into a pocket. Perhaps the publisher could be persuaded to remedy this practical defect of an otherwise excellent guide.

Creagh, Sir O'Moore, and Humphris, E. M. (eds.), *The VC and DSO*, 3 vols., Standard Art Book Co., London, n.d. These three volumes list all the recipients of the VC and DSO from the Crimean War to the end of the First World War. In nearly every case there is a photograph and a biographical note of the recipient, with an extract from the citation.

Ellis, John, *Eye-deep in Hell: the Western Front, 1914–1918*, Croom Helm, 1976. A very good account of trench warfare and life behind the line on the western front, utilising new primary sources.

Essame, Brigadier H., *The Battle for Europe, 1918*, Batsford, 1972. The author of this useful account of the final year of the war, was commissioned in 1915 and was adjutant of the 2nd Northamptonshire Regiment after 1917.

Falls, Captain Cyril, *Armageddon, 1918*, Weidenfeld and Nicolson, 1964. There are few modern accounts of the collapse of the Turkish armies in Palestine, and this one is a good supplement to the official history.

Farrar-Hockley, Anthony, *The Somme*, Batsford, 1964. Although somewhat dated now, still worth reading as a background to the battle.

Farrar-Hockley, Anthony, *Death of an Army*, Barker, 1967. A readable history of the first battle of Ypres, based upon German and French as well as British sources.

Foulkes, Major-General C. H., *Gas*, Blackwood, 1934. A good detailed history of the development and use of gas by the British army during the First World War.

Fosten, D. S. V., and Marrion, R. J., *The British Army, 1914–1918*, Osprey, 1978. There is no one good guide to uniforms and personal equipment in the First World War comparable to Brian Davis's *British Army Uniforms and Insignia of World War Two* (Arms and Armour Press, 1983), but this slim volume illustrated by colour sketches and contemporary photographs is of some help.

Frederick, J. B. M., *Lineage Book of the British Army: Mounted Corps and Infantry, 1660–1968*, Hope Farm Press, New York, 1969. An indispensable guide to the lineage of regiments and corps.

French, Field Marshal Lord, *1914*, Constable, 1919. An unreliable account of events in France and Belgium as seen by the first C-in-C of the BEF. Much of the text was ghosted and its publication was part of the conflict involving French, Kitchener and Haig.

Gardner, Brian, *German East*, Cassell, 1963. A general history of one of the 'sideshows' of the First World War, complementing the official history, which only reached 1916.

A General's Letters to his Son on Obtaining his Commission, Cassell, 1917. A fascinating selection of letters showing what a British general expected from his son on being commissioned, and how important the gentlemanly concept of soldiering was still considered even in 1917.

Germains, Victor Wallace, *The Kitchener Armies*, Peter Davies, 1930. A rather romantic account of the raising of the New Armies, it does contain some good individual unit histories at an anecdotal level.

Gibbs, Philip, *Realities of War*, Heinemann, 1920. Gibbs was a war correspondent in France, and this book is basically an attack on Haig and GHQ. Despite its strident tone it does have some interesting comments about some of Haig's subordinate commanders.

Gough, General Sir Hubert, *The Fifth Army*, Hodder and Stoughton, 1931. An obviously partisan account of the German March offensive of 1918 by the commander of the Fifth Army, which bore the brunt of the attack. Basically, Gough felt let down by GHQ and believed that he and his army were made scapegoats for higher political and military incompetence.

Green, Lieutenant-Colonel H., *The British Army in the First World War*, Clowes, 1955. A short general history.

Hankey, Donald, *The Beloved Captain*, Bles, 1956. A series of essays by Donald Hankey about junior officers' leadership during the First World War, the central figure being an officer whom Hankey admired and made an object of hero-worship.

Hay, Ian, *The First Hundred Thousand*, Blackwood, 1916. A popular account of life in the Kitchener armies, by John Hay Beith, a temporary officer in the 10th Argyll and Sutherland Highlanders. A further volume, *Carrying on – after the First Hundred Thousand*, was published in 1917. Beith was later to work as a journalist and intelligence officer for the War Office and was sent to Hollywood as a 'technical' adviser.

Hutchison, Lieutenant-Colonel Graham Seton, *Machine-guns*, Macmillan, 1938. Hutchison commanded a machine-gun battalion in 1918, and this volume is an unofficial history of the Machine Gun Corps, which existed only from 1916 to 1922.

Hughes, Colin, *Mametz: Lloyd George's 'Welsh Army' at the Battle of the Somme*, Orion Press, 1982. An excellent study of the raising, training and operations of the 38th (Welsh) Division up to the battle of the Somme, based on public and private collections of papers as well as interviews with surviving veterans. Hughes rehabilitates the reputation of this division, which had come in for considerable and unjustified contemporary criticism for its performance at Mametz Wood.

Ironside, Field Marshal Lord, *Archangel, 1918–1919*, Constable, 1953. Brigadier-General Ironside commanded the British troops who served in north Russia against the Bolsheviks in 1918. His memoir if this short and controversial episode reveals the kind of *ad hoc* campaigning the army was involved in throughout the world at the end of the war.

James, Brigadier E. A., *British Regiments, 1914–1918*, Samson Books, London, 1978. An indispensable guide to the service records of British cavalry, yeomanry and infantry regiments during the war, including details on the Officer Cadet Battalions.

James, Robert Rhodes, *Gallipoli*, Batsford, 1965. Although somewhat dated, still the most scholarly and readable account based on secondary sources.

Jones, Nigel H., *The War Walk: a Journey along the Western Front*, Robert Hale, 1983. An interesting approach to the western front based upon the author's walks over the old battlefields. He brings together observations from contemporary sources, memoirs and his own experiences. However, the book does lack the detailed maps necessary to make it a useful guide.

Kipling, Arthur., and King, Hugh L., *Head-dress Badges of the British Army*, I, *Up to the End of the Great War*, Frederic Muller, London, 1973. A meticulously researched and lavishly illustrated book which should appeal to the social and military historian as well as the badge enthusiast. For those attempting to identify photographs of soldiers, a knowledge of cap badges is a considerable advantage.

Liddle, Peter, *Men of Gallipoli*, Allen Lane, 1976. Peter Liddle has become a rival to the Imperial War Museum through his work in collecting documents relating to the First World War. From this collection, and from sources in France, Germany, Turkey and Australia, he has written a detailed account of the Gallipoli campaign. A more rigorous selection of sources might have prevented some degree of repetition.

Liddell Hart, B. H., *A History of the World War, 1914–1918*, Faber, 1934. Since this history was first published in 1934 it has been reprinted many times, with some revisions by the author. Liddell Hart was the doyen of British military historians and a bitter critic of Haig and the 'westerners'. New evidence and new interpretations have since made many of the conclusions out of date. Nevertheless, it represents a formidable work and illustrates an important school of thought about the First World War.

Liddell Hart, B. H., *Through the Fog of War*, Faber, 1938. This series of penetrating essays on leading commanders in the First World War includes some critical comments about many senior British commanders, reflecting Liddell Hart's change from uncritical admiration as a young subaltern in 1915.

Liddell Hart, B. H., *The Tanks: the History of the Royal Tank Regiment*, I, Cassell, 1959. This first volume is also a history of the development of tanks during the First World War. Because of his own personal involvement with many of the leading proponents and opponents of tanks Liddell Hart was able to write a detailed and useful history, which also includes insights into general aspects of strategy and tactics.

Luvaas, Jay, *The Education of an Army*, Cassell, 1965. An excellent survey of the leading British military thinkers and writers in the nineteenth and twentieth centuries. An important chapter is the one on Colonel G. F. Henderson, who taught the future generation of army and corps commanders when they were at the Staff College in the 1890s.

Macdonald, Lyn, *They Called it Passchendaele*, Michael Joseph, 1978. An account of Third Ypres, based upon the author's interviews with surviving veterans and the use of original diaries and letters.

Macdonald, Lyn, *Somme*, Michael Joseph, 1983. An account of the battle based upon the author's interviews with surviving veterans and original diaries and letters.

Middlebrook, Martin, *The First Day of the Somme*, Allen Lane, 1971. Another study based upon interviews of veterans and diaries and letters. Middlebrook used German as well as British sources. Other historians criticised him for concentrating on the first day of what became a campaign which lasted until September 1916.

Middlebrook, Martin, *The Kaiser's Battle: 21 March 1918, the First Day of the German Spring Offensive*, Allen Lane, 1978. Middlebrook used the same methodology in this book. He has some interesting conclusions about the will of the British defenders to continue to fight on after they had been by-passed and surrounded by the enemy.

Moore, William, *See how they Ran*, Leo Cooper, 1970. With an emotive title and a journalistic style, Moore's study of the German spring offensive in 1918 does not readily gain the reader's sympathy. The book is based almost entirely on secondary sources, but presents the main political and military issues.

Moorehead, Alan, *Gallipoli*, Hamish Hamilton, 1956. Although now rather dated, this account is still worth consulting.

Moynihan, Michael (ed.), *Black Bread and Barbed Wire: Prisoners in the First*

World War, Leo Cooper, 1978. There is no definitive study of British p.o.w.s in the First World War, although in the 1920s a number of personal experiences were published. This volume is a selection from the collection of diaries and journals of British p.o.w.s held by the Imperial War Museum, and includes experiences in France and Mesopotamia.

Mr. Punch and the Services, The New Punch Library, No. 7, n.d. A collection of articles and cartoons of the services which contains a number relating to the First World War.

Mr. Punch in Wartime, The New Punch Library, No. 20, n.d. This collection of articles and cartoons is entirely representative of those published in *Punch* during the war. Although they are often fatuous, they are a social commentary on how civilians wanted to see the services and the war.

Palmer, Alan, *The Gardeners of Salonika*, Andre Deutsch, 1965. A reasonably accurate modern study of the campaign which supplements the official history.

Richards, Jeffrey, *Visions of Empire*, Routledge and Kegan Paul, 1973. Jeffrey Richards has now written a number of excellent books on the history of films and the cinema. *Visions of Empire* examines the films of American populism, German Nazism and British imperialism. Those films forming part of the book on British imperialism are a useful social commentary on attitudes prevalent before, during and after the First World War towards duty and service. Chapter 10, 'Officers and other ranks', discusses the way in which these two groups were portrayed in British and American films.

Simpson, Keith, *The Old Comtemptibles: a Photographic History of the British Expeditionary Force, August – December 1914*, Allen and Unwin, 1981. Includes a large selection of original photographs taken by contemporary participants, including journalists and soldiers. It is a photographic history of the regular army in 1914.

Sir Douglas Haig's Great Push: the Battle of the Somme, Hutchinson, 1916. A narrative and photographic history. The photographs were stills taken from the film made at the time and shown to the British public.

Sixsmith, Major-General E. K. G., *British Generalship in the Twentieth Century*, Arms and Armour Press, 1969. General Sixsmith's study has some shrewd points to make about military training before and during the First World War that draw heavily upon the papers of General Maxse.

Terraine, John, *Mons: the Retreat to Victory*, Batsford, 1960. Despite the specific title, this book looks at the campaign in France from the beginning of the war to the battle of the Marne.

Terraine, John, *The Western Front*, Hutchinson, 1964. A selection of John Terraine's articles which tend to support Haig and the 'westerners'.

Terraine, John, *The Smoke and the Fire: Myths and Anti-myths of War, 1861–1945*, Sidgwick and Jackson, 1980. Terraine refighting old battles from the First World War and earlier and restating his belief in the inevitability of the British effort on the western front.

Turner, E. S., *Gallant Gentlemen: a Portrait of the British Officer, 1660–1956*, Michael Joseph, 1956. This general and rather flippant study has a few points to make about the army officer in the First World War.

Wallace, Edgar, *Kitchener's Army and the Territorial Forces*, Newnes, 1916. A contemporary illustrated history of the raising of the New Armies and the expansion of the Territorial Force.

Williams, Captain B., *Raising and Training the New Armies*, Constable, 1918. A useful contemporary account, particularly good on the officers.

Williams, M. J., 'The treatment of the German losses on the Somme in the British official history,' *Journal of the Royal United Services Institute*, February 1966. There is no one agreed set of British casualty figures for the battle of the Somme. In this excellent article M. J. Williams dissects those given in the official history and concludes that they were 'massaged' by Edmonds.

Wilkinson, Alan, *The Church of England and the First World War*, SPCK, London, 1978. Although this scholarly study looks at the wider questions of Church, State and society in the war, it does make some interesting points specifically about the Church and the army.

Wolff, Leon, *In Flanders Fields*, Longmans, 1959. Leon Wolff's study of the Third Battle of Ypres has become something of a classic, and it probably dates the post-Second World War revival of interest in the Great War, which was to reach a peak at the fiftieth anniversary in the 1960s.

Literature and poetry

Adcock, A. St John, *For Remembrance: Soldier Poets who have Fallen in the War*, Hodder and Stoughton, 1920. Short biographical sketches of soldier poets who were killed in the war, interesting because it lists many minor ones.

Aldington, Richard, *Death of a Hero*, Chatto and Windus, 1929. This novel is about the generation who fought in the war, and is critical of the parents of that generation.

Barnett, Correlli, 'A military historian's view of the Great War', in *Essays by Divers Hands*, Royal Society of Literature, 1970. Correlli Barnett advances the thesis that life for the British soldier in the First World War was not noticeably more dreadful than in previous wars, or for that matter much worse than the living conditions of some of the British working class before the war. He argues that many of the most outspoken literary critics of the army and the war who were influential through their prose and poetry were not typical of the broad mass of men who served in the army.

Bergonzi, Bernard, *Heroes' Twilight*, Constable, 1965. An important literary analysis of prose and poetry of the First World War which ranges beyond the inter-war period.

Cloete, Stuart, *How Young they Died*, Collins, 1969. A popular novel about a young British infantry officer and his war experiences.

Cohen, Joseph, *Journey to the Trenches: the Life of Isaac Rosenberg, 1890–1918*, Robson Books, 1975. A biography of the poet, who served as a private soldier in the 12th South Lancashire Regiment and then the 11th King's Own Royal Lancaster Regiment. This biography shows the difficult time he had in the army and the antisemitism he faced.

Deane, Peter, *The Victors*, Constable, 1925. This novel appears to have been a piece of propaganda on behalf of ex-officers. The hero is a young man who served as an officer in the war and remained in the army after the armistice.

Forester, C. S., *The General*, Michael Joseph, 1936. A brilliant, underrated novel about the life of a regular army officer, spanning his career from a young subaltern in South Africa through various levels of command in the First World War to his invalided retirement after the war. Forester magnificently captures the atmosphere of the period, and the novel says more about middle-class society, the army and the First World War than many memoirs and histories.

Fussell, Paul, *The Great War and Modern Memory*, Oxford University Press, 1975. When this study of the literary experiences of the British on the western front was published it received critical acclaim. However, it needs to be treated with caution, as some of the literary illustrations taken from contemporary sources were rather selective.

Harris, John, *Covenant with Death*, Hutchinson, 1961. As a novel *Covenant with Death* is a remarkable literary reconstruction of the raising, training and eventual destruction of a Yorkshire New Army battalion on the first day of the battle of the Somme.

Hurd, Michael, *The Ordeal of Ivor Gurney*, Oxford University Press, 1978. Ivor Gurney served with the 2/5th Gloucestershire Regiment and wrote some fine war poetry. This biography shows the effect the war had on him and his subsequent mental breakdown.

Jones, David, *In Parenthesis*, Faber, 1929. David Jones served as a private in the 15th (1st London Welsh) Royal Welsh Fusiliers. He uses a combination of prose and free verse to tell the story of John Ball, a private soldier serving in a Welsh New Army battalion who is eventually wounded on the Somme.

Klein, Holger (ed.), *The First World War in Fiction*, Macmillan, 1976. This volume of essays contains a useful chapter on the literary importance of R. H. Mottram, Frederick Manning and Henry Williamson.

Manning, Frederick (Private 19022), *Her Privates We*, Peter Davies, 1930. Originally this novel was published anonymously in 1929 in a two-volume limited edition of 520 numbered copies under the title *The Middle Parts of Fortune*. It was then published in an expurgated version as *Her Privates We* in 1930. The author used the pseudonym 'Private 19022' until his identity was revealed for the first time on the title page in the 1943 edition. Frederick Manning was an Australian man of letters who served as a private soldier in the 7th King's Shropshire Light Infantry. Despite his limited literary reputation, he produced one of the finest novels about soldiering in the First World War. Written with an impressive style and using Shakespearian imagery, *Her Privates We* is about a comradeship among soldiers. The unexpurgated edition, *The Middle Parts of Fortune*, was reprinted as a single-volume paperback in 1977.

Maurois, André, *The Silence of Colonel Bramble*, Bodley Head, 1930. André Maurois served as a French liaison officer attached to the BEF in France during the war. The novel is an amusing impression of the British army seen through the eyes of a Frenchman. The sequel, *General Bramble*, was published in 1931.

Mottram, R. H., *The Spanish Farm Trilogy, 1914–1918*, Chatto and Windus, 1927. Mottram served as a temporary officer in the 9th Norfolk Regiment, and this trilogy of novels is primarily concerned with the continuity in experience of a Flanders farm and its occupants.

Parsons, I. M. (ed.), *Men who March Away: Poems of the First World War*, Chatto and Windus, 1965. A useful selection.

Rutter, Captain Owen, *The Song of Tiadatha*, Fisher Unwin, 1920. A parody of *Hiawatha*, the song of 'Tired Arthur' contains some amusing comments about the progress of a young officer in the army and the operations in Salonika.

Sherriff, R. C., and Bartlett, V., *Journey's End*, Gollancz, 1930. Following the success of the play *Journey's End*, R. C. Sherriff, in collaboration with V. Bartlett, adapted it as a novel. Both the play and the novel were largely autobiographical fiction, as Sherriff had served as a temporary officer in the 9th East Surrey Regiment.

Silkin, Jon, *Out of Battle: the Poetry of the Great War*, Oxford University Press, 1972. A good readable commentary and analysis.

Stallworthy, Jon, *Wilfred Owen*, Chatto and Windus, 1974. A scholarly biography showing what a complex and sensitive man Owen was. Owen served as a temporary officer, first with the 5th Manchester Regiment and then in France with the 2nd Manchester Regiment.

Williamson, Henry, *The Patriot's Progress*, Geoffrey Bles, 1930. An anti-war and anti-army novel. The central character is John Bullock, Williamson's Everyman of the First World War.

Williamson, Henry, *A Chronicle of Ancient Sunlight*, Macdonald, 1955–69. Fifteen novels written over a period of nearly fifteen years. The central character, undoubtedly autobiographical, is Philip Maddison, who progresses from his lower middle-class suburban youth in Edwardian London through two world wars to eventual retirement in Devon. The core of the *Chronicle* is provided by five novels which span the First World War – *How Dear is Life*, *A Fox under my Cloak*, *The Golden Virgin*, *Love and the Loveless* and *A Test to Destruction*. Uneven in style and prone to inaccuracy of detail, they nevertheless portray vividly the life of a sensitive young lower middle-class man, his service in the army, life at the front in France and at home in Britain, and the tensions between the generations. Williamson was greatly influenced by the comradeship between British and German soldiers during the Christmas truce of 1914. Williamson served as a rifleman in the 1st London Rifle Brigade in 1914 and then as a temporary officer in the 10th Bedfordshire Regiment.

Morale and leadership

Allison, W., and Fairley J., *The Monocled Mutineer*, Quartet, 1978. This inaccurate and sensational book purports to tell the story of the man who was at the centre of the mutiny among British troops at the base camp at Etaples in 1917.

Babington, A., *For the Sake of Example*, Leo Cooper at Secker and Warburg, 1983. The author was permitted to examine the court-martial documents of British soldiers executed for desertion during the First World War. Unfortunately he was unable to refer to names, and this, coupled with a lack of reference to well known secondary sources, means a rather inadequate book. The whole question of discipline and morale requires a major study.

Baynes, John, *Morale: a Study of Men and Courage*, Cassell, 1967. An excellent study of the 2nd Scottish Rifles, a pre-war regular battalion. John Baynes, himself an officer in the regiment, asked why it was that this battalion continued to press home attacks in Flanders in 1915 in the face of heavy casualties. He concludes that morale was the most important factor, and that it depended on a number of things. Baynes looked at the organisation of the pre-war regiment and its battalions, at the social backgrounds of the officers, NCOs and men, and at their professional relations. However, it would be erroneous to assume that the conclusions could necessarily be applied to every other regular battalion.

Brent Wilson, J., 'The Morale and Discipline of the BEF, 1914–1918', M.A. thesis, University of New Brunswick, Canada, 1978. A very interesting study based upon official documents and papers, showing the concern felt by GHQ about maintaining an aggressive spirit among troops during long periods of static warfare.

Dixon, Norman F., *On the Psychology of Military Incompetence*, Cape, 1976. This provocative book examines military leadership from the basis of psychology and has an interesting chapter on Haig. Although some of the supporting military history is weak and some of the psychology debatable, the analysis does much to counter the 'bloody fools' interpretation of British generalship in the First World War.

Englander, D., and Osborne, J., 'Jack, Tommy and Henry Dubb: the armed forces and the working class', *Historical Journal*, 21, 3, 1978, pp. 593–621, is concerned with the army and navy veteran movements and the attitude of the

Labour Party and the trade unions. It is interesting that acts of indiscipline were usually perpetrated by regular rather than conscript soldiers.

Gill, Douglas, and Dallas, Gloden, 'Mutiny at Etaples base in 1917', *Past and Present*, 69, 1975, pp. 88–112, looks at the series of mutinies which occurred in the base training camps at Etaples in 1917. The authors conclude that they were more widespread than was hitherto been thought, and that they began from variety of causes. There were even greater disorders elsewhere in France at the end of the war involving both British and dominion troops.

Lamb, D., *Mutinies*, Solidarity, n.d. A thin publication, short on facts and accuracy, and largely a political polemic.

L'Etang, Hugh, *The Pathology of Leadership*, Heinemann, 1969. As a medical doctor Hugh L'Etang is concerned to show that the behaviour of men and women in authority and the decisions they make often depend upon the state of their health. He shows that, among others, many of the political and military leaders in the First World War suffered from poor health which probably affected their judgement.

Lynch, P. J., 'The Exploitation of Courage: Psychiatric Care in the British Army, 1914 – 1918' M.Phil. thesis, University of London, 1977. This thesis is very much concerned with examining the contemporary medical profession, understanding of stress and shell-shock, and the distinction made between officers and other ranks.

Moore, William, *The Thin Yellow Line*, Leo Cooper, 1974. With an emotive title, Moore's book is a study of cowardice and fear in the British army. The core of the book is concerned with the question of shell-shock in the First World War. Despite its limitations, this is quite a reasonable introduction to the subject, and Moore revals the divided opinion within the army and the medical profession.

Moran, Lord, *The Anatomy of Courage*, Constable, 1966. Lord Moran served as a regimental medical officer with the 1st Royal Fusiliers during the First World War. He based this book on his experience and observations of soldiers then, and later as Churchill's physician in the Second World War, to write this important analysis of how men bear fear and display courage.

Rothstein, A., *The Soldier's Strikes of 1919*, Macmillan, 1980. A personal and somewhat unreliable account of the disorders and acts of ill-discipline among British troops in 1919.

Official publications

Aspinall-Oglander, Cecil, *Military Operations: Gallipoli*, 2 vols. HMSO, 1929–32. The official history leaves many questions unanswered.

Baker Brown, Brigadier-General W., *History of the Corps of Royal Engineers*, IV, *1885–1914*, Institution of Royal Engineers, Chatham, 1952. A detailed history of the Royal Engineers before the war which provides useful background information about organisation, training and manpower.

Beadon, Colonel R. H., *The Royal Army Service Corps: a History of Transport and Supply in the British Army*, II, Cambridge University Press, 1931. This second volume of the official history of the RASC covers the period from the end of the South African War until 1920.

Becke, Major A. F., *The Order of Battle of Divisions*, I–IV, HMSO, 1935–45. A detailed guide to the organisation and movements of British military formations from army down to brigade level. It also includes the names of commanders and senior staff officers and their dates of appointment.

Dardanelles Commission, First Report and Supplement, 1917, and Final Report and Appendices, 1919, Cmd 8490, Cmd 371, HMSO. These reports are a useful supplement to the official history, although they do not reveal all the disagreements over strategy.

Edmonds, Brigadier-General Sir J. E. (ed.), *Military Operations: France and Belgium*, 14 vols., Macmillan and HMSO 1922–49. This substantial official history of the war on the western front has long been a target of criticism. Edmonds, the official historian, found he had to write the official history in such a way so as to protect the reputations of senior British officers. This meant that although the history is full of a mass of detailed information there is very little critical analysis. As a result of the way in which facts relating to casualties suffered by the army on the Somme and the strategy of the Third Ypres offensive were distorted, one of the assistant official historians asked for his name to be removed from the title page. For Edmonds's role in the writing of the official history and the pressures on him see Jay Luvaas, 'The first British official historians', under the General section of this bibliography. A number of these volumes were reprinted with amendments, and revisions and correspondence relating to the official histories can be found in the Cabinet Papers at the Public Record Office; it is advisable to consult them when studying a specific battle or period of military operations.

Edmonds, Brigadier-General Sir J. E., *Military Operations: Italy, 1915–1919*, HMSO, 1949. A solid and rather uninspring account.

Falls, Captain Cyril, *Military Operations: Macedonia*, 2 vol., HMSO, 1933–35. A well written two-volume history of the British military involvement in the Balkans and the considerable commitment required for one 'sideshow'.

Field Service Pocket Book, 1914, HMSO, 1914. This official handbook, which anybody could purchase from the Stationery Office, was issued before and during the war as a kind of 'bluffers' guide for young officers. It contained a mass of military and administrative information and was frequently the only guide for temporary officers of the New Armies.

Forbes, Major-General A., *A History of the Army Ordnance Services*, III, *The Great War*, Medici Society, London, *1929*. A good introduction to the expansion of the ordnance services during the First World War.

General Annual Reports on the British Army for the Period from 1st October 1913 to 30th September 1919, Cmd 1193, HMSO, 1921. This slim volume contains a wealth of statistics relating to recruitment, casualties and courts-martial and in certain cases is more accurate than the *Statistics of the Military Effort of the British Empire, 1914–1920*.

Heniker, Colonel A. M., *Transportation on the Western Front, 1914–1918*, HMSO, 1937. This detailed history shows the importance of rail, motor and horse transport in supporting the army on the western front.

Hordern, Lieutenant-Colonel Charles, *Military Operations: East Africa, August 1914 – September 1916*, I, HMSO, 1941. Regarded as one of the 'sideshows' of the First World War, the campaign in East Africa was left until nearly last before it received the attention of the official historians. Even then, a combination of the disruption caused by a Second World War and the incompleteness of the surviving documentation ensured that only the first volume was ever published.

Macpherson, Major-General Sir W. G. (ed.), *History of the Great War: Medical Services*, 12 vols., HMSO, 1928–31. A detailed history of the organisation and deployment of the Army Medical Services. One of the most interesting volumes is that relating to *Casualties and Medical Statistics*.

Macmunn, Lieutenant-General Sir George, *Military Operations: Egypt and Palestine*, 2 vols., HMSO, 1928–30. A solid and detailed history of the campaign.

Moberly, F. J., *Military Operations: Mesopotamia*, 4 vols., HMSO, 1923–27. A well written official history which does not fail to censure some of the incompetence displayed at the beginning of the campaign.

Moberly, F. J., *Togoland and the Cameroons, 1914–1916*, HMSO, 1931. It seems surprising today that one comprehensive volume of the official history should have been devoted to this 'sideshow'.

Nalder, Major-General R. F. H., *The Royal Corps of Signals: a Short History of its Antecedents and Development, 1800–1955*, Royal Signals Institution, London, 1958. The development of the signals section of the Royal Engineers before and during the First World War is covered in this official history.

Officers Died in the Great War, 1914–1919, HMSO, 1919. This volume was incomplete when published owing to the problems of accurately documenting the deaths of officers in the war. There is no alphabetical listing of officers except under the relevant battalion or arm of service, so, unless this detail is known, checking a reference is a tedious business.

Priestley, R. E., *The Signal Service in the European War of 1914 to 1918 (France)*, Mackay, Chatham, 1921. This volume on the signal service was one of a series on the work of the Royal Engineers in the First World War. It is useful in understanding the problems of communications between front-line units and higher formations in France.

Pritchard, Major-General, H. L. (ed.), *History of the Corps of Royal Engineers*, V, *The Home Front, France, Flanders and Italy in the First World War*, Institution of Royal Engineers, Chatham, 1952; VI, *Gallipoli, Macedonia, Egypt and Palestine*; VII, *Campaigns in Mesopotamia and East Africa and the Inter-war period*, 1918 to 1938. These three excellent volumes cover the organisation, manpower, training and operational role of the Royal Engineers in the various theatres of war and on the home front.

Raleigh, Sir Walter, and Jones, H. A., *The War in the Air*, 6 vols., Oxford, Clarendon Press, 1922–37. A useful source for the history and development of the RFC and its importance for military operations.

Report of the War Office Committee of Enquiry into 'Shell-shock', HMSO, 1922. An important report looking at what had been a controversial question for the army during the war. The evidence of the witnesses is particularly interesting.

Statistics of the Military Effort of the British Empire, 1914–1920, HMSO, 1922. An invaluable reference work containing statistics and details about nearly every aspect of the organisation of the army during the war.

Organisation and planning

French, David, *British Economic and Strategic Planning, 1905–1915*, Allen and Unwin, 1982. Particularly useful for understanding problems relating to the production and supply of munitions before and during the first year of the war.

Perry, F. W., 'Manpower and Organisational Problems in the Expansion of the British and other Commonwealth Armies during the two World Wars', Ph.D. thesis, University of London, 1982. The author shows that in both world wars the British government was injudicious in raising large numbers of military formations for which there were inadequate supplies of manpower. Hence the disbandment of many formations and at times severe manpower shortages.

Simkins, Peter, 'Kitchener and the expansion of the army' in Beckett, Ian, and Gooch, John (eds.), *Politicians and Defence: Studies in the Formulation of British Defence Policy, 1845–1970*, Manchester University Press, 1981. A timely analysis of what Kitchener actually did at the War Office at the beginning of the war and the policy he pursued towards both the New Armies and the Territorial Force.

Trebilock, Clive, 'War and the failure of industrial mobilisation: 1899 and 1914', in Winter, J. M. (ed.), *War and Economic Development*, Cambridge University Press, 1975. A useful study of the failure of industrial planning in Britain before the war.

Personal experiences

Andrews, William Linton, *Haunting Years: the Commentaries of a War Territorial*, Hutchinson, n.d. The author served as a volunteer in the 1/4th Black Watch, and saw active service in 1915 at Festubert, Neuve Chapelle, Loos and then in 1916 on the Somme.

Barrow, General Sir George, *The Fire of Life*, Hutchinson, 1942. George Barrow served in the Indian Army and his memoirs are perceptively written. He attended the Staff College in the 1890s with Haig, Allenby and Rawlinson. Barrow has some interesting comments about many officers who were later to hold senior appointments. He was to serve under Allenby, first in France and then in Palestine.

Begg, R. Campbell, *Surgery on Trestles: a Saga of Suffering and Triumph*, Jarrold, 1967. A memoir of surgery under field conditions in Mesopotamia.

Behrend, Arthur, *Make me a Soldier*, Eyre and Spottiswoode, 1961. An excellent memoir by a temporary territorial officer serving with the 4th East Lancashire Regiment at Gallipoli.

Behrend, Arthur, *As from Kemmel Hill: an Adjutant in France and Flanders, 1917 and 1918*, Eyre and Spottiswoode, 1963. Behrends's war service in France as adjutant to his battalion.

Bell, Captain D. H., *A Soldier's Diary of the Great War*, Faber, 1929. Henry Williamson edited this diary and served with the author in 1914 in the 1st London Rifle Brigade. Later Bell was commissioned into the 1st Queen's Own Cameron Highlanders.

Blunden, Edmund, *Undertones of War*, Collins, 1965. The wartime memoirs of the poet, who served as a temporary officer in the 11th Royal Sussex Regiment. The first part is prose narrative concerned with the small events of everyday life in France, the second a sheaf of poems illustrating the various phases of the first.

Bolwell, F. A., *With a Reservist in France*, Routledge, n.d. Bolwell was a regular reservist in 1914 recalled to the colours with the 1st Loyal North Lancashire Regiment, and this book is an account of his service with the BEF in the first six months of the war.

Callwell, Major-General Sir C. E., *Experiences of a Dug-out, 1914–1918*, Constable, 1920. Callwell had retired from the army before the war but was recalled to active service as a 'dug-out' in 1914. He served in the War Office as Director of Military Operations and his memoirs contain some interesting insights into the workings of that organisation and some amusing tittle-tattle about personalities.

Campbell, P. J., *The Ebb and Flow of Battle*, Hamish Hamilton, 1977. A beautifully written account of the last year of war service by a temporary officer serving in a territorial field artillery battery from the German March offensive to the armistice in November 1918.

Campbell, P. J., *In the Cannon's Mouth*, Hamish Hamilton, 1979. Encouraged by the success of his first book, Campbell wrote this companion volume, which covers the period from his being commissioned straight from school in 1917 and his experiences during the Third Battle of Ypres.

Carrington, C. E., *Soldier from the Wars Returning*, Hutchinson, 1964. Partly based on *A Subaltern's War*, which Charles Carrington had written in 1929 under the pseudonym Charles Edmonds. In this more comprehensive memoir the author not only describes his military service as a young temporary officer in the 1/5th Royal Warwickshire Regiment but also gives his pungent opinion about the nature of the war and the conduct of operations. Carrington has little sympathy with those who criticise the army's high command or who complain about the casualties of the war. He has been one of the most articulate spokesmen of the generation of 1914.

Casson, Stanley, *Steady, Drummer*, Bell, 1935. A somewhat sardonically written memoir of service life in France and Salonika.

Chapman, Guy, *A Passionate Prodigality*, Nicholson and Watson, 1933. A sensitively written memoir of a temporary officer who served in the 13th Royal Fusiliers; in the same class as Carrington's memoirs.

Chapman, Guy, *A Kind of Survivor*, Gollancz, 1975. This extended memoir was published after Chapman's death and reveals the haunting nature the experiences of the First World War had on his generation.

Charteris, Brigadier-General John, *At GHQ*, Cassell, 1931. Charteris was Haig's over-optimistic head of intelligence at GHQ from 1916 until his fall from grace in 1917. His memoirs form a diary which covers the whole period of the war. In fact they are based not on a diary but on the letters he wrote almost daily to his wife, later written up in the form of a diary. Charteris has a lot of interesting gossip about Haig, GHQ and various political and military figures.

Cloete, Stuart, *A Victorian Son*, Collins, 1972. A very good memoir of a young middle-class man who was commissioned as a temporary officer in the 9th King's Own Yorkshire Light Infantry.

Coppard, George, *With a Machine-gun to Cambrai*, Imperial War Museum, 1969. A short, well written memoir of the experiences of a Kitchener volunteer in the 6th Queen's Royal West Surrey Regiment, who adopted the style and attitude of an 'Old Bill'.

Craig Barr, Lieutenant-Colonel J., *Home Service*, Gardner, 1920. A badly written and tedious wartime memoir of a Territorial officer in the Argyll and Sutherland Highlanders who commanded a Home Service training battalion during the war. It is of interest because the author's attitude to the war and the training of soldiers for active service was probably representative of that generation of officers who were either too old or too inefficient to see active service themselves.

Craster, J. M. *'Fifteen Rounds a Minute': the Grenadiers at War, August to December 1914*, Macmillan, 1976. A detailed account of the action of the 2nd Grenadier Guards with the BEF in the first six months of the war. The basic source is the diary kept by Major 'Ma' Jeffreys, supplemented by the diaries and letters of other officers.

Crozier, F. P., *A Brass Hat in No Man's Land*, Cape, 1930. A pugnacious view of soldiering by an officer who left the regular army before the war, and who in 1914 was an officer in the Ulster Volunteers. By 1916 Crozier was commanding the 9th Royal Irish Rifles and by the end of the war had commanded the 119th Brigade. A tough soldier, he enjoyed the war and mastered the art of trench fighting.

Crozier, F. P. *The Men I Killed*, Michael Joseph, 1937. Slightly more sophisticated than the title might imply. Crozier reflects on the war and the men he had killed and those he had had shot for cowardice.

Crutchlow, William *Tale of an old Soldier*, Robert Hale, 1937. Crutchlow was a pre-war regular in the 1st Connaught Rangers who served in France and then Mesopotamia. After being wounded he transferred to less hazardous duties.

Douie, Charles, *The Weary Road: Recollections of a Subaltern of Infantry*, Murray, 1929. Charles Douie served as a temporary officer in the 1st Dorsetshire Regiment. He was a young man who was proud to serve in a regular battalion and had no doubts about the war.

Eberle, Lieutenant-Colonel V. F., *My Sapper Venture*, Pitman, 1973. A very good

detailed memoir of a young sapper officer who served in France and Italy
during the war.

Eden, Anthony, *Another World, 1897–1917*, Allen Lane, 1976. A short, languid
memoir by the former Conservative Prime Minister, looking back to the
Edwardian world of his youth. Anthony Eden was a temporary officer in the
21st King's Royal Rifles Corps (Yeoman Rifles) and was one of the army's
youngest brigade majors at the end of the war.

Edmonds, Charles, *A Subaltern's War*, Peter Davies, 1929. Charles Carrington
wrote this memoir of his experiences at the battle of the Somme under the
pseudonym of Charles Edmonds. It remains today a minor classic of the First
World War.

Ex-Private X, *War is War*, Gollancz, 1930. A. Burrage wrote this rather bitter
book about his experiences as a private soldier and makes some forceful
comments about what he saw as the army's class system.

Fielding, Rowland, *War Letters to a Wife: France and Flanders, 1915–1919*,
Medici Society, 1929. Fielding was a pre-war regular officer in the 1st
Coldstream Guards who later commanded the 6th Connaught Rifles and then
the 1st Civil Service Rifles. The letters he wrote to his wife contain a wealth of
information about his experience and observations.

Fitzwilliams, John, *Letters from a Gunner, 1914–1918*, private printing, 1935.
Fitzwilliams was a pre-war regular gunner officer. The letters he wrote to his
wife give a vivid picture of life in France and the problems he faced as a battery
commander. He was wounded in 1917, and then sent by the War Office as a
propaganda officer to the Russian armies on the Roumanian border, where he
saw the effects of the revolution.

*Four years on the Western Front, by a Rifleman: being the Experiences of a
Ranker in the London Rifle Brigade*, Odhams, 1922. This account was based
upon the letters Aubrey M. Smith wrote home. A well educated and very
literate public school volunteer, Smith's observations about people, incidents
and places are astute and colourful.

Fraser-Tytler, Major Neil, *Field Guns in France, 1915–1918*, Hutchinson, 1922.
This memoir by a Territorial gunner officer is based upon letters he wrote to his
father from France.

Fuller, J. F. C. *Memoirs of an Unconventional Soldier*, Nicholson and Watson,
1936. Fuller was one of the leading advocates of tanks after the First World
War. A brilliant, if at times erratic and controversial, figure, Fuller's memoirs
show the work of a staff officer and how he developed his ideas on the use of
tanks. Written with wit and critical asides, they give an unconventional
regular officer's view of the army and the war. However, Fuller's account of his
own role in the development of tanks should be treated with caution.

Gladden, Norman, *Ypres, 1917: a Personal Account*, William Kimber, 1967.
Gladden served as a temporary officer in the 11th Northumberland Fusiliers,
and this memoir is an interesting account of his experiences at Ypres from June
to November 1917.

Gladden, Norman, *Across the Piave: a Personal Account of the British Forces in
Italy, 1917–1919*, HMSO, 1971. After surviving the bitter fighting at Ypres in
November 1917, Gladden served with his battalion in Italy until the collapse of
Austria-Hungary in October 1918.

Gladden, Norman, *The Somme, 1916: a Personal Account*, William Kimber,
1974. Gladden's earlier experiences on the Somme in 1916 with the 7th
Northumberland Fusiliers.

Glubb, John, *Into Battle: a Soldier's Diary of the Great War*, Cassell, 1978.
Glubb served as a young sapper officer during the war. Most of his experiences
were with support units in France.

Gough, General Sir Hubert, *Soldiering on*, Arthur Barker, 1954. Gough was one of the youngest British generals, and he gained a bad reputation during the battles of the Somme, Third Ypres and in the March offensive of 1918. In this volume of memoirs he is concerned to put his case, particularly with regard to his command of the Fifth Army.

Graham, Stephen, *A Private in the Guards*, Macmillan, 1919. Stephen Graham was a well known writer when he enlisted as a private soldier in the 2nd Scots Guards in 1917. He gives a detailed description of life as a Guardsman in France at the end of the war.

Graves, Robert, *Goodbye to all that*, Cape, 1929. Generally regarded as anti-war, when analysed more closely it reveals Graves's ambivalence towards the war and soldiering. He was not a typical young temporary officer, and he served in a regular battalion, the 2nd Royal Welsh Fusiliers. The book should be regarded as a work of literature rather than an accurate account.

Greenwell, Graham, *An Infant in Arms: War Letters of a Company Officer, 1914–1918*, Dickson and Thompson, 1935. Greenwell was a temporary officer in the 1/4th Oxford and Buckinghamshire Light Infantry and served in France and Italy. No real self-doubts or fears can be found in this memoir, which brims over with schoolboy zest for everyday life. Greenwell concludes that on the whole he had a good war.

Griffith, Wyn, *Up to Mametz,* Faber, 1931. Wyn Griffith served as a private soldier in the 15th (1st London Welch) Royal Welch Fusiliers. This memoir deals with his experiences on the Somme and reflects the author's eye for detail and the noting of the seemingly trivial aspects of everyday life.

Groom, W. H. A., *Poor Bloody Infantry*, William Kimber, 1976. Groom served as a private in a battalion of the London Rifle Brigade in France from 1916 to 1918. He saw the war as a hideous experience, more than the ordinary soldier could bear. His view is in sharp contrast to that of other veterans like Charles Carrington.

Haigh, R. H., and Turner P. W., (eds.), *The Long Carry: the Journal of Stretcher Bearer Frank Dunham, 1916–1918*, Pergamon, 1970. The majority of wartime memoirs were written by those serving in the combatant arms, and this book makes a pleasant contrast, as it views the war from the perspective of a stretcher bearer who faced the same dangers as an infantryman.

Hanbury-Sparrow, A., *The Land-locked Lake*, Arthur Barker, 1932. A blunt and perceptive memoir by a pre-war regular officer of the 1st Royal Berkshire Regiment who served in France, off and on, from 1914 until the end of the war. Hanbury-Sparrow's comments on the differences between regular and New Army units are particularly interesting.

Hankey, Donald, *A Student in Arms*, Melrose, 1916. In this influential, yet strange, book the author, who served as a temporary officer in the Royal Warwickshire Regiment, mixes fact with fiction.

Harington, General Sir Charles, *Tim Harington looks back*, John Murray, 1941. Harington was Plumer's chief of staff for an important part of the war and gained a formidable reputation among front line soldiers for professionalism and competence. Yet these rather self-effacing memoirs tell little about the conduct of operations.

Hart-Davis, Rupert (ed.), *Siegfried Sassoon Diaries, 1915–1918*, Faber, 1983. This edition is a valuable contribution to the literature of the First World War. From the diaries it is possible to identify many of the characters mentioned in Sassoon's memoirs. The early entries show how naive and pretentious he was at the beginning of the war.

Head, Lieutenant-Colonel C. O., *No Great Shakes*, Robert Hale, 1943. Head, a regular gunner officer before the war, was recalled from the reserve. He is particularly useful in his comments about the repetitiveness and boredom of so much peacetime soldiering.

Hiscock, Eric, *The Bells of Hell go Ting-a-ling-a-ling,* Arlington, 1976. Hiscock enlisted as a private soldier in the 29th Royal Fusiliers when he was under age. He served in France at the end of the war and stayed on in the army of occupation. A somewhat sensational memoir, but, if some of the social experiences are exaggerated, it mentions aspects of soldiering which others usually leave unwritten.

Hitchcock, Captain F. C., *'Stand to': a Diary of the Trenches, 1915–1918,* Hurst and Blackett, 1937. The experiences of a regular officer in the 2nd Leinster Regiment. Hitchcock's diary reveals the relentless nature of trench warfare and the effect this had on both officers and men. It also reveals the physical and mental strength of the pre-war army.

Housman, Laurence (ed.), *War Letters of Fallen Englishmen,* Gollancz, 1930. A fascinating seleection of letters written by soldiers, sailors and airmen who were killed during the war. They reveal a wide variety of reactions and feelings about the war and military life.

Philip Howell: a Memoir, by his Wife, Allen and Unwin, 1942. Howell was a talented young regular officer who had gained the attention of Haig. He was a man of wide interests and had travelled widely before the war. This memoir by his wife is based on his letters and the articles he wrote for the press. Howell served as chief of staff in Salonika, then in France, where he was killed in 1916.

Hutchison, Lieutenant-Colonel Graham Seton, *Footslogger,* Hutchinson, 1931. Hutchison was an unconventional pre-war regular officer who left the army and drifted around the world doing a number of jobs. In 1914 he volunteered and served as an officer with the 2nd Argyll and Sutherland Highlanders. In 1918 he commanded a battalion of the Machine Gun Corps. A tough, able soldier, he had a natural aptitude for war. His memoirs reveal his ruthlessness towards panic in the army during the German Lys offensive in 1918.

Liddell Hart, Sir Basil Henry, *Memoirs,* I, Cassell, 1965. Liddell Hart's memoirs are important because they reveal how one of the most influential post-war military thinkers was affected by his military experiences. Liddell Hart was a temporary officer in the 9th King's Own Yorkshire Light Infantry. An enthusiastic volunteer, he became disillusioned when he studied the war in retrospect. At its end he was responsible for a new infantry training manual; he later stimulated thinking within the army about mechanised warfare. After the war he became a leading critic of British military strategy and tactics during the war.

Liveing, Edward G. D., *Attack: an Infantry Subaltern's Impressions of July 1st 1916,* Heinemann, 1918. A short but detailed account of one junior officer's experiences during the first few hours of the first day of the battle of the Somme. The author served with the 12th (County of London) London Regiment TF.

Lloyd, R. A., *A Trooper in the 'Tins',* Hurst and Blacklett, 1938. Lloyd was a regular with the 1st Life Guards. This is quite a useful memoir of life in army before and during the war, seen from the perspective of a regular soldier.

Lucy, John, *There's a Devil in the Drum,* Faber, 1938. John Lucy was an articulate young man who with his brother enlisted as a private soldier in the 2nd Royal Irish Rifles before the war. He gives a vivid account of life for the rank and file before the war, and is very good about the actions of his battalion for the first six months of the war in France and Belgium. Lucy was eventually commissioned in 1917.

Macmillan, Harold, *Winds of Change, 1914–1939,* Macmillan, 1966. Harold Macmillan served as a temporary officer in the Grenadier Guards during the war. His observations about life in the army, particularly in the Guards, are very perceptive. He was greatly influenced by his time in the Guards.

Maze, Paul, *A Frenchman in Khaki*, Heinemann, 1934. The artist Paul Maze began the war as an interpreter with the British army, and served in France throughout. He has some interesting comments about the British army and some of the leading personalities.

Meinertzhagen, Richard, *Army Diary, 1899–1926*, Oliver and Boyd, 1960. Meinertzhagen was a clever, unconventional regular officer who worked for military intelligence. He served in East Africa and Palestine during the war, and this edited diary is full of uncomplimentary comments about many senior officers. Lloyd George thought Meinertzhagen the cleverest officer he had ever met, a compliment Meinertzhagen might well have done without.

Mellersh, H. E. L., *Schoolboy into War*, William Kimber, 1978. A perceptive memoir of a temporary Special Reserve officer commissioned in the 2nd East Lancashire Regiment.

Molesworth, Lieutenant-General G. N. (ed.), *A Soldier's War: being the diary of Arthur Cook, DCM, MM, 1st the Somerset Light Infantry, 1914–1918* Goodman, Taunton, 1957. Arthur Cook was a regular and kept a slim diary during the war. Nothing very dramatic, but probably more representative of the usual kind of diary hastily written by the average soldier.

Montague, C. E., *Disenchantment*, Chatto and Windus, 1922. Montague was disenchanted by all the worst aspects of human nature brought out by the war, and he saw army life as dismal indeed.

Montgomery, Bernard, *The Memoirs of Field Marshal the Viscount Montgomery of Alamein*, Collins, 1958. The early chapters cover his time at Sandhurst and the First World War. One can see the effect the war had on Montgomery as a junior officer and how he became determined that when he eventually held command he would avoid the kind of operations which so cruelly affected the regimental soldier.

Moynihan, Michael, *God on our side: the British Padre in World War I*, Leo Cooper, 1983. A selection of letters and diaries kept by British padres and now held by the Imperial War Museum.

Nicholson, W. N., *Behind the Lines*, Cape, 1939. The staff received a bad press during and after the war, and it is useful to have this memoir by a regular who spent most of the war on the staff of divisional headquarters. Nicholson believed that many of the criticisms were uninformed and unfair.

Osburn, Arthur, *Unwilling Passenger*, Faber, 1932. A medical officer before the war, Arthur Osburn served with the 4th Royal Irish Dragoon Guards. His account of the first four months of the war appears to have been overlooked by many historians.

Panichas, George A. (ed.), *Promise of Greatness: the War of 1914–1918*, Cassell, 1968. Essays by distinguished men who lived through the war; many of them give valuable insights into military service and life in the army.

Plowman, Mark, *A Subaltern on the Somme*, Dent, 1927. Mark Plowman wrote this memoir of his experiences on the Somme as a temporary officer in the 10th West Yorkshire Regiment under the pseudonym Mark VII.

Pollard, Captain A. O., *Fire Eater*, Hutchinson, 1932. Pollard served in the H.A.C. in the first year of the war and was then commissioned. He was to win the VC, MC and DCM. A brash, arrogant man, he enjoyed the war and was an adept trench fighter.

Repington, C. à C. *The First World War, 1914–1918*, 2 vols, Constable, 1920. Repington had been a regular officer before the war and a contemporary of Haig, Wilson and Rawlinson. He was forced to resign following an affair and went into journalism, becoming a military correspondent. He was a born intriguer. His war diaries are amusing, snobbish and unreliable.

Reitz, Denys, *Trekking on*, Faber, 1933. Reitz was a Boer who had fought the British but loyally volunteered in 1914. He served in France during the last two years of the war, commanding the 7th Royal Irish Rifles. He has some interesting comments about the British army.

Richards, Frank, *Old Soldiers never Die*, Faber, 1933. A classic. Richards had been a regular in the 2nd Royal Welsh Fusiliers before the war, and went on to the reserve. Recalled to the colours in 1914, he served throughout the war as a private with his old battalion in France. Afterwards he began to write these memoirs, and they were eventually published through the efforts of Robert Graves, who had served in the same battalion. The result is a superb book by a regular soldier whose views are sometimes quite different from those of the volunteer or conscript.

Richards, Frank, *Old Soldier Sahib*, Faber, 1936. Following the success of *Old Soldiers never Die*, Richards wrote about his experiences as a regular before the war, from enlistment through his service with the 2nd Royal Welsh Fusiliers in India.

Robertson, Field Marshal Sir William, *From Private to Field Marshal*, Constable, 1921. Robertson was one of the few who made it from private to field marshal at a time when social mobility from the lower classes was extremely difficult. His memoirs are excellent on his early life in the army, and he was an astute observer of contemporary military personalities. He was less forthcoming about the major issues of the war. In later life Robertson was to assume a bluff and hearty working-class manner which disguised a clever and calculating mind. These memoirs show that he was an excellent administrator and staff officer.

Rogerson, Sidney, *Twelve Days*, Arthur Barker, n.d. Rogerson was adjutant in the 2nd West Yorkshire Regiment, and this is a moving account of one of the many twelve-day periods the battalion spent in the front line during 1916.

Rogerson, Sidney, *The Last of the Ebb*, Arthur Barker, 1937. Rogerson's battalion was badly mauled in the German March offensive in 1918, so it was sent to rest on a quiet sector along the Lys, where it bore the brunt of the German April offensive. Rogerson was captured during this battle and writes about his period of imprisonment in German hands.

Sansom, A. J., *Letters from France: June 1915–July 1917*, Melrose, n.d. Sansom was a schoolmaster who in 1914 was commissioned into the 1/5th Royal Sussex. He served on the staff of VIII Corps in 1916 and was killed whilst commanding the 7th Royal Sussex Regiment in July 1917. These very detailed letters were written to his wife.

Sassoon, Siegfried, *Memoirs of a Fox-hunting Man*, Faber, 1928. Pre-war life in the shires; sets the scene for the next volume.

Sassoon, Siegfried, *Memoirs of an Infantry Officer*, Faber, 1931. Like Robert Graves, Sassoon was not typical of the temporary officers, as he shared the same social background and tastes as the regulars. He served in the 1st Royal Welsh Fusiliers and later in other battalions of the same regiment. Despite his protests against the war he reveals a strong attraction to soldiering and trench warfare.

Severn, Mark, *The Gambardier*, Ernest Benn, 1930. The author served in the Royal Garrison Artillery, and his memoirs are interesting about his training in Britain and service in France.

Scrivenor, J. B., *Brigade Signals*, Blackwell, 1932. Memoir by a middle-aged man who was commissioned as a temporary officer in 1914 and then served in various signal units in France. Scrivenor is particularly useful when describing the duties of a signal officer.

Slack, Cecil M., *Grandfather's Adventures in the Great War, 1914–1918*, Arthur Stockwell, 1977. There are plenty of memoirs by former temporary officers, but Slack's is unique because he includes not only his letters from France but the ones he received from family and friends. Slack served in the 1/4th East Yorkshire Regiment and, like Greenwell, was an enthusiastic amateur soldier who saw the war as a challenge, and appears never to have become disillusioned.

Sitwell, Osbert, *Great Morning*, Macmillan, 1949. This volume of Sitwell's memoirs deals with the period before the war when he was an ensign in the Guards, and he has some astute comments to make about the pre-war army.

Spears, Sir E. L., *Liaison, 1914*, Heinemann, 1930. As a junior regular officer in 1914 Spears had the responsible job of liaison between the French Fifth Army and the BEF. He had to interpret and advise senior French and British officers. The book is an important source of information about Anglo-French military relations during the first six months of the war.

Spears, Sir E. L., *Prelude to Victory*, Cape, 1939. Later Spears held an even more responsible job as a liaison officer between the French and British armies. In this subsequent volume he is particularly interesting about the ill-fated Nivelle offensive.

Spicer, Lancelot Dykes, *Letters from France, 1915–1918*, Robert York, 1979. Lancelot Spicer was a temporary officer in the 9th King's Own Yorkshire Light Infantry, and these letters were written to his mother.

Stuart Dolden, A., *Cannon Fodder: an Infantryman's Life on the Western Front, 1914–1918*, Blandford Press, 1980. The author served as a private soldier in the 1st London Scottish and has some valuable observations from the other ranks' point of view.

Terraine, John (ed.), *General Jack's Diary, 1914–1918*, Eyre and Spottiswoode, 1964. Jack was a regular officer in the 2nd Scottish Rifles. He served almost continuously in France, in 1916 commanding the 2nd West Yorkshire Regiment, in 1918 the 1st Cameronians, and finally the 28th Brigade. His diaries are revealing of a rather serious-minded man who exercised command at different levels. They show just how much strain was placed on regulars like himself.

The War the Infantry knew, 1914–1919: a Chronicle of Service in France and Belgium with the Second Battalion, His Majesty's Twenty-third Foot, the Royal Welsh Fusiliers, King, 1939. A marvellous history of a regular battalion compiled by the medical officer from the personal reminiscences of former officers, NCOs and men, including Frank Richards and Siegfried Sassoon.

Tilsley, W. V., *Other Ranks*, Cobden-Sanderson, 1931. Written in prose form, this memoir has some useful points about the everyday life of an infantryman.

Turner, P. W., and Haigh, R. H., *Not for Glory*, Maxwell, 1969. A memoir of Gilbert Hall, a Kitchener volunteer who served as a private in the 13th (1st Barnsley) Yorkshire and Lancashire Regiment and was commissioned in the 2/4th King's Own Yorkshire Light Infantry.

Vaughan, Edwin Campion, *Some Desperate Glory: the Diary of a Young Officer, 1917*, Frederick Warne, 1981. Vaughan was a temporary officer in the 1/8th Royal Warwickshire Regiment. This diary of a platoon officer has much detail about his soldiers and their hopes and fears.

Vivian, A. P. G., *The Phantom Brigade*, Ernest Benn, 1930. A remarkably good account of the first few months of the war in France as experienced by a regular lance-corporal in the 4th Middlesex Regiment.

Voigt, F. A., *Combed out*, 1929. Essays about various aspects of the author's experiences during the war. Generally, they cover some of the less attractive aspects of soldiering, including fatigues and working in a hospital.

Wade, Aubrey, *The War of the Guns*, Batsford, 1936. Memoir by a gunner subaltern serving in a territorial field artillery battery in France. It was reprinted in 1959 under the title *Gunner on the Western Front*.

The post-war army

Bond, Brian, *British Military Policy between the two world wars*, Oxford University Press, 1980. The best scholarly account of the army during this period.

Higham, Robin, *Armed Forces in Peacetime Britain, 1918–1940: a Case Study*, Foulis, 1962. This general survey is now rather dated but is a useful introduction to the subject.

Jeffery, Keith, and Hennessy, Peter, *States of Emergency: British Governments and Strikebreaking since 1919*, Routledge and Kegan Paul, 1983. The early chapters cover the use of the army after the First World War in giving military aid to the civil power.

Jeffery, Keith, *The British Army and the Crisis of Empire, 1918–22*, Manchester University Press, 1984. In this new book Keith Jeffery examines the way in which after the war the British government used military methods, largely unsuccessfully, to deal with problems of nationalism and internal unrest.

Townshend, Charles, *The British Campaign in Ireland, 1919–1921: the Development of Political and Military Policies*, Oxford University Press, 1975. A considerable military effort was required in Ireland after the war. This scholarly study of the campaign covers not only operations against Sinn Fein and the IRA but the difficult relations between civil and military authorities.

Ward, S. R., 'Intelligence surveillance of British ex-servicemen, 1918–1920', *Historical Journal*, XVI, 1, 1973, pp. 179–88. This article shows the concern felt by British intelligence after the war that subversive Bolshevik elements were active among British ex-servicemen.

Ward, S. R., *The War Generation: Veterans of the First World War*, Kennikat, New York, 1975. This study compares the veteran organisations of Great Britain, the USA, France, Italy and Germany. In Britain the ex-servicemen's organisations had little influence.

The pre-war army

Allison, M., 'The National Service Issue, 1899–1914', Ph.D. thesis, University of London, 1975. Despite some public support and pressure, national service was unknown in Britain until 1916. The author outlines the main issues involved and the opinions of both politicians and soldiers.

Bond, Brian, *The Victorian Army and the Staff College, 1854–1914*, Eyre Methuen, 1972. This study of the development of the Staff College before the First World War is particularly good in showing how attendance at the college influenced the generation that was to command and staff the British armies during the war. Bond also attempts to correct the imbalance of criticism levelled against the staff during the war.

Fergusson, Sir James, *The Curragh Incident*, Faber, 1964. In spring 1914 a serious crisis appeared possible in British civil–military relations, owing to the reluctance of many army officers to coerce Ulster into Home Rule. Fergusson's is a balanced account, based upon his father's and other senior officers' papers.

Fergusson, T. G., *British Military Intelligence, 1870–1914*, Arms and Armour Press, 1984. A solid study of a previously neglected topic.

Harries-Jenkins, Gwyn, *The Army in Victorian Society*, Routledge and Kegan

Paul, 1977. This sociological study of the Victorian army is really about the officers. Some of the conclusions about their social background and their lack of professionalism are questionable.

Packenham, Thomas, *The Boer War*, Weidenfeld and Nicolson, 1979. This modern study provides a useful background to personalities and debates over professionalism and modernisation within the army.

Spiers, E. M. *Army and Society, 1815–1914*, Longman, 1980. The best modern study of the army and its relationship with society for the period between the Napoleonic Wars and the First World War.

Recruitment

Dewey, P. E., 'Military recruiting and the British labour force during the First World War', *Historical Journal*, 27, 1, 1984, pp. 199–224. Draws, as did Jay Winter, upon the Board of Trade's wartime employment surveys to highlight the differing rates of enlistment in industries and among occupational groups.

Douglas, R. 'Voluntary enlistment in the First World War and the work of the PRC', *Journal of Modern History*, 42, 1970, pp. 564–85. A lot of research is going on into the problems of maintaining voluntary enlistment in the period 1914–16. This article looks at the work of the Parliamentary Recruiting Committee, based on its minute books.

Hughes, Clive, 'Army Recruitment in Gwynedd, 1914–1916', M.A. thesis, University of Wales, 1983. A very useful study of recruitment in one area of Wales, showing the methods used to maintain the momentum.

Kennedy, T. C., *The Hound of Conscience: a History of the No Conscription Fellowship, 1914–1919*, Arkansas University Press, 1981. A more detailed account than Rae's, looking at one aspect of conscientious objection.

Osborne, J. M., *The Voluntary Recruiting Movement in Britain, 1914–1916*, Garland, New York, 1982. This study, based on the author's Ph.D. thesis, looks in particular at the work of the Voluntary Recruiting Movement in Bristol.

Rae, John, *Conscience and Politics: the British Government and the Conscientious Objector to Military Service, 1916–1919*, Oxford University Press, 1970. John Rae looks at the policy of the army and the advice it gave to the government concerning the question of conscientious objection to military service.

Women

Buckley, Suzann, 'The failure to resolve the problem of V.D. among the troops in Britain during World War I', in Bond, Brian, and Roy, Ian (eds.), *War and Society: a Yearbook of Military History*, II, Croom Helm, 1977. A large number of casualties in all armies during the First World War were due to VD. This limited study of the problem among troops in Britain reveals its extent and the inability of the authorities to deal with it.

Crosthwaite, E., 'The Girl behind the Man behind the Gun: the Position of the WAAC in World War I', M.A. thesis, University of Essex, 1980. A short but valuable study of the importance of the Women's Auxiliary Army Corps during the war.

Macdonald, Lyn, *The Roses of No Man's Land*, Michael Joseph, 1980. A popular account of British nurses in France, based upon personal accounts, letters and diaries.

Marwick, Arthur, *Women at War, 1914–1918*, Fontana, 1977. A lively popular history of the voluntary and compulsory involvement of women in war work in Britain.

Index